Private Equity as an Asset Class

Private Equity as an Asset Class

Second Edition

Guy Fraser-Sampson

A John Wiley & Sons, Ltd., Publication

This edition first published 2010
© 2010 John Wiley & Sons, Ltd

Registered office
John Wiley & Sons Ltd, The Atrium, Southern Gate, Chichester, West Sussex, PO19 8SQ, United Kingdom

For details of our global editorial offices, for customer services and for information about how to apply for permission to reuse the copyright material in this book please see our website at www.wiley.com.

The right of the author to be identified as the author of this work has been asserted in accordance with the Copyright, Designs and Patents Act 1988.

Reprinted in January 2012

A catalogue record for this book is available from the British Library.

Library of Congress Cataloging-in-Publication Data

Fraser-Sampson, Guy.
    Private equity as an asset class/Guy Fraser-Sampson. – 2nd ed.
      p. cm. – (The Wiley finance series)
    Includes bibliographical references and index.
    ISBN 978-0-470-66138-3 (cloth)
  1. Private equity.   2. Venture capital.   3. Investments.   I. Title.
    HG4751.F72   2010
    332.6–dc22
                                            2010008441

ISBN 978-0-470-66138-3

Set in 10/12pt Times by Toppan Best-set Premedia Limited
Printed in Great Britain by CPI Group (UK) Ltd, Croydon, CR0 4YY

Contents

About the Author

Guy Fraser-Sampson draws on over twenty years' practical experience of Private Equity, having held a number of senior positions within the industry, including setting up and running for several years the international operations of the leading Fund of Funds manager Horsley Bridge. He previously lived in the Middle East while working with the Abu Dhabi Investment Authority. He now performs consultancy and executive training for investors, both LPs and GPs, around the world.

He has, for the last few years, designed and taught various modules at Cass Business School in the City of London. His module on Private Equity fund investing is believed to be the only course in the world which teaches the skills required to operate successfully as an LP. He also holds public workshops around the world on subjects including Private Equity, Investment Strategy, Asset Allocation and Alternative Assets. He is well known as a keynote speaker at conferences and investor meetings. He writes for a number of pension and investment publications, including his influential regular column in *Real Deals*.

Guy is the author of two titles in the Wiley Finance series: *Multi Asset Class Investment Strategy* and *Private Equity as an Asset Class*. Both have been Amazon best-sellers. The first edition of this book has been in the best-seller lists continuously for three years from publication, regularly featuring at number one, and its Chinese edition has the distinction of being the first book on Private Equity ever to be published in China. It has been adopted as the standard textbook on Private Equity by business schools around the world. It is also viewed as an indispensable reference and learning tool by investors and advisers.

In addition to numerous professional qualifications, Guy has an LLB with honours from King's College London, and an MBA majoring in finance from Warwick Business School. He lives in London.

Acknowledgements

Acknowledgements are due to:

The students from my various modules at Cass Business School for their lively and challenging feedback over the last few years, both in class and in their coursework. This has always been useful in testing my assumptions and has, in some cases, prompted new teaching approaches, which have been incorporated in this new edition.

Chris Jeffery for encouraging me to teach at Cass in the first place, and him, Scott Moeller and Terry Ilott for their support and encouragement since.

My friend and former colleague Alan Kirkpatrick, now with the Business School at Bournemouth University, who has been an invaluable source of help and advice on accounting and valuation matters.

Pete Baker and Caitlin Cornish of Wiley, who were quick to acknowledge the need for a new edition of this work even though a relatively short time had elapsed since its initial publication. They have, as usual, been helpful, professional and supportive.

Samantha Hartley of Wiley, who has once again shepherded the book through its production process.

Thomson Reuters, as they are now called, who once again generously allowed me to use their industry data throughout.

Finally, my wife, who has not only endured several months of me analysing Private Equity data until late at night, but has also contributed some of the graphics.

Introduction

It is only three years since this book was first published, and the need for a new edition after such a short space of time is an indication of how much the world has changed in the meantime. The financial crisis began to unfold when the book was just six months old, and the resulting credit crunch, together with a fall in both earnings and valuation multiples, has had a profound effect on the Buyout industry, particularly so in the case of the mega funds.

In the flight to liquidity which followed, many fund investors found themselves in what came to be dubbed 'Cash 22', needing to meet Capital Calls yet unable to generate the cash with which to do so from supposedly liquid assets. We will examine just what went wrong here, and note the potential buying opportunity which this represents in the secondary market.

Perhaps partly as a result of this, the Private Equity industry has begun to experience LP defaults, both actual and potential. By the end of 2009 we had also seen instances of LPs refusing to extend investment periods, and forcing fund size reductions. It is clear that the traditional cosy LP/GP relationship has changed, just as it did way back in 1989/90 and again in 2000/1. On both of those occasions, the cooling off was a short-term phenomenon and in both cases the industry went rapidly on to renewed growth. It is, as yet, unclear how long the current investor anxiety will last, and to what extent the industry can grow yet larger.

For growth has been the name of the game. You will see that it is strongly arguable that a whole new era of Private Equity began around 2001, one in which much, much more money has been poured into funds, and invested by them in companies. In fact, the world of Private Equity has changed so dramatically that what we see now is, in many cases, radically different from what went before. Not least has been the very significant increase in holding periods, and thus in investor payback periods, which has, in turn, been a major contributor to Cash 22.

So, much needed changing in the book, not least the guidelines to LPs as to how to plan a fund investment programme. The fact that this edition is half as long again as its predecessor indicates that much new material also needed to be included. Both secondary investing and Growth and Development Capital were now thought to merit their own chapters. Emerging markets do too, but sadly this is just not possible as yet given the paucity of really good and mature data. This is currently the most exciting area of Private Equity, and thus the most intriguing challenge for investors.

The opportunity has also been taken to update the data and expand the Glossary. In addition, some new graphics which have been used by the author to teach Private Equity, both in business school classes and in public workshops, have been included where these have been found to be useful as aids to understanding.

Some things, alas, have not changed. European Venture Capital remains an endangered species, an undeserving victim of investor prejudice. The economic model of GP remuneration remains largely intact. Misplaced LP loyalty continues to enable mediocre GPs to remain in business. The asset class as a whole continues to be neglected by many of the world's investors, most notably UK pension funds. Incidentally, while a full discussion of asset allocation lies beyond the scope of this book, we will at least note for the record the extent to which industry performance figures have been cynically manipulated and misrepresented by some pension consultants.

The fact that such crude and prejudiced views are still able to hold sway in some quarters points to the widespread lack of knowledge of Private Equity which still exists. Many investors, for example, continue to believe that Private Equity and mega Buyout are one and the same thing (whereas by number of funds the latter is only about 6% of the former). To add yet further to the confusion, many seem unable to distinguish between Private Equity funds and Hedge funds, and so a new section has been included in the book to address this problem. This is, of course, highly topical at the time of writing (late 2009) as we are currently seeing ill-judged regulation proposed by the EU which clearly demonstrates an inability to understand this distinction.

This, in turn, shows that the industry as a whole still has a lot of work to do in educating people around the world: educating those investors who are currently unable to take an informed view on the asset class; educating regulators to understand the different characteristics of different types of investment funds both within and outside the asset class; educating politicians, particularly in Asia, to see that Private Equity can safely be embraced, and can represent a powerful economic driver.

This is a challenge to which the industry can, and should, rise. Lack of transparency remains a problem, with many GPs, not just in emerging markets but even in places like America, still failing to register their data with the various providers. This is foolish and short-sighted. The more data sets which are available, and the more complex the ways in which they can be analysed, the more comfortable investors will feel about allocating money to the asset class. LPs can also play a role here, by insisting that an obligation to register fund- and company-level data should be a term of the Limited Partnership Agreement.

There is a challenge here, too, for some of the data providers, some of whose efforts have been overtaken by growth and change in the industry. It seems clear, for example, that growth, development and secondary activity all merit their own representation, and that the traditional classification of Venture activity into IT, Telecoms and Life Science is now outdated. Also, it seems to make little sense to find that sometimes holding periods to IPO are available, but not holding periods to sale or writing-off. Given the weight of accumulated data, none of these would be easy tasks to undertake, yet they seem more pressing with each year that passes.

It is vital that these challenges are met. Private Equity today is a much more complex animal than it was a decade or so ago, yet it remains surely the most fascinating of all asset classes.

Finally a stylistic point. Throughout this book both Private Equity as a whole and its constituent parts have been accorded capital letters, while in all other cases lower case is used. Thus 'Buyout' refers either to Buyout investing as a whole or to a type of fund, while 'buyout' refers to individual transactions.

1

What is Private Equity?

Perhaps never has an asset class been so misunderstood as Private Equity. There is a branch of philosophy which contends that all problems are essentially linguistic; that if one can only properly define precisely what one means then the problem effectively solves itself. All problems, they say, are problems of meaning, and usually arise because two people are using language in different ways.[1] While this may seem a rather extreme view, it does go a long way to explaining many, though not all, of the problems which currently arise when people try to understand Private Equity.

This has become of particular importance since the publication of the first edition in February 2007. There is no need to detail for the reader what has happened since then in the fields of finance and investment. Suffice it to say that events have prompted a wholesale re-evaluation of Private Equity, thrown into doubt some of the traditional approaches of both managers (GPs) and investors (LPs) and made necessary a new edition of this book. It is in the blizzard of media stories and political sound-bites that have bombarded investors and others during the last three years that the root cause of our problem may be found. Many of the authors of these comments did not, in fact, understand what they meant when referring to 'Private Equity', and this has, in turn, clouded attitudes and reactions around the world.

Many, for example, have behaved as though large and mega Buyout funds were synonymous with 'Private Equity', rather than merely a small part of Private Equity funds globally by number (probably no more than about 5% since 2001). This is a mistake of huge proportions since, as we will see, Buyout funds, and in particular those very large ones which have come to be described as the mega funds, are so completely different from, say, early-stage Venture Capital funds in just about every respect as almost to constitute a different asset class altogether. In fact, there are those who suggest that the gulf between them is so wide that perhaps there is no such thing as 'Private Equity as an asset class' at all.

We see the obvious result of such muddled use of language in the current attempts by legislators worldwide to bind Private Equity funds tightly in a straightjacket of new regulation. Even if this were a valid response to the problems currently being experienced by (and, some legislators argue, caused by) the mega Buyout funds (which is highly questionable), it would still be a response to the wrong problem, since they would actually be regulating something very different from their intended target.

We also see it in the reaction by many investors when Private Equity is mentioned of 'don't you mean illiquid, leveraged equity?'. Quite apart from the ignorance (most of the world's Private Equity transactions are entirely unleveraged) and prejudice embodied in such a remark, this leads to dangerous practices and misleading advice.

---

[1] See, for example, Ayer, A.J. (2001) *Language, Truth and Logic*, Penguin, London.

Dangerous practices in that many investors either decide not to make an allocation to Private Equity based upon such mistaken beliefs, or believe that they can achieve the same result by taking a leveraged position in a quoted equity index.

Misleading advice in that many large consultancy firms are telling their pension fund clients that in terms both of its likely returns and its 'risk' (though what they are really referring to is the volatility of historic returns), Private Equity can be safely considered to behave in exactly the same way as quoted equities, but with everything increased by a given multiple (usually about 1.6). Worse even than this, when the real life figures stubbornly refuse to support this assumption, then those figures are assumed to be wrong and notional ones substituted which are reassuringly in line with the originally suggested approach. It may seem absurd that supposedly reputable and professional consultancy firms should be using their assumptions to create data rather than vice versa, but that is exactly what is happening in many cases.

Equally dangerously, this misuse of language has led many investors to believe that they need only invest in the mega funds, and that the rest of the industry (about 95% of funds worldwide) can safely be ignored. There are various investors, for example, whose initial screening process is to filter out all those funds which are less than US$1 billion, and which are not managed by a select short list comprising the big names that regularly make it into the media. The fact that this results in a dramatically undiversified portfolio is masked in many cases by the underlying assumption that 'Private Equity' and 'mega Buyout' are, in fact, one and the same, when they are not: the latter is simply one component of the former.

Further confusion has arisen over the difference between Private Equity funds and Hedge funds, with many investors assuming that they are simply the same animal in different clothing. Some investors simply refer to them all dismissively as 'vulture funds', which is actually an insult to both, since very few of either category prey on failing companies. For this reason a whole new section has been included in the next chapter setting out the different structures, objectives and workings of both Hedge funds and Private Equity funds. As will be seen, there are fundamental differences in each of these areas.

The need for a precise definition having been demonstrated, let us move on to ask the vital question 'what is Private Equity?'. However, here, too, there is a need for discussion, since the traditional classifications are coming to be seen as unduly restrictive.

WHAT IS PRIVATE EQUITY?

It used to be quite easy to define what was and was not Private Equity investment: 'any equity investment in a company which is not quoted on a stock exchange'. This statement still holds true for the overwhelming majority of the world's Private Equity transactions. If you are looking for one definition of universal truth, however, this rather simplistic description has been in trouble for a long time. What about investments which are structured as convertible debt? What about companies which are publicly listed but are taken private? Or where the company remains listed but the particular instrument into which the new investment occurs is not?

Clearly the question 'what is Private Equity?' is no longer capable of being answered quickly and simply, even if it ever was. Without wishing to confuse the reader still further, there was, in the period up to about the middle of 2007, an increasing convergence between the activities of Private Equity funds, Hedge funds and Property (real estate) funds. However, there was a well-known law case in England many years ago when a judge famously said that although you cannot define an elephant you still recognise one when you see it (though some believe he may have pinched this idea from Doctor Johnson without acknowledgement). Hopefully, after reading this book everyone will have an instinct for what a Private Equity transaction is or is not, but it is growing increasingly difficult to be certain about this as the parameters of the asset class are being stretched all the time.

In the rest of this chapter I am going to set out some sub-divisions within the overall Private Equity asset class, many of which will then be developed in more detail in the following chapters. However, it will be necessary first to look at the different levels at which Private Equity investment operates.

Fund Investing versus Direct Investing

There is a fundamental distinction in the Private Equity world between those who invest in funds and those who then manage the capital invested in those funds by making investments into companies. This distinction is sometimes defined by the terms 'fund investing' and 'direct investing', and people will be heard referring to 'investing at the fund level' or 'at the direct level' or 'at the company level' (the last two being different ways of expressing the same thing).

We also have to deal with what Oscar Wilde described as 'a single people divided by a common language', although, to be fair, US Private Equity terminology has become increasingly common in Europe and I shall usually be adopting it as industry standard, except where it is absolutely essential to draw some particular distinction of meaning.

In America, those who invest in funds are called 'LPs', since the most common form of Private Equity fund is a Limited Partnership, the passive investors in which are called Limited Partners. In Europe, such folk have historically been called simply 'investors'. There are various different types of LP and it is worth spending some time examining these here, since they will all have different investment criteria and, most importantly of all, different levels of knowledge of the asset class (with higher levels of knowledge being typically referred to rather arrogantly as 'sophistication').

At the top end of the scale are the Fund of Funds managers. These usually do nothing except invest in Private Equity (though some have branched out into other areas such as real estate), and the best of them will have staff with perhaps twenty years' specialist experience. Some (Horsley Bridge would be a good example) might specialise in one particular area (traditionally early-stage US Venture in their case) whereas others (Harborvest, to give an example of similar vintage) are generalist both as to the type of investments which they make and the geographical areas which they cover. As far as geography is concerned, however, the bulk of Private Equity activity to date has occurred in the US and in Europe and it is these two areas into which the Private Equity world has traditionally been sub-divided. While this will undoubtedly change (some investors are targeting Asian funds for 30% or more of their portfolio), the transition is being hampered by reluctance on the part of GPs in areas such as Asia and South America to lodge their fund data with the industry's data providers, an essential prerequisite to investment for many LPs.

For most investors seeking to enter the asset class, the Fund of Funds approach will be preferred. Few will have the relevant levels of specialist expertise available in-house to be able consistently to select the best partnerships and, even if one could, many of the best are 'invitation only' so that gaining access to them may well prove impossible anyway; this is a particular issue with US Venture funds. Outside the US there is a further issue which is that allocations to Private Equity are usually unrealistically low (so low, in fact, that most investors would do better not to be making any allocation at all) so that not only can the cost of acquiring such expertise never be contemplated, but there is no way in which even unskilled time can be made available to study and analyse the several hundred fund offerings which are likely to be received in any one year.

The Fund of Funds approach provides skilled fund selection expertise. It also ensures that capital will be committed on a scientific basis every year (very important to obtain diversification by time, as we will see), and that all reporting and accounting at the partnership level will be taken care of. In fact, the Fund of Funds route into the asset class can be thought of as the 'fire and forget' option. Provided one commits to each successive Fund of Funds vehicle from that manager (typically every three years), then one can simply sit back and manage the cash inflows and outflows.

The next step up might be to use some aspects of the Fund of Funds approach but perhaps supplemented by one's own efforts. For example, a European investor who has taken the trouble to set a proper allocation level and to acquire relevant internal expertise, may feel confident enough to start making, say, European Buyout selections but may wish to use specialist Fund of Fund products aimed at, for example, US Buyout and Venture. Alternatively, such specialist funds can be used simply to add a 'tilt' to a Private Equity programme by going underweight or overweight in a particular area.

Direct investment is the final layer in the Private Equity environment, where money actually gets channelled into investee companies, and this is the role of the Private Equity manager ('GP'), although sometimes making use of co-investment by LPs. The investment process may therefore be seen as consisting broadly of three levels: the Fund of Funds level, the fund level and the company level, and it is the distinction between the last two of these which we label the difference between 'fund investment' and 'direct investment'.

Each requires its own particular modelling and analysis, and we will be looking at this in more detail in later chapters. Importantly, each also requires its own skills. This is often overlooked by investors who, not content with fund investing, decide they would also like to share in some of the 'fun' of direct investing. As we will see in a moment, where this takes the form of co-investment alongside a fund, it will usually have an adverse impact on diversification. Where it takes place directly, without even the comforting umbrella of a fund co-investor, then it is frequently a recipe for disaster since few investors have the skills of a specialist GP. This was a particular problem during the dot com bubble, as various family offices, banks and large corporates scrambled to take stakes in technology and Internet companies without the relevant company-building skills to ensure their success, and also without the discipline and mental toughness to ride out the bad times when they inevitably arrived. Many of these companies would have been doomed in any event, with hopelessly ill-conceived business plans and poor management, but not all. Who knows how many struggling but worthwhile companies might have survived the post-bubble maelstrom if the business of direct investing had been left to the professionals?

Co-investment

It may seem perverse that many Fund of Funds and other investors should also make direct investments alongside their fund investments (this is known as 'co-investment' because it usually takes the form of persuading the manager of a fund into which you have put money to allow you to invest alongside the fund in one or more of its portfolio companies). I say 'perverse' because there is an obvious argument that by indulging in co-investment one actually harms exactly that diversification which is one of the advantages usually cited by Fund of Funds managers of investing in their programmes. They would argue, on the contrary, that the amounts involved are relatively small, that the overall impact of management fees is lessened, albeit very slightly, and that it enables investors to put more money to work in the asset class than would otherwise be the case.

There has, however, been an interesting development here in recent years. Let us first see what it is, and then understand the reasons behind it.

The development has been the introduction of dedicated co-investment vehicles by Fund of Funds managers. Previously (though these are still sometimes encountered), where these were found they took the form of a pool of additional capital being managed by the GP of a Private Equity fund alongside the fund itself. In some cases this was because the GP had transitioned from being the manager of a quoted vehicle, such as an investment trust in the UK (Candover would be one example), and decided to keep that pool of money alive so that investments made by the GP would be drawn partly from the quoted vehicle and partly from the fund.

These were an accident of history, however, rather than a deliberately introduced measure. In the latter such case, a GP would offer certain LPs (usually the biggest few within the fund) the option of also committing capital to a special co-investment vehicle, which would participate alongside the fund in its larger deals. The co-investment pool would typically have a lower cost to the LP than the main fund, sometimes very much lower indeed.

What is important to understand here, and highly significant in terms of its implications for the Private Equity industry, is that the motivation behind co-investment vehicles has changed dramatically. The traditional form of co-investment pool was attractive to manager (GP) and investor (LP) alike. For the GP, it gave them the opportunity to target much bigger companies than would otherwise have been the case given the size of their fund. This would often be described as 'punching above our weight'. What became clear in the early years of the Buyout industry was that the internal processes of investors who asked for the opportunity to co-invest alongside the fund were often incapable of producing decisions within the required time frame. A distinct pool managed by the GP, on the other hand, was subject to exactly the same decision process as the fund itself, and the GP could thus safely enter into a purchase contract without having to worry about whether a piece of their intended equity finance might fall away at the last minute. The advantage conferred by such certainty was worth paying for, in the shape of lower charges to the LP on that additional capital.

For the LP, the main motivation was usually being able to put more capital to work than might otherwise be the case. Until the explosion in average fund size from about 2003 onwards, it was frequently the case that investors were simply unable to secure as large a commitment to a particular fund as they would like, and thus the co-investment pool was a welcome, though uncertain, addition. This is still the case with the world's largest investors, many of whom have been forced to scale back their percentage allocations to Private Equity because of problems in finding sufficient amounts of quality product.

Nowadays, things are different. The main motivating factor has become the lower cost that such investment carries. Buyout returns have been squeezed in recent years, particularly in Europe when viewed in comparison to the very high returns earned during the 90s, and, as we will see, the cost to the LP of investing in a particular pool has become a major factor when calculating their net return.

Terminology

I have referred to the Oscar Wilde factor above and while I propose to deal with this largely by ignoring it, there are some important points to make right at the outset, since there are some differences in terminology which go to the very heart of understanding the asset class, and which are a constant source of confusion for the uninitiated.

In Europe, the asset class as a whole is called 'Private Equity', and has traditionally been broadly sub-divided into 'Buyout' and 'Venture Capital' (or just 'Venture'), as we will see below. While this broad classification has also held good in the US, different terms have frequently been used. There, the asset class as a whole has sometimes been called 'Venture Capital', and Buyouts (particularly large ones) have usually been referred to as 'Private Equity'. I think you will see at once the huge scope for confusion which this creates. I am frequently consulted by journalists working for national newspapers who are about to write an article on the sector, and find myself having to make this point again and again; it seems that I have been only partially successful, since I have lost count of the number of times I have seen large European Buyout firms referred to as 'Venture Capitalists'.

In fairness to the journalists involved, none of whom pretend to be experts on the sector, this confusion is, to a certain extent, perpetuated and encouraged within Europe for the rather cynical purposes of those concerned. In the right hands, Venture Capital is a powerful tool for economic growth. Research suggests that already by the end of 2000, Venture Capital had directly created about 8 million new jobs in the US (roughly equivalent to one job for every $36 000 of investment), and that if one added into the mix the jobs created indirectly in supporting and related businesses, then the total rose to a staggering 27 million.[2] No comparable studies have been made in Europe; the deliberate confusion between Venture and Buyout makes any reference to 'Venture-backed' companies meaningless in this context. However, it is logically impossible that Venture has had no effect whatever. It must therefore be accepted that Venture Capital is socially and economically desirable, since it has a clear tendency to boost both GDP and employment. Venture Capital typically represents less than 1% of total capital investment in any one year in the US, yet venture-backed companies are said to create about 13% of GDP.[3]

Buyout, by contrast, can be seen by those European governments who practice what might be termed a 'social economic' model (most of the continental countries, and increasingly the UK) as undesirable. As we discuss how Buyout operates it will become clear why Buyout transactions are frequently attacked as having the effect of reducing employment through restructuring and rationalisation,[4] and certainly of decreasing tax yield, since financial structuring will use loan interest to reduce taxable earnings. It is for this reason that, unlike in the United States, where there are rigidly separate industry bodies for Venture Capital and 'Private Equity' (Buyout), industry bodies in Europe have sought to wrap themselves in the flag of Venture Capital.

It used to be the case that wherever you saw the word 'Democratic' as part of the name of a country, then you could be absolutely sure that, far from being 'democratic' the country

---

[2] Public Sector Review: Finance, Summer 2004 pp 62–63.

[3] Public Sector Review, as before.

[4] Though this is hotly disputed by the Private Equity industry. Indeed, these objections were largely abandoned during the Parliamentary Committee proceedings in the UK in 2008 when figures were released by the Centre for Management Buyout Research at the University of Nottingham which strongly suggested that across the whole period of Private Equity ownership (as opposed to the first few months), average headcount actually increased.

would, on the contrary, be a totalitarian police state (the former East Germany would be a prime example). So it is with the word 'Venture' in Europe. The British Venture Capital Association, for example, speaks (despite its name), not, as one might expect, for the Venture community in the UK but overwhelmingly by member fund size for the Buyout community transacting deals across Europe. The European Venture Capital Association suffers from a similar identity crisis.

This is unfortunate for all sorts of reasons, not least that the Venture community in Europe is left without any representative body of its own. Fortunately for the BVCA and the European Buyout community, European politicians are sufficiently, er, unsophisticated that this deception goes unmasked. Unfortunately for the European Venture community, they are forced unjustly to endure the brickbats which are regularly aimed at 'Venture Capitalists' (meaning Buyout firms) by left-wing politicians, which may, in the future, include draconian regulation.

It will be apparent from the title of this book that I have chosen to adopt 'Private Equity' as the name of the asset class as a whole, and 'Buyout' and 'Venture' as its two main constituents. I believe that this is the least confusing approach available and it reflects the way in which I have always viewed the asset class. I will generally be adopting the US expressions 'LP' (Limited Partner) and 'GP' (General Partner) for 'investor' and 'firm' or 'manager' respectively, but there will be occasions when the context suggests that the European terms should be preferred. Incidentally, it may come as a surprise for American readers to learn that the terms 'LP' and 'GP' were entirely unknown in the European Private Equity industry until about ten years ago.

However, while investors and data providers alike cling to this traditional binary classification of funds into 'Buyout' and 'Venture', it is inadequate to describe the various types of Private Equity activity that actually take place. In particular, both Growth Capital and Development Capital are distinct types of investment that currently have to be shoe-horned into one of these categories. In consequence, while we will examine later in this chapter the traditional division of Private Equity into 'Venture' and 'Buyout', Growth and Development Capital can no longer be ignored, not least since they are dominant forms of Private Equity investment in the new, but rapidly growing, markets of Asia, Eastern Europe and South America. Thus, the reader will find both an outline description of them in this chapter and also a whole new chapter describing Growth and Development Capital, which may conveniently be studied together since they are similar in appearance.

Having done that, we will be in a position to set out in summary form all the different kinds of Private Equity investment which occur both at the company and the fund level, but in case you would like to glance ahead, please see Table 1.2 on page 13.

Different Types of Private Equity Investment

There are four main types of what might be termed 'pure' Private Equity investment at the company level: Buyout, Development (Capital), Growth (Capital) and Venture (Capital). It is almost certainly simplest to think of these in terms of the type of company in which they invest, and here it is useful to refer to the Product Life Cycle, see Figure 1.1 (though this can equally well apply to a new service as to a new product).

Many will already be familiar with this basic tool of business analysis, which is widely used by marketing strategists. However, it may also be thought of as very conveniently delineating the 'hunting ground' of each of the four main types of Private Equity activity.

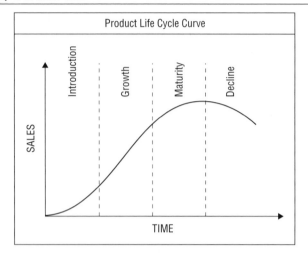

Figure 1.1   Private Equity type by PLC stage

The key thing to bear in mind (and indeed the main driver behind the development of the PLC in the first place) is that a company's cash flow should become steadily stronger as it moves to the right in time along the PLC (as we will see when we look at Growth Capital, things are slightly more complex than this, but this is the basic principle).

In other words, when a company is in the 'Introduction' stage it will initially have no cash inflows at all, since it will still be developing its offering and will thus have nothing to sell. By the time it moves into the 'Growth' stage, it will be generating some income but, given the very substantial cost of promoting its offering in a growing market, overall cash flow is likely still to be strongly negative. Once the 'Mature' stage arrives, then the company should be both profitable and have positive cash flow. However, the strongest cash flows are usually to be found in the 'Decline' stage of the PLC. This may seem counter-intuitive; how can a market be attractive where demand is falling? The answer (or at least the theory) is that by this time the least successful competitors will have exited the market ('market consolidation') and relatively little money will need to be spent on development and promotion.

At the same time, as a company moves to the right along the PLC its risk of not surviving will decrease steadily. For those who work in the Private Equity industry this is really just two different ways of stating the same thing, since until cash flow break-even is reached, the Private Equity investor faces a continuing decision as to whether or not to continue to inject fresh capital into the business, whereas once cash flow turns positive, the business can theoretically at least survive without the need for further outside support. These two closely related trends should be borne in mind as we look at each type of Private Equity in turn.

Venture Capital targets the Introduction stage of the PLC. Thus, Venture-backed companies will be at a very young stage of their life, and perhaps even total start-ups which have been conceived but not yet born. The question of whether or not it will survive until adulthood will be a constant issue hanging over each one, as there is a very high rate of infant mortality.

Growth Capital targets, unsurprisingly, the Growth stage of the PLC. Growth companies are characterised by the need to ramp up their sales very quickly so as to be able at least to hold steady their percentage share of a rapidly growing market, and, as with Venture companies, cash flow will therefore almost always be negative because of the costs of promotion and business development.

Both *Buyout* and *Development Capital* target the Mature and Decline stages of the PLC. Later, we will examine more fully the difference between them, but in this case it has to do not with the type of company being targeted but with the way(s) in which the investment is carried out. Buyout will involve the taking of a majority stake, whereas Development funds take a minority stake. This is often referred to as 'control' and 'non-control' investing respectively, although we will see that this is a rather simplistic view. Partly because of this, Buyout investments will always be leveraged by the use of acquisition debt and related finance, whereas Development deals will not.

A broad delineation: Buyout and Venture

There is, however, a practical problem here which we will encounter in different guises as we explore the Private Equity industry, which is that its members and data providers do not always divide things as neatly as we would wish, or in the same way. We stub our toe straight away here, as the data providers do not recognise the same compartments that we wish to study. There are, for example, no industry figures which break out returns for Growth or Development, these being lumped into either Buyout or Venture, and not always on a consistent basis. In the past, it was felt by many that this did little harm. While there are very many Growth and Development deals done every year, these are typically relatively small in size individually and definitely very small in total value compared to either Buyout or Venture. This effect is compounded by the reluctance of many of those firms who make such investments to register their data, thus rendering Growth and Development statistically even more insignificant. In this case, the argument runs, if one is looking to research the performance of the industry as a whole from the available figures, then little harm is done in practice by the traditional approach.

It is difficult to refute this view, unless one is a statistician of a purist nature. However, it will almost certainly become easier, and indeed more necessary, to do so with each passing year. One of the clear trends in Private Equity activity in recent years has been an increasing amount of money being raised for investment in newly emerging geographic markets, and here, for various reasons which we will explore, Growth and Development predominate. As more and more of these players begin to make their fund data available, it will become vital to be able to differentiate between the performance of, say, Development and Buyout deals, and unless the present system is reformed, then the relevant data will simply not be available to allow this to be done.

It should also be understood that many firms in continental Europe have, for many years, traditionally pursued both Buyout and Development Capital deals within the same fund, usually confusingly referred to as a 'Buyout' fund. So, unless data were available at the level of the individual company, and could be extracted and evaluated separately, then fund returns still might not be very meaningful. These points will be better understood after we have examined the way in which Private Equity returns are measured.

It is also undeniable that the vast majority of the world's Private Equity fund investors (LPs) refer simply to 'Buyout' and 'Venture' when discussing their Private Equity allocations and investments. It is almost unknown (though logically this should change) for them to have any specific allocation to 'Growth' or 'Development'. The data providers might therefore argue, with every justification, that the way they divide up Private Equity returns simply reflects the way in which their clients view the world.

For all these reasons, it was decided that Growth and Development Capital did not merit their own chapter in the first edition of this book, though even then this was a marginal decision. Partly, it was felt that introducing yet another source of complexity into an asset class which is already very difficult to understand might serve simply to confuse people unnecessarily. Given the continued expansion of these sectors since 2006, though, this is no longer a tenable approach and so the reader will find a new chapter dealing specifically with such investment.

Now that we know that is coming, however, let us, for the moment, explore the traditional classification of the Private Equity world into Buyout and Venture. We have already seen that their respective investment focus is to be found at different ends of the PLC, but what does this mean in practical terms?

Buyout can be distinguished from Venture Capital in a number of ways. Chief among these are the fact that it generally focuses on established companies rather than young businesses. It is also generally true that it tends to concern itself with 'traditional' business activities rather than technology, although this distinction is becoming somewhat blurred as former 'dot com' and technology businesses mature. We have already seen a number of Buyouts in the Telecoms space (some of them very large) and there is no logical reason why a company which has originally been Venture-backed should not, in the full course of time, be the subject of a Buyout transaction. It is, however, fair to say that, while the businesses of Buyout companies may be increasingly technology-related, they will never carry any pure technology risk.

Size is also often advanced as a differentiating factor, and now that the excessive valuations of the dot com bubble have subsided, this can also probably be adopted with some confidence as a general truth. However, this, too, should be treated with some caution. While it is certainly true that the average size of Buyout funds is getting larger and larger, enabling them, in turn, to transact larger and larger deals, there are still a few Buyout firms who are happy to operate at the smaller end of the market, while some Venture funds are well in excess of $1 billion.

Another important distinction is that between 'control' and 'non-control' investing, the former being where the Private Equity manager either owns a majority of the shares in the company or at least has control over the majority of the voting rights. It is extremely unusual to find a Venture Capitalist having control over a company, except where this may have occurred through the failure of the company to achieve its targets and the triggering of default and/or preference rights.

A further important distinction, and one of some political sensitivity, lies in the use of leverage. Buyout transactions are structured using both equity (provided by the fund) and debt[5] (from external providers), whereas Venture transactions use only equity. There are two main reasons for this. First, for financial engineering purposes, a major controlling shareholding is required in order to structure a debt package in a tax-effective manner. Second, in order to service the debt, the company must be producing cash flow and usually also earnings, though the two are not, of course, the same thing. Venture Capital investments do not satisfy either of these requirements.

---

[5]This description is deliberately simplistic. In reality there may be both debt and mezzanine, and often several layers of each.

Table 1.1   Traditional guidelines for classifying private equity transactions

Venture	Buyout
Small enterprise value (particularly in Europe)	Large enterprise value, sometimes very large (multi-billion)
Bank debt almost never used	Bank debt almost always used
Young companies, even start-up	Generally mature, established companies
Investee companies rarely profit-making	Profit levels of investee companies crucial (although turnaround situations are considered)
Investee company will always be developing or applying new technology	Technology considerations largely irrelevant
A minority stake will always be taken. Control will usually only arise through default and/or refinancing	Control always present in true Buyouts, though some firms practise Development Capital
Valuation largely a matter of instinct and experience	Firm rules of financial theory available with which to calculate valuation (e.g. earnings multiple)
Venture managers will often have been successful start-up entrepreneurs and/or will have specialist technology expertise	Buyout managers typically come from an accountancy, investment banking or management consultancy background

These factors are advanced as suggested guidelines and while they will prove helpful, and perhaps even definitive in most cases, I think it will be obvious even from the brief outline above that there will always be some that defy precise definition. How would you classify, for example, a firm that took majority stakes in fairly mature technology companies using only equity, or a firm that used debt financing to take a majority stake in a troubled early-stage company? Happily, common sense will usually prevail but Table 1.1, which may be thought of as a sort of Private Equity litmus test, may prove helpful.

Secondary fund investing

When the first edition of this book was being written and discussed in 2006, it seemed as though secondary transactions did not represent a sufficiently large part of the industry as a whole to warrant a separate chapter. Again, this was a borderline decision (I did actually draft a chapter, but finally decided not to use it) but it has become even more obvious since then that secondary investing has become a very significant part of the Private Equity landscape, and also has an important part to play in the planning of Private Equity fund programmes, particularly in the early stages. We will examine both these areas in more detail later, but for the moment I am happy to advance a preliminary explanation of what secondary transactions are and how they work.

It is widely assumed by investors that Private Equity funds are illiquid investments. While this is strictly true as a matter of law (in the sense that they are not quoted on an exchange), it is not true as a matter of practice, because of the very active secondary market which exists. Briefly, if you hold an interest in a Private Equity fund and wish, for whatever reason, to sell it (thus also bringing to an end your obligation to continue to fund capital calls), then there are a significant number of specialist secondary purchasers who will be happy to quote you a price for it. Various investors and Funds of Funds also play in this space, though it does not form the main thrust of their activities.

Secondary transactions also take place at the company level, typically taking the form of a GP seeking to sell the remaining portfolio of a fund in order to be able to wind it up in a timely fashion. Very rarely one may see a GP who has been unable to raise a new fund selling the active portfolio of their existing fund or funds at the urging of their LPs; more often, it will be a question of practical convenience as a fund approaches its scheduled end date.

The skills of a secondary investor are different again to those of a GP or a conventional LP, but are probably the closest of all to standard finance theory and thus the easiest to learn. Certainly they are at the most objective and quantitative ends of the relevant continuum.

As explained above, given the growth in size and importance of the secondary market, a separate chapter has been included later in the book looking at how such investments are analysed and made.

Mezzanine

A further type of Private Equity investment is the provision of mezzanine finance to Buyout transactions. Again, there is potential for misunderstanding here as the word 'mezzanine' can be used differently on each side of the Atlantic, but we will use it in the sense of convertible debt instruments. In other words, a mezzanine investor will lend money into a Buyout transaction, but with the right to convert all or part of it into shares in the target company. In practice, the conversion rights tend to be in addition to, rather than an alternative to, the right to have the debt repaid, and are referred to as a 'kicker'. Mezzanine will typically be unsecured, or have only security rights which rank below that of the senior debt, but the mezzanine provider will charge a higher rate of interest than the senior debt provider in recognition of this lack of security, which exposes the mezzanine holder to greater liquidation risk.

Mezzanine and 'junior debt' are often treated as if they are the same, at least in Europe, but in reality this is not the case and mezzanine is simply one form (though by far the most common in Europe) of junior debt. The other most common form (particularly in the US) is the use of junk bonds.[6] There is yet another type of borrowing known as Second Lien and some believe this, too, forms part of junior debt, though it can more properly be seen as sitting between the senior and junior levels.

Specialist mezzanine funds earned good returns in the 90s while interest rates were relatively high and senior debt relatively limited, since the banks were cautious about increasing their exposure to leveraged transactions. All this changed as the 90s progressed. Not only did the banks embrace the Buyout debt market enthusiastically, they also began arranging and providing the mezzanine requirement. In consequence, mezzanine funds were little seen. Writing in 2009, the wheel has come full circle once again, and the banks have become extremely reluctant to lend money at all, let alone into leveraged transactions. It is no coincidence that a number of mezzanine funds are currently in the market, and this is widely tipped, along with the secondary market, to be a very attractive Private Equity segment over the next few years.

Private Equity at the company level

Table 1.2 may be helpful in remembering the salient characteristics of the four types of pure Private Equity at the company level. 'Pure' because mezzanine is, of course, not strictly

---

[6]See Burrough and Helyar (2004) *Barbarians at the Gate*, Arrow Books Ltd, London, or Anders, G. (2002) *Merchants of Debt*, Beard Books, New York.

Table 1.2 The four main types of Private Equity at the company level

	Leverage	PLC	Stake	Technology	Profits
Buyout	Yes	Mature/Decline	Maj	No	Yes
Development	No	Mature/Decline	Min	No	Yes
Growth	No	Growth	Min	Usually	Sometimes
Venture	No	Introduction	Min	Yes	No

speaking equity at all, but convertible debt. Please note in particular that Buyout is the only one of the four to involve the use of acquisition debt, thus giving the lie to those who describe Private Equity as 'leveraged equity'.

In addition to these four, there is mezzanine, which is used as an add-on to Buyout transactions.

Private Equity at the fund level

Table 1.3

Fund of Funds	Makes commitments to new Private Equity funds, acting just like any other investor (LP)
Secondary	Buys current commitments in existing funds from any investor (LP) who wishes to sell
Buyout	May also make Development Capital deals
Development	May not specifically use the word 'Development' in the fund name
Growth	Can be confused with late-stage Venture or Development (see later)
Venture	Usually fairly clearly labelled, though the words 'Seed' (for early stage) or 'Capital'* (for mid to late stage) may appear in the name instead.
Mezzanine	Invests by way of convertible debt in the deals of various Buyout funds

*Confusingly, the word 'Capital' may be used by any type of Private Equity fund manager, and others beside (Real Estate, Infrastructure, Hedge funds, etc.)

SUMMARY

There is widespread misunderstanding about what 'Private Equity' actually is. In particular, many people believe that Private Equity consists only of the large Buyout transactions which feature regularly in the media, or confuse Private Equity funds with Hedge funds.

Private Equity investing can be divided generally into two streams: fund investing and company investing. Fund investing is essentially one level above company investing, as the fund will, in turn, invest in underlying portfolio companies. For this reason, company investing is often called 'direct' investing.

Fund investments are, in turn, divided into primary and secondary investments. A primary investment is a commitment to invest in a new fund which is, as yet, unformed. A secondary investment is the purchase and transfer of an interest in an existing fund from another investor.

Direct Private Equity investing, i.e. at the company rather than the fund level, can be described as typically being an investment of an equity nature in a company which is not listed on any public equity market. While there are a number of possible exceptions, this definition remains broadly true.

All Private Equity investing, whether at the fund or company level, has traditionally been sub-divided into Buyout and Venture. Buyout transactions typically include debt and involve established and usually profitable companies. Venture transactions typically do not include debt and involve young, even start-up, companies and some element of technological innovation.

In addition to these two traditional categories, it is necessary also to include Growth and Development Capital, which both involve taking minority stakes in companies. These transactions almost never involve the use of debt.

Mezzanine investing is the provision of junior debt to Buyout transactions in the form of high-yield debt instruments which offer the right also to take a small part of the company's equity, usually subject to certain conditions being met. This equity conversion right is usually referred to as a 'kicker' or 'equity kicker'.

2

What are Private Equity Funds, and How do They Work?

For the first of many times in this book, let us note that Private Equity is very different in many important respects from just about any other asset class. One of the most significant of these differences is the way in which Private Equity funds work. Perversely, the more one knows about the world of finance, and the closer the acquaintance one has with investment funds in general, then the more confusing are Private Equity funds likely to be; in practice, it is often easier to teach lay people, such as pension fund trustees, about them since they come to them with no preconceived notions.

It may be easiest to think of a Private Equity fund as a water pipe, since this is, in practice, all it really is, see Figure 2.1.

Imagine that a farmer has access to a communal water tank. When he needs water to irrigate his crops, he turns on a tap and draws as much water as he needs down a pipe from the tank. Imagine that he lives in a region which is subject to monsoons, so every so often his fields will be flooded. Now he is able to turn on a pump and send the excess water up a different pipe back into the tank.

Subject to a few minor refinements, this is essentially what a Private Equity fund does, see Figure 2.2.

When the fund begins its life the investors do not give the farmer all their water (money) at once, since (1) he would have nothing to do with it right away and (2) it is designed to last him for a lengthy period, usually at least three years. Instead this water (money) becomes a reserve.

When he needs some, he issues a capital call for the amount he needs, addressed to each LP pro rata to their share of the fund's committed capital. They pay it into the fund; this process is known as a drawdown. The GP then takes it out of the fund and uses it to make an investment.

When the investment is sold, the process now goes into reverse, this time known as a distribution. The proceeds are pumped back up a different pipe, but here there is a filtering out process. The original cost of the investment plus (typically) 80% of the gain goes back to the LPs. The remainder, (typically) 20% of the gain, goes to the GP; this share of the gain is called the carry or carried interest.

This may seem a simplistic image, but it is actually a very good representation of how a Private Equity fund works in practice, and this has gained greatly added significance over the last few years, given the widespread confusion between Private Equity funds and Hedge funds. Private Equity funds behave in this way; Hedge funds do not. We will examine this in more detail later in the chapter.

If you only ever remember one thing about Private Equity funds, let it be this image of a water pipe. A Private Equity fund will never normally hold cash. It operates simply as a conduit, allowing water (money) to flow down from the investors (LPs) through the fund into

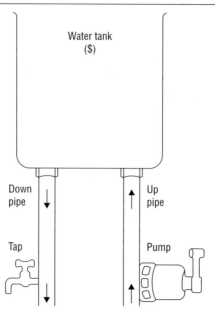

Figure 2.1   Water Pump

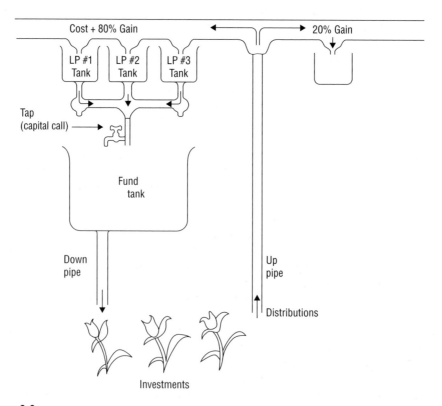

Figure 2.2

investments, and then to flow up through the fund back to investors once an investment is realised. With only one small exception, no other type of investment fund in the world operates on this basis.

CAPITAL: ALLOCATED, COMMITTED, DRAWN DOWN AND INVESTED

We will be examining in some detail how Private Equity funds and transactions work, but this may be greatly facilitated by an explanation right at the outset of the different categories of capital which one encounters. This point is absolutely key as, for example, a failure to understand the difference between committed and invested capital lies at the heart of the fundamental mistakes which one sees being made habitually by investors who have either recently entered the asset class for the first time, or who see it as a tiresome distraction from the main business of investing in bonds and quoted equities, and thus never bother to acquire the required level of knowledge. Without wishing to be unduly paranoid or cynical, could it be that it is perhaps in the interests of such people, who may never have really believed in the asset class anyway, to see its returns artificially depressed in their hands? At the very least, they are unlikely to be unhappy should such an eventuality occur.

It may be helpful first to see a basic graphic (Figure 2.3) showing the way in which Private Equity funds work.

Just before we press on with examining the different categories of capital, let us note one very important thing, which is the subject of much misunderstanding. These two streams of cash flow in and out of the fund, from and to investors, do not net off against each other. In other words, if you have committed $10M to a fund, $6M has been drawn down, and you suddenly receive a distribution of $1M from an early realisation, you still have an outstanding commitment of $4M.

There is a very good reason for this. Under usual circumstances, a distribution, once made to an investor, may not be recalled. This allows the GP to distribute money to investors as it becomes available, thus boosting capital efficiency, without worrying about having to maintain a reserve. Remember, a Private Equity fund operates simply as a pipe, allowing water (money) to move up and down. So, this is a necessary trade-off. Distributions, once made, may not be recalled. Distributions and drawdowns do not net off against each other.

Allocated capital is that amount of their capital which an investor notionally sets aside in their mind to be devoted to Private Equity. For example, if a €500M pension fund decides

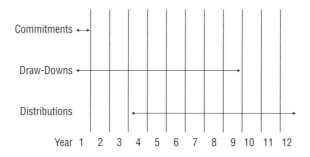

Figure 2.3

to make a 15% allocation to Private Equity, then its allocated capital will be €75M. Allocated capital can be thought of as roughly representing the total amount of capital which an investor would ideally like to have actually invested in Private Equity investments (i.e. companies) at any one time.

Committed capital is that amount of capital which an investor has actually legally promised to provide to Private Equity funds by signing Limited Partnership Agreements. An obvious point needs to be made here, since it is so frequently not appreciated; in the early years of a Private Equity fund programme, this figure will necessarily be quite small, and the difference between committed capital and allocated capital very large.

Drawn down capital is that amount of your committed capital which has actually been drawn down (i.e. requested by a Private Equity fund by way of a capital call or drawdown notice and paid to them). This will include both capital to be invested in companies and also money required for fees and expenses. Again, in the first year or two of any individual Private Equity fund, there may be a big difference between the amount of committed capital and the amount of drawn down capital.

Invested capital, as the name suggests, is that part of drawn down capital which has actually been invested in companies. In the early part of a Private Equity fund a surprisingly large proportion of capital drawn down can actually be going to fees and costs, and thus there can be a big difference between drawn down capital and invested capital.

I think it will be apparent from all of this that there can be a dramatic difference between allocated capital and invested capital. A common misconception amongst those who have been used to investing in quoted shares and bonds is that one can somehow pick up the phone and order a certain amount of Private Equity, thus fully investing your allocation all at once, rather than realising that it is likely to take at least eight years of careful planning and execution to get anywhere near your objective.

HOW DO PRIVATE EQUITY FUNDS WORK?

Structure

We have already seen that Private Equity funds are invariably structured as Limited Partnerships, thus leading to the steady adoption of the American terminology 'LP' (for Limited Partner) for an investor in such funds and 'GP' (for General Partner) for a manager. The basic concept of a Limited Partnership is that there can be any number of passive investors, who take no part in the business and have limited liability (limited to the amount of their committed capital), but there must always be at least one General Partner, who has unlimited liability[1] and actually takes the necessary decisions and actions required to run the business.

There are two main practical reasons why a Limited Partnership is almost always the ideal choice:

1. US pension funds, which still constitute the largest single class of investor in Private Equity funds worldwide, are governed by a regulatory regime known as ERISA.[2] Fortunately, since it is a subject of somewhat limited interest, we have no need to delve into the complexities of these regulations, though there is some very basic discussion in

---

[1] Avoided in practice by using a limited liability vehicle, such as a company, as the GP of any individual fund.
[2] Employee Retirement Income Security Act.

the following parts of this chapter. Suffice it to say at this stage that the Limited Partnership structure proved ideal for accommodating some of their more arcane requirements.

2. Limited Partnerships are treated as being tax transparent. What does this mean? Take a look at the nearest window. You know there is a pane of glass in it, because you can reach out and touch it. Yet when you look at it, you see not the pane of glass but whatever lies behind it. Limited Partnerships operate in much the same way. When they realise an investment, no local tax is paid, since the Limited Partnership is not itself a taxable entity. Instead, you look through it to its Limited Partners (for this reason, Limited Partnerships and other tax transparent structures are frequently called 'look through' vehicles by tax lawyers), who pay tax on their percentage share of the gain (calculated pro rata with their share of the fund's committed capital) in their own jurisdiction.

Why is this so important? Because many LPs are tax exempt in their own country, and thus would find themselves paying tax which they would not otherwise incur, since frequently they are unable for various reasons to reclaim tax paid locally. Worse still, in the case of US pension plans, these deductions of tax and any necessary related tax filings would almost certainly breach the dreaded ERISA rules and put their very tax exempt status in jeopardy.

By the way, there is one small but important point which needs to be grasped. Please note that the penultimate paragraph talked about 'gain', and this word was chosen very deliberately. Generally speaking, this system works for capital gains, since these are not taxed at the local level in the hands of non-residents, but *not* for income. For this reason, Private Equity funds and transactions are structured with a view to producing capital gains, but no income.[3]

For both these reasons, then, the vast majority of the world's Private Equity capital is raised and managed through Limited Partnerships. While true, it is nonetheless important to understand that, if funds were to be measured by number rather than by size, then a rather different picture would emerge.

It is probably more correct to say that institutional Private Equity funds are customarily structured as Limited Partnerships. Many funds which are intended for retail use are structured as quoted vehicles, and these have also been used by investors looking to 'park' uninvested allocated capital. As we will see in a later chapter, these vehicles have at different times frequently been cash rich, and rarely approach the level of returns achieved by institutional partnerships, at least measured in IRR terms. We will also see that quoted status can give rise to other (very significant) problems.

There have been other funds aimed predominantly at retail investors and driven by tax breaks: examples would be a VCT (Venture Capital Trust) in the UK or an FCPR[4] (Fonds Commun de Placement à Risques) in France. In these cases, again, high quality institutional returns are unlikely to be achieved, but investors will hope that the benefit of the associated tax breaks will make up for this.

In certain countries, legal and regulatory reform has been slow to catch up with investor requirements, with the result that even today some rather bizarre legal forms are sometimes

---

[3]This bland statement is a gross oversimplification, but this is not a book on tax law. Clearly some very complex structuring may be required, particularly where (in, say, a Development Capital deal) it is desired to use loan notes. Often, separate vehicles will be set up within the deal structure to facilitate this.

[4]This does not even need to invest exclusively in Private Equity. An FCPR will enjoy special fiscal advantages if even 50% of its capital is invested in European unlisted securities.

forced upon an institutional fund; a good example would be India, where Private Equity funds currently have to be structured as a trust, with the added complication of an offshore vehicle in Mauritius, which has a double tax treaty with India. However, many institutional investors quite understandably take the view that if no Limited Partnership is available in a given jurisdiction then they would rather wait until it is; this is a particular issue for ERISA investors (see below, and the note at the end of this chapter).

Some jurisdictions more or less force a Limited Partnership structure on an investor. In America, for example, pension funds are subject to ERISA regulations, as we have seen. While these do not impose any strict requirement to restrict Private Equity investment to Limited Partnerships (reference is to Venture Capital operating companies (VCOCs) and there is a particular issue with regard to the making of capital contributions before the date of the fund's first investment[5]), in practice US lawyers have become adept at drafting LPAs (Limited Partnership Agreements) in such a way as to accommodate these, and so as a matter of practice few American pension funds will contemplate any other structure.[6]

A Limited Partnership is known as a closed-end fund since it has a finite lifetime (typically for either ten or twelve years, depending on whether it is a Buyout or Venture fund respectively, but in each case with the option of two annual extensions). This has always been the model in the US and the UK (at least for institutional funds) where the Limited Partnership has long been accepted as a way of doing business, but less so in other regions.

In continental Europe, for example, much Private Equity investing traditionally took place through open-ended structures. These 'evergreen' vehicles were the subject of much criticism from Anglo-Saxon observers, who claimed that they provided little incentive to managers to force exits from their investments, and that their returns could not validly be compared with Limited Partnerships because typically there was no mechanism for them to return capital to investors. These are now largely consigned to history as occasional curiosities, and indeed Thomson Reuters have recently removed these evergreens from their industry data.

Cash Flow

Private Equity funds are unlike any other form of investment in that they represent a stream of unpredictable cash flows over the life of the fund, both inward and outward. These cash flows are unpredictable not only as to their amount, but also as to their timing. For example, while funds will typically select their investments over a three-year period, the period during which they are legally able to do so (the 'investment period') is usually set at five years to provide flexibility, and even then some funds (particularly Venture funds) will make follow-on investments into their portfolio companies for some years thereafter. We will be considering later what this means for the way in which we should model Private Equity funds and analyse returns, but let us for the moment abandon our simplistic water tank model and examine how this all actually happens in practice.

When a fund needs cash, either for the payment of fees or the making of investments, the GP will issue a Drawdown Notice (sometimes called a Capital Call, though strictly speaking the Capital Call is the process to which the Drawdown Notice gives effect). This will ask for

---

[5]Broadly, to qualify as a VCOC, at least 50% of capital must be invested in Venture Capital investments and the entity must exercise actual management rights in respect of at least one of the underlying companies.
[6]But please see the note at the end of this chapter.

a certain amount of money to be paid into a specified bank account by a certain date and will give brief details of what the money is required for.

The LP will check that the purposes for which the money is required are valid according to the terms of the LPA (is the investment within the stated scope of the fund? Is there a restriction on the amount of money that may be called in any one year, or for any one investment? etc) and that the amount has been correctly calculated. It will then take steps to honour the Drawdown Notice by making the required bank transfer. An important point to note here is that funds are generally not allowed to draw down money to hold generally on account, although they are allowed to do so in anticipation of a specific transaction which they hope to close shortly, and frequently to return it and draw it down again if the transaction does not complete, although this can give certain types of investors, particularly Funds of Funds, procedural headaches of their own.

Distributions are the other side of the cash flow coin. Whenever a fund exits an investment by sale or flotation (American: IPO) then it will have cash available to return to investors. This is usually effected by a Distribution Notice, which is just the opposite of a Drawdown Notice, and will notify each individual investor of how much money they may expect to have transferred into their bank account, and when. Since the timing of exits is unpredictable, then so, necessarily, is the timing of distributions. To inject yet further uncertainty into the situation, a fund may actually sell its holding in a particular company in tranches over time, particularly where the exit is by flotation.

One important point which is often overlooked is the tendency of some Private Equity funds, particularly US Venture funds, to make distributions 'in specie'. All this means is that instead of selling shares in an underlying company and then distributing cash, they distribute the shares themselves, leaving the individual investors to decide when and how to sell them. Indeed, with US Venture funds, distributions in specie are probably more numerous than cash distributions. A further complication is that such shares are frequently restricted stock, i.e. they cannot be traded (sold) for a certain length of time (usually six months). This imposes a requirement for a specialist 'end game' team within any investor in such funds, firstly because that investor may not already have a mechanism in place for trading quoted stocks (it may, for example, be a specialist Private Equity Fund of Funds), secondly because the management of restricted stocks requires complex compliance and regulatory systems, and finally because even if the investor does already deal in quoted stocks they are unlikely to have an analyst covering the company in question. This means that most investors simply sell their shares on the first available day, which can obviously lead to them having to accept a disappointing price as many shares are thrown into the market together.

There were some European funds which used this practice in the mid-90s, but the problems described above led to such adverse investor reaction that almost without exception European funds decided to eschew such measures, and the practice will now be found only in the very unusual and highly theoretical circumstance of a fund being wound up while still holding active investments. However, in the US it is commonplace and those who rush into investing directly in US funds, particularly of the Venture Capital variety, without putting in place mechanisms for dealing with it (there are various third party quoted distribution management services that are prepared to provide the service for a fee) may be in for an unpleasant surprise. In fairness, the widespread adoption of electronic registration and dealing services in recent years have made this less onerous than once it was, but it still imposes a prodigious regulatory burden, and in any event only a specialist professional investor is likely to have access to these expensive facilities.

Investment

The most important thing to understand about the way in which a Private Equity fund invests is that investment power is confined to the manager (GP). The LPs have no voice at all in the investment process and, indeed, should not want to have, since there is a significant risk of them losing their limited liability if they can be shown to have played an active part in the management of the partnership.

The combination of passive investing and long fund lifetimes has made Private Equity an unpalatable dish for some, and emphasises the need for extreme care and specialist skills in the selection of managers in the first place. Any Private Equity fund is likely to last longer than the average marriage, and while an active secondary market does exist, a Private Equity fund commitment should be thought of as essentially long term.

There are some investors who chafe at the bit and find ways of influencing the investment process, either from behind the scenes, or through sitting on the investment committee or even quite blatantly with a power of veto. This will be dramatically unpopular with most investors, however, even to the extent of putting them off committing to the fund at all. A golden rule of Private Equity fund selection is that those responsible for the investment process should be members of the full-time executive team, but nobody else.

Historically there was an interesting juxtaposition here between practice and attitudes in continental Europe and elsewhere. On the continent, it was commonplace for Private Equity funds to be affiliated to, or even owned by, entities such as banks and insurance companies. Even where this was not openly the case, GPs would seek to position themselves within the semi-formal networks that permeated all local business dealings by bringing senior people from such organisations into the investment decision process. The juxtaposition arose because this was found to be very attractive to local investors (who liked both the idea of enhanced dealflow and some check or balance on the investment team) but deeply unpopular with Anglo-Saxon investors, who deplored the lack of independence and possible interference with the investment process for reasons which might not be purely financial. There was a period in France, for example, when banks were inclined simply to park troublesome debtors in their captive Private Equity portfolio.

To be fair, there were instances of this in the UK and the US as well, but these were mostly resolved some years ago by the executive team buying themselves out from their parent organisation (CVC splitting away from Citibank would be an obvious example). This took much longer on the continent, where many GPs were curiously reluctant to go it on their own, and indeed there are still many captive and semi-captive firms in operation, including many in Asia. Interestingly, however, the teams are at least at great pains nowadays to stress their independence.

This is a delicate matter and I do not wish to provoke controversy. However, it does seem to me that even where there may be no outsiders involved on the investment committee, it is probably illusory to talk about independence within any large group. Deutsche Bank, for example, simply closed down its supposedly independent Private Equity operation in London one day, regardless of the interests of the outside investors which the team had managed to attract into the fund. All in all, I would agree wholeheartedly with an aphorism which is credited to Phil Horsley, a very senior and respected Private Equity fund investor (and a former partner of mine), to the effect that you should never invest with a Private Equity team if you have to go to somebody else's office to meet them.

Fundraising

In a sense we should have discussed fundraising first, since it is chronologically at the beginning of the fund cycle and forms an obvious prerequisite to any form of investment activity. You cannot invest money unless you have it in the first place. Let us explore briefly how the fundraising process plays itself out in practice.

Most funds (including Funds of Funds) tend to work to a three-year fund cycle, which means that in the third year of Fund I they will be out fundraising for Fund II, and so on. This is an important factor which is often overlooked by those seeking to enter the sector for the first time. For example, European pension funds will frequently put a desired Private Equity allocation out to tender, ignoring the fact that (1) some of the best Private Equity managers do not participate in such processes, and that (2) on average only a third of them will be fundraising at any one time. There are many other objections to the tendering process which probably lie beyond the scope of this book but let us simply note that this is a deeply sub-optimal way of choosing Private Equity managers; indeed, as you will see when we come to look at manager selection, this is really just a complete abrogation of responsibility when compared to best practice.

The first step in the fundraising process should be for the GP team to sit down and plan its investment model for the next fund. This should consist of mapping out where the most lucrative returns are likely to be made, assessing how many of these investments they can secure (this is likely to be a strictly limited number in most circumstances), and thus how many are likely to be made in a three-year period and how much money is required for them. They will then resolve to raise exactly that amount of money (plus a small contingency) and no more, since to do so would pull them away from the sweet spot which they have identified.

You will notice the use of the word 'should'. Sadly, what I have just described is best practice but is increasingly now honoured in the breach rather than the observance. Particularly in the case of the large Buyout funds, there is an increasing feeling that they will simply adjust their target fund size to meet investor demand. This is not necessarily damaging, or even reprehensible (see my comments on fund size in Chapter 5) but it is certainly not best practice, and does raise worrying issues about what exactly motivates Buyout managers. In fairness, I should point out that if one glosses over the unfortunate excesses of the dot com bubble, then this best practice is still largely observed in other quarters, most notably by the best US Venture firms.

The next stage in the process is to prepare an Offering Memorandum (sometimes called a Private Placement Memorandum) which is the legal document on the basis of which investment will take place, although the actual contractual document is, of course, the Limited Partnership Agreement, which will be signed separately by each investor, or made the subject of a Subscription Agreement, which will be signed separately by each investor. While the precise status of an OM in relation to a Private Equity fund has never been definitively established (and would, in any event, differ from one jurisdiction to another), it does seem that its representations will be incorporated into the resulting contract,[7] whether expressly or

---

[7] It is probably more correct to say that the contract will be deemed to have been entered into by the parties on the basis of the representations made in the OM.

impliedly, and that knowingly making a false or misleading statement within an OM could well leave one open to criminal charges.

In practice, marketing often takes place without an OM, at least in final form, and I have known the OM to be produced right at the end, and delivered to investors with all the other contractual documentation, i.e. after they have actually taken their decision to invest, which would doubtless raise a number of nice legal points. For marketing purposes, the most important documentation is the Presentation, which is exactly what it sounds like: a set of PowerPoint slides which are used as the focus for a face-to-face fundraising meeting. There are some investors who ask to see the Presentation in advance. Personally, I would discourage this practice. A well-crafted Presentation will act merely as a counterpoint or backdrop to what the team wants to say and should not be considered as a stand-alone document. If the investor wants to know specific information to help decide whether or not to take the meeting, then why not simply ask for it? GPs could be better prepared here. It should be possible, for example, to have ready to hand a standard form fund performance slide (preferably on a single sheet of paper) which can be updated quarterly. Once the meeting has taken place, the Presentation will act as a useful aide memoire in conjunction with the meeting note which will be prepared by a member of the investor's team.

Practice is divided amongst LPs as to what happens next. This is a complex area and most investment decision processes pass through several stages. However, in broad terms the decision process will be either preceded or followed by a period of due diligence, during which the LP's team will endeavour to carry out as much analysis and as many background checks as possible on the GPs. In practice, it is probably more accurate to say that in most cases the decision process will be accompanied by the due diligence process, since some analysis may well be done at a very early stage (on the historic financial performance, for example) while the final decision may well be expressly subject to due diligence which has yet to be carried out.

My views on due diligence may be slightly eccentric, but I must say that in my opinion much of the due diligence which is performed by LPs is excessive, and in many cases ineffective or even irrelevant. Due diligence should be an intelligent exercise during which the LP team members discuss the issues that they see with the offering, and set out specific steps to answer these particular questions. Unfortunately, in practice one is more likely to meet the scattergun approach, which I once heard described as 'asking for my grandmother's birth certificate', and which is aptly known as 'papering the file' in the US.

The really ironic thing is that the intelligent approach is much more likely to disclose useful information than the scattergun approach. Approaching the referees proposed by the GPs, for example, particularly with a standard form set of questions, is unlikely to yield any surprises; the GP would hardly have suggested them in the first place unless they knew in advance roughly what they were going to say. One or two of these calls should be made as a matter of form, but far more interesting will be approaching people 'off the list' as it were. Particular attention should be paid to tracking down anyone who has recently left the firm, the CEO of any portfolio company which has got into difficulties, and any other Private Equity professionals with whom the GP habitually co-invests. Investment bankers and head-hunters can also prove productive sources of intelligence.

Once an investor is ready to indicate that they are minded to invest a certain amount, they become a 'soft circle', and once they have actually taken a firm decision to invest subject only to due diligence and agreement on the legal terms, they become a 'hard circle'. This is what GPs and their placing agents are referring to when they talk of having a certain amount 'hard circled' or 'soft circled'. With successful, established groups it is not unusual to find that existing investors from prior funds are already hard circles before the offering goes out to potential new investors; indeed, it would be surprising if it were otherwise, since the existing LPs will want to make sure of their allocations.

The final stage in the process sees the lawyers being unleashed as the terms of the LPA are debated and negotiated. In truth, such is the bargaining strength of the GPs in desirable funds that little of any substance is usually conceded to LPs, and their choice is effectively between signing the LPA or walking away. Perhaps surprisingly, there is little attempt made by LPs to get together and negotiate terms collectively, nor to agree 'industry standard' terms amongst themselves and then say that they will invest only on this basis, though common sense would appear to commend both these courses of action. A cynic would doubtless venture that, human nature being what it is, LPs might never be able to trust each other sufficiently not to break ranks, thus leaving the remainder horribly exposed.

PRIVATE EQUITY FUNDS DISTINGUISHED FROM OTHER FUND TYPES

Hedge Funds

There are many who seem unable to distinguish between a Hedge fund and a Buyout fund (which they will probably, in turn, see as a 'Private Equity' fund, as if this were the only type of Private Equity there were). This is unfortunate, since there are fundamental differences between just about every feature of each.

First let us consider the matter of what type of *investments* Hedge funds make. They deal in public markets; that is, quoted instruments. Moreover, these quoted instruments will not normally be investments directly into shares, debt securities, or whatever, but derivatives. Many Hedge funds will, for example, look to set up matched pairs of trades, such as taking a derivative position both over the US dollar and the price of oil, or over the equity and debt instruments of the same company, or over the equity of two different companies in the same sector.

So, Hedge funds deal in public markets, such as stock exchanges, currency markets and futures exchanges. Private Equity funds do not. There are two small exceptions to this rule, both of which are natural extensions of what they do. They may hold publicly quoted shares where these have been issued by a company which they held as a private company, there has been a flotation (IPO), and they are now awaiting an opportunity and/or permission to sell them for cash. They may also buy the shares of a public company intending to take it private. These two exceptions apart, it is almost unthinkable that a Private Equity fund would ever trade on a public market.

This is a very significant difference. Many journalists and politicians are very nervous that Hedge funds, given the amounts of leverage they have had available (see below), have been able to build large derivative positions, particularly as their investment model frequently encourages very short holding periods (in extreme cases perhaps minutes or even seconds, though some may have a time horizon of several months). This raises the possibility of market abuse by the unscrupulous. Even in the absence of such abuse, there is the potential for causing much market volatility. For example, many blamed Hedge funds, rightly or wrongly, for introducing unnecessary stress into the system during the early part of 2008 by shorting bank shares.

None of these issues arise in connection with Private Equity funds, since they do not deal in public markets, much less in derivatives.

All of which may make you feel it is rather strange that many of the world's Hedge funds and their managers are entirely *unregulated*, whereas (at least in Europe) registration with and supervision by a regulatory authority has been mandatory for years in the case of Private Equity managers. Given the differences between the two, one would logically expect Hedge funds to be regulated many times more heavily than Private Equity funds.

Another important difference lies in the use of debt as *leverage*. Only one type of Private Equity (Buyout) uses leverage, and, as we will see in Chapter 6, this is employed at the company level, not the fund level. In other words, it is not the fund itself which borrows money but the holding company set up in respect of each individual transaction, and this borrowing is what bankers call 'non-recourse' or 'ring-fenced'. In other words, it is specific to that transaction, and is not guaranteed, whether by the fund, the GP or any other portfolio companies. If the deal goes bad, then the banks lose their money (or some of it) on that deal, and cannot claim against the fund for any shortfall.

Hedge funds, by contrast, borrow at the fund level from a prime broker, which will be part of a banking group. They mix this debt together with the equity which their investors have subscribed, and then use these mixed funds to fund their deals. Naturally, the debt providers have the right to be paid back first, so that if the value of a Hedge fund's assets falls below that of the outstanding debt, the value of the investors' equity will fall to zero, just as in the case of somebody who buys a house with a mortgage and then finds themselves with 'negative equity' when a sudden property slump sends the value of the house plunging below the amount of the mortgage debt.

There is one very important consequence to all this. Hedge funds can (and do) go bust. Private Equity funds cannot. A Private Equity fund never has any liabilities. It does not guarantee any debt, nor does it employ anybody or enter into any property transactions, such as leases. Remember, it functions simply as a conduit for money moving up and down between the investors (LPs) and the fund's investments.

Finally, there is the matter of *fund structure*. As we have seen, a Private Equity fund will invariably take the form of a Limited Partnership. This is a private form of investment vehicle, both in the sense of being unquoted on any public exchange, and also in the sense that as a matter of basic law it will not usually be required to file any accounts (though it will be required to deliver them to its LPs). The partnership will be expressed to come to an end on a fixed date, subject to the clearly defined possibility of some limited extension. As we saw (above), lawyers call it a closed-end fund for this very reason. It stays open until a particular date and, generally speaking, its investors are not entitled to remove their capital before then, though this will be paid back to them as each investment is realised.

A Hedge fund's structure and workings are different in just about every respect. Though its precise legal form may vary (some are companies, others various types of investment fund structure recognised by different jurisdictions around the world), many are quoted (at least nominally) and all are open-end funds. In other words, they have no definite end date; they continue unless and until they are wound up. To get around this, there needs to be some mechanism for investors to be able to withdraw their capital, and this is the area that has generated enormous controversy and ill-feeling over the last few years.

Hedge funds mostly employ a redemption structure, a concept which will be familiar to investors who have dealt with unit trusts or mutual funds, depending upon your country of residence. You may think of it like buying shares in an investment company quoted on a stock exchange, but there is an important difference. In that case you are buying shares that are currently owned by somebody else; this is what is generally referred to as a 'secondary' purchase. In the case of a redemption-based structure, you are actually buying new shares, or units, from the fund itself, and the only way for you to sell them is for the fund to buy them back from you or 'redeem' them. In former days this was not always obvious, as the fund manager would, whenever possible, seek to match a request for the issue of new units from one investor with a request to redeem a similar number of units from another.

Some time around the latter half of 2007, however, the machine ground to a halt. Suddenly the number of redemption requests far outweighed the appetite of new investors. As 2007 moved into 2008, Hedge funds began to be hit by a tidal wave of redemptions. In many cases, they found that they would not be able to generate the cash required to honour these without unwinding complex investment positions, some of which had been designed to last for a long period, and the untangling of which at short notice might cause significant loss.

Fortunately (for the Hedge funds – unfortunately for their investors), there was a mechanism in place to deal with this. Under the terms of most Hedge funds there were circumstances in which they could effectively put redemptions on hold. Investors submitted redemption requests, and the fund said 'no', citing the relevant paragraph of the fund's documentation. This is called being 'gated'; in layman's terms, the investors are locked-in. By the way, in the interests of fairness it should be said (1) many of these redemption requests were driven by panic rather than logic, (2) that there are strong arguments that in some circumstances gating provisions actually impose fairness across the fund's investors as a whole and (3) much bad feeling has been caused by those managers who placed the Hedge fund interests with investors, having dwelt at the time in their sales spiel on their apparent liquidity.

None of this applies to Private Equity funds, at least to that overwhelming majority of them which are Limited Partnerships. They are long-term, closed-end funds and have never pretended to be anything else. There is no possibility of redemption. The only way to exit a Private Equity fund is to sell your LP interest in the secondary market, of which more later. Private Equity funds are designed for that part of an investor's portfolio in respect of which they can afford to give up short-term liquidity in exchange for the expectation of higher long-term returns. That is why they are ideal for long-term investors such as life insurance companies and pension funds (as well as family offices, sovereign wealth funds, endowments and foundations) and not at all suitable for short-term investors such as non-life insurance companies, banks and corporate treasury departments.

Infrastructure

Infrastructure has become much more widely known as an asset class in recent years, and takes different forms in different countries. Briefly, there are infrastructure funds available, some of which are structured as Limited Partnerships, and some investors, notably in North America, have begun including infrastructure as part of their Private Equity allocation.

People are free to do as they wish, and increasingly investment thinkers are beginning to ask if it actually matters at all what an asset is called, as opposed to how it behaves. However, the fact remains that infrastructure and Private Equity are radically different as investments. Infrastructure returns will tend to be lower but less uncertain, as one is investing in individual projects at the direct level rather than in individual businesses. These projects have been meticulously planned, and there is often a measure of governmental guarantee of at least some level of return. Also, cash inflows will often be regular and predictable, rather than irregular and unpredictable. In fact, infrastructure funds often have a cash flow pattern that more closely resembles a bond rather than a Private Equity fund.

So, infrastructure funds have a perfectly valid role to play within a portfolio, but they are not Private Equity funds.

Private (Equity) Real Estate

There has always been a class of funds available in the United States called Private Equity Real Estate (usually abbreviated for some reason to PERA, rather than PERE). However, it is important to be aware of the reason for this.

It is not, as some people believe, because they seek out Private Equity deals from which they can strip out the real estate (property) assets. It is simply because they adopt the Private Equity fund structure. Remember I said there was only one exception to the principle that Private Equity funds operated differently to every other type of investment fund? This is it.

The fact remains, however, that these funds are set up to make property investments (office blocks and the like), not Private Equity investments. Again, they have a perfectly valid role to play within a portfolio, but they are not Private Equity funds. In recognition of this fact, they are increasingly being called simply 'Private Real Estate', which seems a much better description.

A NOTE ON INTERNATIONAL ISSUES

This chapter has assumed the use of the Limited Partnership as the default Private Equity investment vehicle, and in the UK and the US, where the overwhelming majority of fund capital is still managed, this is indeed the case. However, as noted above, there are various jurisdictions around the world where this is not possible, either because the concept of a Limited Partnership is not itself recognised, or because the surrounding tax laws do not permit tax transparency.

This is a whole subject in itself, but in summary the main problems (for LPs) are usually one, or some combination, of the following:

- Limited Partnership vehicles are not recognised by local law;
- ditto even the basic concept of a partnership;
- capital gains are taxed in the hands of non-residents;
- even if a Limited Partnership is recognised, tax transparency may not be.

These issues would happily fill a book, let alone a chapter, by themselves. This is, however, not that book. If it were, it would describe the efforts that have been made in respect of various countries to deal with these issues in practice through the use of offshore vehicles and double tax treaties. There remain, however, a number of countries where the problems are, as yet, insurmountable. In addition, there are some countries where only non-Buyout Private Equity may be practised, either because the purchase of controlling stakes is forbidden by law, or where the concept of consolidating different vehicles for tax purposes is, as yet, unknown.

While predictions are always dangerous, it does seem to be the case that there is a very slow but steady evolution taking place towards adopting what is often described as 'the Anglo-Saxon model'. In recent years, for example, Australia has embraced it almost wholly, while other countries, such as Taiwan and China, have taken the first steps along the path by introducing Partnership Laws. It is likely, however, to be a lengthy, and at times frustrating, path. 'Frustrating' because there are many countries in the world, particularly in Asia, which seem hugely attractive as potential Private Equity markets, but where Private Equity activity is being held back or prevented altogether by unsympathetic legislative regimes.

SUMMARY

An investor in a Private Equity fund is called an LP. A manager of a Private Equity fund is called a GP. This is because the vast majority of Private Equity funds worldwide are Limited Partnerships. There remain, however, a number of jurisdictions, particularly in Asia, where this is impossible or impractical.

A Private Equity fund is different to just about every other type of investment fund. The most obvious difference is that investors' capital is not paid into the fund up front, as with, say, a mutual fund, but is 'committed' (promised) and then drawn down as needed.

This means that the cash flows of a Private Equity fund are unpredictable, both as to their timing and as to their amounts.

It is most important to grasp the difference between allocated, committed, drawn down and invested capital. See the glossary at the end of the book for formal definitions.

The process of asking LPs for part of their capital and receiving it into the fund is called a Draw Down or Capital Call.

As investments are realised, the proceeds are paid back to LPs; this is known as a distribution. In the case of US Venture funds, distributions may be in specie; that is to say, in shares rather than cash.

A Private Equity fund is a closed-end fund with a definite finishing date. Open-end funds such as Hedge funds continue to exist for an indefinite period unless and until they are wound up.

Private Equity funds are very different from Hedge funds. The latter deal in public markets, use derivatives and borrow at the fund level. Private Equity funds do none of these things.

Private Equity funds are long-term investment vehicles for long-term investors, in respect of that part of their portfolio for which they can afford to give up short-term liquidity in exchange for the expectation of higher long-term returns.

Neither infrastructure nor real estate funds are Private Equity funds, even though they be may be referred to as such. Look at what they invest in rather than what they are called, or how they are structured.

3
Private Equity Returns – The Basics

We are going to dive straight into an explanation of Private Equity returns at this point, first because it follows on logically from what we were discussing in the first two chapters, and second because learning Private Equity without first understanding how the returns work is rather like learning to play bridge without understanding how to score. In Private Equity, there are interconnections which mean that the nature and circumstances of a deal, and of the firm which transacts it, will tend to operate in a certain way on its likely return, both as to amount and to timing. Ideally one could discuss both of these aspects at once, but of course that is impossible in practice and so it is best if we first familiarise ourselves with the general characteristics of Private Equity returns. How are these measured, and why? How will they tend to react in different circumstances? How may we compare them with the returns of other asset classes? What industry benchmarks are available to assist us, and how should we seek to use these?

UNDERSTANDING THE J-CURVE AND COMPOUND RETURNS

If people with no prior experience of Private Equity have ever heard one thing about it in passing, it tends to be the J-curve. Sadly, since this lies at the heart of comprehending how Private Equity returns work, it is widely misunderstood, sometimes even after several attempts at explanation. This is not because it is an unduly difficult or complex concept, or that the people struggling with it are unintelligent. It is because the background to it is (to those brought up in a conventional investment environment of bonds and equities) somewhat revolutionary, and unless and until one can grasp and accept this background, then the concept of the J-curve makes little sense or, even worse, can be seen as some sort of attempted confidence trick on behalf of the Private Equity industry to extract money from gullible investors.

This is another time in this book that we have to note that Private Equity is different from just about any other asset class. For our present purposes, one of the main differences is that periodic returns (and particularly annual returns) cannot be used as a guide to Private Equity performance, whereas for most people this is the only return that matters for every other asset class. The reason that annual returns are not a valid measure of Private Equity performance rests on one of the other differences with other asset classes.

Unlike other asset classes, an investment in a Private Equity fund represents an investment in a stream of cash flows. Of course there are other assets which would appear to satisfy this definition, most notably bonds, but in fact there is a huge difference between the two. When you buy a bond you typically have just one cash outflow (on day one, when you buy the bond) and then a series of cash inflows (the coupon payments and then the face value of the bond at the end of its life), the dates and amounts of which can be precisely predicted. That is why, for example, you can calculate the redemption yield of a bond at any time.

Many types of infrastructure project and fund also satisfy this basic definition, but these more closely resemble a bond-type investment in that the cash flows are usually very predictable (where single projects are concerned) or become very predictable (in the case of funds), particularly where we are talking about usage-based developments such as roads, bridges and tunnels where the amount of a payable toll is fixed in advance, as is the period for which it is payable.

With a Private Equity fund, you will have a whole series of cash outflows as money is drawn down by the GP, but both the timing and the amount of these outflows is totally uncertain (the only thing you do know is that their total value cannot exceed the amount of your committed capital). Similarly there will be a number of cash inflows as the GP distributes the proceeds of investments as they are realised, but again it is completely impossible to predict in advance how much each one of these will amount to, or when it will occur. You might like to look back at the graphics in Chapter 2 to refresh yourself on this.

So, yes, the way of calculating the total return of both a bond and a Private Equity fund can be by calculating a compound return over time, but there the similarity ends. The calculation in respect of a bond can be done on the day of purchase; indeed it is this very certainty which is a major selling point for things such as so-called Liability Driven Investment schemes. The calculation in respect of a Private Equity fund can only be made once the very last cash flow has occurred; in other words, the true return will only be known retrospectively at the end of a fund's life. It will hopefully be obvious, though, that the later in the lifetime of the Private Equity fund you find yourself, then the more accurate your guesstimate of the final result is likely to be, since the outcome will become steadily less uncertain with every passing year and every recorded cash flow.

Of course there is also some element of this in the case of the bond, but it is really nothing more than the normal operation of the time value of money. As you approach the redemption date, the redemption amount will play a bigger and bigger part in the total return calculation, but this is only because it is becoming closer in time terms. Thus, looking only at the annual return in terms of the coupon received could actually give a very misleading result, especially in the case of a short bond that has only a few years left to run. However, the bond markets are as near perfect as makes no difference, and this difference would, of course, be reflected in the market price of the bond, which is, after all, only a simple arithmetic calculation. Thus, provided that you take into account both the coupon (the running yield) and the redemption effect, a perfectly valid annual return can be calculated for any bond at any time.

Not so with a Private Equity fund. The cash flows are unpredictable, as we have seen, and to complicate matters still further, the best is often kept until last from an investor's point of view, as the biggest inflows tend to occur towards the end of the fund's life rather than towards the beginning (this is particularly the case with Venture funds, whose average investment holding period will be longer than that of a Buyout fund). Thus, any attempt to calculate an annual return will be hostage to fortune; the fortune being the uncertainty as to how many cash flows might be received that year. Increases in capital values do not work here either, as most Private Equity firms are very conservative on valuation, particularly in Europe where uniform valuation guidelines are enforced. A company will often be sold for much more than its latest valuation in the fund's accounts.

A further problem occurs when the impact of fees and costs is considered. Because the management fee of a Private Equity fund operates on the committed capital of the fund rather than its invested capital, this impact will be very high in the early years of a fund's life. In a typical mutual fund, a dollar paid into the fund buys about 99 cents of net asset value (the difference being a 1%[1] management fee). In the case of a Private Equity fund, a dollar paid into the fund in year one or two will only be translated into somewhere between 50 and 90 cents of net asset value depending on various factors such as the pace of investment. Thus, on any measurement methodology, the annual returns of a Private Equity fund in its early years *must* be negative.

It is grasping this essential truth – that annual returns are not only irrelevant but can be downright misleading in assessing Private Equity fund performance – that represents the biggest barrier to an understanding of the asset class. It is, in fact, too big a barrier for many to surmount. For a great proportion of the world's pension trustees and consultants, for example, any attempt to move away from the comfort blanket of annual returns proves too traumatic to contemplate, no matter how many times this truth is explained, and any suggestion that they look at compound returns instead is viewed as a confidence trick by East Coast snake-oil salesmen aimed at inducing them to part with their money on false pretences. Sadly, this will probably always prove the case, no matter how much education on the subject takes place. Let us simply note the point and move on.

It is clear, then, that we need to look at the compound return over time of the cash flows of a Private Equity fund in order validly to assess its performance. Happily, such a measure is readily available in the shape of an IRR. Before we move on to consider this, however, let us be quite sure that we understand the shape of the cash flows we will be dealing with.

In the last chapter we saw that there were two distinct streams of cash flow in operation over time: (1) drawdowns moving from the LPs to the fund and representing money needed for investments, fees and costs and (2) distributions moving from the fund back to LPs and representing sale or flotation proceeds less the GP's carried interest. The first will obviously predominate in the early part of a fund's life, while the latter will occur mostly in the later stages of the fund's life. Thus, the net annual and cumulative annual cash flows will look something like this (Figure 3.1):

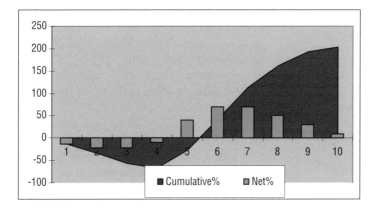

Figure 3.1   The cashflows of a Private Equity fund

---

[1]This is a deliberate generalisation for illustrative purposes.

Please note that the actual shape we are looking at follows what today seems a rather idealised pattern, and is based on a typical fund of 1990s vintage. Today we would expect the maximum drawdown of capital to be much more (perhaps even 90%), and the payback point to be much later. This is deliberate, as this has become a very significant issue, to which a later section will be entirely devoted.

Please note that every Private Equity fund, with the exception only of some secondary funds, will have a similar cash flow pattern, though it may be much more stretched in the case of a Venture fund than in the case of a Buyout fund. All will share the characteristics of hugely negative cash flow in the early years and (hopefully) hugely positive cash flow in the later years.

Given that the outline of the cumulative cash flow chart follows the rough shape of the letter 'J', this has prompted many people to believe that this is the famous 'J-curve' of which they have heard. In fact, it is not, though it is closely related to it. To encounter the real thing, we have to look at what happens if we attempt to measure the IRR of a fund at different stages of its life.

I hope that if you have understood what I have been saying about the nature of Private Equity returns then this part will now seem very obvious. Briefly, the J-curve is produced by looking at the cumulative return of a fund to each year of its life. In other words, the first entry will represent the IRR of the fund for the first year of its life. The second entry will represent the IRR of the fund for the first two years of its life, the third the IRR for the first three years, and so on.

How do we calculate this? Well, there is a 'cheat' which we must recognise up front. Whenever we calculate the IRR, we assume that the book value of all remaining assets comes in as a final cash flow at that time. Arithmetically, there is no other way of doing it. Yes, this means that the IRR calculations at the end of each early year of the fund's life give little clue to the final outcome, but actually this does no more than to recognise and reflect reality. Incidentally, where GPs are holding their investments at cost (which, in the case of a Venture fund, will usually mean the post-money valuation of the last funding round), then generally running IRRs of this nature will tend to be a better pointer to the lifetime performance of a Buyout or Development Capital fund than to that of a Growth or Venture fund, where there tends to be much more uncertainty as to the final outcome of any one investment.

It is these running IRRs (i.e. starting from the beginning of the fund's life and calculated at the end of each year) which produce the J-curve. Again, please note that this is stylised for illustrative purposes, but that every Private Equity fund will have a J-curve (the only exception being the possibility of a secondary fund which has some very early exits), though its length and depth will be different in each case.

A particular problem which arises with Figure 3.2 is that people are so used to looking at annual returns that, try as they will, they find it very difficult to grasp what the chart is depicting. It is *not* saying that the fund returned minus 25% in year three. It *is* saying that if you map all the cash flows from the beginning of the fund to the end of year three, you may calculate an IRR of minus 25%. Similarly, if you look at year six, it is *not* saying that the fund's performance for that year was flat. It *is* saying that from the beginning of the fund to the end of year six the positive cash flows exactly match the negative cash flows, so that the IRR of the first six years is zero.

It is this difficulty in being able to abandon the blinkers of annual returns and view the world afresh from the perspective of compound returns that gets in the way of people understanding Private Equity returns. Once this has been grasped, then everything else falls

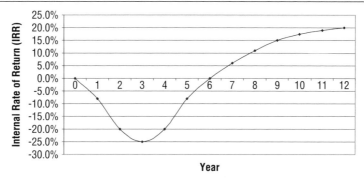

Figure 3.2   J Curve illustration

Table 3.1   Vintage year returns to December 2008, Cumulative IRR to date (%)

1996	1997	1998	1999	2000	2001	2002	2003
22.5	17.5	10.2	11.8	18.2	25.2	28.1	30.5

Source: Thomson Reuters

very easily into place. Private Equity returns are calculated and stated not as the annual returns of any particular year, but as compound returns *from* a certain year (the year of formation of the fund) *to* a specified year. When looking at benchmark figures for the industry as a whole, or indeed any part of it, then all the funds which form part of the sample which were formed in the same year are grouped together and their returns become the vintage year return.

Again, this concept seems to cause even intelligent, well-educated people a lot of problems, so let me expand on it a little to make quite sure that the concept is fully understood. This is important since from now on we will be making frequent references to vintage year returns.

Take the following example shown in Table 3.1, which shows a simple sequence of returns. I have chosen a few years of upper quartile European Buyout returns and presented them as a table:

The 1996 figure shows *not* the annual return for all constituent funds during 1996, but the compound return (the IRR) for all constituent funds which were formed during 1996, from 1996 to date. Similarly, the 1997 figure shows not the annual return for all constituent funds during 1997, but the compound return for all constituent funds formed during 1997, from 1997 to date.

*Rule: the vintage year return will always show (in respect of any one vintage year) the compound return of all constituent funds formed during the vintage year, **from** the vintage year **to** the date specified.*

(In practice, because of the way in which the figures are compiled and released, the specified date will usually be the end of the last complete year for which the figures are available, with the switch typically taking place in about May of each year.) For those who are familiar with such terms, it may help to think of them as 'from inception' returns.

Now if you look at the J-curve you will realise something else. At any one time, the vintage year returns for the last few years (i.e. most recent) should be very low – even negative. That is because they represent the equivalent of the first few years of the J-curve, a time when even the best Private Equity fund in the world will show negative returns. There may be times when this does not appear to be the case, usually when a bumper exit market exists and some funds have an opportunity to 'turn' some investments very quickly, thus resulting in some very high IRRs which badly skew the figures. There was one 2003 vintage European Buyout fund, for example, which, as at December 2005, boasted an IRR of over 1200%! This is clearly both unrealistic and unsustainable. The normal situation is for recent vintage year returns to be either negative or very low depending on their age, and any time when this does not appear to be the case may be regarded as an aberration.

This does, however, illustrate another important principle when it comes to looking at vintage year returns, namely that figures which are very 'young' are inherently unreliable. Indeed, in normal circumstances as a guideline to what the final performance of the fund is likely to be, they are all but meaningless. You can be certain only of one thing: they will most certainly not be the same as the final result. The effect of the time value of money, however, means that the more years a rolling compound return gets under its belt, the closer it will be to the final result. By the end of a fund's life it becomes increasingly difficult to influence the outcome of the final figure – if a fund has achieved 15% IRR for the first eleven years of its life, then even a 50% one-year return in year twelve will only lift it to about 16.6% overall. It is for this reason that I have, in the past, suggested weighting vintage year returns for asset allocation purposes in order to recognise that a young return gained over just a couple of years is largely meaningless, while an old return gained over ten or more years is very robust, but this idea has yet to gain the acceptance of the industry benchmark providers.[2]

Rule: the greater the number of years over which a vintage year compound return is calculated, the more robust it becomes, i.e. the less deviation there is likely to be between it and the final fund return.

Given the current anomalies in the figures, I must stress that the J-curve here does not represent the J-curve of any particular fund in real life, but it is a broad generalisation of what you can expect to find in every case. The only difference will be the shape of the curve; a Buyout fund, for example, will tend to pay back its capital more quickly than a Venture fund. Yet even this generalisation is enough to show us that it is meaningless to look at the performance of a Private Equity fund in its early years. Opinion may vary as to what that period might be (and it will certainly be longer in the case of a Venture fund than in the case of a Buyout fund) but there is no dispute that it exists. I tend typically to ignore the last five years' or so vintage year returns when looking at industry figures and I would urge you to do the same.

Having now explained how Private Equity returns are measured and presented, we are able to understand a basic set of vintage year return figures and also how the J-curve operates. We now need to look at the basics of how these figures are 'sliced and diced', and the first concept we need to grasp is that of the upper quartile.

---

[2]For some worked examples, see my earlier book *Multi-Asset Class Investment Strategy*, already referenced.

UPPER QUARTILE FIGURES

The upper quartile is that data point in a sample population that stands exactly one quarter down from the top in order of ranking. This may seem a rather simplistic point, but I make no apology for it, since it is widely and surprisingly misunderstood when it comes to Private Equity. There are two aspects in particular which I wish to stress because they seem to cause the most confusion.

The first is that the upper quartile is one quarter below the top in terms of rankings, not amount. Let us take a random list of values shown in Table 3.2:

In the above list of values, 18 will be the upper quartile, since it is the fourth of the observations by ranking. It has no reference at all to the values of the other observations save in this sense. I am labouring this point because there are those who seem to believe that it is a number which lies halfway between the average (about 11.56) and the value of the top observation (31), i.e. 19.44. This is not the case.

Neither is it the return of all the funds within the upper quartile grouped together. It is, quite simply, the return of the individual fund which sits at the bottom of the upper quartile, i.e. one quarter of the way down the ranked list of observations. This is one of the worst misunderstandings which bedevils investors' view of Private Equity. They believe that the 'upper quartile return' means the pooled return of all the funds at and above the upper quartile, which can often be a very significantly greater amount. Thus, when an investment manager of, say, a Fund of Funds claims to be targeting 'upper quartile performance' all they are saying is that they want to at least equal the return of the one upper quartile fund in each vintage year. Investors and their consultants, who are usually receiving on a different wavelength, often discount and disbelieve such claims in consequence.

The reason for this is not difficult to spot. The upper quartile can be a very useful statistical device but, as all statisticians know but many investors overlook, it takes no account of the spread of the observations. In particular, it takes no account of the spread of the individual

Table 3.2   Illustration of ranked performance statistics

Ranking	Performance (% IRR)
1	31
2	29
3	23
Upper quartile 4	18
5	17
6	17
7	16
8	11
9	10
10	6
11	5
12	4
13	3
14	1
15	−1
16	−5

(Average = 11.56)
Note: Each individual fund is called an 'observation'.

Table 3.3 US Venture funds cumulative IRRs (%)

	1991	1992	1993	1994	1995	1996	1997	1998	1999	2000
U/Q	25.6	38.9	39.1	41.0	66.4	113.9	59.7	10.7	0.7	1.9
Top	61.3	116.3	98.6	112.9	247.8	415.9	296.0	721.0	140.0	27.6

Source: Thomson Reuters
Figures prepared to 31.12.08

values within the upper quartile. It marks the bottom of the upper quartile, but gives no clue as to where the top might lie. Perhaps surprisingly, since the 'upper quartile' figures are bandied around so readily, the return of the top fund in any vintage year is not.

The significance of this will be apparent from Table 3.3 (above), which sets out the upper quartile and top fund vintage year performance for US Venture funds from 1991 to 2000. While the years are chosen more or less at random, the picture they paint is roughly typical of all vintage years. I hope it will be obvious that this is a point of crucial importance and is, sadly, yet another example of people looking at Private Equity returns without really understanding what they are looking at, or at least being willing to engage their brain and think about what lies behind them. Look, for example, at the dramatic differences between the two figures for 1998, 1999 and 2000. We will see later that this is a particular problem with European Venture returns.

MEDIAN RETURNS

You will see from the list of random numbers above that the median is simply the halfway point equivalent of the upper quartile. It is that individual fund which sits at the halfway point of the sample population. Again, this is an important point since many confuse it with the average (or mean, as it is properly called). There are those who suggest that the median is a good expression of Private Equity returns to adopt on the basis that if one is choosing from a set number of funds each year (the sample population), then the median represents what one is most likely to end up with. This proposition is highly questionable.

Firstly, it assumes that we will be making just one selection, whereas in reality one would be making several. We will be discussing later just how many funds one needs for a properly balanced portfolio, but it is certainly more than one (even from each category) in any one vintage year.

Secondly, just as the upper quartile measure ignores the spread within the upper quartile itself, so the median will underplay the effect of any particularly low (but also, and more to the point, high) values. As we will see later, particularly with regard to Venture funds, it is these few very high values that we are seeking to capture and the median simply does not reflect this.

Thirdly, any good professional fund investor will be looking to invest consistently from amongst the upper quartile. Of course this cannot be guaranteed, but with experience comes judgement and a high quality Fund of Funds, for example, would be looking to have at least two-thirds of its fund picks end up in the upper quartile (the author used to be a partner in a firm which had approximately a 70% success record over a twenty-year period). Taking the median as any sort of guideline in these circumstances is plainly misleading.

Finally, there are some sample populations, European Venture being the most obvious example, which contain a lot of very small funds, so small in fact that they simply would not be considered for investment purposes by any institution. The median will take all of these very small funds into account and treat them in exactly the same way as a large, institutional-grade fund, which is again clearly misleading.

AVERAGE RETURNS

I am a firm believer in taking upper quartile returns as the appropriate measure because they most closely approximate what an individual investor may expect in practice, provided that a reasonable degree of professional skill is exercised. The two main reasons for this are:

- that a competent investor will be able to select pretty consistently a good two-thirds of its funds from within the potential upper quartile, and
- that since the upper quartile measure marks only the bottom of the upper quartile but gives no indication of the top (which may be five, or even ten times higher), then it is likely to be a conservative estimate of what may be achieved.

However, as we have noted, there are unfortunately many in the investment world who view Private Equity as an asset class with grave suspicion, and point to any attempt to use upper quartile returns as some sort of marketing confidence trick. This is not entirely their fault in that if they have been brought up on a diet of quoted investments, then this will, of course, seem correct. It is, however, their fault in that they are not willing to dive into the Private Equity performance figures in detail and get a grip of what lies behind them rather than turning automatically to the median or average figures.

It is sadly also the case that (in Europe) many pension fund investors and their consultants do not even look at the industry figures *at all*, but make their assessment of Private Equity based entirely on made-up figures calculated as a certain proportion of (annual, of course) quoted equity returns. Unsurprisingly, this also results in some very high correlation figures!

Returning from the realms of consultants' fantasy to real life, however, it is a matter of necessity also to look at the figures on an average performance basis, if only to have the answers to these sorts of objections readily to hand. However, one encounters an immediate statistical problem here which will, I hope, be obvious in the light of what we have already been discussing. An average, or mean, is calculated by adding up the individual returns and then dividing them by the number of individual observations (i.e. the total number of funds in the sample), thus:

$$\mu = \frac{\sum r}{n}$$

where μ (the Greek letter mu) is the arithmetic mean (the average), r is the return of any individual fund, and n is the number of funds within the sample population. For those that may not have met it before, Σ (the Greek capital letter sigma) simply means 'the sum of'; in other words it denotes adding up all the individual returns. Do not worry if you do not understand the formula; it simply expresses mathematically the principle set out in the last paragraph immediately before the word 'thus'.

Can you see the potential problem here? Where our sample includes a large number of very small funds, we are giving them the same weighting that we would accord to a very large one, regardless of the fact that they are not deemed to be of institutional investment grade, and that they will generally (the very small ones anyway) create very low returns.[3] The very large funds, conversely, are likely to have attracted money entirely from institutional investors, and may, in many cases, have been the only funds within the sample that such institutions were prepared even to consider.

Clearly, then, we are faced with the need to create a measure that satisfies the 'average fetish' but still gives the best realistic guide to returns that we can manage. This is done by calculating a capital weighted average:

$$CWA = \frac{\sum rc}{\sum c}$$

Where CWA is the capital weighted average and c is the capital raised by each individual fund.

It may all seem a bit complicated, but in fact is not. All the formula is telling you to do is first to multiply the return of each fund by its committed capital, then add all these values up and then divide the resulting total by the total amount of committed capital. Again, however, please do not worry if you do not understand the formula; it is not necessary. It is far more important to understand the principle.

Given the availability of the necessary figures, this calculation can easily be done for any sector within Private Equity, indeed some of the industry data providers such as Thomson actually calculate it for you. There is one surprising omission, however. Believe it or not there is no CWA available for Private Equity as a whole, i.e. the whole asset class on a global basis. It is a baffling absence; surely it is the most important figure of all for the asset allocation purposes of investors worldwide?

The disadvantage of such a method is the converse of its attraction. If you are looking at Private Equity as a whole, where the size of small but successful Venture funds may be swamped by large but relatively unsuccessful Buyout funds, is this really a valid way of looking at things? Similarly, does it really matter to an LP if they are invested in one fund of $5 billion and one fund of $50 million, provided that the size of their commitment to each is $10 million? Surely, as far as they are concerned, each fund will make an equal contribution to the LP's overall return?

These questions suggest their own answers. If you are looking at the performance of the industry as a whole, or of individual sectors within it, then a capital weighted average can be a sensible way of doing this, provided you bear in mind how it has been calculated and thus what it is telling you. However, a professional investor should always prefer the upper quartile as a performance indicator or benchmark. If, on the other hand, you need specific information for specific purposes, then you have to be intelligent about what figures you prepare and, where possible, these should match the individual requirements of a particular investor. If an LP invests only in US Venture funds, for example, then how valid is it to benchmark their performance against the global industry across all fund types? (Actually, it may be *very* valid, since their investment focus was their decision in the first place, but that is another story.)

---

[3] Such a discussion lies beyond the scope of this book, or at least of this chapter, but many such funds are government inspired/ related (either at national or local level) or attached to universities or research institutes. In all such cases, 'investment' in companies is likely to take place on a basis that is not strictly commercial, i.e. perhaps with the objective of supporting a particular line of research, or promoting new companies in a particular area rather than with a view purely to investment gain.

POOLED RETURNS

Pooled returns attempt to address the same issues as capital weighted average returns, but in a different way. Here, all the funds are combined and treated as if they were one giant fund, and the IRR of the pooled cash flows is calculated. Obviously large cash flows, whether positive or negative, will have a disproportionate effect, just as the returns of a large fund will have a disproportionate effect within a capital weighted average. The advantage of a pooled return is that it probably most closely approximates how an individual investor will measure the performance of their Private Equity fund programme. The disadvantage is that it may be heavily skewed by the timing of particular cash flows within one or two very large funds.

This last disadvantage is a significant one, and frequently ignored (usually because it is not understood) by many industry observers, who tout it as the best record of industry performance. For this reason, the capital weighted average should be preferred as a measure, and let any who think this may be a self-serving suggestion from a Private Equity supporter look to the figures, from which they will see that the pooled return is often more flattering, particularly in the case of US Venture funds.

USING VINTAGE YEAR RETURNS FOR BENCHMARKING PURPOSES

We have so far been looking at vintage year returns largely in their capacity as indicators of industry performance. There is, however, an even more valuable role which they fulfill, and that is as a benchmark for the performance of individual Private Equity funds.

Consider for a moment the following situation. You are looking at the performance to date of a US Buyout fund which was formed in 2004. You would like to compare its performance to other Private Equity funds, but are faced with two particular problems. First, we know that all Private Equity funds will show different performance at different times of their lives, so we need some way of knowing that the funds with which we compare this one will all be at exactly the same point on the J-curve. Second, we know that the length and depth of the J-curve will differ according to what type of Private Equity investment the fund undertakes and (possibly) whereabouts in the world it does it.

Vintage year returns are the answer to the first problem. By looking only at those which share the same vintage year, in this case 2004, we can guarantee that we are comparing this fund only with others which should currently be at exactly the same point on the J-curve. Remember that the vintage year return records the returns of all the funds which were created in that year, thus, by definition, they will all be the same age, and therefore at the same stage of their progress along the J-curve.

Segmentation within the industry databases is the answer to the second problem. It is a matter of only a few mouse clicks and suddenly we are able to compare our 2004 US Buyout fund only with other 2004 US Buyout funds. All 2004 vintage US Buyout funds should have the same shape of J-curve, since they will all be targeting similar transactions and similar holding periods. Now we can at least see whether the cumulative IRR of our fund looks high or low in comparison to other similar funds at the same point in their life, and draft the questions for our next update meeting with the GP accordingly.

TIME-WEIGHTED RETURNS

Before we close this chapter, one must say something on the subject of so-called time-weighted returns because these are sometimes quoted as a performance measurement and there is considerable (and understandable) confusion as to what they represent. In particular, it is not well understood how these differ from IRRs. In fact, they are completely different, and it is something of a mystery why they should be quoted in industry databases alongside IRRs without making it quite clear what they are.

In reality, these 'time-weighted' returns are not actually time-based at all, in that they completely ignore the time value of money. Essentially, they calculate the average annual return, but assume that the impact of each year is the same, when clearly this is not the case. A return, whether positive or negative, should have a much greater impact on the return over time if it occurs towards the beginning of the period rather than towards the end. It is one of the more ludicrous aspects of the world of finance that returns paraded as 'time-weighted' can validly ignore this fact.

These so-called 'time-weighted' returns are calculated by taking the returns of different periods and calculating their geometric mean. The geometric mean sounds complicated but really isn't. It is generally recognised as the best way of calculating an average of percentage rates in different periods. It is simply the nth root of the product of all the values, where n is the number of values. In other words, the geometric mean of a series of 26 valuations would be found by multiplying them all together and then finding the 26th root. In formulaic terms, it would be:

$$\sqrt[26]{(v_1 v_2 v_3 \ldots v_{26})}$$

Let us forget the formula and the maths, however, and concentrate on what is actually being calculated in practice. Effectively what we are doing is finding the average of the returns in each year of a fund's life, and it is this that renders time-weighted returns completely inappropriate as a measure of Private Equity fund performance, since they completely ignore the time value of money. For a time-weighted return, it is irrelevant whether a return of, say, 85% is made in year one of a fund's life or in year ten, which is, of course, ridiculous. Private Equity is a cash flow business. Private Equity funds represent nothing except a stream of cash flows and the time value of money is paramount. The only proper measure of a stream of cash flows is an IRR.

So, how did time-weighted returns come to be used at all? Well, for those who are old enough to remember a time before computer spreadsheets, calculating IRRs could be a laborious process, and in the days before electronic calculators could be more laborious still, requiring the use of slide rules or logarithms and repeated 'trial and error' attempts. A time-weighted return was much easier to calculate since all you had to do was look at one page of your list of tables (the roots).

The other reason was that they were already in use in the quoted markets. Here, there is at least some sense to them, since money can be moved in and out of the control of managers, or in and out of different stocks, at any time by investors and thus an average return is quite acceptable. If timing is out of the manager's control, then there is no point in calculating a compound return over time. The real pity is that these came to be called 'time' weighted returns in the first place, since 'time' is the one thing to which they specifically do not apply. For this reason, crazy though it may seem (logically it would have to be the other way around!), IRRs have come to be called 'dollar-weighted' returns in Private Equity circles.

Time-weighted returns are a perfect example of how many intelligent and well-educated people are capable of completely failing to understand how Private Equity returns operate, and leaping to an impressive arithmetic solution without first stopping to ask what it is they should actually be trying to measure. Hopefully they are now of largely historic interest, but they continue to be quoted among the various industry benchmarks and it is important that you should understand what they represent, since it is all too easy for the unwary to confuse them with IRRs. Understand them, yes by all means. Use them? No. Not ever. Not under any circumstances.

SUMMARY

Private Equity returns are measured on a compound, not an annual, basis. It is essential to remember this when comparing them to the returns of other asset classes.

The cash flows of any Private Equity fund will be negative in its early years as money is paid into (drawn down by) the fund before any money is paid back (distributed) by the fund as investments are realised. In due course, there will be a moment when the value of inflows exactly matches the value of outflows. This represents the payback point. The period before the payback point is sometimes referred to as the payback period.

The returns of any Private Equity fund will be negative in its early years as money is paid into (drawn down by) the fund not just for investment but also for fees and costs. In the early years, this 'drag' of fees and costs can be very significant. It is for this reason that annual returns are not normally considered a valid measure of Private Equity fund performance, since even very good funds will show negative annual returns in their early years, and even mediocre funds may show strong annual performance in their later years.

Instead, fund performance is measured by calculating its LPs' IRR from the inception of the fund to date. The book value of remaining investments is assumed to be received as a final cash flow at the date to which the return is calculated.

If the cumulative IRR is calculated for each successive year of a typical fund's life and plotted on a graph, it results in a J-curve, showing negative IRRs in the early years of a fund, and positive ones towards the end. All Private Equity funds will experience a J-curve irrespective of their type (though its length and depth will differ), save only for occasional secondary funds which may achieve a significant early exit.

Returns are measured on a vintage years basis, i.e. from the year in which the fund was formed to a specified date. This allows Private Equity funds to be compared directly with others of the same age. Segmentation within the industry data allows them also to be compared with other funds of the same geography and type.

The best measure of vintage year returns is the upper quartile. However, scepticism and suspicion from outside the industry frequently force the adoption of other measures. If so, it is most important that the measure adopted is a capital weighted average, rather than an average or median return.

The upper quartile figure states the performance of the individual fund at the bottom of the upper quartile, not the pooled performance of all funds within the upper quartile. It gives no indication of the range of returns contained within the upper quartile, which can be huge, particularly in the case of Venture funds.

Time-weighted returns are misleadingly so-called since, in fact, they do not take timing into account at all. For this reason, they are largely meaningless and should be avoided. Because of this anomalous terminology, IRRs are often referred to as 'dollar-weighted' returns within the Private Equity industry in order to distinguish them from 'time-weighted' returns. Time-weighted returns are calculated as the geometric mean of all the funds' annual percentage returns.

4

Private Equity Returns – Multiples and Muddles

MULTIPLES

While compound returns have been universally accepted (at least within the industry itself) as the appropriate measure of performance, there is, however, a totally different way of looking at Private Equity returns which is rapidly gaining ground. As we have seen, Private Equity funds may be thought of as a series of individual cash flows, and IRRs are, of course, usually the best way of measuring these. But IRRs have one practical drawback. Ignoring, for the moment, drawdowns for fees and costs, they measure the return which is earned on money while it is invested in a project (in this case an investee company), but they take no account of the length of time for which it remains invested. Why is this relevant?

The difficulty of maintaining an IRR increases dramatically with each passing year. Remember that an IRR is a measure of compound return, which means that the return must at least compound itself with each passing year in order to stay the same. By way of illustration, let us look at the rate of change of $100 compounding at 25% a year (see Table 4.1).

Note that an investment only has to double over three years to produce a 25% IRR, but must treble over five years to achieve the same result. Incidentally, these figures have been chosen deliberately since 25% is usually the minimum target transaction IRR to which any Private Equity manager would admit, and three years and five years may be thought of as the typical holding periods for Buyout and Venture funds respectively. In other words, the target money multiple at the company level for a Buyout firm could be thought of as 2×, while for a Venture firm it would need to be 3× to produce the same IRR.

There is, thus, an implicit trade-off between the three-way relationship of holding period, IRR and multiple which needs to be understood by any investor entering the Private Equity arena. A Venture fund will keep your money for longer, but will need to deliver a higher money multiple than a Buyout fund, which can traditionally be relied upon to give you each of your drawdowns[1] back more quickly on average. Right at the end of the scale will be secondary funds, which we will be considering in detail later, but suffice it to say that they tend to return money in the shortest time of all, and thus may be expected to produce a reasonable IRR but a relatively low multiple. The sophisticated investor will understand these differences, and use them to their advantage in planning and managing their Private Equity fund portfolio.

Mention of investors brings us rather neatly to the other point about the trade-off between IRR and money multiple. As we shall be discussing in more detail later, it is very difficult indeed to get money to work quickly in a Private Equity fund programme, both because funds

---

[1] Not strictly true, of course, since I am not taking any account here of drawdowns for fees.

Table 4.1   Money Multiple required to maintain an IRR of 25%

After n years	1	2	3	4	5
Amount	125	156	195	244	305

draw down their money over several years and also because you can only commit a small part of your allocated capital every year if you want to achieve proper diversification by time. Given the way in which Private Equity funds operate, it can also be difficult to keep your money at work, depending on market conditions; at one time, some Buyout firms were actually using each tranche of capital drawn down for only about three years before paying it back again, plus the related gains.

Since it is difficult for an LP both to put capital to work in the first place and also to keep it at work, it is strongly arguable that a money multiple is a much more meaningful measure than an IRR. Certainly it is more desirable as a target. Consider for a moment the position of an LP who has an allocated capital of $500M but currently only has about $75M actually invested (far from impossible in the early years of a programme). If that LP is offered a choice between earning 35% on some capital for three years or 25% for five years, which do you think they should take? The answer is 25% for five years, since you have to consider what the alternative use of those funds might be. Unless you have the opportunity immediately to re-invest that capital in another project which is likely to produce an ongoing IRR of more than 25%, then leaving it where it is represents the smart option.

The truth is that most investors will only be able to earn either a bond or money market return on such money. Therefore, the rational investor would accept any rate of return that is higher than that. That is the reductio ad absurdam, of course. I am not suggesting that in practice an LP should be satisfied with a Private Equity return of, say, 9%. If that is all that is on offer then changes within the GP base are clearly indicated. However, this does make a very important point; namely that you cannot and should not consider the returns of any asset class in a vacuum, but only in the context of the total circumstances of the individual investor in question.

This raises another interesting point, to which we will return. Private Equity is unlike any other asset class, and one of the distinctions is the big difference that will usually exist between allocated capital and invested capital. The only other asset class that has this to any real extent is Property, and there one has a myriad of indirect vehicles and instruments to consider for interim investment purposes. Thus, it could be argued that all Private Equity returns are, in a sense, artificial, since they are calculated on invested capital rather than on the totality of the Private Equity allocation. Of course, once one has a mature programme this argument loses much of its force, but even then there will always be a difference between the two.

The issue, though, is not that the stated returns are artificial, but simply that one needs to understand the distinction and take it into account in one's planning. If you believe that you can make an allocation to Private Equity one day and instantly start earning a Private Equity return on your entire allocation, then you are bound to be sorely disappointed. If, on the other hand, you accept that the Private Equity return is a target towards which to work, and make plans as to how to deploy the uninvested capital to advantage in the interim, then you will, within a reasonable time, be getting close to your goal. Private Equity is a long-term asset class, and is suitable only for long-term investors. This point was widely ignored by new investors who came into the asset class during the dot com bubble period, and then found it easier to blame the asset class for their poor performance rather than their own mistakes. It is highly likely that we have just witnessed the same phenomenon with new entrants who rushed into mega Buyout funds in recent years.

Enough theorising, however. Let us examine which multiples we can use for practical purposes in analysing Private Equity returns. I am here going to restrict the discussion to analysing Private Equity *fund* returns. We will be looking in detail later at how we can analyse the performance of individual transactions and use this to build a model of an entire fund. I mention this at this stage only because we shall be meeting some other types of multiples there, and I do not wish this to confuse matters. So, to be clear, the following multiples apply to funds, *not* individual company investments.

Distributed over Paid In (DPI)

This does exactly what it says. It compares the total amount of money paid out (distributed) by a fund to its LPs to date against the total amount of money paid into the fund by LPs. This is the best possible multiple to use for measuring the performance of a fund once it is at the end of its life, since it shows the performance relative to *all* money paid in, i.e. money that has been used to pay fees as well as money that has been invested in companies. All too frequently, GPs try to fob investors off by showing them the multiple to *invested* capital, which is not the same thing at all. Recognising this, most American GPs in the 1990s (at least in the Venture space) attempted to recycle some of their early realisations rather than distributing them to LPs, thus creating a higher multiple, but European GPs were slow to catch on. Given longer holding periods, this point has lost much of its potency in recent years, though it did have a big impact on relative returns at the time. We will consider both these issues in detail later.

However, DPI is not a good measure in two situations. First: where the fund is not yet either at the end of its life, or so close to the end and so nearly fully paid out that it makes little difference. Second: where a fund has failed to invest all its capital. Here, there will have been an excessive draining of fees, and the LP, having allocated the money to this fund, will have been unable to use it within another fund of the same vintage year. For this reason, I would personally favour a multiple of distributed over committed capital. This is commonly abbreviated as DCC.

Paid In to Committed Capital (PICC)

This multiple is of little value in assessing returns. It simply shows how much money has been drawn down, and thus how much remains to be drawn down in the future. This multiple is of most use in the secondary market, which we will be considering later.

Residual Value to Paid In (RVPI)

This is really the other side to the realisation ratio. It shows the current value of all remaining investments (companies) within the fund expressed as a ratio to the total amount paid in to date. This is obviously most useful as a measure early on in the life of a fund before there have been many distributions, in which case it will largely reflect to what extent portfolio

Table 4.2   Upper quartile Buyout and Venture returns, IRR/multiple trade-off

Fund Type	IRR	TVPI
Early-stage Venture	15.1%	2.1
Mega Buyout	14.7%	1.6

Source: Thomson Reuters
Note: figures are for the US upper quartile in each case as measured by the Thomson database covering all US Private Equity funds from inception to the end of 2008.

companies may have been revalued. It is also one of the measures that will be used when looking at an LP interest in a fund on the secondary market.

The disadvantage of residual value as a measure is that it may give a misleadingly low return expectation, particularly early on in the life of a fund, because companies are typically sold for more than their current valuation, especially in the case of Buyout funds.

Total Value to Paid In (TVPI)

This is one of the most useful ratios, and indeed one of the most useful measures of all for evaluating Private Equity fund returns. Total value adds together both the residual value and the distributions to date. It is obviously subject to the same possible drawbacks as RVPI early in the life of a fund, but if you are going to use a ratio based on paid in capital, then this is probably the one to use. For those who believe that multiples give a better idea of fund returns than IRR, the TVPI will be watched very carefully as the fund nears the end of its life, and compared with the same ratio for other funds of the same vintage year.

Incidentally, this is also a very good measure for looking at the different return expectations (and indeed requirements) of Venture funds as against Buyout. Remember that we discussed the trade-off between IRR and multiple? Well, if we look at all the US funds in the Thomson database, we find (Table 4.2).

Not quite a perfect illustration of the principle, but good enough. Because Venture funds have longer holding periods, they have to generate higher multiples to earn roughly the same IRR.

Use of Multiples in Industry Research

Multiples also offer a powerful tool when analysing trends or patterns within the Private Equity industry, whether as a whole or on a segmented basis. In fact, in many cases, they can be the only means of finding out what you want to know. Often this is not obvious, however, and the trick is to think not so much about the available multiples themselves as about what they can indicate regarding a certain issue. This, in turn, necessitates an understanding of how Private Equity funds work (see Chapter 2) and a certain ability for creative, or at least lateral, thinking.

Suppose, for example, that you wanted to look at Private Equity holding periods. At first sight there may seem an obvious answer to this, since Thomson provide details of the average number of months a company is held within a Private Equity portfolio prior to an IPO (flotation). However, this only tells part of the story, since there are no comparable figures for the age of a company at exit by M&A (a sale of the company rather than a float). Nor does it

Table 4.3 US Venture capital weighted average DPI by vintage year

Vintage Year	CWA DPI (x)
1996	4.10
1997	2.16
1998	1.26
1999	0.43
2000	0.44
2001	0.40
2002	0.17
2003	0.29
2004	0.17
2005	0.11
2006	0.03
2007	0.01
2008	0.00

Source: Thomson Reuters

take any account of the large number of companies that are written off and/or closed down (some may not be total write-offs since they may have some cash remaining, or it may be possible to sell some Intellectual Property to a third party), and this can be a large proportion, at least within Venture portfolios.

So, we seem to have a real puzzle here. We are trying to find out if average holding periods have changed over time, but it seems that the data we need is unavailable. It is here that the lateral thinking comes in. Is there a multiple which might prove to be some sort of proxy for what we are looking for?

Well, when a company is sold or floated, then either cash or shares are returned to LPs. This would come under the heading of 'distributed capital'. So, one thing we could do is see what proportion of the money that has been drawn down by GPs into their funds (which is, of course, the same thing as 'paid-in capital') has so far been paid back (distributed). There is a multiple which admirably fits our purpose here: DPI, which measures the multiple of paid-in capital represented by distributed capital. In other words, if this figure were one, then LPs would have so far received back exactly the same amount that they had paid in by way of drawdowns (Capital Calls).

What do these figures in Table 4.3 tell us? Well, let us first think about what we would *expect* to see in the normal course of events. Obviously very young Venture funds will have no exits at all, whereas we would expect very mature ones to be more or less fully exited. Therefore, the figures do follow exactly the broad pattern which we would expect, with the oldest funds having the highest DPI, and the youngest ones the lowest.

Look more closely, however, for the figures have much more to tell us. Would you really expect a fund which is nearly seven years old to have paid back only 17% of LPs' drawdowns? Or one which is ten years old to have returned only 43%? Might these figures not be suggesting that something has changed radically in the length of holding periods, and with them expectations of the likely payback period?

Remember the payback period is the period in a fund's life up until the payback point, the point where the DPI will measure exactly one, where the amount of money received by way of distributions will be exactly equal to the amount of money paid in by way of drawdowns. Back in the 1990s there was an expectation that most US Venture funds would have reached this point within five years or so; this may seem a questionable assumption bearing in mind that we traditionally equate early-stage investment with a lengthy period of 'value add' company building, but nonetheless it was so. This, in turn, had significant consequences for expected levels of IRRs (high, because of relatively short holding periods), and for attitudes to overcommitment. LPs routinely committed more money to funds than the amount of their allocated capital, in the settled expectation that their Buyout funds would be paying them back at least some money after three years or so, and their Venture funds paying them back at least some money after five years or so. Thus, these anticipated distributions would cover any possible shortfall in the capital available to meet future Capital Calls.

Given what had happened to date, this did not seem a particularly controversial approach. Indeed, a version of it was advocated in the first edition of this book. Arguably, it remains a valid approach if used with moderation, and if one plans for future Capital Calls as part of one's likely outgoings, rather than simply modelling one's operating outflows, but that discussion lies elsewhere. It is enough at this stage simply to note that both in the context of return expectations and payback expectations, this is a point of crucial importance. How, then, might we try to get a better handle on the numbers in order to test our hypothesis that holding periods have indeed lengthened considerably?

The Thomson database gives us the ability to make calculations as at different dates. While our default approach will always be to calculate them to the most recent date available, so as to ensure that our workings are as up to date as possible, there is no reason at all why, if we wish, we cannot run the figures as they would have looked at the end of 2005, or in June 2001, or the end of any other quarter. Again, let us think about the question to which we actually wish to know the answer (have holding periods lengthened?), use some lateral thinking and see if there is another question, which the available data *can* answer, and which will act as a good proxy for our real question.

Well, suppose we ran the DPI calculation for the first five years of each vintage year. This would show us the extent to which funds of each vintage year had paid back capital in the first five years of their life. We could actually repeat this exercise for other numbers of years as well, but there is only need for one example just to show you how the figures can be handled.

Clearly if we want to calculate a five-year DPI then we cannot look at any vintage years later than 2003. So, to stay as uniform as possible with our last data set, let us look at US Venture funds for vintage years 1996 to 2003, calculating each of them five years later, i.e. we will calculate the 1996 vintage year figure as at the end of 2001, and so on, see Figure 4.4.

Table 4.4   US Venture Capital, capital weighted average 5-year DPI by vintage year

Vintage Year	5-year CWA DPI (x)
1996	3.84
1997	1.68
1998	0.76
1999	0.26
2000	0.22
2001	0.25
2002	0.15
2003	0.29

Source: Thomson Reuters

These figures clearly show where the expectation of a five-year payback came from, but also that any such expectation has been a dead duck since about 2003. Indeed, if you take a look at the figures for yourself, you will see that, as at today looking backwards, you would have to go back to vintage year 2001 before even the best fund would have paid you back, and all the way back to vintage year 1998 for the upper quartile fund to perform the same feat. Clearly then, holding periods must have lengthened very considerably, and expectations based upon the aberrant conditions of the late 1990s are no longer valid.

This is but one example of what can be done with fund multiples, but hopefully one that is both useful as an illustration of the general technique, and of topical importance.

MUDDLES, MUGGLES AND MARKOWITZ

We have so far considered Private Equity returns in the context both of the Private Equity industry as a whole (including segmentation) and as a way of benchmarking the performance of individual funds. For the first edition of this book, this was considered sufficient, as it was expected that the book would be read by those who both make and advise on investment decisions, and in particular on asset allocation decisions. Armed with the clear, compelling and frankly brilliant explanation of Private Equity returns which it contained, investors and their advisers could march joyfully hand in hand into the broad sunlit uplands of inspired and enlightened investment strategy.

Sadly, this has proved to be something of a pious hope. Joking aside, however, it has come as a considerable shock over the last few years to learn of the depths of ignorance and antipathy which still exist in some quarters in respect of Private Equity. Clearly, then, it is necessary to look at Private Equity returns also in the context of institutional investors and their advisers, and how they approach basic questions of asset allocation, such as the decision whether or not to include Private Equity within their portfolio. Today, with the honourable exception of a handful of sophisticated investors in the United States, and a very few elsewhere, this is all a dreadful muddle. Anybody who seeks to raise money for a Private Equity fund, or argue for an allocation internally within an investment organisation, needs to understand why this is, and think about how to get their message across notwithstanding the fog of prejudice, misinformation and misunderstanding which they will assuredly encounter.

At the risk of being branded cool or hip (there has to be a first time for everything), there are distinct *Harry Potter* overtones to the position of Private Equity within the investment community, with those who understand the arcane mysteries of the asset class being the wizards, and those who do not (the overwhelming majority) being the muggles, many of them going about their daily tasks oblivious even to the existence of the wizards, let alone what they do. Magic is not a bad analogy either, since when we watch a magician at work we all know secretly that, no matter how impressive and credible his performance and patter might be, it is all really just an impressive illusion, and this is still how the majority of investors view Private Equity. As we will see, when the data with which they are presented does not match their preconceptions, they simply assume that someone has waved a magic wand over the numbers to make them temporarily seem something which they are not, rather like leprechauns' gold.

Again, this is a huge subject and really requires at least one book just to itself,[2] but it is important to understand why this is, and so we need to consider the salient issues here, if only in summary form.

The main stumbling blocks are: (1) returns, (2) risk and (3) liquidity.

---

[2] See *Multi Asset Class Investment Strategy*, Guy Fraser-Sampson, John Wiley & Sons, Chichester, 2006.

Returns

As we have seen, annual or any other type of periodic returns are more or less useless for the purposes of getting any valid appreciation of Private Equity performance. Instead, we use vintage year returns, whether multiples or IRRs. This raises an immediate problem, however, since almost all the investment community use periodic returns for all purposes, and indeed could be said to be obsessed by them.

Even after several attempts at explanation, the true meaning of vintage year returns can quite simply be beyond them. As stated already, this is not because they are unintelligent, but more because they have been brought up on a steady diet of bonds and quoted equities, and these have blinkered their thinking. Accordingly, it is a very common mistake indeed for both investors and their advisers to look at a page of vintage year returns and imagine that they are actually looking at a page of annual returns.

Why should this matter so much? Well, perhaps we could look at this by way of an example (Figure 4.1).

Take a look at this period of returns on the FTSE100, a period which has been chosen at random simply for illustrative purposes.[3] The line shows the movement of the index, while the columns show the annual return of each year. Suppose we wanted to look at a single number: perhaps the 16% return for 1991. What does this tell us?

Simply that between 31 December 1990 and 31 December 2001 the index rose by 16%. This may seem a terribly obvious thing to say, but it tells us nothing about anything which

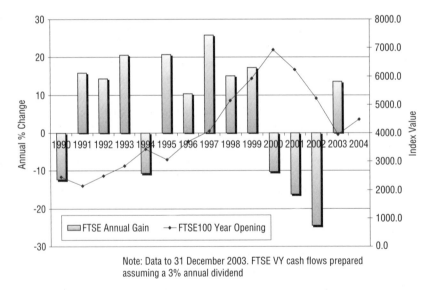

Note: Data to 31 December 2003. FTSE VY cash flows prepared assuming a 3% annual dividend

Figure 4.1   FTSE100 annual returns and index

---

[3] In reality one would, of course, also have to take dividends into account. This example has been deliberately simplified so as not to obscure the salient point.

occurred either before or after that period. Obvious, yet vitally important, since this is exactly the way in which most investors are trained to think.

Suppose now that we were to look at exactly the same numbers, but instead of them being annual returns we were told that they were vintage year returns and that the 1991 vintage year return was 16%. The gulf between the two examples is vast. In the first, we earned 16% *in* 1991. In the second, we earned a *compound* return of 16% *from* 1991. Just see what a difference that makes (Figure 4.2).

Now what we should be imagining is not the return of a single year in isolation, but a stream of cash flows stretching out into the future[4] from 1991, giving us a compound rate of return of 16%. Because it is compounding each year, a notional comparable index would be a steep upward curve. In the first example, we made 16% in 1991. In the second, it is as if we have made 16% not just in 1991, but also in every year thereafter.

A pretty dramatic mistake, then, to confuse annual and vintage year returns, but one which is made routinely. Any time you hear someone say something like 'we've taken a look at the figures and we couldn't see how they justify investing in Private Equity', you know exactly what they have done. Similarly, should you hear someone trying to impress by saying something like 'we've done Monte Carlo analysis on Private Equity returns', you know exactly what they have done. (Monte Carlo analysis can only be performed on periodic returns.)

A further mistake, and one less easy to forgive, is not just to insist on using annual returns where these have been shown to be inappropriate, but to use the wrong ones. If you really *must* use annual returns, then they are available on the Thomson database and can be easily

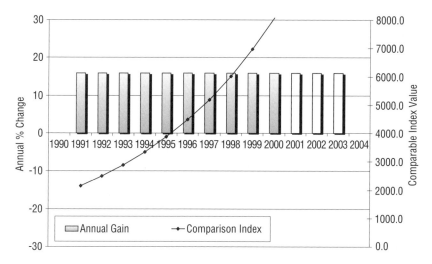

Figure 4.2   1991 European venture vintage year example

---

[4]For page set-up reasons the examples have been cut off after a few years. This is not significant. What is important is to recognise the principle which they demonstrate.

accessed. If you want to measure correlation with other asset classes, for example, then this is probably the only way to do it (though for various reasons the results arrived at will probably be artificially high). Why on earth, then, would people want to make figures up? If real numbers exist, why pluck fantasy ones out of thin air? Yet, believe it or not, this is exactly what happens, even on the part of some of the world's largest pension funds and consultants, at least in Europe.

Rather than spend ten minutes downloading the figures from the industry database, investors and consultants routinely simply apply a factor (perhaps 1.6) to quoted equity returns, so that the two ride up and down together, but with Private Equity obviously moving across a wider range. Unsurprisingly, this results in some very high correlation figures!

It is difficult to know what to say about such an approach, though the words 'incompetent', 'prejudiced' and 'unprofessional' spring readily to mind. It does, however, serve to illustrate the degrees of suspicion, hostility and indifference (if such a combination is possible) with which the asset class is viewed in many quarters. If asset allocation decisions were to be taken in respect of real estate (property), gold, oil or any other investment, then the actual historic performance would be used for analysis purposes. What possible argument can there be for treating Private Equity differently?

The tyranny of periodic percentage returns hits Private Equity particularly hard. First, as we have seen, annual returns are not a good guide, and certainly not if the wider context within which they arise is not understood. Second, they leave no room for money multiples, which are, at the very least, a vital aid to understanding Private Equity fund performance.

The 'annualisation' (averaging) of returns seems difficult to understand in any context anyway, whether for Private Equity or any other asset class, since, as pointed out in the last chapter, this process assumes that the impact of every year is the same when in fact it is not. Surely the performance with which any investor should be concerned is that made during their period of ownership of the investment, and only compound returns calculated across different time periods can measure this. It is quite possible to construct two rows of different annual returns which give the same average annual return, and the same standard deviation, yet a different IRR, a different net present value and a different money multiple.

Risk

The world of traditional finance treats the financial risk of an investment as being the same as the volatility of its historic periodic returns. This is not the place to consider whether or not this is an intelligent thing to do.[5] For our present purposes, imagine a mother finally saying 'it just *is*', in response to her child repeatedly asking 'yes, but *why?*'

The great financial theorist Harry Markowitz, who went on to win the Nobel Prize, usually gets the blame for this, but unfairly. He never actually said that risk and volatility are the same thing. In fact, arguably he never provided us with any specific definition of risk at all. He simply said that certainty of return was desirable, whereas variance (another measure of volatility) of return was undesirable, and few would quarrel with that as a proposition.

---

[5]For a full discussion of risk, see *Multi Asset Class Investment Strategy*, already cited.

Whatever the case, what he called Modern Portfolio Theory, but which today is probably better described as Traditional Finance Theory, proceeded on the mistaken assumption that risk and volatility were, in fact, one and the same, and around this basic and fundamental mistake a whole industry has been erected.

This presents yet another problem when Private Equity comes under consideration, since any calculation of volatility requires periodic returns upon which to operate, and we have already observed that these are not a very good indicator of actual performance. Yet, leaving this to one side and proceeding on the basis of accepting, for the sake of argument, that trying to assess the volatility of the annual returns of Private Equity *is* a valid exercise (since this is what investors are going to do anyway), this runs us straight into another problem, and yet again this is a man-made problem rather than one which arises naturally.

Institutional investors and their advisers are obsessed with calculating a 'risk-adjusted' return for any investment or asset class. Remember that they are using the word 'risk' as if it is synonymous with 'volatility', so what they are really talking about is not a 'risk-adjusted' return at all, but rather a 'volatility-adjusted' return. There is a set way of doing this, which is to use something called the Sharpe Ratio.

For the mathematicians, the Sharpe Ratio is as follows:

$$S = \frac{r - rf}{\sigma}$$

where:

      S is the volatility-adjusted return,
      r is the return (usually the annualised return),
      rf is the risk-free return, and
      σ is the standard deviation of the excess return ($r - rf$).

For the non-mathematicians, all this formula is saying is that you should deduct whatever you decide to take as the risk-free return (such as a T-bill rate for a US dollar investor) from the actual return to arrive at the excess return, i.e. the extent to which you have outperformed the risk-free rate. You then divide this number (the excess return) by its own standard deviation, which is a measure of its volatility over time.

Again, it really is not necessary even to understand this. It is much more important simply to understand that the Sharpe Ratio is a measure of the volatility-adjusted return of an asset or asset class, that the financial community treats this as being the same thing as its risk-adjusted return, and that the higher the Sharpe Ratio, the better. A high Sharpe Ratio (certainly anything above 1) suggests that you are being well rewarded for whatever degree of 'risk' you are incurring. Now, here comes the problem.

Investors and their advisers have an inherent belief that Private Equity must be a 'riskier' investment than, say, quoted equities. This is as a result of another of the conceptual straight-jackets of Traditional Finance, which says that there is a fixed relationship between risk and return, so that wherever an investment exhibits a higher rate of return, it must also necessarily have a higher level of risk. In reality this is not the case, and certainly not if you start calcu-lating 'risk' as, for example, being the chance of losing some or all of your starting capital, but so be it. Because Private Equity has generated higher returns than quoted equities, then it must be 'riskier'.

The problem is that pesky old reality often refuses to co-operate with this tidy theory. For example, measured to the end of 2008, the average annual return of Private Equity was

15.84%, compared to 8.75% for quoted equities.[6] Since Private Equity has produced nearly double the return, one would therefore expect it to exhibit nearly double the volatility. In fact, Private Equity returns have a standard deviation of just 18, compared to 16 for quoted returns, which means that Private Equity's Sharpe Ratio is dramatically higher than that for quoted equities: 0.62, compared to 0.26. Yet investors and their advisers 'know' that Private Equity is the riskier asset class, so these figures are logically impossible.

Can you see how this problem arises, and guess how they solve it?

The first bit is easy. Risk and volatility are *not* the same, and there clearly is *not* a fixed relationship between risk and return, since Sharpe himself explained how it was possible to 'extend the efficient frontier' by building alternative portfolios of uncorrelated assets which could exhibit both higher return and lower risk (volatility). If you base your approach on not just one fallacy but two, then it is hardly surprising if you arrive at results which might appear absurd based on your view of the world.

The second bit is easy too, or at least it is if you think like a European pension consultant. If you can use made-up figures for your calculations in the first place, then hopefully the problem will not arise. If it does, then simply carry things to the next logical step, which is to change not the input figures but the output figure. In other words, if you do not like the result, then change it.[7]

It may seem nonsensical to choose to calculate a particular measure of what you believe to be risk if you are not prepared to abide by the results, but logic and the world of pension fund investment are not always close companions. Essentially what these investors are saying is 'risk and volatility are the same, except when that doesn't suit our purposes, in which case we reserve the right to make up our own figures which are more consistent with our preconceived beliefs.' In practice, what they usually do is to insert what they think is a 'more appropriate' Sharpe Ratio, and use that to calculate the volatility. Life is so much more convenient if you can make up your own answer, and change the question accordingly.

This might seem a lengthy discussion into an area which is of limited relevance to Private Equity practitioners, but sadly that is not the case. Many GPs attempt to go fundraising to institutional investors in their own country only to find that they have no allocation to Private Equity. Sometimes the reason is legal or regulatory constraints to which the investor is subject. More often, though, the answer is that the sort of perverted logic and twisted calculations to which we have just referred are taking place.

Liquidity

It is now three-quarters of a century since the renowned economist John Maynard Keynes bemoaned 'the fetish of liquidity' which strangled investment policy, and yet it is still alive and well. The final stumbling block which the advocate of a Private Equity allocation is likely to meet is 'we must have liquidity', repeated over and over again like a Buddhist mantra, perhaps in the hope that by repetition it will become true.

Again, this is such a huge subject that it could quite properly command a book all to itself, but within the scope of one short section, let us get a few things straight.

---

[6] My calculations, based on the FTSE100 index plus annual dividend yield since inception.

[7] See, for example, de Groot and Swinkels (2008) Incorporating uncertainty about alternative assets in strategic pension fund asset allocation, *International Journal of Pensions*, **13**, 71–77.

Liquidity may be forced upon investors by unintelligent regulation, such as in the case of pension funds in the Netherlands, Denmark or Sweden, or by naked self-interest, whereby governments force public investment bodies to buy only the bonds issued by that government, thus ensuring a constant market for them. In investment terms, however, there probably is not a single institutional investor in the world that requires liquidity in respect of their whole portfolio, not even the mature pension funds which frequently claim that they do.

In investment terms, liquidity is a bad thing, not a good thing. It is very expensive, since it comes at the price of lower returns, and therefore we should actually have as little of it as possible within our investment portfolio, rather than seeking out as much as we can get our hands on.

Expensive, because the reason we look to invest in illiquid assets is precisely because we expect them to give us a higher long-term return, the 'illiquidity premium'. Logically, therefore, if investment criteria were the only considerations (but they rarely are), then the default position would be to invest only in illiquid assets, and have no liquidity at all.

Every investor has some need for liquidity, however. Banks and non-life insurance companies probably need to hold just about all their assets in liquid investments; they are the classic short-term investors. At the other end of the spectrum come pension funds, which, ironically, are the most passionate seekers of liquidity while probably needing less of it than just about any other type of investor.

Investment strategy should start with identifying one's short-term liabilities (usually between three and five years into the future). These should absolutely be held in liquid assets, and they should be truly liquid, such as T-bills (in the case of a dollar investor) or their closest equivalent in the investor's currency. Once this liquidity reserve has been established, however, and kept topped up from one quarter to the next, whatever remains is available for investment in illiquid assets, though some of this will almost certainly end up in quoted equities. In the case of most pension funds, incidentally, the required liquidity reserve is unlikely ever to be more than about 10% of total assets.

The investment rationale for Private Equity is a classic one. It belongs to that remaining part of your portfolio after the liquidity reserve has been established, that part in respect of which you are prepared to give up short-term liquidity against the trade-off of higher expected long-term returns. Every investor will have this; it is just that most either do not recognise the fact, or are too frightened to use it.

Various attempts have been made to graft artificial liquidity onto a Private Equity programme; indeed, this has become the holy grail of many within the structured products business. As a generalisation, such attempts have either been quickly abandoned, or found to be both expensive and ultimately unreliable. Private Equity *is* an illiquid asset class, and it seems only prudent to treat it as such.

There is one exception to this, which is the existence of a thriving secondary market for LPs' interests in Private Equity funds, but we will not discuss this further for the moment as we will be dealing with it separately later in the book. For now, please just be aware that it exists.

So, with liquidity, as with both returns and risk, the only long-term solution is a slow but steady education process aimed at investors and their advisers. Perversely, however, this may not be bad news. There is already a huge debate about large amounts of money flooding into the industry (notwithstanding the apparent slowdown in fundraising in 2009, which is likely to prove only a short-term limitation) and depressing Private Equity returns, though there are many (chiefly the mega funds and their fundraisers) who fiercely contest this view. Whatever the merits of that particular debate, it is strongly arguable that it may actually be beneficial for the industry as a whole that many of the world's investors have set their face resolutely against Private Equity.

SUMMARY

In addition to IRRs, multiples can also be a valuable measure of Private Equity fund returns. Most useful is total value to paid in (TVPI) which measures both the distributions received to date and the residual value of the remaining investments. However, this figure is only truly meaningful towards the end of a fund's life.

There is a direct trade-off between IRR and multiple, with a longer holding period (such as one typically encounters with a Venture fund) needing to result in a higher investment multiple in order to generate the same IRR.

Turning to the perspective of institutional investors and their advisers, vintage year returns are routinely confused with annual returns, a bad mistake with very significant impact.

Even when seeking annual returns for analysis purposes, many investors disregard the actual figures and use fantasy figures, made up according to some notion of their own devising – usually by multiplying quoted equity returns by some arbitrarily chosen factor (1.6 seems particularly popular).

Institutional investors treat risk as being the same thing as the volatility of historic returns. When measured in this way, Private Equity's annual returns in fact show very low 'risk' in relative terms. Because this does not fit with investors' preconceived prejudices, they routinely alter the results to make them fit with what they believe they ought to show.

Liquidity is a bad thing not a good thing in investment terms, and institutional investors routinely have far too much of it in their portfolios (as much as ten times too much in the case of many pension funds). This works against Private Equity, the investment rationale for which is that the investor has some part of their portfolio in respect of which they are prepared to give up short-term liquidity in exchange for higher expected long-term returns.

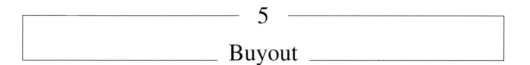

5
Buyout

We will be looking separately at the issue of valuation, how Buyouts work, how and why Buyout returns are generated, how these may be measured and analysed and how we might go about modelling Buyout activity. However, before discussing the 'how' and the 'why', we must turn our attention to the 'what'. What is Buyout? What is a Buyout firm? Can anyone do it? If not, what are the barriers to entry into the Buyout industry?

As we saw earlier, while it is very difficult to arrive at a definition of Buyout that will cover every transaction we are likely to see, it is possible to advance various general characteristics even though in many cases we will also have to acknowledge some specific exceptions. However, before we turn to these aspects which tend to distinguish Buyout from other fields of Private Equity activity, it would be useful to set out the different types of Buyout transaction which can occur.

TYPES OF BUYOUT TRANSACTION

MBO

The classic Buyout has always been an MBO or Management Buyout. In its purest form, this involves the executive team who are managing a particular business activity deciding to buy it out from the parent company or shareholders. This was the bedrock of Buyout activity in the UK, for example, in the early to mid 90s, with the management team typically appointing one of the accountancy firms to act for them, drawing up a business plan and pitching the deal to selected Buyout firms. The management team would be required to put their own money into the deal, usually involving having to borrow in order to do so, but were rewarded with 'sweet equity' issued at preferential rates and ratcheted to pre-agreed performance targets.

The main point which distinguished pure MBOs from other forms of Buyout activity was that these deals were driven, at least in the early stages, by the target company's management team. Once the favoured Private Equity firm had been chosen, however, control of the transaction passed to them, though they were, of course, at pains to keep the management team fully informed, and consult and agree with them on all the key issues. This was only sensible, given that this relationship would prove crucial to the ultimate success of the Buyout. For a rare example of where this did not happen, and the management team retained control of the process throughout, see the contested Buyout of RJR Nabisco in 1988.[1]

While still common, this pure form of MBO has become less prevalent, since dramatic increases in fund sizes, and thus also target transaction sizes, have made it increasingly difficult to find businesses which are not either (1) too small or (2) have already been bought out. It may be that we have seen the last of the old-style MBO, since with the rise of the

---

[1] Helyar and Burrough (1990) *Barbarians at the Gate*, Harper and Row, New York.

mega-deal, many transactions which would previously have been classified as MBOs would probably now more properly be described as 'LBOs' or 'Take Privates' (see below), and a true MBO of a public company would be a very complex operation under existing UK and US stock market regulations.

However, it will be interesting to see if this form of activity takes root in those emerging Private Equity markets in Asia and South America where the legal and tax frameworks do not currently admit Buyout activity. Currently, these markets are dominated by Growth and Development Capital, just as happened originally in turn first in the US, then in the UK and finally in continental Europe. Should this pattern be repeated in other parts of the world, then, as legal and tax requirements are brought more into line with the developed Private Equity markets, there could be a wealth of very exciting MBO opportunities.

MBI

The Management Buy-In evolved from the MBO. It is similar in just about every way apart from the nature of the team or, viewed another way, apart from the way in which the deal initially comes together.

The key difference is that instead of the management team of a business getting together to buy it, a team comes together to buy another company operating in the same sector. This may be because they have tried to buy their own business and been rebuffed by the parent company, or because they wanted to buy it but it was sold to a trade buyer instead.

Pure MBIs are rare, and there was much hearsay evidence back in the 1990s that they tended to perform less well than MBOs.[2] This was almost certainly because the level of knowledge about the target company was inevitably less than would be the case with a team of company insiders. Most Buyout firms maintain a small team of industry-specific executives who work with them in much the same way as an entrepreneur in residence operates inside a Venture firm, helping with due diligence and deal sourcing but with the clear expectation of leading the management team if a transaction comes to fruition in their own sector. However, strictly speaking these deals tend usually to fall into the BIMBO category.

BIMBO

As the acronym suggests, these deals are a combination of an MBO and an MBI, where outside executives are grafted on to the existing executive team in order to facilitate a Buyout. In truth, many Buyout transactions probably fall into this category if one applies the definition strictly. This could range from taking on a finance director for a small Buyout to supplement the existing financial controller, through the return of a recently departed CEO to a team to whom he is well-known, to the effective acquisition by a senior industry figure of a business along with its management team.

LBO

There is a great deal of overlap in these Buyout definitions and in truth most practitioners probably never stop to think about where their current deal falls in the spectrum, and probably

---

[2]Certainly studies by the Centre for Management Buyout Research (CMBOR) at the University of Nottingham tended to confirm this.

wouldn't care anyway. For the student and the LP, though, it is important to try to analyse the sector as fully as possible.

LBO stands for Leveraged Buyout and in a sense all Buyouts are LBOs since 'leverage' is simply the American word for 'gearing', and all true Buyouts will involve the use of some acquisition debt. Indeed, this is one of the main ways in which we distinguish a Buyout from the other types of Private Equity transaction. In the past, this was more an issue than it is today, since there were, in most jurisdictions, restrictions on the 'giving of financial assistance',[3] i.e. the use of the target company's own assets to secure acquisition debt. Acquisition teams had to go through a complicated series of manoeuvres, including a working capital report from the company's auditors, in order to circumvent these. However, legal reform and the growth of more sophisticated cash flow financing have made these issues largely redundant.

Today an LBO has two main connotations which help to distinguish it from other Buyout types, but these are both imprecise and subjective. The first is that it suggests a Buyout which has not been initiated by a management team, either external or internal. Typically today Buyout deals will be initiated by the seller appointing an investment bank to prepare a company for sale, and Buyout firms entering the fray alongside industrial purchasers. The second is that it suggests a transaction where the target company is large enough (or may well be a group of companies) that the typical non-financial purchaser would itself be a comparable large public company. In these circumstances, it may be convenient to think of an LBO as being equivalent to an industrial acquisition, but with the acquirer just happening to be a Buyout firm (or, more frequently these days, a consortium of Buyout firms).

In fact, there are many people today who believe that LBO actually stands for 'Large Buyout' because of this, and it certainly seems to be used in this context when industry observers, particularly in the US, talk of 'LBO activity' or 'LBO firms'. To add yet more confusion, it is common in the US, as we noted at the very beginning of this book, also to use the phrase 'Private Equity' in this regard. This is a most unfortunate usage, and should be corrected and discouraged whenever it is encountered, as it leads to some very serious misunderstandings.

Take Private (P2P)

Again, there is obviously potential for overlap here, but a Take Private is, as the name suggests, a Buyout of a public company removing its listing in the process (or very shortly afterwards once various formalities have been complied with) in order to transform it into a private company. For this reason, such deals are often described as PTP or P2P, meaning 'Public To Private'. As we will examine later, there is considerable scepticism in some quarters as to whether such deals can produce the sort of returns to which investors have become accustomed in the past, but this is a development which has really been forced upon the Buyout sector by the inexorable rise in fund sizes, and thus in target transaction size.

Various arguments are advanced in favour of such transactions. There may well be situations, for example, where very aggressive restructuring is required and it is felt that this might only be effectively accomplished out of the glare of publicity and away from the rigid

---

[3] The phrase that was used in English company law.

reporting regime to which public companies are subject. There is also the consideration that very few public companies actually carry anything like as much debt as a strict application of the Theory of the Levered Firm so beloved of finance lecturers would suggest. As the screenwriters have Henry Kravis say in the film version of *Barbarians at the Gate*,[4] 'debt tightens a company'.

Roll-up

This used to be much more popular than it is today, largely because much larger fund sizes make it a less viable proposition. Basically one targets an industry which is highly fragmented, buys lots of small operators and puts them together. The attraction of such an approach is that not only is it possible to increase profits exponentially by better marketing and management and economies of scale, but the resulting larger entity will merit a higher earnings multiple, thus resulting in an upward valuation curve rather than a straight line.

The reason this approach is now relatively little used is that the growth in fund sizes, and attendant growth in target transaction size, means that Buyout firms are now often targeting either public companies or large subsidiaries of public companies and one is thus thrust instantly into the realm of anti-trust or monopoly regulation, depending on what side of the Atlantic you inhabit. Indeed, it is not unknown for a Buyout firm actually to have to undertake in advance to *sell* parts of a business so as not to run into a potential dominant market position when combined with another company which is already in their portfolio.

Secondary Buyouts

A Secondary Buyout is one which is distinguished by its exit route. Instead of being sold to a trade buyer, or exited by way of an IPO (flotation), it is sold instead to another Buyout firm. For the fund buying it, it will count as a Secondary Buyout. These have become widespread in recent years, sometimes even turning into Tertiary Buyouts when they are sold on to yet a third Buyout fund, reminding the author of a game played many years ago at children's parties, during which a heavily wrapped parcel was passed from hand to hand. With the collapse in both valuations and the debt market since mid-2007, the music can fairly be said to have stopped, and it remains to be seen what will happen when somebody actually has to unwrap it.

Worryingly for LPs, GPs have occasionally been seen to use their current fund to invest in the Secondary Buyout alongside the financial buyer who is purchasing it from one of their prior funds, raising obvious issues of valuation. It is almost inconceivable that it could represent a good deal for both funds, and it would be logical for such transactions to be prohibited by fund documentation in future.

OTHER 'BUYOUT' ACTIVITY

We are going to consider Development Capital deals in a separate category because if one strictly applies the various characteristics to which we have already alluded in outline, they

---

[4] Already cited above.

are clearly not Buyout transactions at all. The key feature of a Development Capital deal is that shareholder control will not pass to the Buyout firm, although some measure of negative control can be granted by reserving the right to veto certain decisions, e.g. relating to capital expenditure, dividends and executive remuneration.

The lack of a majority shareholding also has profound implications for the financial structure of the deal, since it will usually not be possible to use an acquisition vehicle/target company model (see below) where the accounts can be consolidated and the interest on acquisition debt can be set off at the holding company level. Thus, it is frequently not possible to use any debt finance at all.

We will be reviewing Development Capital deals separately, but it is necessary to refer to them here because (particularly in continental Europe) one often finds both Buyout and Development activity being pursued within the same fund, which, confusingly, might be described as 'Buyout', 'Development' or neither, and it is important to be able to distinguish between the two. As an LP, where possible you should be looking to analyse deals falling into the two categories separately, as different considerations will apply.

PIPEs

There is yet a further type of transaction with which a Buyout firm might get involved, and although it has featured to date more in late-stage Venture funds than in Buyout funds, here is probably as good a place to consider it as any, since, like Development Capital, it too defies precise classification. It is a category of deals that have come to be known as PIPEs (Private Investment in Public Equity, or Private Instrument in Public Equity) and occurs when a particular investment instrument is created within a public company that may offer a Private-Equity-type return.

Typically, while the company's equity is quoted, the instrument itself is not. In some circumstances (though there are significant potential regulatory problems here, particularly in Europe) it may be a prelude to a Take Private. The instrument itself is usually a convertible loan note with equity kickers and may carry complex provisions about priority treatment in a liquidation or on the occurrence of a defined act of default.

There have been relatively few such deals to date, but with more and more money coming into the industry, it is possible that there may be more in future. Indeed, various Buyout firms have cited PIPEs as one example of how they would put their newly raised mega funds to work (the others being 'equity only' deals, and moving down into the mid-market) after the debt market shuddered to a halt in 2007.

A cynical observer might suggest that PIPEs tend to occur when private firms find themselves with too much money on their hands and are desperately looking for a way in which to spend it, something which before 2007 last happened in 2001 and 2002 with those US Venture firms who chose not to reduce their fund sizes.

HOW DO BUYOUTS WORK?

It is worth spending some time examining how Buyout transactions are actually structured, since the use of acquisition debt puts them into very different territory compared to their counterpart deals in Venture, Growth and Development.

The essential difference is that, in order to work, Buyout deals need to be able to make use of something which is called by different names in different countries, but to which we

The basic structure of a typical buyout

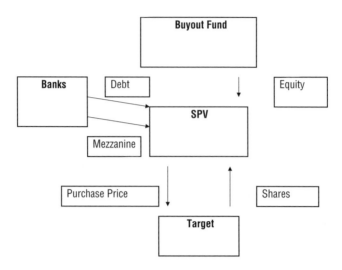

Figure 5.1   The basic structure of a typical buyout

might refer generically as tax consolidation. This is the principle whereby if you have two companies, one of which owns the other, then you may treat both companies as if they were one big company for tax purposes. A detailed discussion of these various provisions lies outside the scope of a book of this nature, but we should note that these rules tend only to exist in the more sophisticated capitalist economies, though we should add 'at the moment', since it seems inevitable that they will be adopted in future much more widely. Briefly, should you happen to live in a country where there is no Buyout activity, the absence of such a regime is very likely to be the reason.[5]

Let us look at an example (Figure 5.1) of how a Buyout might be put together, as once we understand this it will make it much easier to grasp the principle of tax consolidation. This example is useful for two different reasons. Not only will it show how Buyouts are structured, but it will also illustrate in graphic terms one of the things – the lack of borrowing at the fund level – which was referred to in Chapter 2 as distinguishing Private Equity from Hedge funds.

Step One: the Buyout firm identifies a target company which they would like to buy as one of the portfolio companies of their current fund, and agrees a purchase price with the company's current owner.

Step Two: the Buyout firm sets up a new SPV (Special Purpose Vehicle) to act as a holding company.

Step Three: the Buyout firm models a range of future financial scenarios and analyses how much equity it can inject into the deal from its current fund without dropping below its target transaction IRR. It draws down this amount of capital from its LPs by way of a Capital Call.

---

[5]The other main candidate being the existence of regulations banning the taking of control of domestic companies.

Step Four: the difference between the amount of the equity drawn down from LPs and the purchase price is made good by a package of debt and mezzanine finance extended to the SPV by third party providers. In normal market conditions, it is customary for the whole package to be underwritten in advance by a large bank, which will then 'lay off' the various components to a range of different participants.

Step Five: the SPV now has enough money to be able to pay the purchase price to the owner of the target company, receiving in return all the shares in the target, and becoming its 100% owner.

Please note that this explanation is necessarily simplistic, since this is a book on Private Equity as an asset class, not on Buyout structuring. However, to forestall a flood of letters to the publishers, particular attention should be paid to the following points.

In practice, it is much more likely that the first step will be driven by the vendor rather than the purchaser, since these days any corporate transaction of any size will be dealt with by way of a controlled auction run by an investment bank.

The financing package will be dramatically more complicated than this bald analysis suggests. There may be several layers of both debt (referred to as A, B, C, etc) and mezzanine (usually at least A and B), leading to the Inter-Creditor Agreement (the contract regulating the rights and obligations of the finance providers amongst themselves) often being called an Alphabet Note. In addition, something called Second Lien lending seems to have been making something of a comeback as part of the package. Each layer of debt will be extended on different conditions, with the level of security typically falling, but the interest rate rising, the further one drops down the layers.

Incidentally, it is here we find the concept of a 'strip', which sadly turns out not to be nearly as much fun as it sounds. It simply means a vertical section through the funding structure, like cutting a slice of a multi-layered cake so as to end up with a small piece of each different layer.

There may be several different funding vehicles set up to facilitate the different requirements of each type of finance. Similarly to act as vesting vehicles for various share option arrangements.

Because the management team who are actually running the company will be pressed to buy some sweet equity, and occasionally the vendor will want to keep an ongoing stake in the company, the actual ultimate ownership of the target company by the fund may end up being less than 100%, and will almost always diminish again on or just before an exit. However, for practical purposes this is usually done at the level of the SPV, not the target.

It is also necessary to mention 'cov-lite' lending. Alongside the Inter-Creditor Agreement, which binds the various providers of the funding package to each other on specified terms (including the circumstances in which their freedom to pursue a remedy for breach may be restricted), the other main agreement will be the contract entered into between the third party funders, or the lead bank as their agent, and the SPV, commonly called the Loan Agreement, though in reality it is far more complex than this. This contains various covenants designed to protect the lenders, including things like Loan to Value, interest cover, etc. It is these covenants that began to be significantly relaxed by the banks during the feeding frenzy that attended the last year or two of the Buyout bubble, hence the expression 'cov-lite'.

Just circling back for a moment to the distinction to be drawn with Hedge funds, it is most important to understand that all of this Buyout funding is what is called 'non-recourse'; in

Before the transaction

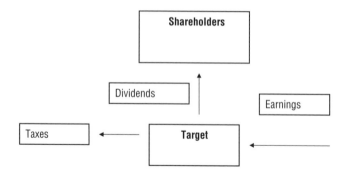

Figure 5.2   Before the transaction

other words it is not guaranteed by any third party, whether the fund, the GP or the LPs. There is not even any cross-default across different portfolio companies. Each single Buyout is totally ring-fenced; if it goes wrong, the banks run a real risk of losing some money. This point is totally lost on many journalists, who continue to run stories speculating on whether a Buyout fund will go bust; as we have just seen, this is not possible, since, unlike a Hedge fund, a Buyout fund never has any obligations.

Now that we understand how the basic Buyout structure operates, the idea of tax consolidation should be relatively easy to grasp. Let us use a simple illustration of the picture 'before' and 'after' the transaction takes place (Figure 5.2).

Here we see the normal condition of a profitable company. It runs a business, from which it earns profits. It pays some of these profits to the Government by way of taxes and can then pay the rest, if it wishes, to its shareholders by way of dividends. Note, therefore, that dividends are paid *after* tax.

Now let us take a look at the same company after the Buyout has taken place (Figure 5.3).

Remember that now we can treat both these companies as though they were one big company for tax purposes. This means that we can set the loan interest being paid by the holding company off against the profits being earned by the target, just as if that interest was being paid by the target company itself, since, unlike dividends, loan interest is paid *before* tax.

In this example, the tax that would otherwise be payable has disappeared completely. Again, this is a simplistic example, but it is undeniably the objective of the financial engineering that goes into creating Buyouts that, if possible, no tax at all will be payable. This was one of the main criticisms that was levelled against the 'Private Equity industry' (though in reality only the mega Buyout sector) during the great Buyout debate that raged in Government and media circles throughout 2007.[6]

For the record, many argue that while it is technically correct that Buyouts reduce tax yield, they probably only do so in the short term, since, in normal market conditions, the interest payable would flow through into the profits of the lending banks and be taxed in their hands

---

[6]There were many other issues as well, such as the tax treatment of carried interest, and disclosure and transparency.

After the transaction

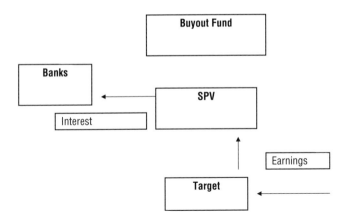

Figure 5.3   After the transaction

in due course. While this particular debate seems largely to have died down, many countries either already have, or are considering introducing, 'thin equity' rules, which will limit the amount of relief that can be claimed on acquisition debt by reference to percentage levels of gearing.

CHARACTERISTICS OF BUYOUT

Established Businesses

As we saw in the first chapter, Buyout practitioners are concerned with established companies which are usually in either the Mature or Decline stage of their relevant product life cycle. There are sound business reasons for this. As we have just seen, Buyout transactions usually incorporate financial structuring that requires cash flow to service debt. Companies which are at an earlier stage of the life cycle are typically cash-hungry, needing to grow quickly so as not to lose ground on the competition. They may also exhibit what would, to a Buyout firm, be unacceptable levels of market risk, or even product risk, thus raising the possibility that the firm may actually fail.

Growth companies might seem attractive because they offer the opportunity for increased earnings, which are one of the three main drivers of Buyout returns. However, the choice of the right place on the growth curve, neither too late to lose out on the potential for increased earnings nor too early to generate sufficient free cash flow, is an extremely delicate one, and an area where experience may confer a considerable competitive advantage. Thus, while it is not unknown for Buyout funds to invest in Growth companies, it is relatively unusual and only entered into after very careful consideration. The risk of outright failure, for example, is one which no Buyout firm can afford to contemplate. As we will see when we come to consider the Buyout fund model and the nature of Buyout returns, there is little room in a Buyout portfolio for companies which fail to return their invested capital. Thus, it is likely, indeed even desirable, that they should err on the side of caution. Incidentally, this is an area where the new entrant (as a Buyout firm) may well hit problems, either through inexperience or through pressure to invest at a time of dealflow paucity.

Mature companies are attractive because they will have become 'cash cows', throwing off cash from well-established business activities which have lost the capacity for rapid growth. In a strategic corporate portfolio as envisaged by the classic Boston Consulting Group matrix, these will support the cash flow requirements of the 'stars', which need to grow at least as quickly as the competition just to stand still in relative terms. In a Buyout portfolio, these companies' cash flow can be channelled into servicing debt and even paying off loan principal. This means both that relatively high levels of gearing can be used initially, and that the company can be recapitalised periodically while it remains within the portfolio, using new debt to replace equity being returned to the fund.

These 'recaps' are a significant contributor to Buyout returns, but their prevalence and importance has not always been properly recognised outside the industry. Because recaps allow capital to be returned to investors early, i.e. before any formal exit has been achieved in respect of the underlying company itself, they can have a substantial impact on the compound rate of return used to measure Private Equity performance, since this focuses on the time value of money and here cash flows are being dragged to an earlier point on the timeline.

There has, from time to time, been talk of Buyout firms moving to an earlier stage of company development for their investment focus. Such talk was prevalent at the time of the technology bubble, with some Buyout firms looking at pre-IPO funding rounds for Venture companies, and some even looking at a number of Internet start-ups, frequently at the urging of their LPs. Fortunately, however, the vast majority of the Buyout sector held their discipline and the amount of money actually invested in such deals was small. In retrospect it may seem strange that such a discussion should ever have taken place at all. The skills of Buyout and Venture managers are demonstrably different, and aimed efficiently at the types of companies in which they respectively invest. To attempt to cross between the two seems to make little sense, yet so strong was the pull of the new, and the feeding frenzy which overtook investors everywhere, that there was a serious danger that many Buyout firms could have been pulled totally off course, and it is to the great credit of the sector that these siren calls were largely resisted.

In the context of the day-to-day terminological confusion between Venture and Buyout, it is this concentration on established businesses rather than on nurturing new and young ones that is the most commonly misunderstood. Hopefully for those who have read this chapter, any reference to Buyout firms coming together to mount a multi-billion dollar bid for an international industrial conglomerate or public utility as 'Venture Capitalists' will, in future, be seen as the basic factual error that it is.

Incidentally, the inexorable growth in average size of Buyout funds has led to questions of just how many established businesses will remain as fresh pickings for Buyout firms. This is actually a more valid concern in the US than it is in Europe. In Europe, industrial consolidation and rationalisation is generally, even now, at an earlier, or at least less-developed, stage than it is across the Atlantic. Almost whatever business sector one examines (telecommunications, banking, etc.) will show many more individual operators in an economy of roughly equal size. Historically this has been partly due to political reasons, every country, or sometimes even region, wanting its own airline, bank, brewery, etc. However, the Buyout firms would argue that, even in the US, the problem is less pronounced than might be thought. The growth in Buyout fund size effectively drives a self-perpetuating cycle in which more capital becomes available for investment, allowing larger and larger deals to be attempted.

We have probably now reached a stage where no company in the world is too large to be safe from the attentions of the Buyout industry, and this obviously in turn raises interesting questions as to the interaction of Private Equity with quoted markets in years to come. With the current pause in Buyout fundraising, it remains to be seen how quickly and how strongly this trend will resume, but it is quite possible that the world will be faced with a fundamental long-term change in the balance between Private and Public Equity.

Debt

It is the use of debt finance that most obviously distinguishes Buyouts from other Private Equity transactions such as Venture and Development Capital. However, for the sake of completeness, we should note that (1) Venture companies can be partly financed by trade credit (e.g. from suppliers of equipment) which, from a strictly accounting point of view, would be classified as 'debt', and that the very late stages of Venture financing can include convertible instruments which may be structured as loan notes and (2) that though it is difficult to inject acquisition debt into Development Capital deal structures, it is not impossible (though usually inefficient from a tax point of view).

We explored above a simple model for explanatory purposes, but it bears repeating that Buyout transactions are structurally very complex indeed, frequently with many different layers of debt, and that no two are the same. Indeed, it is in such structuring that a lot of key Buyout skills lie, and in the ability to obtain advantageous terms from banks through a course of dealings over the years that we find a key barrier to entry for new Buyout firms, or at least a source of competitive advantage to the established players.

We are examining separately exactly how Buyouts work, and can be modelled, but this would be a good moment to examine in a little more detail the sort of funding package to which we referred above. Basically, there are three main types of debt with which we need to be concerned.

First, and this is often overlooked, there is the existing debt that will already be present within a business for working capital purposes. Because the target company is usually going to be viewed on a consolidated basis with the SPV acquisition vehicle (often referred to as 'Newco'), banks will take into account the totality of all debt that is to be present once the deal is completed. Thus, a company which already has high levels of operating debt will be less attractive as a Buyout target, whereas one which has low levels of debt, and possibly even a cash pile, will be highly attractive.

Buyout firms will usually seek to reduce the level of operating debt within a business once they have acquired it. Since operating debt finances the working capital cycle, this may logically be reduced in any one of three ways: lower stock levels, fewer debtor days (i.e. the number of days taken on average for debtors to pay their invoices) or more creditor days (the opposite). Lower operating debt requirement will mean that the bank may be persuaded to issue more acquisition debt in its place, thus enabling some equity to be released back to the Buyout fund as part of a recapitalisation.

The second type of debt is straight acquisition debt, which is often referred to as 'senior' debt because it will take priority in repayment and on any liquidation of the company over other types of debt in the Buyout structure. This will usually have some measure of security, though typically these days this will normally take the form of a floating charge over the company's assets in general rather than a fixed charge over specific assets (since these will frequently be sold off and leased back where necessary to free up cash). There will also be covenants in the loan agreement which will strictly control what the company can do with its cash, though some of these can be to the benefit of both parties; a cash sweep would be a good example.

The third type of debt is variously referred to as 'convertible' or 'mezzanine', though a caveat should be entered at this stage in that, in America, 'mezzanine' can also refer to pre-IPO funding of Venture companies. In its Buyout sense, 'mezzanine' simply means the layer of debt which sits below senior debt and, in contrast, is usually both convertible and unsecured. The derivation of the term is clear: it is a financing layer which sits between the two floors of the structuring house – debt and equity. Indeed, it shares the characteristics of both. (Corporate bonds may also be used, particularly in the US.)

Mezzanine financing has developed into a specialist area of its own, with dedicated funds being raised to operate in the space, and with senior debt providers (at least until 2007) being increasingly interested in providing the mezzanine element of a deal as well. Sometimes one bank or, in the case of a very large deal, a consortium of banks, will combine to underwrite the whole financial requirement and will then seek to sell down parts of it, like a bookie laying off his bets, either horizontally (i.e. asking someone else to provide the whole of a particular layer of mezzanine) or vertically in 'strips'.

Again, for the sake of completeness, I mentioned above something known as 'Second Lien' which, as its name suggests, is debt which takes a second rather than a first charge over the company's assets by way of security, for which reason it is also sometimes referred to as 'Last Out' lending. It is more expensive than senior debt, but less so than mezzanine. Traditionally, it was often used to fill small holes in the funding package where the amount of senior debt on offer was not quite enough for the GPs' purposes. It fell largely out of use in relative terms during the lending frenzy leading up to 2007, but there are those who predict that, as leveraged activity begins to pick up, Second Lien lending may once again have a significant role to play.

Earnings

We will be looking at earnings in detail when we come to see how Buyout transactions are put together, and valuations arrived at. Suffice it to say at this stage that the presence of earnings within a company will usually point to any Private Equity transaction in respect of that company being a Buyout or a Development Capital deal. However, as so often in Private Equity, there are a couple of exceptions which should be noted.

Some late-stage Venture companies may have earnings. This is actually not a real exception at all but rather the result of people having traditionally spoken of 'earnings' when what is really important is cash flow. Venture (and Growth) companies may have earnings, but will almost certainly still have negative cash flow because they need to plough all their earnings and more back into the business in order to fund rapid growth. Buyout companies require cash flow to service debt and while it is often conveniently assumed that, for an established business, earnings (at least at the operating level) may be a good proxy for cash flow, this is not always the case and can sometimes actually be very misleading.

It is also necessary to consider the case of turnaround situations, which one hesitates to describe as a different category of transaction in their own right, since they are frequently

executed by Buyout firms and viewed in much the same way as their other transactions.[7]
However, as we will see when we look at valuation and modelling, they can pose significant
problems and are generally undertaken only with extreme caution, and even then only when
significant sector expertise is available.

Size

Here there is much that is controversial and much that is self-evident. Self-evident is that the
average size of Buyout funds has risen steadily on both sides of the Atlantic. Since there are
only two ways in which this extra capital can be deployed (either doing more deals within a
fund or doing bigger deals within a fund), and since the time and resources required to execute
a large deal are, in many cases, similar to those required to execute a small one, then unsurprisingly the average size of Buyout transactions has also risen quite explosively, see Figures
5.4 and 5.5).

We shall be looking in detail at the whole issue of fund size when we discuss how to
analyse a Buyout firm, but we should note here that the rapid and explosive rise in Buyout
fund size has changed dramatically the sorts of deals which get done. We will see in Chapter
7 how European Buyout returns were at their best in the early to mid 1990s. This was a time
when fund sizes were fairly small and firms were, for the most part, looking to pick off
individual subsidiaries of public companies or, better still, medium-sized owner-managed
companies. This market was characterised by various factors.

Firms were able to seek out deals proactively, and to agree exclusivity with a vendor once
the target had been identified. This was particularly prevalent at the time in countries such
as Germany[8] and Sweden, and it is no accident that it is in these countries that firms such as

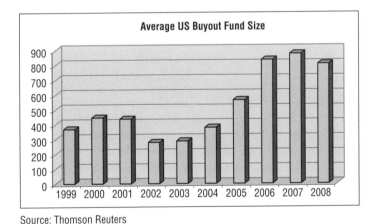

Source: Thomson Reuters

Figure 5.4   Average US buyout fund size

---

[7]As with just about everything one can say about Private Equity, I do not pretend this to be universally true. There are some
firms which specialise in turnaround situations and do nothing else. However, they are generally few in number and small in fund
size, and in the interests of space, if nothing else, I have decided not to consider them separately.

[8]There was, at the time, no phrase in the German language for 'shareholder value'.

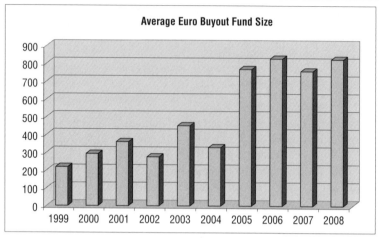

Figure 5.5   Average Euro buyout fund size

Doughty Hanson, IndustriKapital and Nordic Capital made their early stellar returns. Today this is no longer the case, with any deal of any size being put through a controlled auction process.

Target companies frequently had low levels of gearing, particularly owner-managed companies, which could be very debt-averse. This facilitated the use of quite aggressive acquisition debt programmes. To be fair, this was also a time of imagination and innovation within the Buyout community; it was in the mid-1990s, for example, that we saw the first European Buyout ever to be financed by a US bond issue (Doughty Hanson was the firm in question). Today this is hardly ever the case; indeed, operational gearing is sometimes kept at a high level deliberately simply to deter any acquisitive thoughts by third parties.

These companies frequently also had a layer of management effectively missing, since, in the case of an owner-managed company, the owner was accustomed to performing most of these functions himself and, in the case of a subsidiary, they were usually performed at the holding company level. Thus, one might find a financial controller where a finance director was required, and so on. By replacing this missing layer, the skill-base of the business could often be dramatically increased, thus facilitating both revenue and earnings growth. In addition, working capital practices had normally not been the most stringent, and extra cash flow could be squeezed out to service and retire debt.

What has just been described was a legendary golden age of European Buyout activity, a happy hunting time when great returns could be made; funds frequently returned well over three times their capital to investors. These conditions no longer apply, and Buyout firms have had to hone their skills to squeeze out value in other ways.

There are those who claim that, in large part, this transition has been forced upon the industry by the rise in fund sizes, which, in turn, make it unrealistic to pursue smaller companies (Bridgepoint, who execute a large number of transactions within a fund, are a notable exception, but most Buyout firms have been driven to doing roughly the same number of deals as before, but of a correspondingly greater size). However, many firms have been loath to admit this openly and thus we have the rather silly spectacle of some multi-billion dollar funds claiming that they are 'mid-market'. Of course, it is entirely possible that the definition of what is or is not 'mid-market' may have changed significantly, but it is difficult to believe that, if the mid-market could be efficiently served by a fund of no more than about $350M a decade or so ago, then it can equally well be served by a fund of five or six times that size today. Given the effect of gearing, one might be talking about a difference in enterprise value of the target companies between about $30M and anything up to about $200M.

It may be convenient to adopt the classification used by Thomson's industry database, since we shall be using their figures to look at the performance of Buyout funds later. They currently class anything over $500M as 'large' and anything over $1 billion as 'mega'. With due respect, one cannot help feeling that these definitions have been overtaken by events, but let us happily adopt them as a matter of convenience. They would classify $250M to $500M as 'medium', and anything less than $250M as 'small'. An alternative view of the mid-market, as set out above, would probably only extend about halfway into their 'medium' classification, but we will not do any undue violence to the concept by accepting a $500M fund size as its upper limit.

The search for the mid-market in Private Equity today, in the US as well as in Europe, is beginning to resemble the quest for the holy grail; everybody wants it, but many are beginning to wonder whether it actually exists. A common pattern is to see a first-time fund raise a relatively modest amount and then, driven by the LP feeding frenzy created by mid-market fever, raise some multiple of that two or three years later. Thus, the ultimate irony is that many LPs will not invest (because many have blanket bans against first-time funds) when the firm is genuinely able to pursue mid-market opportunities, but will invest when it is no longer able to do so (and, perversely, when that very inability has been created by LP behaviour).

A cynic might say that the Buyout industry today is like a clothes shop which only stocks one size – large. However, Buyout supporters would say that the ability of Buyout activity to include even the world's largest companies has forced them to become more competitive and to give more regard to shareholder value. This is undoubtedly true, and there was, until 2007, talk of 'jug' (juggernaut) funds of perhaps $100 billion, from whose reach no company in the world would be immune. On any view, the industry has become something of a victim of its own success, though most European investors have been very slow to realise this.

Be that as it may, we are clearly caught up in an upward spiral of fund sizes. For example, let us look at the first four and five funds respectively of two typical Buyout firms, one from each side of the Atlantic: Permira and Blackstone (Table 5.1).

Table 5.1 Real life examples of fund size growth

Fund	Permira	Blackstone
	$M	$M
I	1 000 (1997)	810 (1987)
II	3 850 (2000)	1 300 (1993)
III	6 400 (2003)	4 000 (1997)
IV	14 000 (2006)	6 500 (2002)
V		21 700 (2006)

Note: calculated at $1 = €0.78

We see from these figures that the fund size of each firm increased by a factor of about fifteen and twenty-five respectively in the period in question, but that European fund size has grown much more quickly, as Permira raised its first fund only in 1997 (when it spun out of Schroders) while Blackstone raised its as long ago as 1987. Consequently, Permira's fund size grew fifteen times in less than ten years and over only four fund cycles, while Blackstone's grew twenty-five times in twenty years over five fund cycles. Permira is a particularly good example to take since Schroders (as they then were) and Apax used to be seen as very high quality players in certain specialist sectors within the mid-market,[9] but both were subsequently driven to large deals (and exclusively Buyouts – Apax had previously executed a considerable volume of Venture deals as well) by the increase in their fund sizes.

An article in 2006[10] confirmed what one had already suspected: by mid-2006, Private Equity firms accounted for more than 15% of M&A activity worldwide. It remains to be seen how quickly Buyout activity will pick up again, but it seems unlikely that things will stop there; this raises important issues for investment generally which lie beyond the scope of this book. What happens when a significant portion of the world's quoted equity has been taken private by Private Equity firms? Just how much money can the Buyout industry absorb before cost-adjusted returns regress too closely to quoted indices? What happens if a whole generation of senior Buyout managers, made wealthy by large management fees, retire more or less together, leaving a large amount of capital in less-experienced hands (which, some argue, is already happening)? Yes, these questions are alarmist, but they are currently being asked and it would be wrong not to record the fact.

Control

As we have seen already, control is the one element which really does distinguish Buyouts from other forms of Private Equity activity. Indeed, in certain quarters the phrase 'control investing' is virtually synonymous with 'Buyout'. Control will almost always take the form of having a majority of the issued shares in the company. However, it is possible to have a minority holding yet have a majority of the votes, either because certain shares have weighted voting rights or because other shareholders are contractually bound to vote with the Buyout firm in respect of at least part of their shares. This varies from country to country, though. In some countries there can be legal difficulties about enforcing these sorts of agreements and one can also encounter unwillingness on the part of the Buyout firm to be seen to be throwing its weight around.

We have also referred already to negative control, and will consider this in more detail when we look at Growth Capital and Development Capital.

While the advantage of being able to control the day-to-day operations and key staffing of the target may seem obvious, the real benefit of having control is the ability to exit the investment exactly when, and how, one wishes. Again, we will deal with exit protection when we consider Growth Capital and Development Capital, but it may perhaps be helpful to set the historical perspective which one used to find, particularly in continental Europe. Here, where non-control investing used to be much more prevalent than control investing, the former holding company or owner-manager of the firm would frequently remain as a significant, sometimes even a majority, shareholder. While day-to-day disagreements could hopefully be

---

[9] Apax also used to do true Venture deals within the same fund as its Buyouts.
[10] *The Times*, 4 July 2006.

resolved under the negative control procedures, the real fun would begin when the end of the Private Equity investor's target holding period (usually three years) approached.

At this point, the owner-manager would be faced with the prospect of having to sell his remaining shares and finally retire. Often, this would be something which he had been unwillingly deferring for some time, and perhaps he would have been persuaded into the Private Equity deal in the first place only by the lure of generating some free capital. A holding company might have been prepared to bring a junior partner into the business, but the prospect of the company now being bought by someone who might introduce restructuring and redundancies in a town where it still saw itself as the moral guardian of local interests might look a very different kettle of fish. If the prospective purchase was foreign or, even worse, American, then the problem was compounded many times over.

While there were exit provisions in the original contract, Private Equity firms would be loath to enforce these as they wanted to be seen as friendly partners with whom to do business in that country by other prospective sellers, and in any event there were usually no legal precedents available to give guidance as to exactly what extent a local court might be prepared to grant enforcement of these novel provisions in favour of a foreign 'Vulture Capitalist'. One could thus be treated to the spectacle of Private Equity firm and fellow shareholders dancing an increasingly distracted minuet around each other to the rival themes of exit, delay and possible compromise.

Other aspects could be difficult without overall control, too. Owner-managers, for example, are usually debt-averse and so their businesses are frequently cash flow inefficient from a strict financial theory viewpoint. They will also often have irrational attachments to certain business activities or product lines which may prevent these from being eliminated or rationalised when logic would otherwise demand this. Above all, they will often resist the introduction of high-quality senior management, especially a CEO to take over the day-to-day running of the business.

Happily, time has moved on and there is, today, general recognition that the interests of all parties must be adequately protected, and that control investing can and should be the norm. However, history is cyclical and I now see exactly the same sorts of issues which plagued continental Europe in the past rearing their heads anew in developing Private Equity areas such as Asia (particularly India) and Latin America. For those in such places who are willing to listen, the European experience has some valuable lessons.

Barriers to Entry

As the Buyout market has matured and developed, the issue of barriers to entry has become a frequent topic of discussion. There is general acceptance that, as it has matured, the market has become more 'perfect' in financial theory terms. There is much less scope for exclusive, proactively sourced deals (indeed, virtually none at the top end of the market). Pricing and valuation data are much more widely available. Most vendors are now much more sophisticated when it comes to dealing with Private Equity purchasers than they were ten or fifteen years ago. Both Europe and North America are now covered and served by a very competitive and efficient investment banking sector.

This is not all bad news for the Private Equity industry. The other side of the coin is that Private Equity buyers are now widely accepted as an established part of the landscape and indeed at least two or three of them are routinely included in the list of potential purchasers to whom every 'book' is sent. In most countries, any perceived stigma which may once have attached to selling a business to a Private Equity firm has now largely dissipated. Indeed, some governments have willingly embraced Private Equity consortia as a means to privatise certain utilities (the Italian government being but one recent obvious example).

So what does all this mean for new entrants to the market? For, defying strict business school theory about the undesirability of entering a mature market, that is exactly what teams regularly attempt to do. In many cases, of course, these will not be first-time funds, strictly so-called since they may represent a breakaway from one or more established firms.

The answer to this question depends upon exactly what the new entrant is seeking to achieve and, in particular, on what part of the market they are seeking to address. We have alluded already to the vanishing mid-market and this point is particularly relevant here.

As the larger firms get even larger and move to target bigger and bigger deals, they leave something of a vacuum behind them. The classic Private Equity fund economic model (certainly the theoretical ideal) is for the GPs to be motivated by carry, with the management fee simply covering their operating overheads. In very simplified terms, this is an essential element of what you will often hear referred to as 'alignment of interests' in the GP/LP relationship. However, it would be idle to suggest that this has represented even an approximation of the real situation in the Buyout arena (Venture is a different matter) for some years. In practice, firms are driven by the lure of larger pro rata management fees to raise larger and larger funds and this, in turn, necessitates them moving to target larger and larger deals in order to deploy the extra capital. Yes, LPs will, to some extent, be able to reduce the percentage fee rates on larger funds, but such is the bargaining power of the best Buyout firms (because of the weight of the capital trying to crowd into each new fund) that usually at the end of the day they manage to achieve a significant fee increase overall.

There are some honourable exceptions here. Some firms offset fees and incidental income which they may receive from portfolio companies, and/or bear the cost of aborted transactions in such a way that the net fee impact on LPs can be significantly reduced. However, it is undeniable that there are many Buyout professionals on both sides of the Atlantic who have become very wealthy on management fee profits, and while they are to be congratulated as successful businessmen, this is a long way from what the classical Private Equity fund model ever envisaged.

This rather lengthy digression has been embarked upon simply to explain the dynamic which pulls Buyout firms inexorably towards larger fund and deal sizes. There is one European Buyout fund whose fund size increased by a factor of 25 in just two fund cycles. Therefore, if one was sitting down as a strategy consultant logically to plan how a new Private Equity firm might best enter the market, a mid-market focus would seem to present the most attractive option.

This does occasionally happen and despite the fact that a mid-market focus normally requires a highly localised geographical approach (usually single country within Europe), these offerings are rightly regarded as highly attractive in principle, though one always has to balance the 'first-time fund' factor against the attractiveness of the market niche. Indeed, many investors have a blanket ban on first-time funds and while they would argue that this is a sensible precaution to minimise risk, others feel that a blanket ban goes too far and prevents investors from being able to take advantage of the occasional 'nugget' that survives rigorous due diligence.

So for a mid-market firm, the main barrier to entry is the first-time fund factor, and if a compelling team can overcome the 'first-time fund' issues then they have a very good chance of attracting funding. Once having done so, they are likely to find rich pickings, since the bulk of the Buyout capital available will be targeted at much larger companies than they are seeking. This is probably a classic example of a more extreme version of the 80/20 rule (we will encounter something similar in Venture in a different context): probably about 95% of available Buyout capital in Europe and North America combined is targeted at no more than 5% of total companies by number.

For a team attempting to enter the large Buyout sector, the issues are very different.

We have already touched on the issue of dealflow. These days almost all deals will go through the investment banking network and the vendor will normally stipulate that no more than three or four potential purchasers of each type, including Private Equity houses, should be included. Thus, the ability to feature on the investment bank's 'hit list' is key and will be largely determined by a track record of past transactions. Any new entrant is thus likely to be in danger of hanging around the edges of the feeding tray, either trying to persuade an established player to adopt them as a consortium partner, or being left the crumbs which everyone else has rejected.

An element of these relationships which is often overlooked is that it is these same investment banks who will be pitching for the job of arranging exits for the Buyout firms from their companies, either by way of sale or more usually (since often the Buyout firms will handle their own sales) IPO (flotation). One would not wish to suggest that there would ever be any overt connection between the two, but human nature being what it is, an existing and/ or potential relationship with a Buyout firm for IPO work is likely to weight heavily with an investment bank when selecting a list of addressees for their next book.

Similar issues will apply to the question of debt. Contrary to popular opinion, there is only so much acquisition debt available in the Buyout market, and in normal market conditions banks will be constantly adjusting their position as the year progresses by syndicating with other banks to make sure they will be able to meet their commitments should more deals than anticipated actually complete. Thus, not only are they unlikely to be eager to finance a new Buyout firm where they may be in competition with an established one (since they will judge the established one to be the more likely to emerge as the eventual winner), but this may well be reflected in the terms and gearing offered. Since these are key factors in the relative performance of Buyout transactions, banking relationships in general are likely to prove a difficult obstacle to overcome.

There is, too, the question of raising capital in the first place. This is clearly not an insuperable obstacle, since new players do, in fact, successfully enter the Buyout arena almost yearly. However, it must be the case that if an investor who has a finite amount of money to commit is considering the rival attractions of an established player and a new entrant, they are likely to favour the established player, particularly if they have an existing relationship with them. In fact, the situation is likely to be even more depressing for the new entrant since the investor may already be faced with a difficult choice between two firms, both of which they like, but both of which they cannot accommodate within their cash flow constraints.

SUMMARY

It used to be possible to classify most Buyouts neatly into categories such as MBO, MBI, etc. but today the situation is more complex, perhaps because the average Buyout is much larger than used to be the case.

A Buyout transaction will always involve an established, profitable business, though the latter condition may obviously not apply in the case of a turnaround transaction in respect of a troubled company.

A Buyout will invariably involve the use of debt. Indeed, today's financial engineering solutions for Buyouts will often involve various different layers of debt, ranging from straight senior debt secured on assets of the company to pure cash flow lending with equity kickers (mezzanine).

Buyout properly so-called will always be control (majority stake) investing. Development Capital may be distinguished from Buyout on this ground and also because it may be much more difficult, for legal and accounting reasons, to introduce significant acquisition debt.

Cash flow is key to Buyout transactions, since success depends on the ability to service debt, and as much debt as possible.

Recapitalisations (recaps) offer an alternative to an exit where the exit window may be temporarily closed or where cash flow levels may have exceeded expectations. Recaps can have a huge effect on Buyout returns, a fact which is not widely appreciated.

The Thomson database definition of a mid-market fund ($250M to $500M) may happily be adopted, since this will make it much easier to work with the available figures, though a personal estimation would be a little lower. Even adopting this definition, genuine mid-market funds are becoming rare compared to ten years ago, particularly in Europe.

Excessive fund size growth has been the biggest single issue in the Buyout industry in recent years, particularly in Europe. Rising fund sizes have, in turn, driven a rise in target transaction size, since it is easier to do bigger deals than to do more deals.

The main sector-specific barrier to entry for a new Buyout firm is to break into the dealflow channel, much of which is now largely controlled by a relatively small number of investment banks. This is true even moving down the size scale, though it becomes less serious a problem as the number of intermediaries handling smaller deals becomes larger.

6

How to Analyse Buyouts

Our aim in the chapter is to understand how Buyouts actually work. Not so much how they are put together – we have already covered that in the previous chapter – but what drives their returns and how people actually make money out of them. Once we understand this, we will be in a position to move on to discussing how to analyse a Buyout fund. In that last sentence you will already have absorbed one key point, probably without realising it. All Private Equity fund analysis should be 'bottom up'; in other words, it is only by analysing the individual transactions which comprise it (and knowing how to) that one is able to analyse the fund itself.

Of course, the manager of the fund (the GP) will have carried out its own financial analysis of the deal before entering into it, and it can be very instructive to ask to see this if one is in the process of actually performing due diligence on the Private Equity firm concerned. The analysis will model the price to be paid for the company, taking into account how this is to be financed, the length of the period for which it will be held, the exit price and the repayment of restructuring of any financing in the interim. This will produce a modelled transaction IRR. This can be instructive both in terms of what target IRR the firm is willing to accept (are they aiming too low? Are they just desperate to put money to work? Are non-commercial considerations at work? etc) but also in terms of how realistic you feel their various assumptions are (are they assuming an increase in multiple? What level of gearing are they prepared to accept? What debt finance terms are they expecting? etc). These are just a few of the many small pieces of the jigsaw which build up to give you a picture of a Buyout firm.

By the way, the paragraph above is deliberately and necessarily simplistic. In practice there will be much more to the modelling process than this. A wide range of possible scenarios will be considered, and a range of possible outcomes produced. For example, relatively small changes in the financial engineering of the deal can have a large impact on the final result. However, a detailed study of this would require a book all to itself, and would go well beyond the scope of the present publication. The purpose of this book is to explain the basic principles of Buyout analysis. The good news is that once armed with a thorough understanding of these, there is no limit to the sophistication of the model you choose to build.

It will hopefully come as something of a relief, therefore, to hear that there are really only three main drivers of Buyout returns: earnings, multiple and leverage. Actually there is, of course, a fourth –time – but as we will be dealing in compound returns this will automatically form part of our calculations. It needs to be borne strictly in mind, however. The time value of money is an enemy as well as a friend. It is the mouse in the larder of your portfolio nibbling away at the cheese of your returns. The longer you are forced to hold a company for the same multiple, the lower your IRR will be. The sooner you can exit it, the higher your IRR will be.

EARNINGS

Again we must begin with a short terminological detour. The word 'earnings' is used in many senses. While it is generally synonymous with 'profits', it can actually be heard applied to turnover (American: revenues), particularly with regard to Venture companies. So let us be clear from the start; we are talking about earnings in the sense of profits: the turnover of a business less its costs of doing business. Even here, however, there is considerable confusion, since there are various different types of 'earnings'.

The way in which the word 'earnings' on its own is usually used in financial circles is in the sense of that profit which is available for distribution to shareholders, i.e. after deduction not just of the operating costs of the business but also after taking into account tax, interest and depreciation. This is often referred to as 'post-tax profits', 'net profits', 'the bottom line', 'profits attributable to shareholders' (UK) or 'earnings available to common shareholders' (US).

Note, however, that even this measure can be misleading, since it can be heavily influenced by one-off items that are nothing to do with profits generated by the company's ordinary course of business, such as a notional gain on the sale of an asset in excess of its artificially depreciated accounting value. Notwithstanding, this is the figure usually used to calculate earnings per share and thus the PE ratio (the price of a share over its earnings per share, or the value of a company over its earnings). All public companies, for example, are officially priced by reference to their PE ratio.

There are problems in any event with using this number for Buyout analysis purposes. The financial engineering which goes into a Buyout will almost certainly dramatically alter the overall debt structure, and thus the level of interest payments. So far as possible, the Buyout firm will want to ensure that all available earnings are used to service acquisition debt, so as to keep the amount of equity finance required to an absolute minimum. Thus, is it really meaningful to be looking at earnings after interest? Similarly, because loan interest payments will normally be tax deductible, the Buyout structure will normally also dramatically reduce the amount of tax payable, usually to zero. Thus, is it meaningful either to look at earnings after tax?

Also, as we have seen, earnings take into account things such as depreciation and will usually not therefore be the same as cash flow. Because of the need to service debt, it is actually the level of cash flow with which a Buyout firm will be most concerned, and if earnings are not a good approximation, then their value for analysis purposes is highly questionable.

In the light of all these drawbacks you may be wondering why we are concerning ourselves with earnings at all. Alas, Private Equity, like politics, is the art of the possible and there are frequently trade-offs to be made between what is sub-optimal yet possible and that which is optimal but not possible. Briefly, there are generally speaking no publicly available and universally consistent or comparable measures of earnings save that which we have already discussed; in particular, there are no publicly available figures for company cash flows. Thus, one of the very few ways in which we can look at the price paid or realised for a Buyout company as against the valuation of a comparable quoted company is by means of a PE ratio. As a matter of practice, therefore, it is very difficult to build any such functionality into a Buyout model unless we have resort to it.

Which PE ratio should we apply? If the transaction is a 'Take Private' then of course we have an obvious answer: the PE ratio of the company itself in the period leading up to the transaction taking place. Yet even here there can be problems, especially if the deal has elements of a turnaround about it, in which case the last available profits may be historically low. Similarly, as we have already discussed, the figures could be influenced by non cash flow items (such as depreciation) or even non business earnings items, such as profits made on the sale of assets, or the proceeds of a law suit.

Where no such continuity between quoted and private company status is present, we are forced to take either the multiple of a comparable quoted company or that of the sector within which the Buyout company would reside were it itself quoted. The former is open to charges of subjectivity and inconsistency, which can be particularly grave if there is a large range of multiples within the sector, or if there is no directly comparable quoted company of a similar size or scope as that of the Buyout company. Bear in mind, too, that PE ratios can be influenced by things as diverse as the perceived quality of the management team, its level of gearing, its degree of exposure to overseas earnings or its attractiveness as a bid target.

Sector multiples appear to make more sense. At least here there is the advantage of consistency and variation within the sector is smoothed out to a certain extent. Here the two main potential drawbacks are either where the Buyout company is, for some reason, much more attractive than the quoted sector (perhaps because it is enjoying higher growth than otherwise comparable public companies), or where there is confusion or ambiguity about which sector a company might fit into. For example, suppose a company is using proprietary computer technology to make available film previews via the Internet and cable. Is it Media, IT or Telecoms? In many cases there is no clear answer and it is left to the individual company itself to suggest its own classification (in which case they will obviously choose that with the highest sector PE ratio!).

So, as with so many aspects of Private Equity, by all means take full advantage of all the available data, but be aware of what lies behind them and of what allowances have to be made for them being possibly unreliable or even occasionally misleading. If it is any consolation, when a PE ratio works for analysis purposes, it can work very well. If a Buyout fund were to take private a public company at a 35% premium to its PE ratio, and there was no obvious indication that the company was artificially lowly rated, then this would clearly raise some very obvious issues as to valuation.

EBIT

An EBIT ratio would appear to be a better bet. EBIT stands for Earnings Before Interest and Tax, and thus would seem to address some of the above issues. Certainly Buyout firms are understandably suspicious of PE ratios being used for analysis purposes by investors, and have a stated preference for the EBIT ratio. The two problems with this have already been touched upon.

First, it still does not take account of things like depreciation, which can be significant if a company has recently spent heavily on new equipment. Secondly, the EBIT figure is not usually readily publicly available (though it can be calculated from a company's accounts) and is thus difficult from the point of view of plugging a number directly into a computer model.

In the past, I have sought to address this issue by assuming that EBIT will be a pre-stated percentage of earnings, and thus if one has one figure one can calculate the other. This is far from ideal, but is probably an acceptable compromise. At least it delivers consistency of treatment across the whole database population. Also, if a Buyout firm knows that you are going to calculate a possibly erroneous EBIT figure anyway, then it is remarkable how keen they can become actually to provide you with the correct figure!

A word of warning, though, for those who choose to try this approach. Please bear in mind that levels of tax and interest differ with location and currency, as do those of capital allowances, so you cannot just take a particular figure and apply it universally, even within the same region. There may, for example, be a significant difference in writing down allowances between Germany and the UK.

One final point. There can often be some confusion as to the time period in respect of which earnings are being assessed. Is it the earnings of the last completed year (the 'trailing earnings'), or is it the forecast earnings of the current year ('current earnings') or even the projected earnings of next year ('forward earnings')? The rule is that trailing earnings are used as the default, and all quoted PE ratios are calculated on this basis. However, this is a somewhat simplistic answer, as any professional company valuation will take projected future earnings into account as one of its key features.

EBITDA

Earnings Before Interest, Tax, Depreciation and Amortisation is claimed to be a pure cash flow measure since it excludes non-cash flow items such as depreciation, etc. In other words, it eliminates the effect of both financial structuring and accounting policy and decisions. However, this is not strictly true. While EBITDA is a better indicator of likely cash flow than any of the other earnings measures we have been discussing, it does not take into account things such as required capital expenditure or working capital. Of course, a purist would say that this point is well understood and that all EBITDA is supposed to be is a 'top line' entry from which to start your cash flow calculations.

EBITDA is an earnings measure that was more or less invented by the Buyout industry in the late 1980s, initially in the US and then in Europe, as they were looking for a measure that could specifically indicate the ability or otherwise of a company to service certain levels of debt. Such was its effectiveness that it began to be adopted by industrial companies, especially those that were burdened with high asset values and consequently high depreciation numbers stretching over long periods.

While this lies outside the scope of the book, you should be aware that dangers abound in trying to use EBITDA for normal company valuation purposes. Since it is a non-GAAP measure it is not governed by universal accounting conventions, and companies are thus largely free to include or exclude what they like, even changing the way in which they calculate it from one period to the next.

For Buyout purposes its obvious advantage is that it mirrors exactly how a Buyout firm will look at a target company. As we will see later in this chapter, leverage, or debt, makes a huge difference to Buyout returns and a Buyout professional will be primarily concerned in their analysis with how much acquisition debt a company can support. Its disadvantage is the same as for EBIT: one cannot just pick up the FT and find a company's EBITDA figure or indeed multiple. Thus, one is forced back onto the PE ratio for most basic modelling exercises, though there is nothing to stop you adopting the rough rule of thumb approach which we came across when discussing EBIT. However, please be aware that there is even more margin for error here, since EBITDA will be very significantly affected by the age and value of the company's assets, as well as by the nature of its business.

A Buyout firm will typically be happy to reveal an EBITDA multiple to its LPs, and while this is fine for analysing the deal itself, it is largely valueless unless one has some comparable EBITDA figures for similar companies. It is here that the modelling process is likely to break down (unless you are lucky enough to have access to some analysts' research on the relevant sector) and you will find yourself once again being forced back to the sector PE ratio as a default value.

EARNINGS GROWTH

Earnings growth is the holy grail of Buyout investing; the ability consistently to grow the profitability of investee companies is the one thing that every LP looks for when selecting a Buyout fund, and it is accordingly something at which your analysis should look very carefully indeed. The importance of this speaks for itself. If a Buyout firm can grow the earnings of a business, then they have a good chance of being able to make money on the sale of that business in any market conditions. Consequently, many Buyout firms will claim to have 'sector expertise', and will have experienced senior industrial executives available as advisers, or even to go into companies and run them. Some, such as Apax and Permira, historically went even further and sub-divided their firm into a number (usually about five) of sector-specific teams.

The best Buyout returns are made when all four of the Buyout factors: earnings, multiple, leverage and timing, all work together, but if one was forced to choose just one of these, then earnings would be the one to achieve. Apart from anything else, increased earnings will often present an opportunity to recapitalise a company, as to which see below. However, there is often a trade-off here which is not fully appreciated. A Buyout firm will often be at least as focused on growing the cash flow of a business ('freeing up working capital') as on earnings, and often earnings growth will come at a price; it may be necessary to buy new equipment, for example, or to grow the workforce to expand into a new area. This requires money. Specifically, it requires working capital, and portfolio decisions within a Buyout firm are therefore complex ones, especially as time's winged chariot will always be hovering overhead. Should we view this as an investment to turn quickly, in which case we forget expensive expansion which will have no effect on short-term earnings, or should we invest judiciously because we believe that we can grow the earnings significantly over a three- to four-year period?

In fact, the decision will often be even more complex than this, since the firm will also have to consider the shape and timing of its portfolio as a whole, the remaining capital and likely cash flows of the fund within which the company sits, and market conditions. There is, for example, little point in deciding to turn a company quickly if exit conditions are currently unfavourable. There may be the possibility of merging the company with another, or selling off individual business units. There may be monopoly (US: anti-trust) considerations to worry about. There is the situation of, and relationship with, the providers of mezzanine and senior debt, etc. Even this brief survey should be enough to convince you that there is much, much more to the skill set of a Buyout firm than just buying a company, loading it up with debt and sitting back for three years to see what happens.

An obvious question here is 'how should we treat inflation'? The answer is that it probably doesn't matter so long as you do it consistently across your model to all Buyout funds. You can either ignore it completely or apply it to earnings by index linking them to something such as the RPI of the country concerned. This is of more importance when analysing historic returns, some of which were made in times of very high inflation.

MULTIPLE

We have mentioned various types of multiples already, so let us be clear what we are talking about here. This is an important point, as many confuse the fund-level multiples which we have been discussing in previous chapters (TVPI, etc.) with the company-level earnings multiples which we are now going to consider. The two are totally different, and are applied to completely different situations for completely different purposes. The former are cash multiples, which are applied to funds for analysis purposes. The latter are either earnings or cash flow multiples, which are applied to companies for valuation purposes.[1]

So, we are here considering an earnings multiple, in other words that multiple which is applied to whatever measure of earnings we care to adopt in order to reach the price agreed to be paid for the company. At the risk of stating the obvious, the resulting valuation will always be the same. What will be different in each case will be the multiplier and the multiplicand.

$$\text{Earnings} \times \text{Earnings Multiple} = \text{EBIT} \times \text{EBIT Multiple} = \text{EBITDA} \times \text{EBITDA Multiple}$$

For example, if a company has been bought for $200M, and we know that its earnings were $15M and its EBIT was $25M, then the earnings multiple will be 13.3 and the EBIT multiple will be 8. The valuation number is fixed, the various earnings measures are given, while the other numbers (the multiples) are variable.

It will hopefully be obvious that in each case if you know any two of these values, you can calculate the other.

Example 1

If a company has been bought for $200M and its last recorded earnings were $20M then it must have been bought on an earnings multiple of 10.

$$\text{Earnings} \times \text{Earnings Multiple} = \text{Enterprise Value}$$

$$20 \times \text{EM} = 200$$

$$\frac{200}{20} = 10$$

Example 2

If a company has been bought for $200M and you are told that it was bought on an earnings multiple of 10, then the trailing earnings must have been $20M.

$$\text{Earnings} \times \text{Earnings Multiple} = \text{Enterprise Value}$$

$$E \times 10 = 200$$

$$\frac{200}{10} = 20$$

---

[1] Without wishing to confuse you further at this stage, we will see when we come to discuss Venture returns that money multiples can also be used at the company level.

Example 3

If a company has trailing earnings of $20M and we know it has been bought on an earnings multiple of 10, then the enterprise value, and thus the price paid, must have been $200M.

$$\text{Earnings} \times \text{Earnings Multiple} = \text{Enterprise Value}$$

$$20 \times 10 = EV$$

$$EV = 200$$

Multiple Increase (Sometimes Called Multiple Arbitrage)

An obvious way in which Buyout firms can make money is to sell a company at a higher multiple than that at which they bought it. This is the Private Equity equivalent of a free lunch. Even if you do not manage to increase the earnings of a company at all, you will still make money. There are two possible reasons for this, largely depending on whether the company was bought in an imperfect or a perfect market.

Multiple Increase in an Imperfect Market

In financial theory, a perfect market is one where all investments are equally accessible to all investors, and all investors have full and equal knowledge of all relevant information. Arguably, there is no such thing as a truly perfect market, but it is certainly the case that some markets are less imperfect than others.

If a company is bought privately, i.e. otherwise than through a market on which its shares are publicly quoted, then in principle this will always be a transaction on an imperfect market. It is true that this distinction is blurring, chiefly because any private transaction of any appreciable size will now be subject to some form of auction process. However, there are limits to such openness. Only a certain number of potential purchasers will be admitted into the process, which usually means that only two or three Buyout firms will be included in the list of possible buyers to whom the book is sent. Another issue, less prevalent than before but still discernible, is where a potential buyer will be preferred because of nationality, or some other such quality (for example, a bank may not wish to sell a subsidiary to another bank). This used to be a particular problem in France, where most large companies were at one time para-statal, and when occasionally one had to be disposed of because it could not be propped up for any longer, there used to be earnest talk about 'finding a French solution'. This, in turn, gave rise to the term 'French auction' which means an auction in which the highest bidder is not guaranteed to win and where the auction may be re-opened so that the preferred purchaser can be given an opportunity to match the other bidders. There were also instances where trifling technical irregularities in the bid document, or issues which had not even been raised during the offering stage, were used to disqualify particular candidates.

There are some instances where the transaction has clearly been bought in imperfect market conditions, and we will see in a later chapter how such conditions dominated Buyout returns in Europe in the late 1980s and early 1990s, for example. Let us simply agree for the present that any company which is bought on an exclusive basis (i.e. where the vendor agrees to deal only with one particular purchaser) will, for our purposes, be 'imperfect'.

In such circumstances an increase in multiple may occur simply because the company in question has been bought on a lower multiple than it should actually enjoy. This may seem unlikely to a contemporary reader, but it must be remembered that the Buyout environment has changed dramatically in recent years, not least because of much higher average fund sizes. So has the deal environment in many countries. In Germany and Italy, for example, historically only a small number of companies were actually quoted compared to the UK, and even then these would usually contain a blocking family interest (such as still exists within BMW, for example) making the company immune to takeover, and thus meaning that it would be quoted on a lower multiple than should be the case anyway because of the absence of a bid premium.

Given that the average German vendor fifteen to twenty years ago was also obsessed with secrecy, and a desire not be seen to be making a large profit on a financial transaction,[2] it will become more credible, I trust, that Buyout firms could and did regularly buy companies effectively at an undervalue. In these imperfect market conditions, an increase in multiple could be achieved simply through listing the company in due course, at which time it would simply be acquiring the multiple which should probably always have been applied to it in the first place.

Market conditions were reflected in the analysis procedures of Buyout firms at the time, which would always include at least one scenario in which the exit multiple would exceed the entry multiple. Significantly, multiple increase is no longer routinely assumed in Buyout analysis; on the contrary, in recent years such analysis has often contained at least one scenario in which a *decrease* in multiple is assumed.

The other way in which multiple increase can occur is by the business being made more attractive in some way (perhaps by selling off a mature business unit and retaining an exciting, high growth one) or even just bigger. Large companies generally command higher multiples than smaller ones, which opens up the interesting prospect of company value being an upward curve rather than a straight line. Roll-ups are a very good example of how this may be exploited. In one celebrated instance in Italy during the early 1990s, a small road haulage company was bought and no less than about eighteen subsequent acquisitions were bolted onto it.

Of course there comes a size beyond which multiple increase is unlikely to occur, and it is almost certainly the case that the 'mega' (>$1 billion) funds have reached this point with regard to the size of company which they need to target. So, apart from rare instances where it may be possible to reposition a company into a different sector which commands a higher multiple, this sort of increase is, in future, likely to be of benefit only to the mid-market.

Having said this, the strength or weakness of quoted markets will play a significant role in Buyout valuations, particularly through the use of comparable multiples. It is thus inevitable that in certain situations (where quoted PE ratios rise significantly through the period of ownership), companies may nonetheless be sold at a higher multiple. As we

---

[2] The German language at this time contained no word or phrase meaning 'shareholder value'. This absence may be instructive in understanding the attitude adopted by many German corporate groups at the time.

will see in the next chapter, for example, this was undoubtedly a factor during the 1990s, both in Europe and in the US. Similarly, it will undoubtedly work heavily to the detriment of those Buyout funds which invested heavily in the two years or so leading up to mid-2007.

Without wishing to muddy the waters, it may be both convenient and apposite to think of these two types of multiple increase as 'beta' and 'alpha' in quoted market terms.[3] The way in which a multiple goes up and down with the market is systemic, just like the sort of 'beta' return which will be earned by buying the market index. The other way is something which is open to the manager (Buyout firm) to control, influence or create and thus represents an additional, non-systemic source of return. As with all investment manager selection, it is this sort of 'alpha' return in which one is particularly interested.

Multiple Increase in a Perfect Market

For our present purposes, it is generally safe to assume that any public company which has been taken private has probably been bought in perfect market conditions. The same can probably be assumed for the sake of argument where a large company has been taken through an auction process. However, the possible reservations set out above must always be borne in mind.

In such conditions, there are only two ways in which a multiple increase can be achieved. Before we examine these, though, please bear in mind that any increase at all will be much less likely if a company has been taken private, since in order to buy it in the first place the Buyout firm will have had to pay a premium to the quoted multiple (varying with time and market conditions, but typically anywhere between about 20% and 35%).

The first, and most obvious, is where there is a general increase in company valuations, resulting in higher earnings multiples. In strict theory this should only happen in periods of falling interest rates (if you look at earnings multiples the other way round you can view them as a means of implicitly discounting the future value of a company; if the risk-free rate falls, then so does the rate by which you should discount the company's future value, resulting in a higher present value and a higher earnings multiple), but unfortunately for financial theorists markets do not always behave so rationally. A general increase in multiples can be indicative of nothing more than a need to justify higher valuations brought about by a period of irrational exuberance (in which case it is probably a good time to be selling rather than buying).

In passing, I should warn against reading too much into quoted multiples when it comes to the analysis of Private Equity returns in general. Many very clever people have tried to find trends and correlations between patterns of quoted and Private Equity returns and have largely failed. The reasons are partly that Private Equity funds invest across long periods, and therefore tend to be largely unaffected by short-term public market movements (unless they are extreme and part of a larger phenomenon, such as the collapse of the technology bubble), and partly that people's pricing expectations do not move strictly in line with current

---

[3] I am, of course, aware that these terms can unfortunately be used in a number of different ways. For example, Beta can be used as a measure of the volatility of any one stock against a market portfolio, and there are different connotations again when considering the analysis of investment managers. That is why I make the point as lightly as possible, but I do think it is an interesting analogy.

multiples, but may lag them by as much as a year or two. If a vendor is told in a certain year that he can sell his business on an EBIT multiple of 12, then he is going to hold onto this expectation even if in the following year the appropriate sector EBIT multiple may have dropped to 10. Thus, Buyout firms are often unable to take full advantage of periods of low multiples because, by the time vendors' valuation expectations have started to adjust, multiples are usually on the rise once again.

The other problem with such an approach, of course, is that it forces the use of annual returns upon anyone attempting it and we have already seen that these are not a good measure of performance. We will examine this further when discussing recent developments and current trends in Chapter 15.

LEVERAGE

Leverage, or the use of debt to help finance an acquisition, is sometimes also called 'gearing' and this is a very good way in which to think about it. If an engineer adds an additional (smaller) gear wheel to an existing one, then he knows that by so doing he is increasing the number of times the spindle attached to the smaller wheel will rotate relative to the rotations of the larger one, thus increasing the speed of the whole mechanical process involved. If a Buyout professional goes in for financial engineering, this involves, in its simplest form, adding debt into the financing mix to increase the impact of the underlying equity. So it is quite apt to think of debt as an extra gear wheel, which does not affect the performance of the equity (just as the smaller gear wheel does not affect the speed of the larger, original, gear wheel), but does greatly increase the impact which it is able to have on the overall return of the transaction, just as the smaller gear wheel enables the large one to have a much greater impact on the speed of the process.

The principle is simple and well known. If a business is bought for $100M and sold for $150M three years later, and is financed entirely with equity, then the equity return will be a money multiple of 1.5× (150M/100M) and the equity IRR will be just under 15%. Replace half of the equity with debt, however, and the equity multiple becomes 3× (150M/50M) while the equity IRR increases to about 44%. See how dramatic is the effect which leverage may have, and now imagine what might happen if you could replace not just half the equity with debt, but 90% of it. (Just to satisfy your curiosity, the multiple would now be 15× and the IRR would be over 145%.)

Such 'thin' financing structures (i.e. having very little equity compared to the amount of debt involved) are the dream of Buyout firms, but the opportunities to employ them are becoming less, partly because most businesses today will already have quite high levels of operating debt (if only to make a take-over or Buyout a less attractive prospect!) and partly because some countries are pursuing tougher and tougher 'thin equity' tax rules under which it can be difficult to make loan interest fully deductible.

We have discussed senior debt and mezzanine in outline already, and will not do so any further, since this is a book about Private Equity, not financial engineering. Suffice it to say that this is a very complex area, and that the financial structure of a Buyout will almost always be far more complicated than the simplistic debt/equity/mezzanine breakdown that this book has used for illustrative purposes. As we have seen, there may well be different levels of senior debt and mezzanine. There will almost always be a separate working capital facility. There may be factoring of invoices, or other trade finance such as operating leases. There may be sale and leaseback of certain assets. Certainly there will always be a separate strip of sweet equity for the management team. However, in complexity lies opportunity, and in financial engineering we find a way in which an experienced and skilful Buyout team can exploit both their financial expertise and their standing with financial institutions to add significant value to a deal.

RECAPITALISATION

Recapitalisations or 'recaps' are a very significant but little appreciated contributor to Buyout returns. Essentially, all that happens is that where the finances of the company have improved to the extent that they have been able to pay down part of the debt, and/or will be able in the future to support a larger burden of debt, then the company is recapitalised. Some or all of the equity is released back to the Buyout fund and replaced with debt. Again, the process can be much more complex than is here described, but what is important for the purposes of this book is that you should understand the effect which a recap has rather than exactly how one might go about it.

By releasing some or all of the equity back to investors, the fund is now essentially 'there for nothing'. The effect is twofold. First, a positive cash flow is pulled into the reckoning early (i.e. well ahead of the exit event which would otherwise have triggered it), thus boosting the IRR. Second, the multiple which will be made on eventual exit is enhanced.

In the past, recaps were usually resorted to when the exit route was blocked, as can happen, for example, when the IPO window is closed, and/or at times of depressed public market valuations. For this reason, little understood by those outside the industry, the returns of 1997 and 1998 vintage year Buyout funds will not actually be as bad as had originally been feared. Finding themselves in danger of being stuck with investments for five years or more, most Buyout houses went in for recaps fairly heavily between about 2000 and 2003.

However, so successful has the technique proved that many Buyout houses now look for recap opportunities within their portfolios as a matter of course (in London, CVC were one of the pioneers of this approach).

It is worth noting in passing that the technique has not been well received when used in public/private partnership projects such as PFI in the UK. Many left-wing politicians had not fully accepted the idea of private financing being used in public sector situations, and there have been vocal protests at the use of what is, after all, a standard Private Equity technique when applied to things like hospitals. Full discussion of PFI-type financing lies beyond the scope of this book but demonstrates the paradox of politicians wanting to attract Private Equity into public projects, yet being unwilling to accept the sort of returns which are expected, and the techniques required to achieve them, thus throwing into question the whole future of such funding.

It follows from all this that whatever Buyout model you create must be capable of handling recaps. In other words, you cannot just assume that a Buyout will be an entry transaction and then an exit transaction three years later. You must be able to accommodate changes in debt and equity levels, and map all the cash flows involved.

TIMING

We noted at the beginning of this chapter that time was the fourth Buyout driver, but one that rarely needs to be considered explicitly since it will be an automatic operator in calculating the IRRs with which we measure Private Equity performance. However, it is worth just running through this very quickly to be sure that the different implications of timing are properly understood.

First, of course, there is time in the sense of absolute time – the day, the month, the year, etc. Market conditions will vary from one year to another, both in the public markets and with respect specifically to Private Equity, even at the fundraising level. For example, healthcare might be popular one year and the German mid-market the next. How should one change one's behaviour to adapt to these changing conditions?

The short answer is that you shouldn't. Market timing is one technique which can be almost guaranteed not to work in Private Equity, and it is not difficult to understand why. If I raise a healthcare fund today I am going to be making investments for at least the next three years, and am likely to be selling the portfolio companies over a period starting in about four years' time and going out perhaps as far as twelve years into the future. How can I or anyone else possibly know what conditions are going to be like in three years' time, let alone ten or twelve? Market timing simply is not possible, and if you ever hear anyone at a conference saying anything such as 'now is a bad time to be investing in Buyout' or 'we have gone overweight in Telecoms because we really like the sector' or even 'we have stopped our commitment programme for the time being' then you will know that you have stumbled across someone who understands absolutely nothing about Private Equity.

At whatever level you are investing in Private Equity (company, fund or fund of funds), it is imperative that you put your money to work steadily year after year. We shall be looking at this in more detail in Chapter 14, but there is an important lesson to be learned here. Diversification should occur naturally in any Private Equity investment programme (largely as a result of the number of underlying companies) but of all the different types of diversification, by far the most important is diversification by time. If you are properly diversified across vintage years, then the returns of the good times should more than compensate for the occasional bad times.

If, on the other hand, you choose to 'blow your wad' in less than a single year on a portfolio of almost exclusively Internet-biased US Venture funds, as many did in 1999/2000, or you out most of your allocation into mega Buyout funds in 2005 and 2006, then you cannot be heard to complain if things go disastrously wrong. Sadly, human nature being what it is, investors do complain, and vociferously at that. It is apparently easier to blame an entire asset class for some supposedly inherent defect than to admit that you got things hopelessly wrong. Diversification is a basic principle of sound investment, though one which is widely misunderstood and largely ignored.

Then there is time in the sense of the life of a fund, or a fund programme. This has probably already been dealt with in the comments above about diversification by time. If you are running a Buyout fund you must keep your discipline and make your investments roughly equally over a three-year period. No matter how attractive the prospects you may see in year one, you must maintain your discipline. Then, once the investment cycle is complete, there will begin the period in which you look first to develop your companies and then to harvest them. This is an art in itself. Which companies should you select for the investment of more time and money to help them grow, and which should you look to sell quickly? Can the former maintain their IRRs over longer periods? Will the latter contribute enough to the eventual fund multiple?

So finally we have come specifically to the question of the holding period of each individual company. As we noted earlier, length of holding period is the continuum along which the IRR/multiple trade-off operates and every Buyout professional will be acutely aware of it at all times. As a rough rule of thumb, a Buyout fund used to expect to hold its companies for an average of about three years, and a Venture fund for about five, but these holding periods have proved impossible to maintain in practice. What is vital is that an LP should, at all times, monitor what is, or has become, the average holding period for a fund of any particular type, and question the GP closely if there is any divergence.

MODELLING AND ANALYSING BUYOUT FUNDS

Now we are ready to start pulling together what we have been discussing. First, we should understand the concept of enterprise value. This simply means the total value of the business, or the price which is paid.[4] The equity value is the amount of equity which has gone into the deal, so:

$$\text{Equity Value} + \text{Debt} = \text{Enterprise Value}$$

Again, as when looking at multiples, if we know any two of these numbers, then we can calculate the third.

So, we now have the full algebra that we need for each individual portfolio company:

$$\text{Earnings} \times \text{Earnings Multiple} = \text{Enterprise Value}$$

$$\text{Enterprise Value } \textit{less} \text{ Debt} = \text{Equity Value}$$

The return made by a fund (and the returns earned by its LPs) will be driven by increases in equity value. That is why we need to be able to isolate this number.

Enterprise Value

The concept of enterprise value is central to any Buyout model. This is the amount of money for which any business is actually sold and which, after repayment of outstanding debt, will belong to the shareholders.

We are using 'equity' and 'debt' here as if they were homogenous generic expressions, but if you bear in mind all that we have already covered, you will realise that you will have to distinguish between different classes of equity (usually the management's sweet equity and then the rest) and various layers of senior debt and mezzanine. Convertible shares (US: convertible stock) should typically be treated as mezzanine. However, remember to treat any convertibles or other mezzanine instruments which are provided by the fund, as opposed to outside sources, as part of the fund's investment in the deal when calculating the fund's total return. It is fine to calculate the mezzanine and the equity returns separately if you wish, but, in practice, LPs will only be concerned about the total return. After all, the mezzanine is

---

[4] I acknowledge that it has become dangerous to assume that the value and the price of an asset are one and the same, but we will use 'Enterprise value' in this sense.

usually just taking the place of equity which the fund would otherwise have been compelled to subscribe.

At the top level of analysis, however, the four values which are essential to our workings are enterprise value, earnings (whichever measure you choose), earnings multiple and debt. The debt figure will be the total of all non-equity financing and will include all mezzanine; in other words, as shown above: Enterprise Value − Equity Value = Debt.

These figures need to be captured both on entry (purchase) and exit (sale or IPO). As already noted, the model must also be able to accommodate interim cash flows such as recaps, but this can happen separately on a time period based model. The important part of the Buyout model is analysing the performance of one Buyout fund against another.

There are some obvious things that can be done, all of which can give clues to how a Buyout firm operates, any strengths or weaknesses which it may have and any problems which it might be encountering. Average leverage and average holding period are two examples. These and other values can, of course, be combined and/or calculated across more than one fund to give a picture of a firm's total history.

Average leverage will be

$$\frac{\sum Debt / n}{\sum EnterpriseValue / n}$$

Expressed as a percentage, where n is the number of companies. However, where a fund has one or two very large transactions, it may be more meaningful to take the capital weighted average, particularly if they have either unusually low or unusually high levels of gearing.

The average holding period is best calculated by the number of quarters, and will simply be:

$$\sum HoldingPeriod / n$$

The interesting part, though, is to see how we can analyse how a Buyout firm is adding value to its investments. In particular, to what extent can we identify the 'alpha' type elements of earnings growth or non-systemic multiple expansion?

A couple of important points need to be made here before we begin. First, if you are planning to take inflation into account, then this is where you need to do it, by indexing the earnings over the length of the holding period. Second, the mathematical purists amongst you will notice that there is an element of double counting about some of the calculations. This is acknowledged and deliberate.

The problem is that you have two variables (earnings and multiple) in operation independently and, to complicate matters still further, the level of debt will act as a gearing factor on both multiples, and may also change itself during the lifetime of the transaction. This is a problem on which I have worked alongside some very clever mathematicians, including one from Harvard and one from Trinity College, Dublin, yet none have thus far been able to arrive at any final conclusion.

For the mathematicians out there, this is apparently a variant of Foucault's three bodies theorem, which states that when you have two bodies moving dependently on each other, then, subject to having certain inputs available, if you know the position of one you can fix the position of the other, but if you add a third body to the mix, this becomes impossible.

So I advocate a simplistic solution which works, at least in terms of adding up to 100%, and in mitigation I would say only that if and when anyone finds a better solution I will happily and gratefully adopt it. As you will see when you consider the basic algebra that follows, the effect of multiple expansion should logically be calculated on the going in earnings, otherwise there is always going to be an element of double counting. Similarly, why not calculate the effect of earnings growth using the exit multiple, since that is what was actually achieved? However, if you do all this, you are left each time with an awkward sort of remainder which does not seem to fit logically anywhere, and ends up getting ascribed to the effect of debt (since this is the only other way of dealing with it).

As you will see, the suggested approach takes into account only the direct impact of any debt paid off during the period of ownership, not the gearing effect of debt upon the equity returns. It is acknowledged that this is imperfect.

Clearly the algebra set out below understates the effect of debt. Strictly speaking we should calculate the transaction twice, once as it actually occurred and once on a notionally debt-free basis and then compare the difference in the two results. Strictly speaking, yes, if we wanted to look at the total effect of debt, but we don't. We want to analyse one Buyout against another, and all Buyouts are going to have high levels of debt, so it is artificial to exclude it all together. With regard to debt, we are principally looking to calculate the level of gearing for each deal and it will be easy to check for correlation between high debt levels and high transaction returns.

Having considered such arithmetical niceties, let us now ignore them and get on with the algebra.

Let:

　　　　Impact of Earnings Increase be A
　　　　Impact of Multiple Increase be B
　　　　Impact of Debt be C

　　　　Going In Earnings be E1
　　　　Going In Multiple be M1
　　　　Going In Debt be D1

　　　　Exit Earnings be E2
　　　　Exit Multiple be M2
　　　　Exit Debt be D2

For each portfolio company,

$$A = (E2 \times M1) - (E1 \times M1)$$
$$B(E2 \times M2) - (E2 \times M1)$$
$$C = D2 - D1$$

Each can then be expressed as a percentage of the total, e.g. $\left(\dfrac{A}{A+B+C} \right) \times 100$

I am deliberately keeping this all at a very straightforward level, since I want to make sure that the basic methodology is understood. Once it is, the only limit is your imagination! You might choose to analyse returns by deal source, country, transaction size, fund size, or any one of a myriad other considerations. For the moment, let us look at a worked example just to make sure that everything is clear.

Example 4

Let us assume that a company with earnings of $10M is bought for $80M, thus on an earning multiple of 8. It is held for three years and then sold for $117M, by which time its earnings have increased to $13M, and so the exit earnings multiple is 9. The original purchase price is funded by $70M of debt and $10M of equity.

Analysis

Going In Earnings	$10M	Exit Earnings	$13M
Going In Multiple	8×___	Exit Multiple	9× ___
Enterprise Value	$80M	Enterprise Value	$117M
Capital Structure:		Capital Structure:	
Equity	$10M	Equity Value	$47M
Debt	$70M	Debt	$70M
Enterprise Value	$80M	Enterprise Value	$117M

Gain ($47M − $10M) = $37M
Money Multiple ($47M/$10M) = 4.7×

IRR	Yr0	Yr1	Yr2	Yr3
	−10M	0	0	47M
68%				

Contribution of Earnings Increase (13M × 8) − (10M × 8) = $24M
Contribution of Multiple Increase (13M × 9) − (13M × 8) = $13M
$37M

Contribution of Earnings Increase = (24M/37M) × 100 = 65%
Contribution of Multiple Increase = (13M/37M) × 100 = 35%

SUMMARY

Fund analysis must be 'bottom up', i.e. modelling the individual Buyout transactions in order to build up a picture of the fund as a whole.

The four drivers of Buyout returns are earnings, earnings multiple, debt (leverage or gearing) and time.

Buyouts are measured both by IRR and by money multiple. Be aware that there is an inherent trade-off between the two over time.

When modelling Buyouts, pseudo cash flow measures such as EBITDA are the closest to what Buyout firms themselves will use, but lack of consistency and public availability of such figures will usually drive the modeller back to earnings and PE ratios.

The ability to grow the earnings of a company is the most highly prized of Buyout firm abilities, and your analysis should focus on identifying this. Be aware, though, of the effect of inflation, especially when modelling returns from the late 1980s and early 1990s.

Multiple increase can be thought of as both systemic (beta-like?) and non-systemic (alpha-like?). The latter is obviously preferable and, like earnings growth, represents highly desirable Buyout firm expertise.

Debt plays a key role in the generation of Buyout returns, operating as gearing to enhance equity returns. The way in which different layers of debt and mezzanine can be structured into a deal is a complex subject and requires separate study.

Timing is largely implicit in Buyout returns, since they are calculated by a time period-based measure (IRR). However, there are some explicit considerations which will impact on decision making and returns, such as the stage of a fund's life cycle and prevailing market conditions.

The effects of earnings increase, multiple increase and debt reduction can and should be broken out and analysed.

Other key factors to capture and analyse include the gearing ratio, length of holding period, type of deal (MBO, MBI, etc), deal source (proactive, auction, etc), country and fund size.

Given the mathematical complexities introduced by multiple variable, some degree of algebraic simplification is required. However, once the basics are grasped, there is no limit to the complexity of model which may be created.

7

Buyout Returns

Having examined how Buyout returns are generated, and thus how they may be analysed both within a single fund and also by comparison between different funds, it is time to look at what returns the asset class has actually generated, and how we should view these.

US VERSUS EUROPEAN BUYOUT

For many years during the 1990s there was an axiom 'Buyout in Europe and Venture in the US' which was often used to express investors' instinctive belief as to where the best returns were to be found. We will be looking at Venture returns in Chapter 10, so let us focus for the time being on the Buyout part of this maxim. The belief was that European Buyout returns generally outperformed US Buyout. Well, let's take a look at the figures in Table 7.1.

As you can see, the axiomatic view seems to hold water. For every vintage year save 1992 the European upper quartile figures are higher, and usually significantly higher. Of course, there are those who argue that looking at upper quartile figures is inherently undesirable for all sorts of reasons, not least that one is looking at the returns of a single fund. However, the capital weighted average figures tell a very similar story; the 1990 and 1992 vintage year returns are less good, but for some of the other years the extent of European outperformance is staggering.

Remember please that we are here looking at vintage year returns; that is, the compound return to date (in this case 31st March 2009) of all qualifying funds (i.e. US or European Buyout funds as appropriate) that were closed ('born') in that year. It may be easier to see the relationship between the two sets of figures if we set them out as graphs (see Figures 7.1 and 7.2).

Again, we see that the difference is most pronounced in the case of the capital weighted average, and this raises two important issues. First, it shows that during the 1990s the famous dictum about Private Equity being an upper quartile game did not, in fact, hold true. If an investor had picked a sample of European Buyout funds almost at random, then they would still have been likely to experience very good performance. We will examine a little later why this might have been so.

Second, since it can serve as a proxy for how the Buyout industry as a whole behaves (or, in this case, the European Buyout industry), then it set expectations of Buyout returns at levels which, by today's standards, are unrealistically high. The 1990s was a wonderful decade in which to be an LP in European Buyout funds. This may still be the case in future, but the days of 40% net IRRs are over, probably for even the upper quartile, let alone the capital weighted average, and certainly in the case of the mega funds.

You will, of course, be thinking back to the previous chapter, which mentioned the importance of always looking at multiples as well as IRRs, so let us run the same calculations again, but this time looking at the TVPI multiple (Figures 7.3 and 7.4).

Table 7.1   IRR by vintage year (%), Calculated to 31.03.09

	US CWA	US UQ	Euro CWA	Euro UQ
1990	11.3	12.3	9.7	19.7
1991	13.2	14.0	15.0	25.9
1992	24.4	29.8	23.0	23.4
1993	21.1	25.8	17.7	28.3
1994	16.2	21.5	42.7	49.2
1995	10.1	15.1	44.8	21.7
1996	6.5	9.9	18.1	22.5
1997	8.9	11.1	16.1	17.5
1998	0.6	9.6	7.8	10.2
1999	8.4	13.9	10.2	11.8

Source: Thomson Reuters

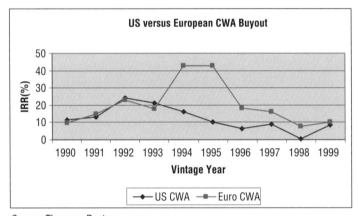

Source: Thomson Reuters

Figure 7.1   US versus European CWA buyout

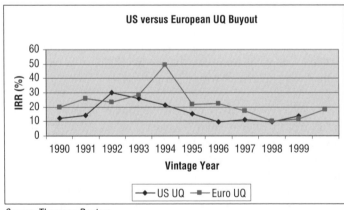

Source: Thomson Reuters

Figure 7.2   US versus European UQ buyout

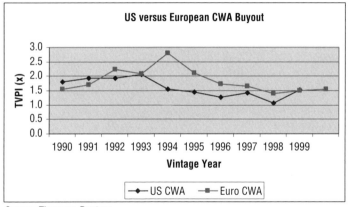

Source: Thomson Reuters

Figure 7.3   US versus European CWA buyout

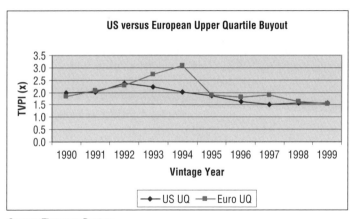

Source: Thomson Reuters

Figure 7.4   US versus European upper quartile buyout

Each graph shows broadly the same story. Note that there is a significant difference in the TVPI (money multiples) generally, particularly the capital weighted average and particularly after 1993. 'Significant' both in range (in 1994 for example) and in effect, since it is generally multiples that drive IRRs, rather than vice versa (for example, there is more than 85% correlation between the European CWA TVPI during the 1990s and the relevant IRR for the same period). The difference in Buyout returns between the US and Europe can be clearly traced to this fundamental difference. In general, European Buyout GPs achieved higher money multiples on their deals, and thus higher money multiples (TVPI, for example) on their funds.

In Europe in the early and mid 1990s it was far from rare for Buyout funds to achieve at least 3×. It occurred regularly and thus set expectations around this level. With US Buyout funds, as with European funds today, that simply did not happen. By about 2000, expectations were for Buyout funds, both in Europe and the US, to achieve only about 1.8×, and today even this figure feels too high. So, again, we need to consider why this might be.

We shall be looking later at the phenomenon of falling Buyout returns generally. For the time being, let us focus on the difference between these historic European and US figures and try to think of some possible explanations for the difference.

Buyout Skill Bases

Let us dispose of one possible suggestion very quickly. Though the situation with Venture was certainly different, there is absolutely no difference between the quality of the skills and expertise of Buyout professionals on either side of the Atlantic, neither has there ever really been, certainly not during the period we are here discussing, although it is broadly true that Buyout activity (certainly in any real volume) started in the US and then spread to Europe via the UK. Nearly $50 billion had already been raised by US Buyout funds prior to 1990, compared to perhaps as little as $6 billion in Europe,[1] but there were, by that date, a number of very active and very professional European Buyout firms based in London such as BC Partners, Doughty Hanson, Duke Street, CVC, Permira,[2] Apax, Cinven and Candover,[3] while in Scandinavia both Industri Kapital and Nordic Capital commenced operations in 1989.

The skills involved in operating as a Buyout professional are profound, and can confer a significant strategic advantage; many of them are essentially financial in nature, which is why Buyout firms favour young accountants and financial analysts when they recruit entry level personnel. For anyone with a good level of financial education, they can be learnt and quickly developed. The basic skills, that is, for of course there are others, such as the ability to source deals, and when and how to exit them, which require considerable judgement and experience, and these need to be acquired over a lengthy period. However, it has never been suggested by anyone that during the 1990s European Buyout houses (at least the major, independent ones – those attached to continental European banks may well have been a different story, but these were frequently practising Development Capital rather than Buyout anyway) had lower levels of professional skills than their US counterparts, or indeed vice versa. So, whatever the reason for the differing levels of returns, we need to look beyond the firms themselves, at the broader environment within which they were operating. We also need to be alive to what lessons this may have for us when looking at Buyout conditions today.

Imperfect Markets

The most frequently heard explanation for the very high European Buyout returns of the early and mid-1990s was the 'imperfect markets' issue which we have already met in an earlier chapter. US markets, both public and private, so the argument goes, were much better developed by 1990 than their European counterparts, certainly so far as continental Europe (that is, Europe excluding the UK) was concerned. Thus, the ability to source a deal proactively

---

[1] My own calculations based on Thomson Financial's VentureXpert system, which may slightly understate the European figures for this early period, as not all European Buyout firms registered their data in those days.

[2] Then called Schroders.

[3] For the sake of convenience, I have used the present names of all these groups. Doughty Hanson was previously CWB Capital Partners, Duke Street was born out of Hambros European Ventures, CVC was originally part of Citibank and Permira was previously part of Schroders.

and be able to transact it on an exclusive basis was still very much alive in Europe at a time when it had already largely disappeared in the US, certainly in respect of a business of any real size.

Like all generalisations, this one is largely true. Nobody would deny, least of all the Private Equity firms involved, that a lot of the Buyouts in countries like Germany and Sweden in the early 1990s fell fairly and squarely into this category. They were rarely put through any sort of auction process, the vendor was frequently either a family owner or a socially embarrassed local corporate group, and as a result they were often bought for values which in retrospect seem generous to the purchaser. However, on the other side of the coin, it should be remembered that these businesses were usually subject to all sorts of restrictions which would simply have been unfathomable to any US purchaser, such as the extreme difficulty in some countries (legal, political and cultural) of any significant rationalisation involving redundancies and/or plant closures. The continental socio-economic model at that time, even more strongly than today, held that a company existed to provide employment and retirement security to the local community at least as much as to make a profit for its shareholders. German companies in the 1980s, for example, were customarily ranked on their turnover (sales revenue) and their number of employees, not on their profits (the figures for which, by the way, were not usually publicly available).

Thus, this combination of historical circumstances might be thought of as a sort of 'happy hunting time' during which Buyout firms were able to conclude difficult but attractive deals largely undisturbed. However, these conditions were largely confined to Scandinavia and German-speaking Europe. Countries such as France and Italy, for example, were largely untouched by large Buyout activity at this time, although this changed as the decade progressed and, indeed, one of the most spectacularly successful Buyouts of all time took place in Italy (the Yellow Pages deal, the chief beneficiaries of which were BC Partners and Investitori Associati).

US Buyout firms were perhaps slower than they might have been in trying to access this particular honey-pot, an interesting parallel with US Venture firms, who have been even slower and more reluctant to seek deals outside their own immediate geographical environment.[4] It was only in the late 1980s that the large US Buyout firms began to set up European operations, and even then these were frequently staffed largely by Americans at senior level, with all investment decisions being taken in America by Americans. This is often cited as a reason why they found it very difficult at first to access deals in continental Europe, particularly those which had a political element (which so many did), but in fairness this was almost certainly also a product of deep anti-American sentiment (particularly a suspicion, often unfounded but not always, that what the American firm was after was a quick return, after mass asset sales and redundancies). Whatever the case, it is certainly true that American firms largely missed out on these early opportunities and this would thus definitely be one plausible reason for the difference in historic returns.

Earnings Multiples

Thinking back to our discussion about the drivers of Buyout returns, it would be instructive to look at how the different drivers might have contributed to the historic situation, but an

---

[4]Though this is easier to understand in the case of Venture Capital, since hands-on company-building skills are best exercised face to face.

immediate caveat must be entered here. This sort of information is available, in so far as it exists at all, only within the Buyout models of professional Funds of Funds and other sophisticated LPs. The Private Equity industry does not handle the concept of transparency very well; indeed there are some US Venture firms who insist on strict secrecy from their LPs on pain of possible expulsion from their funds. They believe that they have all sorts of good reasons for this (chief among which is the problem of performance data falling into unsophisticated hands which do not, for example, understand the effect of the J-curve, or the difference between annual and compound returns), but this view is increasingly hard to stomach.

Investors today expect transparency across all asset classes and are entitled to get it. There are legitimate concerns among GPs that data may be compared across firms in ways which are not fair and consistent, either because the data has been prepared on different bases in the first place, or because the analysis systems used by individual investors make different assumptions, or categorise information in different ways. Buyout firms, for example, can be extremely sensitive about the way in which gearing ratios or earnings multiples are calculated, and as to the attribution of particular deals to particular individuals within the firm. However, these legitimate concerns can be addressed given goodwill and professionalism on both sides, and it is a huge pity for those who take a genuine interest in the analytical side of the industry that there is so little company-level data available with which to work.

The fact that underlying data is not available is a major stumbling block, but not a complete impasse. There are ways in which we can imply or infer the action of Buyout drivers, so let us do the best we can with the information at our disposal.

As we discussed in an earlier chapter, there is a relationship between quoted earnings ratios and those which are applied to Private Equity transactions. While this link exists, let us remind ourselves of its limitations. It works well when a public company is being bought, as the company will have its own irrefutably relevant multiple. However, even here one hits problems immediately, since the Buyout house will be thinking in terms of EBITDA, which may paint a very different picture to the 'earnings' used for the PE ratio. When the transaction is anything other than a Take Private, there will be arguments about the comparative factors (size, growth, business activities) and there will also be a time lag between publicly quoted sectors changing, and private company vendors' pricing expectations making a similar adjustment. In some cases this latter phenomenon may be so extreme that the vendor will simply refuse to sell at any reasonable price, no matter how irrational such behaviour may be given their own particular circumstances or those of the company.

Even taking all this into account, however, we can, at the very least, say that Private Equity multiples are heavily influenced by publicly quoted PE ratios, and that, accordingly, any rise or fall over a period (particularly if it was a fairly steady rise or fall, so as not to confuse people's valuation expectations too much) in the latter would almost certainly be reflected in the former.

As you can see from Figure 7.5, the PE ratio of the FTSE index, which we may take as a proxy for the European Buyout industry since it is likely to be the index to which they would turn first, rose steadily during the 1990s, and so one would expect the earnings multiples available for Buyout transactions to have risen steadily as well. The only problem with this analysis is that the comparable US ratios also increased steadily throughout the 1990s, and so US Buyout funds should have been equally able to profit from rising earnings multiples as their European counterparts. The fact that they apparently did not (or, at least, not to the

PE Ratios 1994–2000

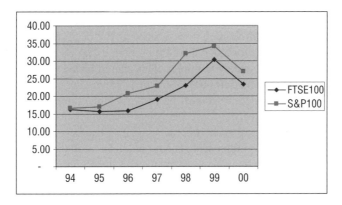

Figure 7.5   PE ratios 1994–2000

same extent) suggests that while there must logically be some force to this argument, it is at best a partial explanation.

In fact, if one tries to measure the correlation between the FTSE PE ratios for the period 1994 to 2000 against first the capital weighted TVPI for European Buyout funds and then the capital weighted IRR for the same vintage years, one finds that, not only is there no correlation, there is actually strong negative correlation!

It therefore seems more logical to ascribe at least a part of the assumed multiple increase in the European arena to 'imperfect market syndrome'. If one is buying on a multiple that does not fully reflect the value of the business on a public market, and subsequently disposes of it either by floating it on a public market or by selling it semi-publicly in a way in which the public multiple will be used as a comparator, then this clearly opens up the potential for greater gain.

One specific situation merits discussion, since it had a major influence on the returns of a number of London-based Buyout funds in the mid-1990s. The Conservative government decided to privatise the railways and chose to do so by offering the various individual companies into which assets and routes had been bundled for sale by tender, rather than offering their shares on the stock exchange as they had done in previous privatisations such as British Telecom. The Labour opposition, unable to halt the process because of their (then) minority in parliament, threatened compulsorily to re-purchase the companies when they returned to power. Because the various transactions were thus subject to a huge amount of political risk (a general election was in the offing), this was reflected in the price, as was the Government's determination to be rid of them well ahead of any possible political interference by the then opposition. In the event, compulsory re-purchase ideas were quietly abandoned after Labour's election victory in 1997, the Buyout firms involved had anyway already been able to sell the companies on almost at once for greatly enhanced prices (geared by substantial amounts of debt) and reap rewards that were almost embarrassing even by the standards of the Private Equity industry. City of London humour being what it is, the various participating funds (who included Candover and Charterhouse) promptly became known collectively as 'the Great Train Robbers', a reference to a famous and highly romanticised (such accounts conveniently ignore the fact that the train driver, who was hit over the head with an iron bar during the raid, later died) British crime which caught the public imagination in the 1960s.

This apparent narrative excursion is important, because these railway privatisation deals had a huge impact on the returns of various European Buyout funds, both because of the gains that were made[5] and also because the holding periods involved were unusually short, thus boosting IRRs as well as money multiples. This should be borne in mind when looking at 1994, since Candover and Charterhouse both had 1994 vintage year funds.

The 1995 figures are also a little strange, particularly since the capital weighted average is so much above the upper quartile fund. This clearly suggests that at least one very large fund in relative terms must have done extremely well; a leading candidate here would be Doughty Hanson, whose Fund II represented about one-fifth of all the capital raised that year. However, there is another possible answer, which is that the aforementioned Candover 'train robbery' fund also had a closing in 1995 as well as 1994, and is double-counted, appearing in both years' figures. Most likely, the apparent anomaly is due to a combination of these two things.

Earnings Growth

Earnings growth can come about in three ways. First, there is the growth that would have occurred naturally anyway from higher revenues (perhaps as a result of a new product coming on stream) or lower costs (for example the removal of the sort of hidden costs that often accompany family ownership). Second, there is growth caused by the effects of inflation. Lastly, there is the sort of 'alpha' earnings growth to which we alluded in an earlier chapter which is brought about by the specific actions of the Buyout group.

Without underlying data of the necessary complexity, we can only attempt conjecture here. The first type of growth can probably be discounted as a distinguishing factor, since logically it would have occurred to the same extent in both the US and Europe. Indeed, given that the US led the way into the intensive computerisation of business processes which occurred during the 1990s, if anything this factor should have favoured American rather than European returns. However, there may have been significant differences in both the other two areas.

The 1990s began as a high inflation decade in Europe, particularly in the UK (less so in countries such as Germany, where it was held in check by high interest rates to the ultimate detriment and effective collapse of the European Monetary System) but ended as a low inflation decade. Thus, some argue, there was a period during the early 1990s when inflation could have played a key role in earnings growth, which would mean that the glory day returns of 1994 and 1995, while still very impressive, may actually be slightly less so than they appear to be. However, one should not overplay this; high inflation was much less of a factor in continental Europe than in the UK (though the UK at the time accounted for about half of all European Buyout activity by value).

In fact, if one looks at the official UK government figures (the various different measures for the Retail Price Index) it is clear that this can have had little real effect on proceedings. Yes, for the whole of 1995 inflation stood at about 3.5%, but it then dropped back pretty quickly before hitting another peak between August 1997 and July 1998. Thus, with the possible exception of 1995, inflation can have had little impact on the stand-out vintage years

---

[5] An equity investment of £70M in Eversholt, a rolling stock leasing company, allegedly turned into over £450M: 'Red faces over rail privatisation', *Sunday Times* 1997.

in question, and if it was a significant factor, then one would have expected the vintage year returns for 1996 and 1997 to have been similarly boosted, which they weren't. Thus, we should be inclined to dismiss inflation as a factor which could provide any significant explanation.

The second factor is much more likely to have been significant. Companies bought from family vendors, and even some which had been owned by public companies, had pursued a deliberate policy of keeping earnings in check, usually by aggressive asset acquisition programmes, in order to avoid as much as possible high rates of taxation. This was a particular problem in Germany, where the real cost of unification on a one-to-one basis between the Deutschmark and the Ostmark had been badly underestimated (or perhaps just swept under the carpet at the time for political reasons). So this was one reason why it might have been quite easy to increase earnings.

Another was the condition which afflicts most owner-managed companies, namely a missing layer of management. Regardless of what titles are in use, there tends to be a Financial Controller rather than a Finance Director, for example, and a similar situation in all the other disciplines. Often simply replacing this missing layer of management can yield quite spectacular results.

Yet another has been referred to obliquely elsewhere in this book. In Europe, the process of industrial consolidation which took place in the US in the 1960s and 1970s had been delayed, and arguably still has not been properly completed forty years later. In part this was due to national and local pride; every country wants its own airline, and every town in Belgium and Germany wants its own brewery, and preferably two or three. In part it was also down to the heterogeneous nature of Europe itself, a factor which is often overlooked by Americans, who find it difficult to conceive of a situation where one can drive a few miles down the road and be confronted by a different language, currency and legal system, together with completely different cultural mores and purchasing habits; the 'white sausage/black sausage' border in Germany is perfectly real, for example, even though it is not marked on any map.

That being so, it was frequently possible to buy a company and put it together with another business in another country, or spin individual business units off for such a purpose, something that would probably have been politically impossible for the previous owner even to contemplate. Indeed, sometimes this possibility was explicitly discussed at the time the original Buyout was done, and the vendor kept a stake in the business precisely to derive some financial benefit from this when it happened.

Because the consolidation process was still in its infancy, the size of the business units involved rarely gave rise to any serious monopoly (anti-trust) problems. Compare and contrast that with the situation today, where much larger fund sizes have led to much larger transaction sizes, which, in turn, frequently raise significant legal and regulatory issues whenever any merger is contemplated.[6]

Leverage

In a sense, leverage, inflation and interest rates are all inter-related. Monetary policy in Europe in the early 1990s was to attack high inflation with high interest rates. Such an approach will,

---

[6]In some cases, where a utility has been purchased, or where a business may have monopoly-like issues, government pricing restrictions may also be in force. This was a factor, for example, in the UK Yellow Pages deal in which Apax participated.

in turn, prompt low earnings multiples, since the perceived risk-free investment return, and thus the discount rate applied to future cash flows, is high. So, in a sense, it is a case of what you gain on the swings you lose on the roundabouts as far as Buyout funds are concerned.

At the beginning of the 1990s, one could look to inflation to flatter one's earnings growth, and buy on low earnings multiples. However, high interest rates made aggressive leverage difficult, or at least very expensive. By the end of the 1990s, Europe (particularly the UK) had become a low inflation, low interest rate environment with plentiful debt available at reasonable prices,[7] and much higher earnings multiples than ten years previously.

Thus, one would expect there to have been a change in the relative impact of the Buyout drivers over the course of the decade in Europe, with earnings growth and multiple expansion playing a large part early on, but diminishing towards the end of the period, perhaps with gearing levels rising. As has been already observed, it is a great pity that this information is not freely available, in which case we would be able to know for sure rather than having to guess, but these seem reasonable assumptions to be drawing.

If so, then this is one area where some of the difference could be explained. The US did not experience anything as extreme as the British conditions, and in particular neither inflation nor interest rates ever got as high as they did in the UK. So, this might explain some of the differential early in the decade. The fly in this particular ointment, however, is that because US interest rates were typically lower, then it should have been that much easier to gear companies up with debt. However, this might, in turn, bear out one's instinctive view that earnings growth and multiple expansion have a higher potential to influence Buyout returns than does the effect of some extra leverage. We are here forced into the realm of pure speculation, but they are important issues which one should bear in mind when analysing Buyout returns.

There is one extra point to be made about leverage. With the rising transaction values brought about by larger fund sizes, the amount of acquisition debt available at any one time is not infinite. Remember that, at least in the early stages, there may be two or three different Buyout funds (or, more usually these days, consortia of Buyout funds) chasing a particular deal, and each will need to have its potential funding firmly in place before making a formal offer (indeed, this is usually a specific requirement of the sale process). Thus, if there are a number of large deals in the market at any one time, and particularly if the bidding process in respect of most of them has not yet been narrowed down to one preferred purchaser, then the banks which habitually supply this acquisition debt start to come under pressure, and may have to start tweaking their terms to regulate supply, or even deciding not to proceed with a particular deal (these days there are also some fairly sophisticated underwriting and syndication techniques entered into between banks). Having the stature, credibility and track record to ensure that you are the bidder proceeded with rather than the bidder who is dumped by the banks, is, in fact, a significant but little recognised strategic advantage.

Contribution of Different Drivers

It is not possible to attempt any specific analysis of the relative contribution of the different return drivers without full company-level information of each transaction of the sort we

---

[7]The actual economic cycles within Europe were different, particularly as between the UK and Germany. Generally speaking, the UK went from low growth to medium/high growth, while the German economy did much the opposite, but that is much less relevant for our purposes.

discussed in the last chapter, and sadly this just is not publicly available. Even where it is privately available, it is unlikely that the firms whose funds make up the population of the relevant database would agree to it being used for external purposes. That is why we have had to indulge in the rather generalised conceptualising which has characterised this chapter to date. We can only examine the big picture and then argue about how this may have affected individual funds at different times.

For the record, some research[8] does claim to have isolated different drivers at work at different times, contending that the 1980s were truly 'The Age of Leverage',[9] the 1990s were, as has been suggested above, a time when multiple expansion played a great role, while Buyout returns in the 2000s were driven by earnings growth. The authors of the report suggest that in future, operational improvements will be key. While it is difficult to disagree with any of this, particularly without knowing precisely what data is being used, it is arguable that operational improvement (margin growth) is really only a sub-set of earnings growth, and has always been something for which Buyout firms have aimed. It is true that, by a process of elimination, margin growth seems about the only possible avenue remaining for existing Buyouts, but it would be a brave observer indeed who would be prepared to predict what is likely to happen for new Buyouts entered into over the next decade or more. We will have more to say about this when we consider the current environment in Chapter 15.

Fund Size

We have already noted the phenomenon of rising Buyout fund sizes and conjectured whether there may be some connection between fund size and return. This may be of particular interest for the period under consideration, since there was a stark difference between Europe and the US.

The average size of European Buyout funds raised between 1990 and 1999 was less than $250M, whereas for US Buyout funds raised during the same period it was nearly $370M.[10] To throw this into starker contrast, US Buyout funds raised a total of $348 billion during the 1990s, while only $66 billion was raised in Europe. In other words, the American Buyout industry was trying to put over five times as much money to work during the 1990s as were their European counterparts in an economic block of roughly equal value. Given that, by common consent, there were more potential Buyout companies in Europe at this time (since industry consolidation in just about every sector was well behind that in the US, thus meaning there were a larger number of (generally smaller) players in each case) then this factor – good, old-fashioned supply and demand – is clearly significant.

It is not just that American GPs had more money to put to work (which would raise obvious implications that they may have been less price sensitive, since they could afford to be less choosy in the face of greater competition) in total, and the Europeans less. It is also that the vast majority of European Buyout capital was being targeted at what we would today call the mid-market. There were only 14 mega funds (more than $1 billion fund size) raised in Europe before 2000, whereas there were 85 in the US. During the 1990s, the amount of capital raised by mega funds in the US fluctuated between 11% and 55%, whereas in Europe it was zero for five of the years in question (Table 7.2):

[8] IESE/Boston Consulting Group 'The Advantage of Persistence', Meerkatt and others, 2008.
[9] Anders (1992) *Merchants of Debt*, Jonathan Cape, London.
[10] All figures taken from Thomson Reuters.

Table 7.2   The impact of mega fund capital in Europe and the US 1990–1999

Europe

Year	#Funds	#Mega	Total Capital $Million	Mega Capital $Million	%
1990	21	0	2 588	0	0
1991	21	0	1 376	0	0
1992	10	0	1 201	0	0
1993	14	0	1 518	0	0
1994	20	1	5 186	1 779	34.31
1995	20	0	2 474	0	0
1996	29	1	7 753	2 038	26.28
1997	38	4	13 489	7 240	53.67
1998	50	5	16 787	10 380	61.83
1999	49	3	14 033	5 485	39.09

USA

Year	#Funds	#Mega	Total Capital $Million	Mega Capital $Million	%
1990	74	1	9 101.20	1 015.50	11.16
1991	36	1	7 889.70	1 944.50	24.65
1992	64	4	14 120.10	4 855.00	34.38
1993	76	2	18 413.00	3 151.40	17.12
1994	105	5	26 087.70	6 524.80	25.01
1995	111	10	32 999.60	14 404.70	43.65
1996	102	4	26 791.20	6 746.10	25.18
1997	128	14	57 101.10	28 147.00	49.29
1998	183	22	88 312.70	46 288.70	52.41
1999	141	22	67 483.80	37 205.50	55.13

Source: Thomson Reuters

Of course we have to keep things in proportion. We are talking about a smaller sample size in Europe, because of a younger, and thus smaller, industry. Even by the end of the decade, the number of European Buyout funds was less than was the case in America at the beginning of the decade (although the difference is less pronounced than it seems, because of the absence of some European funds from the database population). However, there is no getting away from the fact that we are talking about lower average fund sizes, and very significantly less total capital in Europe than in the US. There was also markedly less incidence of mega funds in Europe during the 1990s (the figures pick up after 2000). Since we are clearly also looking at higher vintage year returns in Europe, let us dig a little deeper and see if it is possible to establish any specific connections. Let us also extend our period of enquiry to vintage year 2003, since (1) fund sizes increased dramatically after 2000 and (2) the returns of these funds will be at least five years old and thus becoming meaningful (Table 7.3).

You will see from the above figure that it looks as though our suspicions were largely correct. Here, we take four main measures of return – money multiple and IRR (both capital weighted average and upper quartile in each case) – and measure the correlation in these vintage year data series against the same series for average fund size and total fund capital.

Let's look at the American figures first. Here, there is a very clear and very strong negative correlation with every return measure against both our fundraising figures, save only for the

Table 7.3 Impact of average fund size and total capital on Buyout returns by vintage year 1990–2003

Year	US Buyout					European Buyout				
	CWATVPI X	UQTVPI X	CWAIRR %	UQIRR %	Avge Size $Million	CWATVPI X	UQTVPI X	CWAIRR %	UQIRR %	Avge Size $Million
1990	1.81	1.98	11.30	12.30	125	1.54	1.84	9.70	19.70	120
1991	1.93	2.01	13.20	14.00	227	1.70	2.07	15.00	25.90	76
1992	1.94	2.38	24.00	29.80	220	2.23	2.29	23.00	23.40	119
1993	2.06	2.21	21.10	25.80	243	2.09	2.73	17.70	28.30	104
1994	1.54	2.02	16.20	21.50	252	2.80	3.07	42.70	49.20	267
1995	1.44	1.88	10.10	15.10	300	2.12	1.89	42.80	21.70	139
1996	1.28	1.62	6.50	9.90	263	1.72	1.82	18.10	22.50	264
1997	1.43	1.50	8.90	11.10	461	1.64	1.91	16.10	17.50	290
1998	1.07	1.56	0.60	9.60	485	1.39	1.62	7.80	10.20	316
1999	1.53	1.58	8.40	13.90	458	1.50	1.53	10.20	11.80	240
2000	1.51	1.80	11.50	21.30	626	1.56	1.70	13.40	18.20	309
2001	1.45	1.72	11.20	19.70	665	1.86	1.86	24.50	25.20	518
2002	1.33	1.50	11.30	22.20	308	1.46	1.76	18.80	28.10	426
2003	1.48	1.53	16.80	15.80	501	1.41	2.15	16.70	30.50	494
Correl Avge Size	−51%	−56%	−34%	−10%		−33%	−25%	−5%	9%	
Correl Capital	−66%	−63%	−53%	−20%		−51%	−50%	−29%	−22%	

Source: Author's own calculations, primary data from Thomson Reuters
Note: 'Correl Capital' is the calculated correlation with total Buyout fund capital raised for that region in that vintage year (not shown)

IRR of the upper quartile fund (though even this is still negative). We can conclude from these numbers that if either average fund size or total fundraising is bigger one vintage year than the year before, then it is highly likely that any of the return measures will be lower.

For European funds during the same vintage we see broadly the same relationship, although the degree of negative correlation is lower in the case of IRRs, and is actually slightly positive for the upper quartile IRR. This probably does no more than reflect (1) the much lower incidence of mega funds in Europe during the 1990s and (2) the generally much lower average fund sizes in Europe during the same period, both of which we have already noted above.

In both the US and Europe then, the message seems to be that fund size and capital availability are the enemy of returns; the more capital available for investment, and the higher the average fund size, the lower the returns of that vintage year are likely to be. In both Europe and America, you appear to be much less likely to be affected by these lower return expectations (at least if measured by IRR) if you are able to select the upper quartile fund.

However, the bad news for those favouring the mega funds is that it is difficult to suppose that the upper quartile in any one vintage year is likely to be one of these. Look at the relationship between the capital weighted average IRR (which, by definition, is likely to reflect disproportionately the performance of the mega funds), and the upper quartile. In both the US and Europe, it is lower than the upper quartile in 13 years out of 14, whereas if the mega funds were consistently outperforming, one would expect it to be the other way round.

The good news for mega fund supporters is that in most years the CWA IRR is higher than the average IRR, which strongly suggests that the mega funds as a group generally outperform the market as a whole. However, for those who argue that 'Private Equity is an upper quartile game', the figures strongly suggest that there is a select group of the smaller funds which perform very strongly, and from amongst whose ranks the upper quartile and above are most likely to be drawn. The best performing US mega fund ever has an IRR since inception of 74%, while the best performing smaller fund has doubled that. The upper quartile US mega fund appears to be about 12% since inception, while the corresponding smaller fund is about 15%.[11]

Why is all this so important? Well, as a matter of interest, let us look at what has happened to Buyout fundraising in recent years, see Figure 7.6.

See how the mega funds have come to dominate Buyout fundraising in the US. Over the last four available vintage years, they have averaged nearly 84% of all the capital raised. At the same time, both total fundraising and average fund sizes rose rapidly until the financial crisis started to gather pace in 2007. It is thus vitally important to consider, as we have done above, both the impact of much more available capital upon returns, and also the performance of the megafunds relative to the others.

Some believe that this is a debate which many LPs seem content not to have had. The only alternative view would be that they *have* had the debate, and have concluded that there is overwhelming evidence that it is the mega funds which offer the best returns. However, as we have seen, though direct performance comparison is not possible within the existing structure of the industry database, there is, at the very least, strong circumstantial evidence that, in fact, the opposite is the case, at least at the level of individual fund performance (and therefore, selection).

Whatever the case, the performance of the US market as a whole will clearly be dominated in future by the mega funds. Given the proportion of the total capital for which they account,

---

[11] Neither of these figures are directly available, and have been taken as the mid-point between the 70th and 80th percentiles.

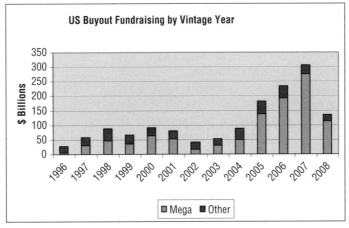

Source: Thomson Reuters

Figure 7.6 US buyout fundraising by vintage year

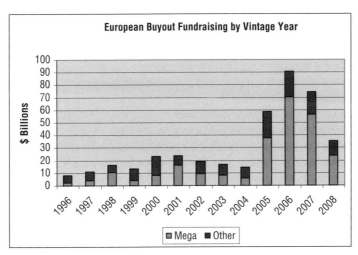

Source: Thomson Reuters

Figure 7.7 European buyout fundraising by vintage year

it could not be otherwise. This could, in turn, represent a major opportunity for smaller funds to demonstrate truly outstanding superior performance, since their own figures will hardly move the needle on the industry's returns overall, thus leading to the potential for huge gaps to open up between the capital weighted average and the upper percentiles.

Let us now consider the situation in Europe (Figure 7.7).

Note how the dominance of the mega funds is spilling over into Europe. The comparable percentage for the proportion of total capital accounted for by the mega funds over the last four years is about 75%. So, here, too, a discussion of the relative merits of the mega funds against the rest of the market seems long overdue.

We will return to these trends in Chapter 15 when we consider the current situation of Private Equity and its prospects for the future.

For the moment though, let us remember, lest we be accused of spreading doom and gloom, that Buyout represents but one strand of the Private Equity industry, and that in the case of the mega funds we are actually talking about a very small part of that industry indeed – by number, that is. Since the beginning of 2001, funds in excess of $1 billion have made up over three-quarters of the total fund capital raised in the global Private Equity market, but they represent less than 6% of global Private Equity funds by number. So, even if you have reservations about the returns likely to be earned by the mega funds (reservations which the above analysis would appear to support, at least in part), then you could simply invest in the other 95% of the market, which by the way would have given you several thousand funds from which to choose!

SUMMARY

Historically, European Buyout funds have consistently outperformed US Buyout funds. In particular, European Buyout funds enjoyed a period of significant outperformance in the mid-1990s, with both 1994 and 1995 being stand-out vintage years.

These, in turn, were facilitated by the existence of market imperfections in Europe, leading to Buyout firms being able to buy companies on a proactive and exclusive basis that had largely ceased to be available by the end of the decade. No comparable conditions existed in America at any time during the decade.

The available data strongly suggests that there is a direct inverse relationship between (1) Buyout returns by vintage year and (2) both total capital raised and average fund size by vintage year. In other words, if either the total capital raised in any one vintage year or the average size of the funds raised in any one vintage year is higher than the corresponding total for the year before, then the returns of the funds raised in the vintage year in question are likely to be lower than for the preceding vintage year. Thus, a period of steadily increasing fund sizes would seem to signal a period of steadily declining returns.

It is unclear that the mega funds offer higher returns in general than their smaller counterparts. On the contrary, it seems likely that most of them offer less than the upper quartile return, otherwise the capital weighted average returns would be closer to the upper quartile, or could even theoretically exceed it on a consistent basis. The figures suggest that in both the US and Europe there is a select group of smaller Buyout funds which offer superior performance, though there are currently no individual fund data (at least, not comprehensive and/or publicly available) with which to test this hypothesis further.

Europe was comparatively little affected by the 'mega fund effect' during the 1990s. For this reason, it is not possible to be so categorical about their relative performance. However, the data appears to support the same suppositions.

The European fundraising pattern has changed dramatically in recent years, so that over the four vintage years from 2005, about 75% of all European Buyout capital raised was for funds in excess of $1 billion.

Those who are concerned by the possible low return potential of mega funds should remember that, since the beginning of 2001 they have represented less than 6% of global Private Equity funds, which would leave several thousand other funds from which to have chosen.

8

Venture Capital

WHAT IS VENTURE CAPITAL?

Just as we have already done for Buyout, we will now take a closer look at Venture Capital. What is it? What are the qualities that characterise a Venture firm? Can anyone do it? If not, what are the barriers to entry? What are the current issues which concern the Venture industry? How might it differ from one geographic area to another?

A glance back at the table in Chapter 1 will remind the reader of those things which tend to distinguish Venture transactions from Buyouts, and it will be useful to bear these in mind. It is time to amplify these very considerably as we look at the types of Venture deals and firms that one may actually encounter in practice.

Unlike Buyouts, which may be classified broadly by the type and size of the deal, most Venture transactions are very similar in their form, while variations in size tend (except during periods of irrational exuberance, such as the two years or so from early 1999) to be a function of stage (see below). It is therefore much more useful to categorise them in terms of their sector and stage. However, geography also plays a part, particularly when we look at historic trends (though this should play much less of a role in the future, and may indeed ultimately become irrelevant as Venture Capital becomes a truly global industry) and we will need to look in particular at the differences between the traditional 'US' and 'European' Venture models.

One point before we begin. In Chapter 1 Buyout and Venture were presented as two distinct and separate entities, and indeed they are. However, as with much of Private Equity, the truth often lies not in black or white but in the intervening shades of grey. We will be discussing early-stage Venture Capital almost exclusively, partly because it represents what has become known as the classic US Venture model, secondly because it is the easiest with which to demonstrate the way in which Venture deals are actually transacted and developed, and last but not least simply because it is so much fun. However, as we will see, there are firms which quite legitimately specialise in later stage Venture and here the rigid differentiations which we laid down earlier begin to creak at the seams a little. For example, the way in which returns can be earned across the portfolio is different (more uniform in the case of later stage, more explosively binary in the case of early stage) and Venture debt can enter the equation. There are specialist providers of Venture debt both in the form of equipment finance (although traditionally in the US this has been handled by the equipment manufacturers themselves) and in the form of working capital facilities for companies which have already become profitable, or at least cash-flow positive. Let us note this point at the outset for the sake of completeness, but not seek to labour it, not least because we should not confuse the very significant distinctions between what really are two very different investment areas. Witness the fact that it is almost unheard of for the same Private Equity firm to conduct both Venture and Buyout transactions, at least within the same fund (Apax did so until the explosion in fund sizes made it impossible, but this is a very rare exception indeed;

a very few others, such as Doughty Hanson and Carlyle, have done so but with separate teams and separate funds).

BACKING NEW APPLICATIONS, NOT NEW TECHNOLOGY

Before we begin our detailed look at Venture, however, let us clear up one widespread misconception. There is a popular belief that Venture Capital exists to fund the development of new technology. This is quite simply untrue. Indeed, there is probably not a single professional Venture Capitalist in the world who would be prepared to invest in pure technology risk of the 'when I switch it on, will it work?' variety. What a Venture GP is looking for is someone who is looking to develop a new application of an existing technology, which has itself been tried and tested. They are, in other words, not prepared to take the 'when I switch it on will it work?' technology risk, but they are prepared, if appropriate, to take the 'when I show it to people will they buy it?' market risk.

You will notice the words 'if appropriate'. In these two words lie the further level of distinction between what Venture Capital actually is and what the misinformed believe it to be. Venture Capitalists are looking for a new application of an existing technology that addresses a commercially significant need or problem. Ideally, the entrepreneurs will have worked in an industry sector, and will there have experienced a particular problem to which they believe they now have the answer; this will, for example, be the classic model of a Venture-backed enterprise software company. Unfortunately, many ideas which are put forward for Venture funding are technology focused rather than commercially focused. As one former chairman of the Irish Software Association said a few years ago: 'every year I see two hundred solutions in search of a problem'. The world is full of engineers who believe they can build a better mousetrap, but it is not the function of Venture Capital to support their endeavours unless somebody somewhere has a significant commercial interest in catching mice.

The words 'commercially significant' also merit further consideration, since it is here that much of a Venture firm's due diligence may take place. If any Venture company is to produce the sort of potential returns for its investors that the Venture model requires (we will see later that this is about 25 times capital invested), then it needs to be able to grow quickly to a significant size and thus the size of the potential market represented by the identified need or problem is crucial, as is the likely presence of any competitors. The word 'size' here not only refers to the totality of the market, but also the number of participants; a product or service for which there may only be a dozen customers worldwide (albeit any customer is likely to be prepared to pay large amounts of money for it) is clearly an inherently riskier proposition than one which can be marketed to tens of thousands.

Given the above, it is unfortunate that such a jaundiced and inaccurate view of Venture Capital should still prevail. Yes, of course there is risk in investing in Venture companies, but given the right investment planning techniques that risk can be reduced to virtually nothing at the LP level,[1] and given the right mind-set and experience it is actually significantly lower than people may believe even at the level of a single Venture fund. We will look at this in more detail when we consider Venture returns.

Historically, this was not always the case, the most obvious exception being drug discovery projects, although the purist might argue that even here this is rarely total innovation,

---

[1] See Multi-Asset Class Investment Strategy, already referenced.

since the research team will frequently be moving onwards or outwards from protein or chemical combinations which are already known to have certain properties. However, the Venture industry, particularly in the US, has shown an enviable ability to develop and evolve by abandoning anything which does not work well, so that this area of Venture investment has, in any event, now been largely discontinued, at least in terms of early-stage deals. Again, we will look at this point in more detail later, since it is one where geography has a part to play.

Just to be clear, then, there are actually two reasons why professional investors will shun technology creation, as opposed to technology application or development. The first is the technology risk issue. The second is that the research teams involved will usually be pre-occupied with investigating a particular scientific area without any particular idea of how this might be applied to commercial uses. It was notable, for example, how little success was enjoyed by the various 'nanotechnology' funds which went out fundraising a few years ago.

It is a sobering thought for a European that just about all the major inventions and discoveries of the modern age have been made in Europe, but commercially exploited in America. Many Americans, for example, quite reasonably (but mistakenly) believe that the computer was invented by Americans, let alone most of the other technology which we take for granted today: jet engines, rockets, antibiotics, DNA, the internal combustion engine, helicopters, radar, yes and even those most ubiquitous technological applications of all – the Internet and television. It is this wonderful ability to commercialise technological developments quickly and successfully, together with the 'can do' attitude that characterises American culture generally, that have together formed the bedrock of American Venture Capital.

CLASSIFICATION BY SECTOR

Having hopefully now clarified exactly what Venture is, let us turn to examining the different sectors within which Venture operates. There are basically three of these: IT, Telecommunications (Telecoms) and Life Science (sometimes called Healthcare or Biotech). Historically a significant amount of Venture funding was also directed towards retail products and services (a branded chain of steak restaurants in the US comes to mind) but I do not propose to consider this further as it is now largely of only historic interest. Of course, many Internet-related projects are aimed at the retail market, but I will consider these within the IT and/or Telecoms sectors. Incidentally, IT and Telecoms are sometimes jointly referred to as 'Technology' or 'Tech' deals, to distinguish them from Life Science.

This lumping together of IT and Telecoms (deals in both sectors being frequently pursued within the same Venture GP team) seems sensible, for it has become increasingly difficult to distinguish between IT and Telecom deals. These categories were dreamt up two decades ago, when the average PC could have an 8-bit 4 MHz processor and only 64 Kb of memory. The computer then was seen as a means of storing and processing information and was typically used for word-processing and spreadsheet work. Today, of course, the computer is viewed primarily as a communication device attached to a global network, and processing and storage capabilities are regarded as commodities, and cheap commodities at that. Indeed, many, particularly under the age of 17 or so, might even say today, if asked, that they view their computer as essentially an entertainment centre.

So, while this book will honour the conventions of Venture deal classification, please be aware that today the issue is frequently not clear cut. How would you classify, for example, a new email application for Microsoft Outlook? Or a new development in wireless networking?

IT

IT deals have traditionally been divided into 'hardware' and 'software'. The nature of the typical hardware deal has changed considerably, but software deals less so.

In the early days of Venture Capital, hardware deals could encompass the development of a new computer itself, or new computer peripherals (there were repeated attempts, for example, to develop an alternative to the QWERTY keyboard), but it is extremely unlikely that such a project would even rate a meeting with a Venture firm these days. There is general acceptance that the basic infrastructure of computer technology is now cast in stone, and that the global market is dominated by a handful of immensely powerful players. There is perhaps one exception to this, and it lies in the field of memory. The computer hard disk suffers from a particular problem in that the speed at which data can be shifted within (and onto and off) the disk is many times faster (some people suggest by as much as a million times) than the speed with which the disk can be mechanically accessed. This might be thought of as a sort of holy grail of computer design, since even a small improvement could have a dramatic effect on performance. There are currently experiments taking place with different storage media and techniques, however, this probably falls foul of the 'technology risk' objections referred to above and is best left to the R&D departments of big computer companies.

These days, hardware deals are more likely to feature chips, data connectors and so forth, although there can be some hardcore production engineering involved as well, such as vacuum automation systems for chip and storage disk manufacturing. It is this hardware section which perhaps strays most insidiously into the Telecoms sector. How would one classify things such as radio baseband processors for wireless networks, or some of the advanced laser components for fibre optic communication? The latter is almost certainly 'Telecoms', but the former could really be either.

Software companies can fall into various different categories. First there are the so-called 'tools' companies which provide utilities that can be used in the design both of hardware and software (particularly where the latter is object oriented), and also in the construction and operation of systems. Where these are used to diagnose and cure particular operating problems they are sometimes referred to as utilities.

Second there is the world of integrating software, which has become a very hot area. Banks and financial institutions are a particular market here. Most banks have legacy systems going back many years (dating from the days of green screens!) and have, over time, bolted on other systems around them, resulting in a huge mish-mash of largely incompatible systems. For most banks it is currently impossible to pull together on screen the full information for any one customer if that customer has a spread of accounts ranging across, say, currency, trade finance, leasing, investments, etc. These will mostly be dealt with separately and in many cases at least two of the various systems will be unable to speak to each other. This raises particular issues regarding compliance with Basel II and other regulatory standards.

So, this is another 'holy grail' area but subject to a large Catch 22. While banks would love to have an integrated system to cope with the demand of new regulatory environments (such as Basel II), they are understandably reluctant to close down their legacy systems and subject themselves to the disruption which we all know attends the introduction of a new computer system, particularly since during any such period of disruption they could hardly avoid being in breach of exactly those regulatory requirements which they were seeking to satisfy. This has, in turn, led to some innovative proposed solutions in the form of software that can act as a 'front-end', making it look as if an integrated system were in place but in fact operating more as a reporting agent, burrowing into each system to extract the required information.

Operating software used to form quite a large part of Venture portfolios, but this is another area which has become of largely historic interest since most operating software is now proprietary and the sector is dominated by one huge player, with whom few are prepared to tangle. Kleiner Perkins, one of the most successful Venture firms in history, has a maxim 'don't stand in the path of an oncoming train', which means 'never invest in anything which may compete with Microsoft'.

Application software, too, has become less attractive of late. An early success story (Sage, which developed some of the first PC-based accounting packages would be a good example), this has become increasingly standardised, based on the Windows platform and bundled with new computers. There are still opportunities here but they are tending now to be based around the email, chat and contact management spaces.

There were great hopes for enterprise software (i.e. software specially tailored to the needs of a particular industry) in years gone by, but these have been largely unfulfilled, despite some individual success stories. One of the problems here has been industry consolidation, with the number of potential customers in some areas (insurance companies, banks, etc) shrinking rapidly. At the other end of the scale, where an industry has an almost infinite number of customers, Venture companies have seemed unable to handle the scale involved, resulting in the enterprise software space becoming highly fragmented, with a large number of small players (perhaps a Roll-up opportunity for a Buyout group?), while copyright piracy has also been a significant problem.

Where software is being created, particular problems are faced by Venture Capitalists. The process itself must be rigorously controlled, but a balance must be struck so as not to alienate the individual developers; as a matter of temperament, software engineers tend not to respond well to discipline. At the very least, a daily development log must be maintained (and it is worth considering hiring one individual to do nothing else) so that in the event of the loss of any one developer or batch of code, everything can be re-created.[2]

The other challenge lies in successfully marrying 'a bunch of guys writing code'[3] with people who can sell the product and people who can run the business. Too often, one or more of the software engineers will believe that they can fill these roles themselves, and may be allowed to do so by inexperienced or irresolute Venture Capitalists.

Internet deals have also traditionally been listed under IT, but this classification is itself becoming much more hazy. It already had to cope with e-commerce, sub-classified into B2B (Business to Business) and B2C (Business to Consumer), as well as various application-type businesses, but there is growing pressure for it now also to include computer gaming.

Gaming has long been a fertile area for Venture investment and, in the UK at least, is a sector in which the angel community is also very interested. Here, too, precise classification is a real issue, however, not least because the sector is evolving rapidly. As a gross simplification, the traditional market model of 'boxed' games which were bought for use on PCs

---

[2]Bronson (1998) The First 20 Million Dollars is Always the Hardest, Vintage, New York. Though a work of fiction, this gives a very authentic flavour of a 1990s Californian technology start-up.

[3]As I once heard software companies described at a Venture firm's annual meeting.

or game-stations, has moved in favour of games which are downloaded digitally and/or multi-player online games (known as MMOGs). Many boxed games are now MMOGs, of which the most successful example is probably the *Warcraft* series. A further development, particularly in Asia, has been the offer of games which are free to play, but then entice the gamer into purchasing virtual items for use in the game. This, in turn, has led to the introduction of game cards, which children can buy in shops and then use as virtual currency.

Incidentally, a further area of rapid development is that of games which can be played on mobile devices and music players. This is leading many entrepreneurs and VCs alike in the gaming industry to argue that there is now effectively little difference between the Internet and mobile devices such as 3G telephones; they are simply different distribution channels for the same content. Yet another sign that the traditional binary classification of all technology deals into either IT or Telecoms is looking increasingly dated.

Telecoms

This has probably been the most exciting sector in recent years, given first the birth of the Internet and then its rapid growth, fuelled in part by the other big factor: fast, affordable broadband. Over the last decade or so we have seen some major technological changes. Analogue communication has given way to digital. Fax has given way to email. Traditional cabling systems have, in many cases, given way to fibre optics, while even old-fashioned copper can carry ADSL. Data communications have overtaken voice conversations on both national and international networks.

Then, of course, there is the whole mobile world, which was part of the analogue to digital progression noted above and has now spawned both 3G (UMTS) and also GPRS, which is colloquially referred to as third generation but is, in reality, 2½G. We now routinely use mobile devices to access email and the Internet, while wireless technology such as Bluetooth enables machines to talk to each other, and Wi-Fi creates wireless networks that allow us to use laptop computers to access the Internet no matter where we are. Yes, there are problems which have not yet been solved, but for the most part these are now practical, commercial problems such as the unwillingness of many hotels, airports, etc. to provide free wireless broadband as the commodity that it is, rather than trying to sell it as a luxury product. The technical problems have been largely overcome, though much has taken longer than originally envisaged, particularly in the fields of battery technology and UMTS handsets.

This is all fertile ground for entrepreneurs and thus also for the Venture Capital community. One particularly popular area of interest (so much so that it became a bubble) was the whole of the optical technology field. There were some exciting successes early on in this area: Chromatis, a metro optical networking company which started life in Israel was bought by Lucent in May 2000 for $4.5 billion in stock, while in the same month Altitun, a Swedish tuneable laser company, was bought by ADC for nearly $900M, representing a multiple of over 80 times the invested capital of its local Venture backers, for one of whom, InnovationsKapital, it was their second big 'home run' (see below). Incidentally, these two examples have been deliberately chosen rather than their many US counterparts, since the ability of Venture Capitalists outside the US to create 'home run' companies has been largely overlooked. We will look at this in more detail later.

Particular problems to which engineers have turned their attention in the optical field have included the ability to split an optical beam into many different signals without any leakage from one to another, and the need to boost the signal at regular intervals to prevent it degrading. Then there is the whole area of the optical routers and switches which are needed to transform an optical signal into a wire-carried one, and vice versa. In the early days, many companies sought to develop the individual items (tuneable lasers being a good example) which went into these devices; this became known as the sub-components field. Today, however, companies will look to provide the whole device, and these are called components companies by way of distinction, though this is not an obvious use of the terminology – it would seem more logical to call them component and device companies respectively.

The optical bubble was as devastating in its way as the dot com bubble, though because it happened in a specialist area with which consumers had no dealings, and which was of interest only to engineers and Venture Capitalists, it received relatively little publicity. In fairness, the problem was not just too many Venture Capitalists putting too much money into too many optical companies (though this certainly happened 'in spades', as the Americans say). More pernicious was the conduct of the incumbent telcos in both Europe and the US in denying new operators access to their exchanges. This prevented the new entrants from rolling out the high-speed networks for which they were purchasing technology from the Venture-backed start-ups, with the result that most of them simply ran out of money and went out of business. Since the telcos themselves were very resistant to the idea of using the new technology (since they could enjoy the position of being able to sell obsolete technology to their existing customers on a monopoly basis at a high price), the Venture companies were faced with a nightmare situation of a dramatic fall in the number of carriers, who were the natural customers for their product. Some were able to sell to equipment manufacturers, and this, in turn, prompted a wave of corporate acquisitions such as the Lucent/Chromatic transaction, but this proved short-lived as the full potential downside of the market crash became evident, and large corporations the world over slashed their budgets for R&D or the purchase of new technology. As this last window closed, the optical sector entered a nuclear winter from which it is only now slowly emerging.

Another area of interest is mobile telephony, where the Nordic area, and particularly Finland, has traditionally led the way. Mobile applications have featured in many Venture Capital portfolios and there is some geographic variation here; for example, SMS messaging has been rampant in Europe for years, particularly among younger people, but took some time to catch on in America. One showing considerable novelty value was a computer dating application that was beta tested among the gay community in Los Angeles. Having fed your preferences (history does not record what categories there might have been) into the system, the application would track your location and if you were found to be within a certain number of feet of someone whose preferences matched your own, then both mobiles would ring simultaneously. Sadly, this service did not survive and was never rolled out to other communities; such imaginative thinking deserved a better fate.

Although the traditional set of mobile technology has been the Nordic area, many innovative applications have originated in Israel. At one time it was envisaged, for example, that you might phone a cinema, theme park, railway station or airline, buy your tickets over the phone, and that these would then be electronically loaded into your phone's SIM card, which could, in turn, be read electronically, thus making queuing and paper tickets a thing of the past. Hopefully these ideas were simply ahead of their time. It certainly seems to have been the case in recent years that the pace of the advance of any particular technology has often outstripped people's willingness to use it.

During the period leading up to the collapse of the dot com bubble, some Venture firms also backed large systems companies, including businesses which were actually installing and operating high-speed metro networks for business customers. However, these proved poor investments, as the large amounts of capital required to fund their roll-out could not be justified in terms of the ultimate valuation of the business, so it is most unlikely that we shall see companies of this type in Venture portfolios in future.

Life Science

Life Science has traditionally been divided into two broad areas, although this classification is no longer exhaustive. The first is the drug discovery area, which, as the name suggests, involves backing research teams who wish to spin out of university laboratories or the R&D departments of large drug companies. This is probably very much the stereotype view of what Venture Capital is all about on the part of those with no actual knowledge of the area. In fact, as we have already seen, there is very little truth in such an image at all.

The other main area of speciality is usually just called 'devices', and, as the name suggests, this dwells on the various sorts of device which are used in the medical profession, ranging from stents (the tiny tubes inserted into blood vessels during surgery), through diagnostic testing equipment to large, expensive scanners. Perhaps the most exotic variants I have encountered were an injection directly into the penis to facilitate erections (this was in the days before Viagra), and what was enthusiastically described as 'a flight simulator for dentists' – an artificial replica of the human mouth on which dentists could practise their gentle arts.[4]

As noted above, these two areas are no longer exhaustive. The major change has been brought about by the success of the human genome project which, as one leading Venture Capitalist said at the time, 'means that everyone is suddenly playing with a new deck of cards'. In addition to pure research projects in the genetic field (usually involving identifying the exact genetic combination which causes a particular condition, and whether this becomes defective in some way which can be reversed, thus forestalling the onset of the condition), there is now specialist genetic software which can greatly speed up this process, as well as assisting drug development by suggesting compounds which are known to have worked (or are close to compounds which have worked) before, and anticipating possible side effects in time for a line of research to be discontinued early, with consequent savings in time and money.

Another area which has grown rapidly is that of specialist services in the healthcare arena, particularly in the field of testing, analysis and diagnostics. Interestingly, this area has also been of interest to Buyout firms, driven in part by the trend for both hospitals and large companies to outsource service provision to specialist third parties.

Life Science investing has increasingly become a tale of two continents. While there are little publicly available data to back this up, apocryphal evidence and personal experience strongly suggest that Life Science Venture deals have performed better in Europe than they have in the US, both in absolute terms (i.e. that European Life Science deals have achieved better multiples on average than their American counterparts) and also in relative terms (i.e. that Life Science has generally performed better than Technology deals in Europe, with the opposite being the case in America). In fairness to the American Venture community, however, it must be admitted that this latter point loses much of its force when one considers

---

[4]Rather than corpses, which can, apparently and surprisingly, be hard to come by.

that Technology Venture returns in Europe (at least as recorded in the available industry databases[5]) have been extremely disappointing for the most part. Whatever the case, this has led to a number of developments.

It used to be the case that Venture firms would routinely practise both Technology and Life Science within the same fund (this was less universal in America, but still a frequent occurrence). In the US, however, this practice has been almost entirely discontinued. Publicly, the stated reason for this is usually a desire for focus, and the desirability of all partners within the Venture firm to be able to understand and discuss everyone else's deals. Privately, the reason is clear. Rightly or wrongly, Life Science is seen as having underperformed, and the Technology-focused GPs want to be free to pursue their business without this perceived drag on their fund returns. Consequently, most Venture firms, and that includes just about all the leading ones, have either hived off their Life Science teams to become separate firms, or closed them down entirely.

It is only fair to record, however, that this was during the period up to around mid-2001, when you heard jokes like 'you know things must be bad when Life Science starts to look attractive' at Venture firms' annual meetings. While at the time this attitude towards Life Science was sincerely felt by many in the American Venture community, the sector never lost a loyal core of LPs and thus continued to attract funding. One wonders what the people who made those jokes might say today nearly a decade later, a period of several years in which there have been almost no exits from their favoured technology funds. Does a decision totally to exclude Life Science seem as sensible today as it did then?

While it may seem a very sweeping (not to mention somewhat jaundiced) attitude, there were a number of very valid reasons behind this attitude, and it may be worth taking a little time to consider some of them.

Chief amongst them is the whole question of the approval process for many Life Science products. In the US, the FDA approval process for new drugs and other therapeutic products, for example, can be very lengthy and involve clinical trials lasting years rather than months, and the situation is similar in most countries around the world (in Europe, EU approval is also required). Given that a new drug has a limited patent period during which to earn royalties before it can quite legally be copied (as a 'generic' drug) by anyone in the world, this has been a major stumbling block to achieving Venture-type returns, particularly when coupled with the very large amounts of money which such a Venture company typically requires. The combination of a long holding period, high capital requirement and limited income period make it very difficult to justify this as a legitimate Venture Capital activity, particularly given the extreme product risk involved (it has been estimated that as few as one in every hundred thousand pharmaceutical research projects ever results in a commercially available drug). In truth, 'pharma' itself mirrors closely the early-stage US Venture model, where the occasional home run such as Viagra or Zantac justifies the very many failures and also-rans. However, here much competing activity is carried on by the big pharma companies themselves, and so there is the added complication that as a Venture firm you do not even have access to all the potential home runs from which to make your selection. This latter point is often overlooked.

The arguments against other forms of Life Science activity are less clear cut. There seems no obvious reason, for example, why medical devices, particularly of the external and/or

---

[5]We will see later that these consistently under-state European Venture returns, but this does not change the point I am making here, it only lessens its extent a little.

diagnostic variety, which require a very light touch on the licensing tiller, should not have the potential to be successful on a similar scale to other forms of Technology project. While the data is not available to support this, it may be that what is lacking here is widespread genuine home run potential. An application such as Google, Skype, Amazon or eBay can meet needs and change behaviour patterns across the globe. In the early days of chip development a relatively small advance in microchip technology could increase the power and speed of a computer by two, or even ten, times. Short of an artificial brain or a functional suspended animation machine, it is difficult to conceive of a medical device that could have a similar impact. Since, as we will see, it is home runs that drive Venture returns, then it may well be that this is a major reason why US Venture firms have shunned this sector in recent years.

There is another possible reason which is more nebulous, but probably still valid. America has led the world in technological advancement in Information Technology, particularly in software, applications and hardware bundling (though not necessarily in chip technology, much of which was developed in the Far East, and certainly not in Telecoms, where much pioneering work was done in Europe). Thus, if one was able to establish a leading position across the US as a provider of, say, an Internet search engine (Google, Yahoo), or operating software (Microsoft) or bundled hardware (Dell), then a position of global leadership followed more or less automatically. In other words, the amount of proactive marketing required in different parts of the world in the very early stages of the company's life is probably negligible. That is not to take anything away from the achievements of such companies, which have been impressive on a truly staggering scale; one is simply seeking to draw a distinction.

Compare and contrast this with the position of a young medical devices company, perhaps the one referred to above which developed a flight simulator for dentists. Almost from the day when they had a test product available, they needed dedicated sales people around the globe trying to sell sometimes individual machines to teaching hospitals, wrestling with different languages, buying practices and regulations. That same teaching hospital would probably have bought Windows software for each new computer without even stopping to think about it, and without Microsoft having to make that sale specifically to them. Thus, companies for which it is possible to establish a position of global leadership without having to step outside their home market in their early days clearly enjoy a significant advantage, and the companies mentioned above have done a great job of exploiting that advantage to its maximum potential.

So, yes, there are some valid reasons why Life Science has lost favour in the US (although it still has a dedicated following amongst many LPs), but this raises two questions to which one cannot know the answers, but could guess at the likely outcomes. First, if US Technology Venture had not been so dramatically successful during the mid-1990s, would the bifurcation in US Venture and the relegation of Life Science to perceived second place necessarily have happened? Second, if one accepts, for the sake of argument, that it is impossible for any LP new to the asset class to access any of the leading technology Venture funds, then which is preferable (in US terms): to invest in upper quartile Life Science, or to invest in second or third quartile Technology?

In Europe, the pattern has been different. Life Science still routinely forms half of the activities of many leading Venture firms (Innovations Kapital in Sweden and Sofinnova in France being two obvious examples), though even here these activities are starting to be split between separate funds, and in addition there are some very respected firms who specialise in nothing but Life Science investing. As mentioned above, this is largely because the sector's performance has been viewed in a much more friendly light. It may also have something to do with the fact that most of the world's leading pharma companies are based in Europe, and that perhaps there are thus more spin-out opportunities available; indeed, Actelion, one of Europe's most lucrative Venture deals to date (a huge success for Joel Besse and the Life Science team at Atlas Venture[6]) was just such a transaction.

However, notwithstanding these apparent differences, it is fair to say that drug discovery deals have been declining in Europe too. In truth, it was probably always difficult for European Venture firms, with their small fund sizes, to finance these sorts of undertakings and there is, in any event, a growing feeling that these projects are probably best left to large pharma companies or university research labs, at least in their early stages. In particular, for them to be funded by very small seed funds, such as those which are sometimes based around a particular university, seems to make no sense whatsoever.

Whatever the case, it seems clear that, one way or another, drug discovery deals will all but disappear from professional Venture fund portfolios, if indeed they have not done so already.

CLASSIFICATION BY STAGE

We have just looked at one of the two main ways of classifying Venture deals, namely by sector. The other is by stage, and this is less clear cut than the former, since there is considerable looseness of terminology. Venture deals, unlike Buyout deals for the most part, will enjoy successive rounds of financing, and the point in the company's development when each of these rounds occurs will determine whether such a round is, for example, 'early' or 'mid'. Certain Venture firms specialise in different stages; thus, a late-stage firm might only invest for the first time in the fourth or fifth round, while a seed firm will tend to invest heavily at the beginning and then seek subsequently to invest the bare minimum necessary to maintain a significant equity position.

At the risk of stating the obvious, the valuation of the company will typically rise with each successive round as its perceived risk decreases, and thus in theory the gains available to the Venture Capitalists involved will correspondingly diminish. It is a classic example of the relationship between risk and reward.

Broadly, the Venture world divides by stage into seed, early stage, mid stage and late stage. Thus, the Venture universe might be thought of as a grid, see Table 8.1:

Table 8.1   Venture Capital classified by stage and sector

Life Science	Telecoms	IT
Seed	Seed	Seed
Early	Early	Early
Mid	Mid	Mid
Late	Late	Late

[6]Actelion went public on the Swiss stock market in April 2000, just two years after its first Venture financing round (there were only ever two) at a valuation in excess of $800M, reputedly gaining its Venture backers a money multiple in excess of 200×.

Let us take a look at each stage in turn, as we need to be quite clear what we mean by the relevant term in each case.

Seed Stage

This term is particularly corrupted in Europe, where a lot of Venture Capitalists claim to be 'seed' investors when they are really nothing of the kind.

The word 'seed' carries very strong implications of a total start-up, and ideally that should be the sense of the word adopted by the industry as a whole to avoid confusion. However, while this is broadly true, industry practice also recognises as a 'seed' round one which occurs very early in the life of a company but not quite at the outset if there has been an 'angel' round to fund the actual start-up. An angel round is one put together by angel investors, i.e. investors who are not professional Venture Capitalists, and there are important differences in practice and possible consequences between the US and Europe relating to angel rounds which merit a separate section below.

The confusion which this introduces into proceedings is regrettable, not least because it can have a knock-on effect so far as the classification of subsequent rounds is concerned. However, let us clarify as best we can the obfuscation that industry practice has created. There are many Venture firms who claim that a 'seed' round is the first one in which at least one professional Venture firm participates, even if this happens one or two years into the life of the company. While every situation is different, and it is hard to lay down universal rules, this definition seems hard to accept.

It is true that, in general, the first round in which a Venture firm participates will be a seed round (particularly in America). However, where there has been a long period between the start-up of a company and the first institutional round (as is frequently the case in Europe), this is not a proper use of the term, and the phrase 'A round' should be preferred. How long is too long? Well, definitely if a company is generating revenues and probably even if they have a test product out with alpha or beta customers. The word 'seed' implies the very early stages of a company's existence and we must not lose sight of this.

So, such a view suggests the following as an answer to the question 'was this a seed round?' in any particular case:

• Where the company is a genuine start-up: definitely.
• Where the company has yet to produce its product or service in even alpha testing form: probably.
• Where a company has product in test: probably not.
• Where a company is generating revenues, no matter how small: definitely not.

As the story of seed funding unfolds, differences between European and US practice become very stark. It is probably not going too far to say that, with a very few honourable exceptions, there are virtually no European Venture firms who are pursuing genuine seed-stage opportunities. To understand why this is, we need to take quite a lengthy excursion into the US Venture model.

The US model

As we will see in Chapter 10, so far as historic returns are concerned, Venture is the mirror image of Buyout; not only have American returns been better, they have been quite dramatically better. This has given rise to an impassioned debate about whether there is something intrinsically superior about the way in which US Venture firms do business, or whether environmental factors produced a 'happy hunting time' in US Venture in the same way that they may well have done in European Buyout. We will be examining this debate later, but suffice it to say for the moment that the answer, as usual, is 'some of both', but we must at this point examine the former of these points, since we cannot sensibly discuss seed funding unless we understand what the US model is.

There are a number of components to the US Venture model, and although they interact to the point that they form a cohesive whole, we will look at each of these in turn for ease of discussion. They are (1) a focus on the seed stage, (2) a home run mentality and (3) 'value add'.

Seed-stage focus

As we will see shortly, two of the things which US Venture Capitalists look to do is to achieve as high a money multiple as possible and to add value in actually building a company along-side an entrepreneur. Both such things are facilitated by trying to invest, wherever possible, at the seed stage. This boosts the chance of being able to achieve a high money multiple (because one is getting into the company at the lowest possible valuation), and also allows the Venture Capitalists to build the company from day one in the way they believe it should be built, rather than getting involved at a later stage and possibly having to unscramble unsatisfactory arrangements that may already have been put in place.

In order to increase the possibility of sourcing quality seed-stage dealflow, and also to increase the chances of being able to work with experienced company builders in that seed-stage dealflow, many US Venture firms adopt an 'EIR programme'. This is an intriguing and exciting process which has not, as yet, been widely copied in Europe. It consists of finding three or four experienced entrepreneurs (who have preferably been backed previously by the firm in successful ventures and are now 'going round again') and designating them as 'entre-preneurs in residence' (EIRs). They are encouraged to spend time in the firm's offices talking to start-up teams about their ideas. The aim is partly that they might be able to join one of these teams (probably to lead it) if they like the idea sufficiently, but this is more the province of so-called 'Venture Partners'. The real objective with an EIR is that they should be per-suaded actually to start their next company right there in the Venture firm's offices, using the firm's facilities, in full discussion with the GPs, and with every expectation of being funded by them. This process is called 'incubation' and is very different from the way in which the term is used in Europe, where frequently all that is provided is a glorified business centre, with little hands-on support.

While it is difficult to be certain, since no performance figures for individual funds are publicly available broken down by stage, there is a general belief that it is seed-stage funds which have consistently scored the best returns in the US. This is borne out by the available industry figures. We will be looking at this in more detail in Chapter 10, but let us glance quickly in passing at the TVPI figures for US Venture since inception, broken down by stage (Table 8.2).

These figures do not seem consistent with the idea of earlier stage Venture companies bearing higher risk, and also producing higher returns, but they tell only part of the story,[7]

---

[7] It is interesting to note, however, that the seed and early-stage multiples have come down quite dramatically since the first edition of this book was published, while the late-stage multiples have increased slightly. Might this indicate late-stage firms having had opportunities to back 'down rounds' and restructurings during the long 'exits desert' since the collapse of the dot com and technology bubble?

Table 8.2   TVPI since inception, 1969 to 2008 inclusive

Stage	Capital weighted average	Upper quartile
Early/Seed	1.29	2.11
Early	1.52	2.11
Balanced	1.51	2.21
Late	1.49	2.12

Source: Thomson Reuters
Note: 'Balanced' refers to funds which invest at all stages.

since the real excitement of Venture returns lies at the upper margins. The best ever early-stage fund had a fund multiple of over 28×, while the most successful late-stage one enjoyed a multiple of 14.6×; the best balanced, i.e. multi-stage fund was in the middle as one might expect at just over 16×, and these figures present a much more potent view of what might be expected.

The real difference comes from the very best funds of all. As we will hear in a later chapter, if you wanted to make ten times your capital on a Venture fund, then, according to the industry figures, you are no less than fifteen times more likely to have done so with an early-stage fund than with a late-stage fund.

Home-run mentality
This phrase is bandied about continually when discussion turns to American Venture practice, but often with little real understanding of what lies behind it. Briefly, as we shall be discussing in more detail in the next chapter, US Venture returns have been dominated at the company level by a small number of very big winners – the home runs. Publicly available evidence is sketchy, but leading US Venture Capital Fund of Funds manager Horsley Bridge released into the public domain some years ago its analysis of its own database (which is generally recognised as being the best in the industry), which was that slightly less than 5% of all companies by cost produced 80% of returns by value, and these conclusions have never been challenged.

A difference which has often been claimed to exist between US and European Venture Capitalists (with much justification) was that American GPs recognised this and adapted their approach accordingly, whereas European GPs did not. We should not get drawn into this discussion too deeply at this stage, as it is one we shall be having in the next chapter, but let us note for our present purposes that this involves trying to grow every company in which they invest into a very large company, instead of just a medium-sized company, and not considering for investment in the first place any company which does not appear to have this potential. It also follows that, unless they have lost confidence in a company, they will resist the temptation of an early exit, preferring to 'swing for the fence'.

'Value add'
This is an American phrase that would perhaps be more elegantly expressed as 'added value'. It describes that ability of American Venture Capitalists to get closely involved with a company's development on a hands-on basis, using their own personal knowledge and contacts gained when they themselves were an entrepreneur founder of a start-up company. It is key

to the US Venture model, and is the one element of it which was undeniably largely absent historically from European Venture activity. When an American entrepreneur tries to attract the attention of a Venture firm, he is not going there primarily for money, but for the first-hand operating experience of its GPs. A European entrepreneur, by contrast, will be desperate for money from any source, since there is much less of it available for early-stage companies in Europe, and will not expect operating experience to be on offer.

The US model comes to Europe

Since we are dealing with the US model at this point, it is only fair to point out, since it does actually impact on the question of stage preference, that while the above distinctions between US and European Venture were largely valid on a historical basis, they are becoming less so with every passing year. There is an increasing number of European Venture firms who recognise the merits of the US model and are making great efforts to apply it in Europe. This will be of particular relevance when we come to consider Venture returns in later chapters.

Why European Venture Capital firms have avoided the seed stage

If you do not have the first-hand operating experience to bring value add to the party, then the picture changes dramatically. From being viewed as an area of opportunity in the US (because you can (1) get in at a low valuation and (2) build the company as you would like it to be from day one), it is viewed as an area of risk in Europe and thus an area to be avoided, rather than sought out. 'Come back when you've got some customers' is a commonly heard refrain.

Incidentally, it is here that a lot of the confusion over terminology arises. There are some European firms who are honest enough to say 'we don't do seed', but there are many others who seek to portray the image of being very early-stage investors without having either the skills or the inclination to do so, and they do this by calling what are essentially A rounds 'seed'. The author's own belief, which is drawn from many years of practical experience, is that there are almost no independent, professional Venture firms in Europe who offer genuine seed-round funding. Some small number may, but they are very, very few in the context of the industry as a whole.

Early Stage

We discussed above the difference between 'seed' and 'early'. Let us take 'early' as meaning a genuine A round together with possibly a B round if the A round is very small and/or very early in a company's life, and/or the B round quickly follows the A round. As with so many aspects of Private Equity, this is an art not a science, and instinct and experience are probably more important than scientific analysis.

It is at early to mid-stage that the bulk of European firms enter the fray. In fairness, it makes comparatively little difference in valuation terms, as shortage of capital ensures that there is usually little difference between the pre-money valuation of a company in the early stages of its life and the post-money valuation of the preceding round, but in the US it can make a dramatic difference.

Mid and Late Stages

The skills required for a later stage Venture investor are different to those needed in the early stage, and start to approach those that one might find in a Buyout firm. Financial analysis becomes increasingly important, and technology skills and sector knowledge less so. Debt can also enter the picture, either by way of working capital facilities (if the company has the cash flow to justify it) or by way of equipment financing (which might actually be present from a very early stage of the company's existence in some circumstances).

Confusingly, the term 'mezzanine' is often used to describe very late stage (typically pre-IPO) Venture investing in the US, whereas in Europe this term is used exclusively to describe convertible debt, almost exclusively for Buyout transactions.

SUMMARY

The main differences between Buyout and Venture are set out in Chapter 1.

Venture can be classified by sector and by stage.

The three main sectors are Life Science, Information Technology ('IT') and Tele-communications ('Telecoms'). The latter two are frequently referred to together as 'Technology' to distinguish them from Life Science and the distinction between them is becoming increasingly blurred.

The main stages of investment are seed, early, mid and late. Again, the distinction between them is frequently blurred and they can mean different things to different individuals. In particular, the usage of 'seed' and 'early' is often confused, especially in Europe.

Historic returns in the US have been driven by a small number of very large winners, which are referred to as home runs. Strictly speaking, a home run is any investment which returns the entire committed capital of the fund which invests in it at least once, but in practice it has come to mean any investment which returns over 25 times its capital ('25×').

It is believed that amongst the leading US Venture firms, about 5% of companies by cost have historically generated about 80% of returns by value.

The traditional US Venture model recognises this and preaches (1) a focus on investing as early as possible, preferably at the seed stage, (2) a focus on producing home runs, not medium-sized companies and (3) value add, which means the ability to contribute personal company-building skills on a hands-on basis.

The US model was not historically practised in Europe, but various European firms are now seeking to implement it, and have, in fact, been doing so for some years.

European firms have, in general, avoided the seed stage, which has been seen in Europe as an area of risk rather than as an area of opportunity.

The skills required for later stage Venture investing start to approach those relevant for Buyout firms, with financial skills becoming more important and technology and sector experience becoming less so.

9
How to Analyse Venture

We have seen that there are three main drivers of Buyout returns: earnings, earnings multiples and the use of debt (usually known as either leverage or gearing, depending on what side of the Atlantic you inhabit). These drivers arise naturally from the way in which Buyouts are transacted, and in particular they reflect the underlying financial engineering that can make the difference between an indifferent Buyout and a really exceptional one.

As we saw in the opening chapter, Venture Capital transactions have different characteristics and operate in a different way (debt, for example, is almost never present, at least in early-stage deals). Since the way in which their returns are generated also differs from Buyout, it follows that the drivers of those returns must themselves be different. So, what do we have to consider when looking at Venture firms and their transactions?

THE FUNDAMENTALS (1) – MONEY MULTIPLES

Let us note from the outset that removing the debt factor renders the basic arithmetic of Venture returns considerably simpler. In very basic terms, a Venture Capitalist buys shares in a company, hoping to be able later to sell those shares at a higher price, thus generating a profit. It is the relationship of the latter figure to the former (the price originally invested in the company in return for the shareholding) which generates the basic money multiple that lies at the heart of analysing Venture returns.

Remember that we looked earlier at the various ways in which the money multiples of funds can be expressed? There are two very important points to bear in mind as we start to consider how actually to use these in practice. The first is that whatever money multiple we decide to use at the fund level, it can only have been generated in gross terms by the money multiples achieved on the fund's underlying portfolio companies. Note the important qualifiation 'in gross terms' because, of course, before being made available to LPs there will be payments of management fees and (if and when appropriate) carried interest to be deducted first. The basic principle will always hold true, however. A Venture fund, just like a Buyout fund, can only ever be a composite of its individual transactions, and this is why we model them on a 'bottom up' basis.

The second point is that there is typically only one way of calculating the money multiple which is earned on a company and that is by looking at the actual amount paid out and the actual amount received. Distinctions such as total value, etc. have traditionally been accorded little significance at the company level. For the purposes of simplicity, and also with a view to keeping the discussion within the proper scope of this book, this view will be accepted, but a very brief digression may be in order to point out why this might be a slightly dangerous assumption to make.

We have seen above that the way in which Venture returns are made is by buying shares and selling them at a profit. Thus, the money multiple is essentially the ratio between those two numbers. All this is true. However, let us consider a couple of different situations where such a measure is either unavailable or potentially misleading.

The first one will become obvious if you stop and think about the way in which a Venture fund operates, and about the different ways in which we looked at fund-level multiples. What do we do about companies which are current investments within the fund's portfolio, but which have not yet been sold? We should not get drawn into a discussion at this stage about how they will be valued, because we are going to look at this in detail a little later, but let us just note for the moment that arguably everybody essentially assumes them to be worth what the Venture Capitalist says they are worth. Since, at the end of the day, they are going to be either written off or sold for some amount of money, little harm is done, since sooner or later we will know the real figure and be able to use it. Thus, everything comes out in the wash at the end of the day, but it does mean that both at the fund and the company level we can never be sure of exactly what the final multiple will be until the very last investment is fully exited.

The second situation arises from the way in which companies are exited, particularly in the US. Where a company is sold to a large corporation, then all or part of the consideration for the sale is typically in shares (stock) of the acquiring company. Where these are readily saleable and do not represent too large a proportion of the total float, then this will not raise any significant issue; the individual vendors can simply sell those shares and pocket the resulting cash. However, there may be legal restraints, either agreed at the time or arising thereafter which can delay things significantly. For example, the acquirer may decide, in the coming weeks or months, to issue new shares, and this can cause regulatory headaches if a Venture firm GP has been welcomed onto the board. Similarly they (and, by extension, their firm) may be barred from dealing in the company's shares at certain times, such as before publication of financial results.

If the portfolio company is exited by way of an IPO (flotation), then similar problems can occur with lock-up provisions, particularly in the US where these may well be regulatory, rather than contractual, in origin. Whatever the case, there may well be a period of considerable uncertainty before all the Venture fund's shares can be sold and the final price established. During the rampant equity market conditions of the late 1990s this could actually work to the Venture firm's advantage, since the shares would usually be sold for considerably more than their original exit valuation. However, the reverse could also be true; the author was personally involved in one Venture transaction where the cash actually received by some investors was only just over 10% of the price originally agreed.

So, let us accept the simplistic approach but subject to these reservations. Certainly anyone who wishes to analyse Venture funds on a sophisticated basis will be alive to these possibilities. At the end of the day, all that matters is the real number actually achieved, but there will always be those who either do not have the perception to realise this, or the patience to wait for it. In fairness, there will, of course, always be situations where LPs feel that they are forced to sell an existing interest (a 'secondary') for some reason or other and then, of course, this becomes a very major issue. We will examine this in more detail when we look specifically at the secondary market.

So, before we move on, let us be quite clear about what the money multiple is *at the company level*.[1] It is simply the ratio between the total cash invested in a company and the

---

[1]This is an important distinction. Many readers of the first edition grew confused about fund-level multiples (TVPI, etc) and company-level multiples (the V/C multiple). At the risk of stating the obvious, the former are used when comparing the performance of different funds, or of similar funds over time. The latter are used for evaluating the performance of single portfolio companies, or of building up a picture of a fund's portfolio of companies as a whole.

total cash realised by disposing of that interest, no matter how many individual cash flows may be involved. For example, if we pay a total of \$2.5M into a portfolio company and we eventually receive back \$5M, then the money multiple will be 2×. It is irrelevant for these purposes how many individual cash flows are involved, or over what period they take place, though this *will* become of great relevance when we move on to look at transaction IRRs.

THE FUNDAMENTALS (2) – VALUATION

Having touched on this above, let us now turn our full attention to the vexed question of valuation.

'Vexed' because this has always been one of the major reservations voiced about Venture returns (particularly in the US), since it is open to much abuse and uncertainty, even though this is usually innocently arrived at. These issues have been given new impetus by concern over the valuation of investment assets generally (which came to a head during the highly abnormal market conditions of September 2008) and what was seen by some as the inability of accounting standards around the world to reflect financial reality. The whole area of 'fair value' is currently the subject of active debate within the accounting community.

Valuation as an Element of Stated Returns

One hears many reasons (excuses?) for not investing in Private Equity funds. One of them is that Private Equity returns contain a large element of illiquid and therefore unrealisable capital gain, which is represented solely by a portfolio company having been written up by the GP. Similar accusations are levelled at asset classes such as Property (real estate). While this is undeniably true, particularly in the case of Venture and particularly in the US (specific valuation guidelines apply in Europe), it fails to grasp the true nature of Venture returns, what they represent and how they should be used.

Let us remember that annual returns are irrelevant when considering how to measure Private Equity fund performance, not least because one is a hostage to circumstances so far as the J-curve is concerned. All that matters are long-term compound returns over time and, as we have seen, these are conventionally expressed in vintage year terms. IRRs measure cash flows; that is what they are designed for and they cannot operate in any other way. Yes, while a fund is not yet fully divested it is necessary to assume that the current valuation of the existing investments will automatically occur as a cash flow at the end of the period in question, but in what other way could this be handled?

Property returns customarily adopt an annual return approach and break down the return into capital gain and rental yield. There are two problems with adopting this approach, however. The first is that with Private Equity, unlike Property, an investment is never made with the objective of creating an income stream,[2] but for generating a capital gain. Secondly, wherever we are concerned with a closed-end fund (and this applies to Private Property funds just as much as to Private Equity funds), then any notional but unrealised capital gain is essentially irrelevant, as it will sooner or later be realised and become a cash flow back to the investor. So it is entirely appropriate to adopt a cash flow measure such as an IRR to

---

[2] Except for certain types of mezzanine investment and even here this rarely tells the whole story.

analyse the overall return to the investor. (There is, in fact, an equally strong argument that compound returns should be adopted by Property and other types of investors, since to do otherwise ignores the time value of money.)

Private Equity funds comprise a stream of cash flows and the true return of a fund can only be measured in retrospect, once all cash flows have been mapped and analysed. Any true Private Equity professional, whether an LP or a GP, knows this. Attempts to impose mensural disciplines on a fund which has not yet run its full course may be necessary for financial accounting purposes, but they will rarely give a true picture of what may actually transpire; certainly they will give little clue to the timing of likely cash flows and it is, of course, this timing which will have a crucial effect on the final IRR. It is in precisely this area of uncertainty that secondary players seek out value. Thus, to criticise the stated returns of half-run funds as containing an element of unrealised valuation is analogous to criticising a long-distance lorry driver for being unable to give a precise ETA for a journey of several hundred miles. All he can do is to provide an estimate based on the time he has taken to cover a certain distance to date and his own experience of what sort of road and traffic conditions he is likely to encounter on the rest of his journey. Of course, the closer he gets to his destination in terms of time and distance, the more accurate his estimates will become, and it is precisely the same with Private Equity funds.

As we will see below, this is, in any event, much less of an issue in Europe than it is in the US, and there are measures which one can take to address unrealistic valuations in individual cases.

Differences in Valuation Approach between Europe and the US

It is generally believed that the Venture industry in the US is ahead of Europe in terms of its development, and this is undeniably true in most areas. When it comes to the field of valuation, however, Europe has led the way.

From the very early days of Private Equity in the UK, the BVCA operated valuation guidelines which had been prepared in consultation with accounting bodies, and similar guidelines were adopted by EVCA, who issued subsequent versions in 2005 and 2009. Sadly, each development seems to have led to less, rather than more, certainty.

Briefly, the original guidelines severely limited the ability of a GP to write up an investment, but provided various circumstances in which it *must* be written down by an arbitrary 25%. Note that there was typically no option here; it *had* to be written down by 25% if, for example, it missed its annual budget or other targets by a significant amount, and by further 25% tranches if similar circumstances re-occurred. Both subsequent sets of guidelines have replaced brevity and clarity with verbosity and obfuscation. Evidently drafted by committee (a phrase which might be thought of as almost an oxymoron), they talk at great length about the nebulous concept of 'fair value', and while they list a great number of things which '*may*' be considered or which '*might*' indicate a decrease or increase in value, they provide few of the obligatory admonitions that were a hallmark of the original version.

It is ironic to reflect that these new guidelines were apparently prepared for the benefit of the LP community. Why should any rational LP who may be concerned about the level of Venture valuations want guidelines which provide less, rather than more, certainty and more, rather than less, room for subjective manoeuvring by the GP?

It also seems to be rather bold to say that compliance with accounting standards can be achieved by following the new guidelines. For example, when dealing with fair value, the accounting standards have some very specific wording concerning 'impairment' in value of an investment as a result of 'a significant or prolonged decline' in its fair value below cost. For another thing, the guidelines say that if a fund was forced to sell an investment today, then that would be a distressed sale and not indicative of fair value, whereas there has been an ongoing argument within the accounting profession that precisely the opposite is the case. Indeed, this was the very issue that led to concerns over the valuation treatment of things like credit derivatives and corporate bonds in September 2008.

It should be stressed that this is, in any case, a somewhat academic debate of interest only to the accountants. As stated above, any experienced Venture fund LP will know exactly how much weight they can or cannot place on company valuations, and if they are uncomfortable with this, they will not commit to Venture funds in the first place. They are concerned with their compound return across the life of the fund, not with what somebody might think a particular three-week-old start-up is 'worth'. There is a very simple general rule: once a Venture investment has been fully exited, and you have all the proceeds actually sitting in your bank account as cash, then you know what it is worth; until then, you frankly have little idea.

At least in Europe there *are* guidelines issued by a reputable industry body after a great deal of discussion, and what they say is generally sensible. This is not the case in the US.

In the US guidelines exist too, but the difference is that these are of a purely advisory nature and many Private Equity firms do not adopt them. At least in Europe there is now almost universal acceptance that all Private Equity fund accounts will be prepared in accordance with the guidelines (and indeed this is usually a legal requirement imposed by the LPs as a matter of contract – it is most unlikely that any institutional investor would consider any fund which did not so undertake). The US guidelines are mistakenly referred to as the NVCA guidelines, but actually all NVCA has ever done is to issue a general letter of support; it has never formally endorsed or adopted them. They were instead prepared by a body called the Private Equity Industry Guidelines Group.[3] As these are neither mandatory nor widely adopted, there is little point in devoting any detailed discussion to them.

One point may be of interest, though. Under the US guidelines, a GP can quite legitimately write up the value of an investment *between* funding rounds, based on an expressed *expectation* of a future funding round being concluded at a particular value. Americans will doubtless argue that this is simply another example of them being able to show considerably more entrepreneurial initiative than Europeans.

Variability of Venture Valuations

Variability of valuation has been a particular problem in the US, though to be fair this became only pronouncedly so during the technology bubble and in its immediate aftermath. To give you a real life example, one American Fund of Funds manager during this period held, at

---

[3] www.peigg.org.

one point, three Venture funds which had participated in the same funding round in the same company. The three different funds had it valued in their audited year-end accounts at $960M, $480M and zero. Even more alarmingly, two of the three Venture groups involved had the same audit firm (so, a resounding raspberry here for the accountancy profession). This is, of course, an extreme example, but it does illustrate just how severe a problem this can be. How can the same company be valued at the same time by one Venture firm at $960M and by another at zero? And what is an LP to do when confronted by such wildly differing assessments? Specifically, what figure is the LP to adopt for inclusion it its own accounts (particularly as 'ask the auditors' does not seem to be a good approach)?

It was because of cases like this that many American LPs yearned for semi-compulsory valuation guidelines such as Europe already enjoyed, but it will be clear from the example given above that it hardly helped matters that the audit community was found wanting. In situations like this surely it is they who should take the lead. Sadly, far from doing so they seemed to go to extraordinary lengths to avoid taking any responsibility whatever, helped in many cases by the terms of the relevant LPA. It is not unknown, for example, for the GPs and the auditors to try to throw the burden of valuation onto the members of the advisory committee, who have no first-hand knowledge of the portfolio at all. Hopefully this is an area where progress will be made in the future. All it really needs is to have a provision in the LPA which says something to the effect of: 'in the event of any dispute or disagreement as to the valuation of any portfolio company, the auditors' view shall prevail' and then go on to detail what they should or should not take into account, perhaps even incorporating the EVCA guidelines by reference.

In fairness, there may be perfectly genuine commercial reasons for a GP not to want to write down the value of a company. They may, for example, be in the throes of negotiating a new funding round, or even a disposal of the business. However, when it comes to a question of what value should be placed on a set of audited accounts, then one runs the risk of straying into fairly dangerous territory.

Why have we focused on this issue when writing about Venture, but not about Buyout? The answer is that it is rarely anything like so difficult an issue. For one thing, there will almost always be a publicly available earnings multiple (or range of multiples) against which to compare a Buyout transaction. This approach is obviously irrelevant for a Venture company which is not yet making any profits; indeed the EVCA guidelines quite properly draw this very distinction.

Second, the range of valuations within which a company can fluctuate is obviously vastly different, and thus the scope of the problem is dramatically bigger with Venture deals. In an extreme case, a Venture fund might invest in a company at an initial post-money valuation of, say, $5M and see it grow to several billion dollars. The range within which a Buyout will fluctuate is much narrower, unless it is a turnaround, or perhaps unless something dramatic and unexpected happens in its business environment. Thus, it probably does not matter too much (at least during the life of the investment) if a Buyout transaction has an earnings multiple of 17 attached to it as opposed to 18. It *does* matter if a Venture company is valued at $960M as opposed to zero.

Finally, as we saw when we looked at the analysis of Buyout funds and transactions, debt makes a key contribution to Buyout returns and, in many cases, the enterprise value of a business may not actually change very much while the equity value could change considerably (due to acquisition debt being repaid). With Venture Capital, the enterprise value is the only value which matters (since debt is normally absent).

Pre-Money and Post-Money Valuations

Before we move on to discuss the nuts and bolts of how Venture returns are actually generated, it is important that we understand the difference between pre-money and post-money valuations, since this is a constant source of some confusion to those new to the asset class.

The distinction is best considered in the context of a single round of funding for a Venture company, and for the sake of argument let us assume that it is the B round, and that there has already been one round of financing (the A round). The pre-money valuation will be the valuation of the company upon which the B round is based, while the post-money valuation will simply be that figure plus the total amount contributed by the B round investors. Perhaps a simple example would be helpful.

Example 1

Suppose that the Venture company is looking for an additional $5M of funding, and that they agree, during the negotiations with the Venture Capitalists they have identified, a pre-money valuation of $8M. They can now calculate how much of the company's equity the new investors will require:

$$\frac{5}{13} \times 100\% = 38.46\%$$

Thus, in principle, the new investors will take 38.46% of the equity in the newly enlarged capital structure. The figure of $13M is the post-money valuation (the pre-money valuation of $8M plus the amount of new money being introduced of $5M).

There are three important points to note here. First, this is deliberately a very simplified example. In reality, things would be much more complicated than this. Certain investors, such as the entrepreneurs who comprise the key executives of the company, may well have anti-dilution rights which prevent their shareholding from ever falling below a certain percentage of the total. Others, typically those who come into later rounds, will have liquidation preferences (we will consider these in detail below). There may also be options attached to some of the shares (particularly those of the founders) and these will also be potentially dilutive.

Second, it is important to understand that the same investors do not participate pro rata in each round of the company. In particular, those who participate in the very early rounds, whether as entrepreneurs, angels or seed-stage Venture Capital funds, will rarely have the large amounts of money available which may be required to fuel the rapid growth of a potentially very large company. In any event, seed-stage funds will want to keep their money available to participate in other early-stage situations, not D and E rounds. This means that some dilution is inevitable (as we will discuss below) and will be built into their plans from the outset.

Third, it is not necessarily the case that the pre-money valuation of one round will be the same as the post-money valuation of the previous one; far from it, in fact. This uplift in valuation is one of the ways in which early-stage investors make their money and, indeed, the main financial argument for investing at an early stage in the first place. In the example given above, for instance, it is quite possible that the A stage was a $2M dollar round at a pre-money valuation of $3M. Thus, there has been an uplift from that post-money valuation ($5M) of $3M to the new pre-money valuation of $8M. Thus, there has already been an increase in the value of the A round investors' investment:

$$\frac{2}{5} \times \$5M = \$2M$$

$$\frac{2}{5} \times \$8M = \$3.2M$$

Thus, before the possibly diluting effects of the B round come into play, the A round investors have already made an unrealised potential gain of $1.2M, or 60% of their original investment. Their V/C (value over cost) multiple on that investment would be 1.6×. In practice they would now take some of the B shares themselves (perhaps half of them) to avoid excessive dilution.

Share Classes

To give expression to the various anti-dilution and liquidation preference provisions referred to above, a different class of shares in the company is typically created for the participants of each funding round, with the relevant protection being given effect as what lawyers term class rights (rights attached to a particular class of shares which cannot be varied except with the consent of the holders of that class of shares). Since any one investor may participate in different funding rounds, it is quite possible for them to end up with shares of several different classes in the same company.

By tradition, the shares issued for the A round are called A shares, the shares issued for the B round are called B shares, and so on.

THE FUNDAMENTALS (3) – COST AND VALUE

Having had fairly complicated discussions about the nature of Buyout returns, it may come as something of a relief to hear that when it comes to Venture we are concerned with such basic topics as cost and value. This initial view might well be mistaken, however. Once you can ignore the debt factor then Buyout returns, too, come down to little more than this, while the way in which cost and value are built up are actually much more complex in a Venture transaction, largely because, unlike the typical Buyout, a Venture company may go through several funding rounds, all at different values and on different terms.

Cost is, of course, a fairly straightforward concept. The cost of an investment is what we pay for it, and so we can and do calculate this simply by adding together all the various amounts which have been contributed by any one fund in the various funding rounds of that one company. However, it is important for us to be able to see how that cost figure has been built up, otherwise we will not be able to conduct any meaningful due diligence.

Thus, the 'cost' side of your model may well look something like this (Figure 9.1):

Let us just be clear what we are looking at. We are modelling an individual Venture fund, and within that we are modelling an individual Venture company. This part of the model is showing us essentially how much the fund has invested to date in that company (cost), what

Fund Name: Allstar Ventures III
Fund Size ($M): 220
Company Name: Crazy New Venture Inc.
Sector: Telecoms
Business description: High-speed optical routers for metro networking

Round	Pre ($000)	Amount ($000)	Post ($000)	%*	Cost ($000)	Co-investors
A	3000	2000	5000	20.0	1000	Baby Seed II
B	8000	5000	13 000	18.0	800	California Warriors IV, Baby Seed II

Total Cost: 1800
Fund %:   0.82

*This column is designed to show the *current* percentage of the company's total issued shares owned by the fund. It will therefore need to have something like the following sitting behind it in the model:

Round	#Shares Pre(000)	#Shares Round(000)	#Shares Post(000)	#Shares Taken(000)	#Shares To Date(000)	% Current
A	3000	2000	5000	1000	1000	20.0
B	5000	5000	10 000	800	1800	18.0

Figure 9.1   An explanation of what you might see in a GP's quarterly report

percentage of the company we currently own in return for that cost and what percentage of the fund as a whole this investment represents.

We can, in turn, use the percentage we own of the company to calculate our current value. Assuming that the valuation of the company has not increased since the time of the B round, we currently own 18% of a company which is valued at $13M. This values our holding at $2.34M, which, in turn, represents a money multiple of 1.3× on our current cost of $1.8M.

Is it really as easy as this? Well, no, actually it isn't. We are happily ignoring, for illustrative purposes, the potentially dilutive effects of any anti-dilution rights, liquidation preferences and options in the hands of either third parties or indeed of the fund which we are analysing. Thus, there would have to be yet another level sitting behind our model which calculated the possible effect of these based on the current value of the company. However, we run very quickly into three major problems here.

First, the full effect of them often cannot be properly appreciated until one knows the final exit value of the company. It may be advantageous to exercise options at one value but not at another, for example. Second, this is an extremely complicated process and many investors may well take the view that it really doesn't matter that much, since they will know at the end of the day exactly what cash multiple results, and in the meantime have a roughly accurate figure which is fine for their everyday monitoring and reporting purposes. Third, the information which you need will frequently simply not be available. The exact terms of funding rounds are usually not disclosed save to those who have signed the relevant documentation, and again the vast majority of LPs will neither need nor want the information, nor would they probably know what to do with it if they had it. Thus, as a matter of practice, most LPs simply ignore this aspect of things and adjust their figures on exit as necessary. Indeed, many LPs do not undertake even the level of analysis which you see set out in the above figure (though it is difficult to see how they can conduct any meaningful monitoring or due diligence without it).

We also need to remember that just as a Venture company may have several rounds of funding, so the exit rarely comprises one single cash flow. Either the company will be floated (IPO'd) and quoted shares may be held within the fund (or distributed in specie to LPs) and sold in tranches over a period of time, or the company may be bought for stock by a public company and a similar process will ensue. It is relatively rare for a Venture company to be bought for a single cash payment, particularly in the US.

Thus, our model will have to distinguish between money that has already been distributed to LPs or, to put it another way, value that they have already realised, and unrealised value that is still sitting within the fund as potential distributions that have not yet occurred. Just as the performance of a fund cannot be properly measured until the end of its life, so an individual investment in a portfolio company can only be properly analysed once there is no remaining value (in other words, once the company has been either fully exited or written off, and cash realised for LPs).

IRRs and Multiples

Discussion as to the timing of cash flows brings us rather neatly to the question of IRRs. You may be wondering why we have been talking about money multiples when analysing Venture transactions rather than IRRs. Well, the answer is that we look at both, but sophisticated investors have always realised that with Venture (and with Buyout too, in truth, but that is more difficult as Buyout LPs and GPs alike seem obsessed with IRRs), the multiple is what matters. If you can get the multiple right, then the IRR will take care of itself. The same is not necessarily true vice versa. Consider what may happen if a Private Equity transaction generates an IRR of 60% over a six-month period. This is all very well, but an LP is most unlikely to be able then to redeploy that money straight away in another Private Equity transaction offering a similar rate of return. On the contrary, the most likely outcome is that it will end up invested at a money market rate of return while some alternative use is found for it. We will come back to this point in a later chapter.

The other side of this particular coin is whether, given the choice, we should rather have the money invested at, say, 20% for ten years than 60% for six months. To say that what we should be concerned about is the money multiple rather than the IRR is simply another way of putting this. As a rough rule of thumb, a Venture fund was traditionally deemed a success if it generated a money multiple of 3×, but usually not if it did not. The ability to generate 3× on previous funds was therefore one of the main things you would be looking for when performing due diligence on a Venture group; those who slavishly rank funds purely by IRR would miss this point entirely.

However, IRR is obviously another valuable dial on the dashboard and our model should be calculating this both at the individual transaction level and also at the fund level (which will, of course, be lower because of the impact of fees and carried interest). Please remember, though, that while the closer one comes to the end of the fund, the more accurate IRR is likely to be as a measure of final performance, the early stages of the fund's life, when it is still subject to the undue influence of the J-curve, will tend to be much longer for a Venture fund relative to a Buyout fund because of the longer average holding periods. This measure should therefore be treated with extreme caution, perhaps for as long as the first eight years or so of a Venture fund's existence.

Let us look briefly at one or two individual components of our model and then turn to considering how the pattern of Venture returns is made up.

Going in Equity (GI%)

This is one of the two factors which make up the cost of any one round and the value of any total investment in a Venture company. Surprisingly, many LPs pay little attention to it, given its vital nature. There is little point in having an investment in a successful company unless one is going to be able to claim a major part of the spoils, and indeed experience shows that levels of equity ownership are a major driver of Venture fund returns. This is particularly important given that early-stage investors will not be able to invest pro rata in later rounds (and sometimes not at all) and must therefore plan both the level of their initial investment and also their strategy for dealing with the capital structure thereafter with this in mind. Traditionally, the very best US Venture firms aim to end up with no less than 20% of a company if at all possible.

We will be looking at this further in the chapter on due diligence, but consistently low levels of equity ownership are indicative of a firm which is (1) piggy-backing on other people's deals rather than sourcing its own, (2) attempting to limit its downside by investing in too many companies rather than looking to maximise its upside by concentrating on fewer and fewer potentially successful companies as the fund progresses or (3) whose fund size is too small to allow it to hold onto a decent equity position once other, larger, investors become involved. None of these are desirable qualities in the eyes of an LP.

Percentage of the Holding within the Fund

This is another key indicator which many LPs ignore. As we will see in a minute, Venture returns are driven by a very small number of very big winners, and there is little point in having a big winner which is not able to make a significant contribution to the overall fund return. As a rough rule of thumb, any one of these big winners (home runs) should be able to return the entire capital of the fund at least once, and since 25× is generally regarded as the hurdle multiple for a home run, this suggests a target of about 5% of the fund, in order to allow for the impact of fees and carried interest.

As we will see when we look at due diligence, one of the key indicators when looking at a Venture firm is the correlation between their biggest bets and their biggest winners. Putting a lot of money into poorly performing companies is indicative of bad judgement. Even worse, putting a small amount of money into very successful companies smacks of a lack of home-run mentality.

Putting a good proportion of your capital into successful companies, on the other hand, speaks not only of being able to choose the right companies behind which to throw the main thrust of your efforts, but also of knowing which companies to kill, and doing so as early as possible.

THE IMPACT OF HOME RUNS

This is the one issue which is fundamental to a proper understanding of Venture Capital; indeed, it is probably the single most important issue to understand in the whole field of Private Equity and so would probably justify a whole chapter (if not a book!) to itself. It is also the one issue which has traditionally most divided the Private Equity industry; there used to be many European LPs, for example, who found the whole concept just too much to stomach, though hopefully this is slowly changing.

We have already looked briefly at the 'US Venture model' and so you will already have an understanding of what a home run is. It is an investment which can return the whole capital of the fund at least once, and a 25× multiple is usually accepted as a proxy for that level of performance.

We also looked in the last chapter at what it means to have a home-run mentality, and there is no need to repeat any of that here. What we need to look at now is the impact which home runs have on Venture returns. There is an immediate difficulty here in that data on individual Venture companies is not as widely available as they are for Venture funds, and what data there is tend to be relatively recent in origin. However, the industry owes a huge debt of gratitude to leading US Fund of Funds manager Horsley Bridge, whose US funds specialised throughout the 1990s in almost nothing but early-stage Venture, and whose in-house database is therefore almost certainly the best repository of Venture company information in the world. While, of course, they cannot do anything which might identify individual funds or companies, they do occasionally release into the public domain summaries of their data on a 'blind' basis, and Figure 9.2 has been widely seen and discussed.

Let us be clear what we are looking at. The figures are drawn from a portfolio of many leading US Venture funds for the period leading up to 2000. It can therefore be argued that they may not be taken as a valid prediction of what will happen in the future, since at least the last three years or so of that period represented abnormal 'bubble' conditions. Actually, this objection is of only limited validity, since many of the greatest money multiples in the Horsley Bridge portfolio occurred before 1998 and were genuine Technology companies, rather than 'dot com' businesses, but let that go. It is not necessarily intended as any sort of prediction of the distribution of future Venture returns. It is, however, undoubtedly an accu-

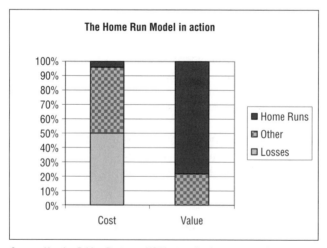

Source: Horsley Bridge Partners, US Venture fund programme based on figures to 2000

Figure 9.2   The home run in action

rate record of a period of many years' fine performance by nearly two hundred different Venture funds, and shows admirably the way in which the home-run model works in action.

The first thing to note is that roughly 50% of all Venture companies will fail. One of the hardest things with which Venture GPs and LPs alike struggle to come to terms is that this is no reflection on anyone's abilities as a Venture Capitalist; it is just the way the awful arithmetic of the Venture model works out. Even if you are the best Venture Capital firm in the world, there is every chance that 50% of your companies by cost will fail to return their capital. However, this doesn't matter, and if you take a look at the home runs category, you will see instantly why it doesn't matter.

The home runs represent less than 5% of companies by cost. Yet, this 4% by cost creates nearly 80% of the value. The stark reality is that, provided you can capture a home run, it is almost completely irrelevant what happens to the other 95% of the portfolio by cost. Yes, the remaining 95% or so make some contribution, but only about 20% of the total. It is the home runs, and the home runs almost alone, which drive Venture returns.

For example, Kleiner Perkins, perhaps the best known of the leading US Venture firms, is rumoured to have bought 25% of Netscape at a post-money valuation of about $20M, to see the company later acquired (having first gone public) by AOL for $4 billion. There are many other examples, and Kleiner Perkins is far from the only firm to have achieved these sorts of multiples on individual deals, but it will give you some idea of the scale of what can be achieved.

This is why home-run mentality is so important, and this is why arguably the main thing you really need to look for in a Venture firm (if you are an LP) is the ability to score home runs. Almost nothing else matters. Every successful Venture fund in history has included at least one home run. One will frequently hear, during industry discussions, comments such as 'oh yes, that was their Ciena fund'; in other words, the fund will often be associated in people's minds with, and thus identified by, the particular home run company which it featured.

We talked in the last chapter, for example, about the way in which many US Venture firms have withdrawn from Life Science activity. One of the main reasons for this was that it was perceived as much more difficult (certainly this is what experience suggested, anyway) to score a home run in that area compared to IT or Telecoms. The European experience, as we noted, has been rather different.

We also need to be aware that there is, in some parts of the world, considerable scepticism as to whether the home-run model constitutes a sustainable model of Venture investment. In the more traditional corridors of European Venture investing, for example, there is deep unease with such a fundamentally binary approach, and a contrary view that returns can and should be earned more evenly across the whole portfolio.

In part this stems from a different cultural background in some countries, particularly amongst, say, the over-fifties. In these more enlightened times it may come as a shock to some younger Europeans to know that only a few years ago the general rule in many European countries, including the UK, was that if you had been a director of a company which had gone into liquidation or receivership, then you could actually be banned for several years from becoming a director of another company; there was very considerable stigma attached to insolvency and corporate failure. Fortunately, a much healthier viewpoint has spread from the US, which sees a failed business venture as worthwhile experience, a campaign medal to be worn with some pride. For example, a study in about 1999 showed that the CEOs of most NASDAQ flotations had previously been the CEO of two failed companies.

However, old habits die hard and the traditional European mindset led to an undoubted reluctance to kill struggling companies and this, combined with a lack of value add skills compared to the US, contributed to a widespread failure by the European industry to generate the number (and scale) of home runs which it needed to establish a record of healthy historic returns. We will look at this area in much more detail in the next chapter.

One small personal recollection may perhaps serve to illustrate this point. The author used to be in the position of monitoring the performance of Venture funds both in the US and in Europe. It seemed in general that the quarter of the year in which companies were written off was fairly random in the US, whereas in Europe there was a heavy concentration in the fourth quarter. This suggests very strongly that in Europe the imperative to kill a company was being largely driven by accounting considerations (i.e. the need to agree the necessary figures for the audited accounts) rather than strategic issues of portfolio management.

The historic figures seem to show very clearly that the Europeans simply got it wrong, and that trying to draw intellectual distinctions about the basic concepts is largely irrelevant. The US experience shows overwhelmingly that the home-run model is valid, and indeed will ultimately impose itself upon any Venture market given the right GP skills and enough capital. It is increasingly being accepted that it can, and indeed does, work not just in America but anywhere in the world given the right legal and regulatory environment.

In particular, an increasing number of European Venture firms (generally the smaller and the newer) are embracing it enthusiastically. It may be significant that it seems to be the smaller and newer European firms that are attracting people with genuine entrepreneurial experience as former company founders, and that it is these operating skills (previously largely absent from European Venture firms) which are required to provide the sort of value add which will allow the home-run model to work successfully. Current developments in Asia, for example in India, give further reassurance that the US Venture model is robust and capable of being readily transplanted.

Ironically, it is precisely this historic strength and success of the US Venture industry which may prove ultimately to have spawned its Achilles heel. The size of the US as a homogenous market, and its willingness eagerly to embrace entrepreneurial activity, has led many to the dangerous belief that it is the only Venture market which matters. It isn't; it just happens to be the easiest. In their failure to recognise that Venture is a global business may perhaps be found the fatal flaw which will be exploited over time by firms operating in other parts of the world, and adopting a more international approach. Predictions are always dangerous, but it is entirely possible that the next generation of golden circle Venture Capitalists will be not those who restrict their scope to an hour's drive from Palo Alto, but firms which operate collaboratively on a global basis. A significant challenge, certainly, but then isn't that what Venture Capital is all about?

SUMMARY

Venture deals, unlike Buyout transactions, typically do not involve debt and so the analysis process is, at first sight, much simpler, at least at the most basic level.

However, the mechanics of Venture returns are, in fact, very complex, since several funding rounds will usually be involved, and each on different terms. The ability to model this, though, is usually restricted by the level of available information.

The basic drivers are the post-money valuation of the round concerned (with the first round in which the fund participates obviously having the most impact) and the percentage of the company's equity which a fund holds.

By far the most important measure of Venture performance is the money multiple. This is known as the V/C multiple (value over cost) and represents the ratio of the total amount of cash generated by an investment to the total amount of cash invested.

IRR is also important, not least for charting the progress of the J-curve, but is largely meaningless in the early to mid stages of a fund – even more so than for Buyout, given the longer average holding periods of Venture funds, and the extreme uncertainty of outcome relating to any individual portfolio company.

Valuation of current investments is much more of an issue for Venture funds than for Buyout, and there have been some extreme variations of approach and procedure, particularly in the US, which have given rise to concern. However, this is probably more of an accounting issue than an investment returns issue.

Historically, European Venture was subject to strict peremptory valuation guidelines while US Venture was not. With the publication of new guidelines in Europe, the situation appears less clear cut going forward. However, the principles behind the EVCA guidelines in Europe are sensible, and the guidelines themselves have been universally adopted.

Home runs have driven Venture returns in the past, and there seems little reason why they should not continue to do so in the future. Historically, less than 5% of companies by cost have generated nearly 80% of final fund value. What happens to the other 95% is largely irrelevant. About 50% of all Venture companies will fail to return their capital. Thus, analysis of Venture funds should concentrate on illuminating the ability (or otherwise) of the relevant Venture Capital team to score home runs.

As well as examining what percentage of a company's equity is held by a fund, one needs also to look at what percentage of the fund itself is represented by any one investment. There is little point in having a company which returns 25× if it is only 1% of the fund.

10

Venture Returns

Just as we examined the historic returns that have actually been earned by Buyout funds, we will now do the same for Venture. Some of the issues which we will be examining will be similar, but some will be rather different. How can we explain the different returns that have been earned in different geographic areas, specifically Europe and the US? Are the European figures really as bad as they appear to be? Is there any correlation between returns and fund size? Can we dig a little more deeply into how returns are influenced by the stage at which one invests? Are the historic figures a good guide to future performance?

US OUTPERFORMANCE VERSUS EUROPE

The really big issue here is the radical difference between the historic returns of Venture funds in Europe and the US. Take a look at Figure 10.1, which shows the historic returns during the 1990s measured by capital weighted IRR.

Look at the huge extent by which US Venture outperformed European Venture during the decade. It looks as though the 'European Buyout and US Venture' mantra really was justified throughout the 1990s. Remember, too, that we are here looking at the capital weighted average rather than the upper quartile fund, which most people in the industry would consider a more realistic measure. Figure 10.2 shows that this difference is even more dramatic.

The conclusion is inescapable. Not only has US Venture as a whole outperformed European Venture significantly throughout the decade, but the best US funds outperformed their European counterparts quite dramatically. We need to consider not only these figures but also the implications and issues which lie behind them to see if they can help us understand just how and why this should have happened.

In this one area we are going to have to dig into the figures rather more deeply than we have hitherto, because one of the issues here is the extent to which the data population is representative and statistically significant. We will see, when we do that, that the contrast between European and US Venture returns is not actually as stark as it might at first appear. However, let us leave this to one side for the moment. Nobody can deny that, throughout the 1990s, there was dramatic outperformance by US Venture, and we need to analyse this so we can better understand it.

Money Multiples Drive IRRs

It is usually money multiples that drive IRRs. Let us see if this is so in this case.

Figure 10.3 clearly suggests a direct connection between higher money multiples and higher IRRs. In fact, there is very high correlation for this period between the capital weighted average TVPI and the capital weighted average IRR for both Europe and the US. In other words, the ability to score high money multiples appears to drive high IRRs, just as we suspected, and this seems to be so in both regions.

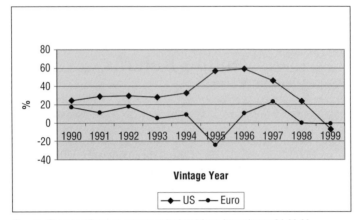

Source: Thomson Reuters, returns calculated from inception to 31.03.09

Figure 10.1   CWA Venture IRRs

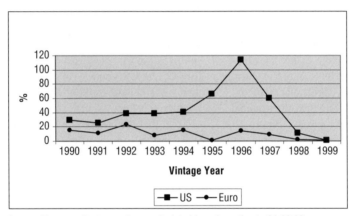

Source: Thomson Reuters, returns calculated from inception to 31.03.09

Figure 10.2   Upper Quartile Venture IRRs

As we have observed many times in the book already, it is multiples that drive IRRs, and not the other way round, at least not directly. The desire to chase a high IRR can result in GPs baling out of an investment before they should, which may, of course, result in a lower multiple than might otherwise be the case. Remember the earlier example of asking you to consider which you would prefer: 60% IRR for six months or 25% IRR for six years? The sophisticated LP will, of course, choose the latter, but a GP who is about to go out fundraising might be tempted to opt for the former. This is an extreme example, but deliberately chosen so that the difference is obvious. More usually in practice it will be a more subtle question of degree.

This example is strictly irrelevant, though, since it requires some form of conscious human intervention. The principle here is that in the absence of any intentional alteration of events,

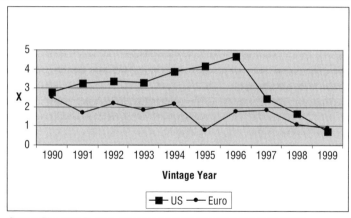

Source: Thomson Reuters, returns calculated from inception to 31.03.09

Figure 10.3   CWA Venture TVPI

it is the multiple that will drive the IRR, rather than vice versa. The third of the figures above supports this view. We can accordingly safely advance the hypothesis that the outperformance achieved by US Venture during the 1990s was actually a manifestation of an ability to achieve high money multiples. Further, if we remember what we said about home runs, it must specifically have been a manifestation of the ability to score home runs. Sadly, that degree of data is not publicly available at the company level, but we may be able to find echoes of it in the data which we *do* have available at the fund level.

Home Runs and the Golden Circle

First, though, a little background: US Venture returns have not only been driven by a relatively very small number of big winners at the company level, but also by a relatively small number of big winners at the fund level (which have been essentially those funds in which the big winners at the company level have been present). These funds have, in turn, been managed by a relatively small number of Venture firms, generally known as the 'golden circle'. While no two Venture industry professionals will agree on precisely the same list of names to include, there is general consensus on who is or is not likely to figure on the list, and it may be as few as a dozen names, and certainly no more than a couple of dozen. It is not suggested that the funds managed by these firms consistently outperform time after time; on the contrary, what research has been done suggests that it is extremely difficult for any two consecutive funds managed by the same Venture firm both to outperform. It is more a general pattern of outperformance, probably about two or three funds out of every five.

These observations are based on personal experience of the industry rather than on any hard, publicly available data but they are broadly correct. In other words, if you had been able consistently to select (and access, which is another point entirely) funds managed by the golden circle, then you would have scored very dramatic returns from your Venture fund portfolio, whereas if you had not been able to select or access these funds, then your returns would have been significantly lower, even if most of your fund picks had been in the upper quartile. As Phil Horsley, the founder of Horsley Bridge, memorably remarked: 'Venture is an upper decile game'. Indeed, many believe that it is the absence of this annual cluster of golden-circle-type returns that has been the major factor in the differential between historic US and European returns.

What we need to try to do, therefore, is somehow to isolate and consider the track record of the (few) very best US Venture funds in each vintage year, since it is here that the home runs are most likely to have been scored. Unfortunately, lack of transparency again arises to thwart our efforts, since the publicly available data in the Thomson Reuters system do not allow one to identify the performance of individual named funds. However, we do know which individual funds make up the sample population in each vintage year, which allows a few educated guesses to be made, and we do know the performance of both the best and the upper quartile funds: in others words we know the spread of the upper quarter of the population since we know both its top and its bottom.

Table 10.1 shows the top and bottom of the upper quartile by TVPI for each of the vintage years we have been considering, and a 'short list' of golden circle candidates from within that year, any one of which may well be represented by the 'maximum' figure. Figures are for US Venture funds, with the data being drawn as usual from Thomson Financial's Venture Xpert system.

You will see that in seven out of the nine vintage years under review there was at least one US Venture fund that returned a very substantial double-digit multiple. In fact, given the very large gap between the top and the bottom of the upper quartile, it is reasonable to assume that in each of those vintage years there were, in fact, three or four that outperformed in this

Table 10.1   Upper Quartile US Venture Analysis by TVPI (x)

Vintage Year	Maximum (Top of UQ)	(Bottom of UQ)	Golden Circle Shortlist
1991	5.7	3.6	Austin Ventures III, IVP V, Sierra IV, Sutter Hill Ventures
1992	16.0	3.6	Highland II, Kleiner Perkins VI, Matrix, Mayfield VII, Mohr Davidow III, Oak V, Sevin Rosen IV
1993	28.0	2.7	Accel IV, Hummer Winblad II, NEA VI, Sequoia VI
1994	13.7	4.7	ARCH II, Battery III, IVP VI, Kleiner Perkins VII, Mohr Davidow IV
1995	21.9	4.6	Benchmark I, Charles River VII, Doll I, Foundation I, Matrix IV, Mayfield VIII, Mohr Davidow V, Sevin Rosen V
1996	19.6	6.0	Accel V, Geocapital IV, Highland III, IVP VII, Kleiner Perkins VIII, Mayfield III Sequoia VII, USVP V, Worldview I
1997	15.8	2.6	Benchmark II, Charles River VIII, Greylock IX, Mayfield IX, Menlo VII
1998	17.7	1.7	Accel VI, Benchmark III, Foundation II, Highland IV, IVP VIII, Matrix V, Mayfield IV, Sequoia VIII, Sevin Rosen VI
1999	5.6	1.0	Accel VII, Battery V, Benchmark IV, Charles River IX and X, Doll II, Kleiner Perkins IX, Mayfield X, Mohr Davidow VI, Sequoia IX, Sevin Rosen VII, WPG V

way. It is these funds that one needed to capture to achieve the sort of returns that were, in fact, achieved by a small number of Private Equity fund LPs in the US during the 1990s. You will see also that, although for the sake of completeness we have included golden circle candidates for 1991 and 1999, the scale of their success at the fund level is not in the same league as for the vintage years comprising the rest of the decade.

There are probably different reasons for this. 1999 was, of course, the last vintage year under review completely to encapsulate the technology and Internet bubble. One would therefore expect performance to be disappointing, given that many investments would have been made at high valuations and then either written off or sold a considerable time later at written-down values. Take a look at the upper quartile TVPI and you will see the stark reality: any GP who returns committed capital on a 1999 vintage year Venture fund will be doing well. To make any significant return would be heroic indeed.

1991 is a different matter. The truth here may be partly that 1991 vintage year funds were too early to capitalise on the huge ramp in company values which occurred during the 1990s. It is also partly that at this time a lot of Venture firms in the US were still transacting a mix of Life Science and Technology deals, and we have already heard that the former performed disappointingly in general. Indeed, it was the fear that these were dragging down overall fund returns that led many American GPs to withdraw from the field and/or to hive off their Life Science teams as separate firms. The final reason is a purely statistical one. The sample population for the 1991 vintage year is only 41 funds, compared with 125 (though out of a possible population of 544 – see below) for fund year 2000. In part this reflects the explosion in Venture activity which took place during the late 1990s, but it may also be a symptom of the fact that collecting fund data was still in its comparative infancy in 1991 and there was considerable resistance to the idea of making performance data public, even on a blinded basis as Thomson Reuters do.

At the end of the day, though, 1991 is probably a very good example of the principle we have been examining. The fact is that not a single fund was closed in 1991 by a clear-cut golden circle candidate, save for a very small ($5.4M) expansion fund by Sevin Rosen. It may well be, therefore, that this provides yet more evidence to suggest that, without the presence of the golden circle, Venture returns will indeed struggle to find break-out performance. Perhaps significantly, the maximum TVPI for both the previous vintage years (when there *were* golden circle firms closing funds) is higher, and the upper quartile TVPI is lower, suggesting significant outperformance by one or two funds within the upper quartile.

Market Conditions

It is tempting to seek to explain US outperformance during the 1990s solely by reference to the amazing market conditions which flourished during the second half of the decade. We have already seen what happened to PE ratios during this period: the S&P PE ratio peaked at nearly 35 in 1999. While it is not strictly relevant to talk about PE ratios in the context of Venture companies, since few have any earnings, this is nonetheless indicative of what happened to equity valuations generally. At the end of 1990 the NASDAQ index stood at a lowly 374, while by the end of 1999 it had risen to 4069. That is why it is tempting to seek to dismiss such outperformance on the grounds that 'a rising tide lifts all ships'. If the equity market which provides your main exit route and your main exit valuation benchmark rises more than tenfold in a decade, then, the argument runs, you would have to have been pretty stupid not to score good returns even if only by accident. Kleiner Perkins, for example, was reputed to have earned a transaction IRR in excess of 50 000% on its investment in Amazon. com based on 1999 stock prices.

However, this argument is simplistic and pays little regard (or respect) to the very real skill base which exists among the best US Venture Capitalists. Yes, by the end of the decade valuations had risen to ridiculous levels for companies which had absorbed, in some cases, hundreds of millions of funding and had yet to turn a profit (and in many cases were based on a business plan that was unlikely *ever* to produce any significant profits). Yes, this was a genuine bubble and, yes, experienced and skilful Venture Capitalists who should have known better fell for its siren call in much the same way as others did, but much was achieved that was genuine and cannot be explained by this simplistic analysis.

Genuinely superb companies were created which stood the test of time and are today acknowledged global leaders, many of which are solid Technology businesses, such as Cisco, Sun, Intuit and Lotus, in addition to Internet success stories such as Google, AOL, eBay and Amazon. These are high quality companies which would have succeeded in any equity market environment because they were based on sound business principles and run by highly talented individuals. Yet the 'value add' which their Venture Capital backers provided also played an essential role in their success.

Thus, while it is undeniable that market conditions boosted US Venture returns during this period, high quality companies, and the high quality Venture Capitalists who backed them, would have thrived in any conditions, and still produced good (though not so exaggerated) returns. It is worth stating, for the sake of balance, though, that the argument does have some relevance in two specific areas.

First, the spectre of almost unbelievable Venture returns drew a large number of new investors into the marketplace. In 1991 $1.9 billion was raised by US Venture funds. This had risen to $60 billion by 1999 and in fact peaked at nearly double that amount in 2000 – a sixty-fold increase in just ten years – though the true figures for 2000 have since been obscured by fund size adjustments. There were only two ways in which this much money could be accommodated. Existing firms increased their fund sizes (in some cases to $1.5 billion – more or less the whole amount that had been raised by just 40 funds in 1991) and many new entrants came into the market (contrast those 42 funds in 1992 with 544 in 2000). This massive influx of new capital, much of it in unskilled hands, acted like air being sucked into the bottom of a furnace and fuelled the massive bubble which grossly inflated Venture company valuations. It is fair to say that while this happened in Europe to some extent, it was not on anything like the same scale. Valuations never reached the peaks they had scaled in the US and, more importantly, everything was a year or two later, which meant that the scope for making high returns by getting into bubble-type companies and out of them again in time before the market collapsed was more limited.

Second, there is no doubt that the absence of anything like NASDAQ was a severe drawback for European Venture Capital firms, and had a definite negative impact on their returns. In retrospect, Europeans should have invited (even implored) NASDAQ to come to Europe with a view to creating a global exit market for Venture companies. A welcome corollary to this would have been that on their coat-tails might have come most of the leading US Venture firms, setting up offices in Europe (as it is only a very few have done so – see below). Instead, the Europeans decided to try to create their own version of NASDAQ. Named EASDAQ, it was a sad failure which only ever attracted a handful of companies and, like all such pan-European projects, became a highly political affair, with nobody being prepared to admit defeat. Ironically NASDAQ was invited to take a controlling interest in it in 2001, by which time the damage had been done and European Venture firms had been denied (though in theory they could have relocated their companies to the US, as Israeli Venture firms did, in order to take advantage of NASDAQ) access to NASDAQ exactly when they could most have profited from it.

Nor does the London Stock Exchange emerge particularly well from the story. Two attempts at providing junior markets, The Third Market and the Unlisted Securities Market, both took hold but were then abruptly closed down by the LSE for no good apparent reason, leading to great scepticism about the LSE's commitment to this area. Ironically, AIM, the LSE's latest offering, has now become what EASDAQ was intended to be and until the onset of the financial crisis attracted IPO candidates from all over the world, including the US. It is a sad indication of just what an opportunity might have been missed as a result of the LSE's arbitrary actions in the past.

EUROPEAN VENTURE – IS IT AS BAD AS IT SEEMS?

The answer to this is 'no', but understanding why it is 'no' requires an explanation of a few things.

We have already discussed a couple of factors (NASDAQ and the bubble) which artificially boosted US Venture returns, thus making European returns look worse in relative terms. We have also discussed the very different skill sets which would have ensured that in any event US Venture would have outperformed European Venture during the 1990s. None of this is in issue. US Venture Capital firms (particularly the golden circle) achieved some amazing things during the 1990s and deserve many congratulations for having done so. We will probably never see the like of those returns again.

However, when we come to look at how European Venture performed in absolute terms, we hit an immediate problem with the available data. Following the publication of the first edition of this book some thought this a controversial topic, but the facts are clear and bear repeating. The industry figures for European Venture include a lot of funds that simply should not be there, and they do this to such an extent that the resulting figures cannot be taken as any valid measurement of European Venture returns.

A lot of this is not the fault of the data providers, and has indeed resulted from excess zeal rather than lack of it. Many very small seed and development funds, usually operating on a very localised basis, and frequently either governmental (local or national) or attached to an academic institution, have been rightly anxious that they should be listed in the Thomson Reuters database. Arguably these are not even practising 'Venture Capital' in the true sense anyway, but whatever the case virtually none of them would be eligible for investment by institutional LPs in any event, either because of their size or their nature. In a market the size of the US, for example, this would not matter very much, though it would introduce some statistical 'noise' into the system, but within a much smaller sample population it matters very much indeed. The average number of European Venture funds tracked in the five vintage years from 1992 to 1996, for example, is only 14; within such a small sample, any sampling error can potentially have a very significant effect.

In addition to these very small quasi-developmental type funds, there are funds run by entities such as banks, media companies and industrial groups which, even if they are technically open to outside investors, would not generally be considered (sophisticated LPs invest only with independent professional firms, to the extent that the merest possibility of any outsider being able to exert influence, either in investment decisions or otherwise, will usually bestow the kiss of death). There are also funds which would be ineligible because of their legal nature; VCTs, for example, are tax-friendly vehicles aimed at British retail investors.

In the first edition, we notionally stripped all these inappropriate funds out of the universe to leave only those which were institutional-grade European Venture funds. The difference really was very dramatic. Even in the best year (1997) only 15 out of the stated 43 funds were eligible, while the average number of eligible funds for any one of the vintage years under consideration was just 27%. Putting this the other way round, we could state that in the average vintage year the figures were 73% inaccurate by number of funds. Needless to say, this was a pretty staggering result, and underlined the fact that, in this one area, the database broke down, and that its numbers could in no way be seen as representative of real life European Venture performance.

In fairness, the total number of funds covered by the system for each of these vintage years has been reduced since then, but while it is impossible to know for certain, since individual fund data is not available, it still seems highly likely that the database is not properly representative of European Venture performance.

So, where does this leave us? If we cannot rely on the figures, what can we do instead? Well, there are a few pointers. First, look at the figures achieved by the 'maximum' fund in each vintage year:

Clearly, there must have been at least one European Venture fund in each vintage year that achieved stand-out performance. The figures shown in Table 10.2 would be completely acceptable as the performance measures of any quality US Venture fund, and in some years (e.g. 1996 and 1997) are the sort of figures that could be achieved by one of the golden circle firms in the US. Thus, it is facile to suggest, as many do, that it is simply not possible to earn decent Venture returns in Europe. Not only is it possible, but people have actually done it.

The question, of course, is 'who?' Unfortunately the figures do not help us very much here as they are 'blinded'. It could be suggested that as we are, for the most part, concerned only with about a quarter of the data, then we should take the upper quartile figure as essentially the bottom of the range, but there can be no guarantee that the quarter with which we are concerned is indeed all clustered within the upper quartile. Just as there is undoubtedly at least one fund in each vintage year which has outperformed, there must surely be others which have underperformed.

Table 10.2   Performance of the best recorded European Venture fund

Year	TVPI(x)	IRR(%)
1990	11.2	54.9
1991	3.3	36.2
1992	2.8	26.2
1993	6.6	43.8
1994	4.5	28.3
1995	3.2	200.1
1996	11.2	88.8
1997	10.0	262.0
1998	9.2	194.1
1999	2.9	357.2

Source: Thomson Reuters

However, experience suggests very strongly that if one is comparing institutional quality funds against non-institutional quality funds, then the former are more likely to have over-performed than underperformed. Thus, it is very probable that most of them will indeed be in the upper quartile, at least half of them anyway. So, if you were approaching the problem with a very broad brush, it is almost certain that the stated upper quartile is, in fact, more of a median, and probably even below that.

At the same time, there could well be an opposite problem with the figures in respect of US Venture, in that underperforming funds may simply stop submitting their data and drop out of the population. This is known as survivorship bias. For example, the fundraising figures show that 544 US Venture funds held closings in 2000, yet only 125 of them still submit performance data.[1] It is thus entirely possible that what the 'industry' figures show are, in fact, not the performance of the industry as a whole at all, but rather the performance of something approximating the upper quartile.

In other words, it may be strongly arguable that if one wishes to look at the whole universe of institutional-grade, professionally managed Venture funds, the available figures under-state, by some significant measure, the European performance, while over-stating the American. To put it another way, it may not be too fanciful to suggest that a fairer comparison might be to graph the European stated upper quartile TVPI against the US stated median (Figure 10.4).

Rough and ready though such an approach may be, it may well be that the position it sug-gests is not unrealistic. Yes, US Venture still outperformed during the middle of the decade but perhaps the scale of it was not quite as dramatic as may appear at first blush. For the rest of the decade, European Venture seems to have been very competitive in terms of the money multiples it generated.

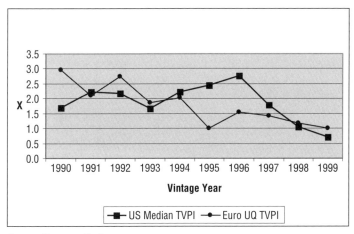

Source: Thomson Reuters

Figure 10.4   A fairer comparison?

---

[1] The Thomson Reuters VentureXpert website acknowledges that the sample Venture funds collected represent only 25.9% of the universe by number, or 29.4% by capital.

We are straying into dangerous territory here, since we are now largely in the realm of supposition, yet when the official figures fail us we have little alternative, and it seems preferable at least to make some attempt at independent thought rather than, as many in the industry do, simply to accept the figures at face value and never even wonder about what may lie behind them. Many will argue that such an approach may flatter actual European Venture returns. However, if it does, then it probably does not do so by very much, and certainly not by as much as the official figures seem to underestimate them.

One other point to bear in mind before we leave this issue and move on is that there is undoubtedly much greater variation in European Venture returns than in American, and in Europe this is concentrated within a much smaller sample. In other words, it must be true that in Europe there is a much greater proportion of funds which make truly awful returns than in the US. In the figures for US Venture, for example, there is only one vintage year in which a fund has made -100% since records began, whereas the European figures show five, and this within a much smaller sample. What does this mean? Simply that in Europe, manager selection is even more important than in the US. This has understandably led to European Venture gaining a reputation as by far the most difficult of the various Private Equity classes, and to many LPs deciding that they simply do not want to be involved with it.

RETURNS AND FUND SIZE

Let us now repeat the exercise which we carried out for Buyout funds by looking at the relationship between historic Venture returns and average fund size. Let us look first at Europe. Figure 10.5 shows the capital weighted average TVPI achieved in each vintage year between 1990 and 1999 against the average fund size of the same vintage year.

This seems to suggest a definite sweet spot in terms of fund size at about $150M, both below and above which returns will suffer. So far as very small funds are concerned, experience does indeed suggest that they tend to fare badly. They are unable to follow-on when

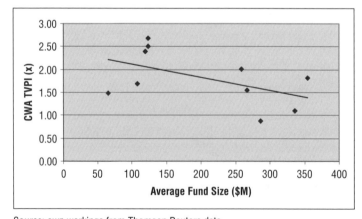

Source: own workings from Thomson Reuters data

Figure 10.5   European Venture vintage years 1990 to 1999: fund size versus performance

other, bigger, sources of funding get involved at later stages and tend to get excessively diluted. Also, they are less likely to be trying to grow really large companies, in part because that is often not their raison d'être (they may, for example, be a university seed fund) and in part because they rightly identify in such efforts a high chance of (as they see it) unnecessary dilution. I can therefore happily accept that there is an efficient fund size in Europe below which returns will suffer; indeed this is currently a very real issue, with even high quality European Venture firms struggling to raise money.

At the other end of the scale, though, I think one needs to be a little more careful about accepting the figures at face value. We have to remember that these figures are highly questionable, particularly when we start talking about average fund size. There are, for example, a number of funds within the database where the fund size is stated as zero, which must inevitably skew the resulting averages. My own personal instinct is that the ideal Venture fund size, certainly for those operating at the seed and early stages, is probably about $250M, so that these figures probably all need shifting notionally to the right as you look at the graph. We will talk a little more about large fund sizes in a moment when we examine the US figures, since the issue is much more relevant there, but certainly there is a point beyond which returns will suffer, if only because a large fund size will inevitably push one's investment focus towards the later stages.

Because these figures seem to be somewhat skewed by false 'zero' fund sizes, I think it be may be more useful to look at returns versus total capital raised in any one vintage year, as Figure 10.6 shows for vintage years 1990 to 1999. Again, I am conscious that such an approach is far from perfect. It ignores, obviously, the number of funds that were raised and the sectors and stages for which the capital was intended. However, if we do not have the data which we need, then we have to make the best of what we do have, and it strikes me that this will at least give us some indication of possible over-capacity in the system.

We have to be careful about what conclusions we draw here, since we cannot ignore the timeline of the 1990s. Yes, commitments to European Venture funds rose quickly towards

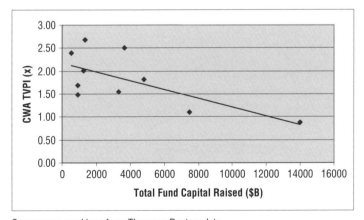

Source: own workings from Thomson Reuters data

Figure 10.6   European Venture vintage years 1990 to 1999: total fund commitments versus performance

the end of the decade, but this was on the back of the bubble and we cannot just ignore the fact that the bubble happened. However, very cautiously I would suggest that these figures do seem to support the common sense hypothesis that the less money there is available in the system, then the better returns are likely to be. Even here, though, we must be careful. It may well be that once the amount of available capital dips below a certain point, then this trend will reverse itself as it becomes difficult or even impossible to raise further financing rounds for companies, or to get funded in the first place. It could also drive firms to invest in fewer companies in each fund, thus lessening their chances of catching that one all-important home run. The years 2002–2005, for example, saw very low levels of fundraising in Europe. The figure above would suggest that they should be very successful vintage years in terms of returns, but there is the very real danger that levels may have been so low that some of the phenomena I mention above may apply.

Let us now look at the same measure for the same vintage years but applied to US Venture funds (Figure 10.7).

Wow! This seems to be sending a very clear picture of a direct inverse correlation between capital raised and vintage year performance. I must say right at the outset that I believe this picture to be broadly true, but there are a number of important caveats to state. First, there is the timeline effect just as with European funds. Second, this is probably exacerbated by the fact that the funds from the last couple of years (which were the really big ones) may not yet have had a chance to develop any realistic indication of their actual lifetime return.

However, these figures again seem to square with the common sense hypothesis that an excess of money in the system will lead to a diminution of returns. This arises in a number of ways. First, American GPs have always drawn a distinction between what they call 'smart money' and 'dumb money'. What made the funding bubble particularly harmful in the US (and, by the way, it was even worse than these figures suggest – the original total raised for 2000 was over $120 billion before fund size reductions started to kick in) was that most of the new influx was 'dumb money' from LPs who were determined to commit to US Venture funds come what may, and did not particularly mind that their capital might fall into

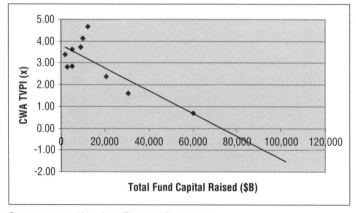

Source: own workings from Thomson Reuters data

Figure 10.7   US Venture vintage years 1990 to 1999: total fund commitments

Table 10.3   US Venture: returns by stage

Stage	UQ TVPI(x)	CWA TVPI(x)	UQ IRR(%)	CWA IRR(%)
Seed	2.12	1.30	13.3	0.2
Early	2.25	1.58	16.3	13.2
Balanced	2.22	1.52	15.4	6.9
Late	2.09	1.44	14.8	5.8

Source: Thomson Reuters
Note: All funds from inception to end 2005 for comparative purposes

inexperienced or inexpert hands; 544 funds were raised in 2000, of which a very large proportion must have been first-time funds. In other words, LPs were prepared to commit to funds which were likely to end up in the third or fourth quartiles of US Venture performance rather than to funds which had every chance of ending up in the upper quartile of, say, European Buyout. Given that even in the glory days of 1995 and 1996 the top of the lower quartile only returned 3.5% and 1.7% whereas the upper quartile European Buyout fund returned 20.3% and 22.9% respectively, then it can readily be appreciated just how tragically mistaken this approach was.

So, quality was undoubtedly a new problem which was forced upon the US Venture industry by LP behaviour, but so was quantity. As more and more money came into the system, company valuations rose dramatically and fund sizes spiralled upwards to try to keep up with them. By 2000, firms which just a few years previously had been raising funds of $300M were suddenly raising $1.5 billion funds. While officially denied at the time, there can be little doubt in retrospect that these larger fund sizes, in turn, played their part in a continued increase in company valuations, even though these were already in many cases at unsustainable levels. I would argue that once the level of available funding reaches a certain level within any Venture environment, then this sort of outcome is inevitable, which is why I am comfortable with the general trend identified for US Venture (Table 10.3), even though I acknowledge that there were specific factors throughout the bubble period and the build up to it which all made their individual contributions.

In fact, what we are seeing here is probably a natural cycle in which perceived outperformance in an asset class sucks more money into it until the excess availability of money pushes down returns sufficiently to make the asset class unattractive in relative terms, at which point allocation levels drop off, returns rise and the whole cycle starts all over again. We see this clearly in the US, where three or four years of bumper fundraising followed two or three years of bumper performance. I think what made this possible was that whereas normally it would take several years for fund performance to become apparent, the prevailing climate of rapidly rising equity markets and fairly rapid Venture company exits into a booming IPO environment made clear very quickly the sort of returns that LPs in the top US Venture funds of that era could reasonably expect. In more normal circumstances I would expect the cycle to develop more slowly.

Hopes that this cycle may have reversed itself very quickly were initially raised by the figures for, say, 2002 and 2003. In both those years roughly $11 billion was raised by roughly 100 funds, even at a time when fund size reductions were taking place and so LPs should logically have had surplus capital to allocate; compare and contrast this with 2000, when 525 funds raised initially over ten times that amount. By 2005 US Venture fundraising had already returned to 1998 levels; indeed the four vintage years to 2008 seem to have averaged well over $30 billion each.

Venture Returns by Stage

Accepted wisdom has it that the earlier the investment stage on which a Venture fund focuses, then the higher the returns it can realistically expect, and vice versa. We have already touched on this briefly, and I have to say that it accords with my own experience gained largely from US Venture funds. Let us see how it works out in practice (Table 10.3):

I think the table above broadly shows what one might expect. Observe that for both IRR and TVPI there is a slow but steady falling off as one progresses from early to later stages of investment. By the way, these figures show the fund's main investment focus, and will therefore be blunted somewhat since there is nothing to stop a later stage fund making a few early-stage investments as well, or vice versa. The seed figures, though, are a bit strange and we need to dig a little deeper to see what has happened here. Note, too, as pointed out elsewhere, that these figures have narrowed very significantly since the data calculations for the first edition were finalised in late 2006.

We spoke earlier about the difficulty which very small Venture funds have in avoiding dilution, and this is what I think we are seeing at work here. This problem is more acute in the US than it is in Europe. In Europe, there is a feeling that a continuing good relationship with the other Venture firm in question is more important than pressing what might be seen as a cruelly hard bargain on any one funding round. In the US, the opposite is the case, and the prevailing maxim is 'if you can't pay, you can't play', or in other words if you cannot participate meaningfully in a funding round then you must expect to be seriously diluted. Incidentally, this caused quite a few ruffled feathers when US firms first started doing deals in Europe in the heady days of 1998 and 1999.

Across business as a whole, and Venture is no exception, US participants tend to be transaction oriented whereas their European counterparts tend to be relationship oriented, and I feel that each side needs to try to understand the other much more in this regard or further bad feeling is inevitable. As the bubble started to burst I lost count of the number of European GPs who complained bitterly to me that they had been badly treated by a US GP 'who I thought we had a relationship with', usually followed by an expressed determination never to have anything to do with that firm again. Naïve, perhaps, but one could argue that the American attitude was just as mistaken in its short-sightedness. What will happen when that US firm tries to re-enter Europe? People have long memories when they think they have been ill-used.

I suspect that the figures for US seed funds are a clear example of this inability to avoid dilution. The vast majority of the US seed-stage funds listed by VentureXpert are less than $25M in fund size, certainly way too small to 'play with the big boys' as I have heard it expressed by US GPs. The absolute minimum effective size for a seed fund, bearing in mind the need to be able to follow in later rounds all the way through to exit, is probably about $100M, and some would probably argue for an even higher figure. In fact, only 34 out of 544 seed funds in the database, or about 6% by number, are bigger than $100M. This also helps to explain why the capital weighted average IRR is so low. Just about all the larger funds were raised at the height of the bubble and their predictably low IRRs will be unduly depressing the result – hence the very large difference between the CWA and the upper quartile.

In general, though, I think the table above does indeed support the general view that later stage funds are likely to see lower returns than early ones. A sceptic might object that the differences are so small that they might safely be ignored; however they are a drawn from a large sample and the trend which they display, though small, is statistically significant. More importantly, there is one key fact that they do not show. Remember that Venture returns are driven by the stand-out funds largely managed by the golden circle firms? Well, you are no less than fifteen times more likely to achieve at least a 10× return by investing in an early-stage US Venture fund than you are by investing in a late-stage one.[2] For anyone who really understands Venture returns, this is a killer point. You cannot achieve the sort of returns we have heard talked about by the likes of Horsley Bridge, the Yale Endowment and others without capturing a good number of these stand-out funds within your portfolio; you have only a limited number of bullets to fire at that particular target, so why waste any of them on such a very long shot (no pun intended)? It is no coincidence that Horsley Bridge traditionally specialised almost exclusively (in the US) in early Stage Venture, though interestingly they now appear to be moving towards a rather more diversified approach.

WHAT OF THE FUTURE?

It is always a difficult business making predictions about what will happen to Private Equity in the future. I felt reasonably confident in doing so when talking about Buyout returns since the prevailing trends seem to be suggested so strongly by the available data. Here, we are obviously in different territory.

First there is the effect of the bubble to consider. This had infinitely more direct impact on Venture returns than it did on Buyout. Buyout suffered indirectly through the associated ramp in equity valuations followed by what was almost a nuclear winter for some years as far as exits were concerned, but Venture caught the full blast of it. This was hopefully a 'once in a generation' event and so it seems hard to take the possibility of another such cataclysmic period into account, but human nature being what it is, one trembles to think what might happen to investor sentiment should things such as stem cell therapy, fuel cell technology or cold fusion ever really take off; there is the even more likely prospect that something as yet completely uncontemplated could suddenly be hailed as 'the next big thing'. So faddism, or irrational exuberance, or cyclicality or whatever you might like to call it is probably something that must be factored into our expectations of Venture returns in the future.

My concerns in this direction are heightened by the fact that Venture fundraising does not appear to have fallen back, as one might have hoped when looking at the figures a few years ago, to the more rational levels of, say, 1994 or 1995. On the contrary, fundraising already seems to have regained the levels it enjoyed at the beginning of the bubble period and my instinct is that it will go higher yet. There are likely to be a good number of investors wishing to enter the Private Equity space over the next few years and the advice they will probably receive is that they should be looking to put their money to work in US Venture funds. Since access to the golden circle will be effectively impossible, this means that we will see the irrational intention of investing with potential third or fourth quartile funds perpetuated. This, in turn, will enable some firms who should probably not be able to raise a new fund in normal circumstances to remain in business.

---

[2]Figures from Thomson Financial's VentureXpert system.

Then there is the problem of coming to any sort of accurate view on what European Venture has actually achieved in terms of historic performance, and in any event is historic European performance necessarily a good guide to future returns?

We have demonstrated that coming to any sort of accurate view of how European Venture has really performed is virtually impossible. There is evidence that at least one fund in each vintage year has usually produced performance that would measure against the golden circle in the US, although the golden circle effect, as such, is absent. However there can be no doubt that European Venture has badly underperformed, though it is impossible to say by exactly how much.

This is due partly to the absence of the golden circle, but this only tells part of the story. The absence of the US model of early-stage investing, and skills, expertise and mind-set that this requires have meant that, with the exception of that odd one or two funds a year, European Venture has underperformed across the board. The really interesting question, of course, is what will happen as the US model starts to be widely employed in Europe? Is there any good reason why it should not generate at least as good returns as it has done in America?

My instinct says 'no'. However, I am in a delicate position here. I am well known as an advocate of European Venture and do not want to be accused of making fanciful claims with little hard data to back them up. It may, I freely admit, be seen as highly convenient that the historic data which seem to damn historic European Venture returns turns out to be unreliable. Very well, here are some hard data. According to data provider VentureOne, there have only been eight Venture exits in the world since the beginning of 2002 with an exit value in excess of $1 billion. It may surprise many that not only have four of these been European, but also that, with the exception of Google, the European realised exit multiples have been higher than the others. Now, one swallow (or even four swallows) doth not a summer make, but surely this is at least circumstantial evidence that European Venture Capitalists are watching what has happened in the US, learning from it and applying it in Europe to good effect.

So, the future for Venture may be unpredictable but certainly, for this most exciting of asset classes, is not going to be boring. Certainly the golden circle will continue consistently to outperform. The question is what happens outside the golden circle. How will the returns of the run-of-the-mill US firms hold up in an environment which still looks over-funded and over-populated? Will the gap between the golden circle and the rest open up still further? Will the bulk of the golden circle come to rue their decision not to expand into Europe in the late 1990s?

My instinct says 'yes', but I am unsure exactly how this might play out. I am aware of at least one European Venture firm which has been approached with a view to becoming the European offshoot of an American firm, and this is certainly one way ahead, but I am not sure that it will prove widespread as an approach. Nor I am sure that US firms will actually come to Europe en masse in the near future. European expansion, or, at least, *successful* European expansion, requires a mind-set which I think simply does not exist in US firms at present. It requires a willingness to adapt where necessary to slightly different ways of doing business, and to accept that companies planted beyond your own garden fence might prove just as successful as your own home-grown variety. It also requires a readiness to work with Europeans as equal partners. There are at least two honourable exceptions here,[3] but for the most part the best US Venture firms seem to believe that none of this is possible without in

---

[3]Accel and Benchmark, though the latter has subsequently gone it alone as Balderton, and neither are doing much in Europe before a B Round.

some way fatally compromising the US model. I think they will come to see that they are mistaken, but it will take time and by then the real opportunity may well have been missed.

In the meantime they may well have decided to expand to Asia first. While illogical, since Europe represents an already established Venture community, and a stable business infrastructure in marked contrast to, say, China, this would be consistent with what has happened in other areas of investment and also with everything I have heard from talking with American LPs. The roots of the American love affair with Asia, and particularly with China, run deep and were planted a long time ago (at least seventy years ago and possibly longer). Asia is hugely seductive and it is a seduction that US investors feel unable to resist. One constant in human affairs is our apparent inability to learn from history. Those few of us with long enough experience of Private Equity will remember the ill-fated China funds which were set up almost exclusively with US money in the early 1990s amid brave talk of expectations of 4× or 5× fund returns (since naturally something which was high risk must also produce high returns, mustn't it?). Yet sadly it seems that this is something that each successive generation of investors must learn for themselves all over again.

Please do not run away with the idea that I am somehow anti-Asian; I am not. Venture Capital has become a global business and Asia has a vital role to play. There are already, for example, exciting things happening in India. However, where there is (as yet) a general lack of transparency in business dealings, a flexible attitude towards contractual commitments, and a lack of sophisticated corporate, insolvency and floatation regimes then investors should exercise caution. A headlong rush into the darkness can easily become a flight to disaster.

SUMMARY

Historically, US Venture has very significantly outperformed European Venture. However, while taking nothing away from the superb achievements of US Venture firms during the 1990s, the difference is not perhaps quite as dramatic as the official figures would have us believe.

The official figures for European Venture contain a large number of funds which either cannot be properly classified as Venture, or are not of institutional investment grade, either because they are very small or because they are not managed by independent Venture firms. The level of accuracy in the average vintage years during the 1990s, measured by the number of such eligible funds, is only about 27%. Thus, while performance has been undeniably disappointing, it is difficult to be sure just *how* disappointing. Individual European funds have proved successful, even achieving 10×, but it seems that such successes have been isolated and not reproduced across any significant portion of the industry.

In statistical terms, much of the difference is due to the consistent success of the 'golden circle' firms in the US in producing funds which can return more than 10×. It is significant that in the only pre-bubble vintage year in the 1990s to produce less than exciting returns (1991) there was not a single such fund formed. Thus, the ability to produce excellent returns from a portfolio of US Venture funds is dependent upon the ability successfully to identify and access these funds.

Early-stage funds seem fifteen times more likely to produce at least 10× than late-stage funds.

There seems to be a direct inverse relationship between the amount of capital raised in any vintage year and the returns of that vintage year, particularly in the US.

In practical terms the main reason for the differing returns was the absence in Europe of the US model, with everything that this implies (mind-set, skills, etc).

However, it should be remembered that no equivalent of NASDAQ existed in Europe to provide exits and drive valuations. Also, the bubble had much more opportunity (because of the relative timelines) to create high returns for a brief time in the US than it did in Europe.

Levels of Venture fundraising remain a concern in the US. There are indications that these are returning to early bubble era proportions, despite a significant overhang of capital already in the system. This could well result in valuations remaining at relatively high historic levels, but will also see LPs being pushed inexorably down the quality chain in their fund selection.

It seems highly likely that the golden circle will continue significantly to outperform the rest of their US competitors. Indeed, it is possible that with high levels of available capital enabling third and fourth quartile firms to stay in business, this difference will become even more pronounced.

The huge unknown is what will happen as the US model becomes increasingly widely practised in Europe. Recent billion dollar exits, though small in number, suggest that Europe may well be able to at least match US returns in future. Given that very small amounts of capital are currently being allocated to this area, European Venture could be seen as representing a classic contrarian opportunity.

It is possible that the vast majority of US Venture firms may live to regret having missed a strategic window for expansion into Europe in the late 1990s. It is unlikely that this situation will change any time soon; indeed, it is quite possible that most US firms have Asia ahead of Europe on the agenda.

Whatever the case, Venture is rapidly becoming a global business, and the key test for any Venture firm in the future may well prove to be how they rise to this challenge. With one or two honourable exceptions, international expansion by Venture firms has proved highly problematic in practice. Indeed, one firm (Atlas Venture) has recently announced the closure of its longstanding European operations, and retrenched to a single office in Boston.

11
Growth and Development Capital

It should be stated straight away that we are here faced with yet another problem of terminology. There has grown up, particularly in the United States, the habit of using the phrase 'Expansion Capital' to cover any type of either Development or Growth Capital transaction. This is undesirable, since it masks the fact that there are, in fact, significant differences between them. So, let us note the fact that the term exists lest we should meet with it in practice, but ignore it henceforth for the purposes of this book since it assumes that Development Capital and Growth Capital are the same, whereas in fact they are not.

Development Capital and Growth Capital deserve serious consideration since they could well represent something like half by number of all the Private Equity transactions which take place worldwide. One has to say 'could' since there are no specific figures available on this. The data providers do not recognise them as separate categories, and, even if they did, many of them take place outside Europe and the US in the (so far as Private Equity is concerned) emerging markets such as South America, Eastern Europe and Asia, where the overwhelming majority of GPs do not file their data anyway. The proviso 'by number' is also an important caveat, since compared to large Buyout transactions these deals can be very small.

It is no accident that it is in the emerging Private Equity markets that Growth and Development deals predominate, since it is with this category that Private Equity markets tend to begin, only later spreading out in each direction into Venture and Buyout. In the 1990s, for example, the US and UK markets had already evolved to include a considerable volume of Buyout activity, while continental European markets were still dominated by Development Capital transactions. Interestingly, even when Buyout activity reached significant proportions, many continental GPs did both Development and Buyout deals within the same fund (yet another reason why precise classification of data is all but impossible).

Even though the markets in the US and the UK were the first to mature, if the development of a fully functioning Buyout market may be taken as a sign of maturity, Development and Growth investing has not gone away. In the US, for example, firms such as Summit and TA have pursued this style of investing, and both have now spread their operations to Europe. In the UK, too, there are long-established players and indeed the author was recently a member of a judging panel for the BVCA 'deal of the year' award which decided in favour of a Growth Capital investment made by ECI Partners.

Development and Growth Capital are often confused with each other since they share many superficial similarities. Chief among these is that they both tend to be relatively small when compared with Buyout transactions, and that they both involve the taking of a minority stake. As we will see, this raises some very important considerations as to how these deals are structured. It is also regarded in many quarters as a significant selling point; many entrepreneurs or family owners will not countenance giving up control of their business, but might be persuaded to give up a minority stake. This is yet another reason why Private Equity activity tends to start with such deals; where the concept of a financial buyer is, as yet, relatively unknown there can be a great deal of trepidation at the idea of entering into a Buyout transaction.

This is a double-edged sword, however. The fact that the existing shareholders do not have to surrender control may lull them into believing that this is a long-term strategic alliance into which they are entering rather than a short-term financial arrangement, no matter how many times they may be told that this is not the case. Even worse, they may believe that, rather than an equity stake, this is, in effect, some sort of disguised loan, which may simply be repaid at some stage in the future.

This phenomenon seems to be particularly pronounced in India for some reason, with entrepreneurs regularly talking of 'paying back' the Private Equity investor. True, the investment may often be made by way of a convertible loan note for tax reasons, but it is important to look at the substance, not the form. As far as the investor is concerned (1) they are taking an equity stake and (2) they require an exit, probably within three years, and both these points need to be emphasised and re-emphasised at every available opportunity.

Since many of the features of Development Capital and Growth Capital investing are, in fact, very similar and can be discussed together, let us focus first on those ways in which these two types of investment differ. Briefly, these are (1) the type of company which they target and (2) the objective which they are trying to achieve.

THE PLC AND THE BCG GROWTH MATRIX

Both of these issues are directly linked to the cash flow characteristics which lie behind the product life cycle (PLC) curve. Let us just remind ourselves what this is (Figure 11.1).

Remember that when we looked at this in Chapter 1 we learned that the main interest in this concept for Private Equity investors was that as a company moved to the right along the

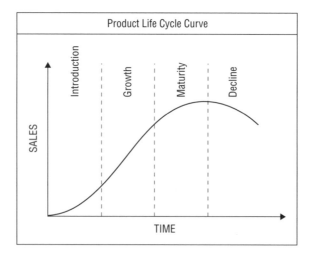

Figure 11.1

curve, its need for cash flow gradually diminished, and that its chances of survival steadily increased. It is time now to look at this in a little more detail.

The reason why cash flow needs decrease as one moves into the 'Mature' stage of the curve is that the product or service has become well established, so that there is no longer as much need to spend money promoting customer awareness of it. Competition will, by this time, have become fairly straightforward, focusing on cost, quality and the perceived relationship between them. There will also, of course, be much less need for any expenditure on product development, let alone R&D.

By the time we move into the 'Decline' section of the curve, industry consolidation will be taking place, with various players dropping out of the market on account of their low market share, thus leaving two or three dominant businesses in place. This, at least, is the theory. The practice tends to be somewhat different, since anti-trust or monopoly authorities may seek to block the sale of small, non-core assets to large players who already have a significant market share, and businesses may decide to hang on to uncompetitive market positions for emotional or political reasons, rather than yielding to cruel commercial logic.

That, however, is the theory, and in general it holds true; certainly the logic is impeccable. Around this theory the Boston Consulting Group constructed a matrix which sets the rate of growth of a particular market against the relative market share of any individual participant, and it is important that we should understand the mechanics of this, since a proper understanding of Growth Capital (and arguably other Private Equity activity as well) is impossible without it.

You will see that the matrix charts relative market position on the horizontal axis and the percentage rate of market growth on the vertical axis (Figure 11.2). Thus, a company which is in the bottom left-hand square has a strong market position in a mature or even declining market, while a business which is in the top right-hand square has a low market share in a rapidly growing market, and so on.

The matrix was developed by BCG as part of its management consultancy activities, and specifically for the new breed of corporate conglomerates that grew rapidly during the 1960s and 1970s. The ultimate objective is to move your business into the bottom left-hand square and become a cash cow, i.e. a business which has strong positive cash flow for the reasons

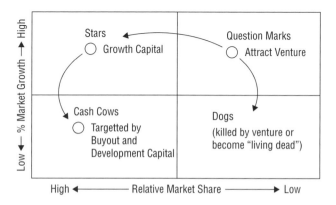

Figure 11.2

we just examined. Conglomerates would, in fact, end up with various product lines all occupying different positions in the matrix representing their own particular market, and the matrix was designed to give guidance on how to manage this portfolio of brands and products. Cash thrown off by the 'cows' could be used to sustain the hungry 'stars' and 'question marks', which typically have negative cash flow, but only a certain number, so the trick was to close down or sell off all the 'dogs' and most of the question marks, retaining only those few voted most likely to succeed.

Why should stars and question marks have poor cash flow? Because they are having to spend heavily on marketing and promotion at the same time as perhaps still spending heavily on R&D and product development. They may also have to be indulging in price-cutting to protect or acquire market share. By the time the market matures and growth levels off, so the theory goes, cash flow should have turned positive as none of these things apply, or at least not to nearly the same extent.

So, the matrix was produced for a specific purpose, and one should always be wary of taking things out of context, especially when this is already done so often in the world of finance, but the matrix does very neatly delineate the areas of activity of each of the main types of Private Equity, as we saw in Chapter 1. When we come to look in detail at Growth Capital, we will see that the particular imperatives of the Growth stage of the PLC have a huge impact on the specific objectives which a Growth Capital GP will seek to achieve.

For the time being, please remember that the PLC, as translated into the BCG matrix, is driven by the strength or weakness of a business's likely cash flow, and its rate of growth relative to the rate of growth of the market within which it operates.

DEVELOPMENT CAPITAL

Target Companies

Like Buyout firms, Development Capital GPs target companies which are in the Mature or Decline sections of the product life cycle. However, the BCG growth matrix also comes into consideration; they do not want 'dogs', but rather 'cash cows'. Thus, they will be well-established businesses with strong cash flows and decent market share.

Why, then, would such businesses seek equity capital when they could, in normal circumstances, obtain bank debt? Partly because the shareholders of some private companies, particularly if they are family owned, tend to be debt-averse. Partly because many such companies actually have the opposite problem and are under-capitalised. Partly also because debt finance for at least one type of Development deal ('money out' deals, which we will consider below) can be hard to obtain for both practical and legal reasons.

Development Capital deals can be divided into two main categories: 'money in' and 'money out'.

Money In Deals

In this case the company requires new capital for expansion or development, usually with a specific purpose in mind, such as expanding into a new geographic market, establishing a new distribution network, building or re-equipping a factory, etc.

Money in deals are so called because the new capital goes into the company in exchange for new shares, though frequently a convertible loan note is used instead. The reason for this is that should it prove possible to pay a coupon on the loan note, then it will be treated as loan interest and be tax deductible, rather than a share dividend which can only be paid after tax (and may be subject to withholding tax together with certain legal restrictions in some circumstances on the right to pay a dividend).

There are some who remember the difference between stalactites and stalagmites as being that stalactites stick tight to the roof of a cave. For those of a similar mind-set, it may be convenient to note that 'money in' ends with the letter n, and that 'new shares' begins with it. This is, after all, the key thing to remember; money in deals always result in an issue of new shares, either directly at once, or indirectly in the future.

Money Out Deals

Money out deals are usually driven by the desire of one or more of the company founders to retire, though also occasionally by the consolidation of various family shareholdings which have become highly fragmented over the years. In this case the new capital does not go into the company, and so there is no issue of new shares. Rather, the Development Capital investor will buy existing shares from the shareholders who own them.

Having said this, it would be very unusual for any experienced Development Capital investor to countenance a purely money out transaction, and so many deals tend, in practice, to be hybrids between the two forms. Even here, it would be rare for one of the founders to be allowed simply to cash in a large part of their chips and walk away from the company. Instead there will usually be a lengthy transition period, perhaps as long as three years, with the departing shareholders being paid out gradually on an earn out based on actual performance.

Again, for tax reasons it may be advantageous to issue loan stock to the departing shareholder if it is desired to pay him money during the earn out period, or this may be structured as a salary or bonus paid under a service (employment) contract with the objective in either case of rendering the payments tax deductible.

Objectives

As we will see when we look at the way in which Development Capital deals are structured, there will rarely be the potential for any leverage within the transaction, at least not in the shape of third party debt such as we would expect to find in the case of Buyouts. This means that the return made by the fund is likely to be largely un-geared, i.e. the increase in equity value will be broadly the same as the increase in enterprise value. This, in turn, means that it will rapidly become very difficult to maintain a respectable IRR for the investment. For example, even if one could achieve an un-geared increase of 2× in the enterprise value (which would imply a similar increase, or close to it, in earnings after tax), then, after three years, the IRR would only be about 26%. Bear in mind that this would be the transaction, or gross, IRR, not that which the LPs would earn on their fund cash flows net of fees, costs and carried interest; that would probably be about 15% for a typically structured fund.

Even today, this would probably represent the minimum return expectation for a Development Capital fund LP, but let us reflect on this a little more. In order for that return to be earned *across the whole fund*, we would have to assume that in respect of each and every one of the fund's investments, the holding period would not exceed three years, and that earnings could be roughly doubled in that period.[1] How likely is this? Not very!

So, the objectives of a Development Capital GP are simple and connected; they must be able to see a way of significantly growing a company's earnings (in the case of a money in deal, attention will focus on the potential for extra profit being generated by the development project, whatever it may be), and they must be out of the investment within three years. We will see shortly that the second of these requirements can become a cause of much friction and bad feeling between the parties.

The former is more likely to be a source of bemusement and irritation when an investment is rejected in the first place. An entrepreneur may believe, quite correctly, that they have 'a good business', but does it have the true potential for the sort of growth that the GP requires for their fund investments, and can this be achieved within a reasonable time frame? There are other issues too. How attractive is the market within which the business operates? Is there an obvious purchaser for this business? Is it likely to make an attractive IPO (flotation) candidate? How comfortable can the GP be that the management team has the ability to execute on the business plan?

GROWTH CAPITAL

Growth Capital is distinguished from Development Capital in two ways. First, the type of company which is targeted, and second the absence of money out deals; all Growth deals are money in.

Target Companies

As might be expected, Growth Capital targets the 'Growth' section of the PLC curve. Here it is clearly necessary to explain in a little more detail exactly what this means. Companies in this section will feature in the top half of the BCG matrix. If they already have a strong market position they will be stars. If not, they will be question marks.

Stars are highly attractive because as long as their market share can be maintained, then, as the rate of market growth slows and the market moves into its Mature phase, the business will fall downwards within the BCG matrix and become a cash cow, that most desirable business of all, so beloved of Buyout and (where possible) Development players. However, it is important to be absolutely clear what this means. In order for a business to maintain its market share, it must grow its sales by at least the same rate that the market as a whole is growing. This is always challenging, and sometimes almost impossibly so. For example, the mobile telephone market in India was, at one time, estimated to be growing at over 2000%, or more than 20× a year. In this situation, even maintaining one's market position would mean generating sales of more than $20 this year for every $1 of sales last year.

This requirement for rapid growth means that Growth companies are extremely cash hungry. We are no longer driven by the risk of not surviving, as is the case with Venture companies. With a Growth company, were one to take one's foot off the accelerator, then a

---

[1]This is not, strictly speaking, true, as some potential leverage may be available through the use of loan notes, but it is still a useful way to think about the situation.

certain base level of profitability would remain, but it would be small. The company would become one of the dreaded 'living dead', too small and unexciting to attract the interest either of a purchaser (except perhaps as an add-on acquisition by a larger player) or the IPO market. In due course, it would fall, as the market matured, not into the 'cash cow' square, but into the 'dog' square.

The need for advertising and promotional spending, as well as the spread of the company's infrastructure demanded by rapid organic growth plus ongoing R&D and product development can generate huge additional cash flow requirements. Just the exercise of entering foreign markets for the first time can be extremely expensive in terms of 'up front' costs as well as massively disruptive, and carries the potential fatally to wound the business should it not be well executed.

Few banks will be prepared to lend to a Growth company since it will not be able to demonstrate the sort of positive cash flows to service the loan, at least not in the near future and not in anything approaching a normal banking environment. Private Equity is thus usually the only practical option, and just as Venture Capital is largely ignored as a force for good in socio-economic terms, so (perhaps even more so since few outsiders even realise that it exists) is Growth Capital.

Question marks raise more difficult issues, and most Growth Capital GPs will tend to avoid these unless there is a very good story to be told. The reason is obvious; if a star has to grow by at least the same rate as the rest of the market simply to stand still, then a question mark has to grow by several times the rate of the rest of the market, and starting at once, since any delay will only make the situation worse still. What might represent a 'good story'? Perhaps some product innovation which would suddenly make the company's offering much more attractive, or the ability quickly to access a new distribution channel or geographic market.

Objectives

The way in which GPs approach Growth deals is very different from the objectives we saw set out for Development Capital. Remember the imperative of a Growth company in terms of the PLC and BCG matrix; to grow by at least the same rate as the rate of the market within which it operates. This is where Development and Growth diverge; Development Capital GPs try to increase the earnings of the company after tax. Growth Capital GPs try to grow the sales (turnover or revenues). Or, as Americans put it, Development Capital, like Buyout, is about growing the bottom line while Growth Capital is about growing the top line.

This is a vitally important distinction and one which is frequently not understood. A Growth Capital firm recently complained about being criticised on the grounds that after it invested in a company, its earnings tended to fall, and that it could even start making losses. Yet, if a Growth Capital GP is doing their job properly, then this is exactly what one would expect to happen in many cases! Extra marketing and promotional spend, plus the sort of R&D and product development which we mentioned above, all represent deductions to be made from top line revenues (sales revenue) and thus profits are likely to fall. Yes, it is hoped that this expenditure will translate into much higher sales, but this benefit will take time to flow through and in a fast-moving market one cannot afford to wait for increased sales, but has rather to be prepared (and able) to build manufacturing and distribution capacity ahead of demand.

Thus, the most successful Growth Capital GPs tend to be those that have business development, marketing and distribution skills within their firm, if not in terms of the individual GPs themselves then definitely within the extended firm network of entrepreneurs and senior corporate managers who get drawn into the firm's portfolio companies.

The task of making and managing a Growth Capital investment might be thought of as being rather like a theme park roller coaster ride. The idea is to jump on as it starts to go uphill, ride it up the PLC and then jump out towards the top. Because the potential for value growth is so much greater than in the case of a Development Capital deal, the length of holding period is not quite so critical; where one has a significant money multiple then an IRR can be sustained for a longer period. However, the timing of the exit is still crucial, and a matter of very fine judgement. One wants to sell when there is still some growth potential left in the company to support a high valuation, but not too early when the high cash flow requirement might be off-putting for investors who are not used to this particularly challenging stage of a company's life.

Growth Capital and Late-Stage Venture

There is much confusion about the difference between Growth Capital and late-stage Venture. Does a company transition to one classification from the other at a particular point on the PLC and, if so, how might this be defined?

The answer to this question is 'yes, it can', but the distinction is more subtle than that. Let us deal with the specific question first. The dividing point can conveniently be taken as the moment when a company becomes profitable for the first time and would, if one took one's foot off the accelerator, be cash flow positive. In other words, the first moment at which the actual survival of the company is probably no longer in question. The question has evolved from 'will this company survive?' to whether it will be a huge success, or fall back to languish in the ranks of the living dead, those companies that can scrape a bare existence, but will never be large enough or exciting enough to attract a buyer, or justify an IPO.

Beyond the question there lies a further distinction which is much more difficult to categorise; it is more a matter of nuances. First, there is the intention with which the GP invests. Late-stage Venture funds typically invest in what they hope will be the last year to eighteen months in a company's life before a sale, or an IPO should no trade buyer materialise. For this reason, late-stage Venture is often referred to in the United States as 'pre-IPO funding' and there are a number of firms which specialise in this area. In other words, a true Venture company tends to be on a short but sharp upward trajectory and will, if necessary, use that part of the proceeds of the IPO which are represented by the sale of new shares to fund continuing growth.

Growth Capital, as we have seen, differs from this. Here, the GP is looking to work with the company over about a three-year period (but perhaps slightly longer) to grow sales and at least maintain market share before an IPO becomes an appropriate option. If you think back to what we said about Private Equity returns in general, this means that a late-stage Venture investor can countenance a lower money multiple because they are looking to calculate an IRR over a shorter period (this is the theory anyway, albeit theory which has come largely unstuck during the fallow exit environment from 2001 onwards). Growth Capital investors have never worked on this basis. They have always planned for a longer holding period, and thus a higher money multiple.

To muddy the waters still further, it is worth pointing out that Growth Capital investors often view valuation as a function of sales. This used to be a traditional way of valuing companies in countries like Germany. Before the discounting of cash flows became widespread, one frequently encountered the idea of a multiple of turnover (sales or revenues) and even an appreciation that this should be higher in respect of companies which were in high growth market sectors. Of course, this is subject to all sorts of fairly obvious objections, not least that it ignores the question of margins and operating efficiency, but it is frequently used, at least on a 'broad brush' basis, to arrive at a valuation of a Growth company, at least for bargaining purposes. This, incidentally, is another reason why Growth Capital GPs are relatively relaxed about the possibility of falling earnings – something which could represent a major tragedy for Buyout and Development Capital GPs.

The second, and more subtle, distinction is linked directly to the first, and is that a Growth company and a late-stage Venture company may, in any event, be rather different animals. Many Growth companies have never actually been on what one might call the Venture Capital curve at all. In many cases they have been bootstrapped; in others they might have been spun out of a larger corporate structure. There is a yet further possibility, which is that they might be a conventional business which now wishes to enter, or is forced into, a much higher growth environment, or a more technology-focused delivery method; hard copy trade directory businesses going online some years ago might be a good example of this.

COMMON ISSUES

Though Development Capital and Growth Capital have different targets and objectives, they do appear superficially the same, since GPs in both these areas will structure their deals in very similar ways. They both involve minority (non-control) investing, and neither will typically feature any third party acquisition debt. We have already noted that this is a frequent source of confusion which can lead to deals being misclassified, and even to a total ignorance that a distinct category of Growth Capital should exist at all.

However, let us now turn our attention to the common issues which arise as a result of such deal structures. There will, of course, be all the usual questions of company analysis and valuation, purchaser due diligence and the negotiation and agreement of vendor reps and warranties. However, these are common to all Private Equity transactions with the possible exception of seed-stage Venture. With both Development Capital and Growth Capital we come across two specific issues, which will together take up a great deal of discussion, negotiation and drafting, the importance of which cannot be underestimated. Both arise as a direct consequence of the taking of a minority shareholding position. The first concerns the question of how to protect your position as a minority shareholder during the period of the investment. The second concerns the question of how to protect your exit route.

Minority Protection

What have generally come to be referred to as Anglo-Saxon legal systems (those based upon or derived from American or English law) will generally provide various mechanisms for the protection of minority shareholders. They may recognise the concept of a fraud on the minority, allow a minority shareholders' action where they allege that they have been treated inequitably, or even a derivative action whereby they can bring an action against a third party in the name of the company.

However, there are many jurisdictions in the world where such rights do not exist, at least not in clear-cut form, and even where they do they are subject to the usual problems of bringing a case, proving the facts and arguing the law, which may take several years. By this time not only will the exit trail long ago have gone cold, but the particular facts complained of will probably have lost both their immediate impact and their overall relevance to the situation. Better by far to take practical steps to protect ourselves, rather than having to rely on the cumbersome and uncertain legal machinery.

Fortunately, there is an easy way of doing this. Every Private Equity transaction will result in a shareholders' agreement being prepared as one of the key documents. It is here that both the issues we have raised will be addressed by suitable wording.

Negative Control

The idea of negative control may sound a bit of an oxymoron, but in fact it describes the situation very well, It refers to a series of provisions in the shareholders' agreement that give the Private Equity investors a right of veto over certain management actions. Again, you need to be a little bit careful here as certain legal jurisdictions around the world can pose problems with creating different classes of shares, class rights and a speedy and effective way of seeking (if necessary) injunctions. These can usually be overcome by the use of an offshore holding company, but this can, in turn, raise problems about (1) the mutual recognition and enforcement of judgements and (2) tax and exchange control issues concerning the transfer of assets and business undertakings. Detailed legal advice should, of course, be sought on all these issues; the object of this book is simply to make the reader aware of the general form which such protection typically takes.

Basically, it revolves around the creation of two different classes of share, one of which is held by the Private Equity investor(s), and the other by everybody else. The shareholders' agreement will then stipulate that certain things cannot happen without the consent of both classes of shareholder (or, in practice, without the consent of the director or directors nominated by the Private Equity shareholder). It creates, in effect, a right of veto.

The chief concerns of a GP will be (1) not to allow money to be taken out of the company rather than being used for operational purposes, (2) to be kept properly aware of what is happening within the company and (3) not to allow the directors to dilute the Private Equity shareholding, whether directly or indirectly. These concerns shine through any list of the typical things to which such veto rights will attach:

• increasing directors' salaries;
• agreeing new directors' service contracts;
• paying dividends;
• issuing new shares;
• issuing new convertible instruments;
• additional bank borrowing beyond agreed limits;
• changing the nature of the business;
• significant asset sales or purchases;
• opening or closing offices or operations;
• hiring new directors or key executives.

This list is not exhaustive, but will give a good flavour of the sort of issues that need to be considered. The question of reporting is more tricky, since negative control works by preventing the company (or, more precisely, its directors) from doing something rather than forcing them to do so. The answer is usually to specify exactly what accounting and reporting is required at what intervals, and then to provide that failure to comply counts as an act of default. Various sanctions can be provided for acts of default, including triggering exit protection (see below).

Incidentally, any failure to provide accounts promptly, even if only the monthly management accounts, should be treated very seriously, as it is often the first warning sign of a founder or entrepreneur who has decided to make the Private Equity investor's life as difficult as possible in the hope that they can be 'paid back' and persuaded to give up their shareholding. At a workshop in India based upon the first edition of this book, one company founder boasted openly of having achieved this feat no less than three times, which says much for the entrepreneur's attitude to Development Capital, but little for the due diligence abilities of the last two in that sequence of three Private Equity firms.

Exit Protection

Consider the situation of a minority shareholder in the absence of any specific legal protection, particularly that of a Private Equity investor. You need an exit after no more than three years. You make this clear to the entrepreneur at the time you make your investment, and they assure you that this is understood, and will not be a problem. Three years later, you broach the question of a sale of the company to provide you with an exit. The entrepreneur stares at you blankly. 'Sale?' they ask. 'Are you crazy? I'm growing this business for my grandchildren to inherit.'

A nightmare scenario certainly, but there is another which you may not have considered. An alternative script might play out something like this. One day the entrepreneur calls you up and proudly announces that they have sold their 70% controlling interest to someone you have never heard of, and that henceforth you will be a 30% minority shareholder alongside this unknown third party.

There are, in fact, yet others, to which we will turn in a moment, but it should be clear even from what we have considered above that a Private Equity investor who is a minority shareholder needs proper exit protection in place. In the course of performing consultancy assignments around the world, the author has, in fact, come across many situations where GPs are effectively taking no exit protection at all because 'the entrepreneurs we deal with would never agree to anything like that'. Without wishing to seem unduly cynical, this probably translates as 'whatever they may say to the contrary, the entrepreneurs we deal with have no intention of giving us an exit'. LPs need to be alert here; as part of your due diligence you should ask to see company-level legal documentation, and ask specific questions about negative control and exit protection. Investing without the latter is like throwing money into a time tunnel that only operates in one direction.

The various types of exit protection can be simply summarised. You should normally expect to encounter the first four in any transaction. The fifth seems to have fallen out of favour. All of these various types of protection could trigger either on the expiry of a certain time period (e.g. three years from the date of investment) or on the occurrence of a specified event (e.g. an act of default, or the company achieving a specified level of profitability).

1. *Tag Along* gives the minority shareholder the right to compel the majority shareholder to sell both classes of shares pro rata if they wish to sell. This deals with the second scenario sketched out above, since the entrepreneur can only sell their own shareholding if they sell yours on the same terms at the same time.

2. *Drag Along* is the opposite of this. If you find a purchaser for your minority interest, but the purchaser is only interested in buying 100% of the company, or some lesser controlling interest, you can force the entrepreneur to sell their shares into the deal alongside your own. Both Tag Along and Drag Along can be facilitated by powers of attorney and/or shares being placed in escrow, with the escrow agent bound by an escrow agreement.

3. A *Put Option* gives you the right, by serving notice in the required form, to force the majority shareholder to buy your shares. Both this and the Call Option referred to below will include some form of agreed valuation formula, usually based on an earnings multiple methodology, and providing for arbitration in the event of disagreement.

4. A *Call Option* is simply the reverse of this. This time the notice will require the majority shareholder to sell their shares to you, based upon the same valuation methodology. This would usually provide for the consideration to be paid on an earn out basis rather than up front, as the majority shareholders will usually be running the company, and their departure as managers could cause serious disruption with attendant decline in profitability. The call option's real usefulness lies simply in its very existence. It represents the nuclear option of Private Equity, and the mere threat of it being used should usually be enough to bring a recalcitrant entrepreneur to heel.

5. A *Shoot Out* used to be quite popular, but seems to have fallen out of use. The agreement will provide that on certain dates either side can give notice to the other, triggering the shoot-out and naming a figure. The other side then has a limited amount of time within which to decide either to buy your shares at that price, or to sell their shares to you at the same price. There will be a default provision covering what happens if the period expires without an election. GPs argue that this is perhaps the fairest provision of all, but this argument is slightly suspect. After all, a GP will have the established banking relationships as well as the financial skills to put a financing package in place very quickly should they decide to buy, whereas an entrepreneur may not.

THE FUTURE

Both Growth and Development Capital have grown rapidly in significance over the last few years, not least because in emerging Private Equity markets they account for most, or even all, of the deals being done. Thus, their emerging as topics of importance has gone hand in glove with the increasing interest and amounts of capital being directed at Private Equity in places like the so-called BRIC economies: Brazil, Russia, India and China.

As so often, the industry as a whole has been slow to recognise the importance of this trend. While the first edition of this book discussed non-control investing, it was not felt that Growth and Development Capital merited their own chapter. Similarly, the various industry data providers do not yet break fund performance and capital raising down into a sufficiently large number of buckets; hence the misclassification of many funds, particularly in Europe, as 'Venture' when actually they are nothing of the sort.

The evolution of Private Equity markets is driven partly by changing social attitudes and increasing financial sophistication and entrepreneurial activity, but these days is even more dependent on the development of suitable legal and fiscal regimes. Where no Private Equity activity at all is to be found (apart, perhaps, from a few local captive players), the answer is likely to be that Limited Partnerships are not recognised as tax transparent, or that they are not even recognised as legal vehicles. Taxation of capital gains in the hands of non-residents can be another problem, even in countries which are generally thought of as developed economies.[2]

It is in the area of tax consolidation, whatever it may be called in different countries, however, that development has been slowest. It was widely predicted back in about 1998 when there was a fresh rush of interest in Asia, particularly from American LPs, that within the next decade Buyout activity would have spread across the region. There were others (chiefly those who had actually done business in Asia, rather than just spent a few days on holiday in Thailand) who found this view naïve and hopelessly optimistic.

The cynics had it right. Over ten years on, we are little closer to most Asian countries (including the two – China and India – in which there has been most interest) being able to operate as fully fledged Private Equity markets. Though political and social acceptance of foreign investment has undoubtedly grown, this has rarely been translated into positive action. Not only has no effort been made to introduce the necessary framework to facilitate Buyout activity, but onerous registration and authorisation procedures for foreign investors remain in place in many countries, exchange controls remain an issue for repatriation of proceeds, and some countries do not yet recognise even a basic partnership structure, let alone more exotic variants. At the time of writing (late 2009) there is even talk of certain countries reviewing existing double taxation arrangements, thus throwing into doubt legal arrangements entered into some years ago with the expectation of certainty of outcome.

Progress will come, but those of us who actually know the relevant investment and political bodies recognise that there is an understandable sense of caution, and of wanting to move only after proper deliberation of all relevant issues. So, progress will come, but it will be slow and move forward in a series of short paces, not one giant leap.

The potential of the BRIC economies, and of others in both Asia and South America, is, however, immense in Private Equity terms and thus the story of that progress is likely to form an increasingly large part of future editions of this book.

SUMMARY

Growth and Development Capital are outwardly similar, at least superficially, since they both involve the taking of minority stakes, and neither makes use of acquisition debt. Incidentally, both these elements distinguish either Growth or Development Capital from Buyout.

Where they differ is in the type of company which they target, and their overall objective.

Development Capital targets companies in the 'Mature' and 'Decline' phases of the PLC, exactly the same sort of companies, in fact, as Buyout GPs will target.

Growth Capital, as the name suggests, targets companies in the 'Growth' phase of the PLC.

Development Capital aims to generate some significant improvements in a company's earnings (profits). This is sometimes referred to as growing the bottom line. Development GPs will be looking for an exit ideally within three years. This can make Development returns very sensitive to exit market conditions.

---

[2] Australia, for example, was very slow to make the switch.

Growth Capital aims greatly to increase the turnover (sales, revenues) of a company. This is sometimes referred to as growing the top line. Provided this objective is achieved, Growth GPs can afford to be a little more relaxed about the timing of an exit.

Both Growth and Development Capital GPs need to pay particular attention to (1) minority shareholder protection and (2) exit protection. The former is achieved largely through 'negative control' provisions. The latter is achieved by various measures, the best known of which are Tag Along and Drag Along.

It is with Growth and Development activity that Private Equity markets tend to begin. Thus, these two types of investment currently dominate deal-making in emerging markets such as China, Russia, South America, India and the Middle East. However, in some of these places, notably India, there is also significant Venture activity.

12

Secondary Private Equity
Fund Investing

It is often said that Private Equity is an illiquid asset class, and strictly speaking that is true. Certainly there is no public market for Private Equity, either at the fund level or the company level. In other words, there is no quoted price for either Limited Partnership interests in Private Equity funds,[1] or for the shares in their portfolio companies. It is therefore definitely the case that, in legal terms, Private Equity is an illiquid asset class. In fact, this is, for many investors, its main attraction. They like the opportunity to take some of their assets in respect of which they have no need of short-term liquidity, and invest them in illiquid investments, trading short-term liquidity for the expectation of higher long-term returns.

The recent financial crisis has exposed yet another advantage of illiquid investment vehicles. They will usually be valued on the basis of their underlying assets, rather than priced at the whim of stock markets. There used, for example, to be many investors who sought some or all of their Private Equity exposure through quoted vehicles; the first edition of this book, written in 2006, suggested this is as one possible way of deploying uninvested capital. The crisis has changed this thinking dramatically, however, or should have if investors have been thinking about the wider implications of what has happened.

What we have seen is quoted alternative asset vehicles across all classes (but most obviously Private Equity and real estate) moving up and down not in response to asset revaluations, but rather in line with stock exchange beta, which might be thought of as the gravitational pull of the stock market. In the UK, for example, 3i, surely the largest Private Equity vehicle in the world, and a key component of the FTSE 100 index, was, early in 2007, trading at about a 30% premium to its net asset value, whereas by early 2009 it dropped as low as a 75% deficit to net assets (having revalued its assets downwards in the meantime). The arithmetic is fairly simple. If one assumes an asset devaluation of 10%, then that is the loss that would have been suffered by an investor holding 3i as a notional private vehicle, such as a Limited Partnership. Holding it as a public company would have caused that same investor a loss of nearly 82%.

In practical terms, however, it is no longer the case that Private Equity is an illiquid asset class, nor has it been for some years, since an active secondary market exists for Limited Partners' interests, and some Private Equity managers specialise in this space, seeking nothing but secondary purchases. Let us look at why people look to buy and sell 'secondaries', and how the process works.

---

[1] Although there is persistent talk of such a market being established, at least for the 'big name' funds.

WHY DO PEOPLE BUY SECONDARIES?

This is obviously an important question for those who raise secondary funds to be able to answer. Indeed, in the early days of the secondary market back in the 1990s it was commonplace to hear investors say 'why should I invest in a fund that is going to buy rubbish that other people don't want?'

The problem here lies in the assumption that secondary interests are unwanted rubbish. In fact, this is very rarely the case, and if it were it is unlikely that anybody holding such 'rubbish' would be able to find a buyer for it. Secondary players are discriminating and, as we will see, there are certain types of interest they would simply not consider.

In the world of secondaries, it is much more likely that it is the seller, rather than the interest they hold, which is distressed. Even this does not apply in many cases, where the seller is not distressed at all but has a valid reason for wanting to sell. We will look at these reasons in due course, but first let us address the question which we posed above: why should people want to buy secondary interests at all, and in particular why should they prefer them to primaries, i.e. committing capital to a Private Equity fund in the usual way when it is formed?

Time and the J-curve

There are some investors who find the idea of a Private Equity type return appealing, but who cannot or will not countenance the very long-term nature of the asset class. To a certain extent, they can seek to mitigate this by avoiding Venture funds, which tend to last longer than some other types of fund, but this is only a partial solution. In many cases even the ten to twelve years which must be assumed for the sake of caution for a Buyout fund may seem too excessive.[2] It is here that the world of secondaries may offer an attractive prospect.

If we think about the way in which a Private Equity fund works, we remember the J-curve, with its early years of negative returns. Suppose, however, we could buy a Private Equity fund not on day one at the beginning of the J-curve but after about five years, when the negative portion of the J-curve has already been played out.

Figure 12.1 shows what happens. The primary investor has to endure an initial period of negative returns (particularly if measured on an annual basis). A sophisticated LP will not

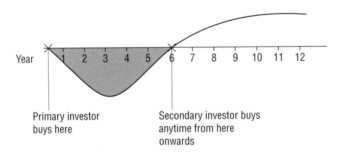

Figure 12.1   A Secondary investor buys only the later stages of the J-curve

---

[2]There have been attempts to address this on the part of some GPs by offering annual commitment periods, i.e. with LPs making rolling one-year commitments either on a pool basis or to successive annual Limited Partnerships, but, by and large, these have not found a wide audience. Alchemy was a well-known example of this in Europe.

be concerned by this as they recognise that this is a natural function of the way in which Private Equity funds work, that annual returns are largely meaningless and that all that is really important is the compound return which a fund earns over its entire lifetime. All well and good.

The secondary investor, on the other hand, will say, 'but I can avoid having that initial period of negative returns. If I wait until the fund is fairly mature and then buy an interest from one of the LPs, I can be reasonably sure that I will never have to suffer that period of returns. On the contrary, I should be able realistically to expect positive returns from day one.' There is also the fact that rather than having to hold the interest for ten to twelve years, it is quite possible that the fund may be fully wound up within five years or so of the secondary investor having bought the interest. Let us consider each of these points in turn.

The idea that a secondary player can sit out the early, negative years of the J-curve and then buy in at a time when only positive returns can be expected in future is broadly sound. However, remember that the secondary player has to pay the vendor for the interest up front as well as honouring any remaining Capital Calls. So, in terms of periodic returns, it may well appear as if a positive return has been made in year one, since if the purchaser has bought the interest at a discount to net asset value they will be able to write it up to the fund's reported values at the end of the year, showing indeed a paper gain.

In cash flow terms, however, this is not the case. If, at the beginning of a year, you pay someone $3.5M for an interest which actually has a book value of $4M, then at the end of the year, assuming nothing else happens in the meantime, you will be able to show a gain of $0.5M and an annual return of 14.3% ($0.5M/$3.5M). The reality, however, is that you have suffered a negative cash flow of $3.5M and do not yet have any positive cash flows to set off against it. Even if we change our assumption about nothing else happening during the year, it is almost inconceivable that the fund will pay back in a single year the whole of the value you have ascribed to the interest you have bought.[3] Thus, you have actually simply started a new J-curve of your own based on your own cash flows rather than those of the fund, and would still show a negative IRR at the end of year one (and quite probably year two as well).

Incidentally, this is another example of how it can be very misleading to use annual returns in respect of funds which, in fact, represent a stream of cash flows. It is also inappropriate. After all, the J-curve is based on cash flow calculations, so in assessing how well or badly you may have done relative to it, you must compare apples with apples. The only way you can gauge your performance against a fund J-curve is to run a J-curve of your own, showing the alternative cash flows.

As for the argument that one is compressing the timeline of the fund, this is undeniably true – but at what price? Since you are compressing the time over which much of the distributions will be earned, you can legitimately expect a higher IRR than a primary investor who has committed on day one, since this is a time-based measure, and we have already seen the power of the time value of money. Yet, research shows (and secondary fund managers will tell you this themselves) that there is an associated trade-off in the shape of lower fund money multiples. In other words, once again there is a relationship between a multiple such as the TVPI and the IRR. Yes, the secondary investor may enjoy a slightly higher

---

[3]This would only be conceivable in the case of an early-stage Venture fund, which secondary investors traditionally avoid.

fund IRR, but they will enjoy it over a shorter period and will thus receive less money in total.

It has to be said, however, that none of this experience of the secondary market has encompassed a period of such dramatic change as we have recently experienced, and it remains to be seen whether it will still hold true. Some argue, for example, that if the impact of fees and costs becomes much greater as a proportion of the gross returns made at the company level, then the traditional assumption may no longer apply. Certainly there were times in 2005 and 2006 when secondary interests were strongly rumoured to be changing hands at a premium to NAV. Others contend, however, that in practice the pricing of secondary interests will adjust (ignoring short-term blips of supply and demand) to ensure that the logical position will be preserved. For those of a financial disposition, this is probably an analogous situation to that of a futures market being either in backwardation or contango; backwardation may occasionally occur, but that does not alter the fact that it is an inherently abnormal condition.

Diversification by Time

No matter how many times you may hear it said, it bears repeating that one of the most important principles with Private Equity, as with any other type of investment, is diversification. Stubbornly sticking to its very different characteristics, however, the most important form of diversification in Private Equity investing, whether at the fund or the company level, is one which does not even feature in most other areas of finance: diversification by time.

As we will see when we come to planning an investment programme, what an LP will end up with is a whole series of J-curves stretching out into the future, each representing a separate fund. What is really important is that those J-curves should, so far as possible, start from different points in time, since (1) different vintage years will perform well or badly and it is almost impossible to decide in advance which it is likely to be and (2) you do not want to have only negative cash flows at any one time (as would be the case if all your Private Equity funds were very young) or only positive cash flows (as would be the case if all your funds were very old).

The first point is significant because you want to be able to take advantage of good vintage years to off-set the poorer ones. The latter point because you want to be able to use incoming cash flows at least partly to seed future investment opportunities, otherwise your Private Equity programme will simply peter out.

It is entirely possible, however, that one might end up with an undiversified portfolio through no fault of one's own. Suppose that the powers that be decide to increase the organisation's percentage allocation to Private Equity. One will now have a situation in which you will be putting much more money to work in each future vintage year than you have in each past vintage year. Worse still, you might inherit a situation where the organisation committed money to the asset class for a few years and then stopped altogether for the next few years, so that there might actually be a yawning hole in the time-line rather than just an imbalance.

These are both situations where an investor should seek to make use of the secondary market to target funds of those specific vintage years so as to restore the necessary balance. A word of caution, however. This is not easy, and this should be borne in mind as a powerful argument against getting into this situation in the first place. Perhaps the most widely ignored advice given to LPs is that they should set their long-term allocation right away and start committing on that basis, rather than starting with a low percentage and then seeking to increase it later.

A more extreme version of this strategy may be found where an investor is looking to enter the asset class for the first time, and decides to target the secondary market at the same time as making primary commitments in an effort to gain exposure to previous vintage years and thus artificially create the position of an investor who has actually been in the market for some years. Incidentally, this is considerably easier to accomplish than what we were considering previously, since that requires the interests purchased to be from particular vintage years, whereas in the case of a new investor it almost does not matter how the interests are spread across years. Thus, the latter can be accomplished by investing in a secondaries fund, whereas the former cannot.

Diversification by Geography and Sector

These more mainstream types of diversification can be addressed in exactly the same way. The most extreme form can be found in the case of LPs who, believe it or not, are allowed to invest only in Private Equity funds investing locally in their own country. Once this restriction is relaxed, the only real option open to the investment team will be to enter the secondaries market and buy a more international coverage (perhaps selling some of their local exposure at the same time).

Similarly, there have been times when it has been fashionable to invest only in Buyout or only in Venture. Again, hopefully, the limitations of either such approach will be obvious, but it has been the norm for many investors. Here, too, the secondary market offers an opportunity to redress the balance when common sense re-establishes itself. There were many investors looking to sell Venture fund interests in 2002 and 2003, for example, just as there will doubtless be many looking to sell Buyout fund interests in 2010 and 2011.

TREASURY AND PORTFOLIO SECONDARIES

This is a distinction which the author first advanced some years ago, and which now seems to have become accepted as a part of doing business in the secondary space. It is a distinction which has a parallel in the world of investment as a whole, namely that between passive and active investing.

Passive investing is designed to capture what is known as the beta of a particular asset class.[4] For example, if you want to invest in the S&P100 index, then you can simply buy the index itself, either by matching your own share portfolio exactly to its own constituents, or by investing in a tracker fund. That return may be good or bad at any particular time, but one thing is guaranteed: it is, and always will be, the return of the S&P100.

If, on the other hand, you want to take a chance of underperforming the index as the trade-off for the chance of outperforming it, then you can hire a manager who will attempt to pick individual stocks from within the S&P100. This is active, as opposed to passive, investing. This may also be good or bad at any particular time, but will never be the same as the index itself (the beta return). Instead it is something called alpha,[5] which will be either more or less

---

[4] What is often referred to misleadingly by traditional finance theory as 'systemic risk', since it actually has very little to do with 'risk' in any real sense at all.

[5] Strictly speaking, the alpha return is actually the return in excess of the beta, but many investors seem not to realise that this means alpha can be (and frequently is) negative, particularly after all the extra fees and costs have been taken into account.

than the index, though it is by reference to the index that the manager's performance will be evaluated. Such an approach is often referred to as 'seeking alpha'.

Of course, strictly speaking, passive investing is not possible in Private Equity since there is no available beta. This is a slightly controversial area, so let us choose our words with care. What is meant by this statement is that there is no beta available which is both (1) truly representative of the Private Equity as a whole and (2) truly 'investable' in the same way as, for example, a quoted index such as the S&P might be.

However, there is a situation which is roughly analogous to it, and that is the treasury secondary. Here, the distinction is not so much the type of return one is chasing, but whether one is chasing a particular manager (GP) in the belief that they will be likely to outperform the market (however one expresses that). With a treasury secondary, then, as long as (1) its vintage year, and geographic and sectoral coverage are consistent with what one is looking for and (2) the numbers make sense (as to which, see below), then one should logically be fairly indifferent as to the name of the manager.

With a portfolio secondary, however, one is actively seeking new or extra exposure to that particular manager because one feels that it would be a welcome addition to the portfolio. For example, you may have committed money for the first time to a particular manager for their Fund IV, and you become aware (probably from them) that there may be a secondary available in one of their prior funds. There are two other possibilities. First, you may not actually have committed money to this GP yet, but have them very firmly on your list of hot prospects. If you are doing your job properly as a proactive LP, they will know this and may well approach you as a favour should this sort of opportunity arise. Second, you may have committed money to a particular fund, but have been unable to satisfy your appetite in full as they were overcommitted. Here, the attractive opportunity would be to pick up a secondary interest in that same fund from anyone who may, for whatever reason, be looking to sell.

Incidentally, a failure to understand this basic difference led to some ill-feeling in the past; GPs who had acquired LPs by way of a secondary purchase looked to them for a commitment to their next fund, and were disappointed. As we will see, this, in turn, led to the creation of a creature called a stapled primary.

WHY DO PEOPLE SELL SECONDARIES?

Easy enough, then, to understand why investors might be looking to buy secondaries. More difficult, perhaps, to understand why they might be looking to sell them, particularly since, apart from abnormal periods such as occurred around 2005 and 2006, a vendor will normally have to accept a discount to book value. Interestingly, what to many people may seem the most obvious answer, namely dissatisfaction with the GP, actually comes fairly low on the list whenever a vendor survey is carried out.

Change of Strategy/Leaving the Asset Class

A 'change of strategy' is usually the euphemism employed by people who have decided they do not want to invest in Private Equity funds any more. Sometimes there is a valid reason for this, such as where a short-term investor (such as a non-life insurance company or a bank) has been lured into the asset class but then realises later that its long-term nature is inconsistent with the organisation's need for liquidity. More often, though, a change of top management is the more prosaic reason. Believe it or not, there are a considerable number of people who simply do not believe in Private Equity, despite the excellent historic performance figures which it has generated. As we noted when we looked at Private Equity returns, this is frequently because they have actually misunderstood the nature of the figures at which they are looking, but so be it.

This was a prevalent reason for secondary sales back in 2002, when many investors who had been drawn into Private Equity during 1999 and 2000 (and committed most of their money to Internet-focused Venture funds) decided to withdraw: Nomura and Bertelsmann were but two examples. While details of secondary transactions are rarely made public, it is difficult to imagine that these were beneficial transactions for the sellers, since not only were early-stage Venture funds deeply unattractive to secondary purchasers, but the sellers had usually openly broadcast their intention of selling off their whole portfolio for strategic reasons.

Overconcentration by Time, Sector or Geography

This is simply the mirror image of what we examined when looking at reasons for buying. Sometimes where additional money may not be immediately available, an investor may look to sell funds in one area and use whatever capital is realised to buy some in others.

Unexpected Need for Cash

This can occur in three ways, one of which we have already met. This is where a short-term investor, such as a corporate treasury department or a non-life insurance company, is drawn into the world of Private Equity funds and then realises too late that this may not be a very good idea given their own liquidity needs.

The second is where a long-term investor has quite properly gone into Private Equity but then faces a need for cash which was entirely unexpected. A good example of this would be where the sponsor of a corporate pension plan embarks upon a programme of plant closures and/or layoffs, which may well involve offers of early retirement.

The third way in which this can arise is something that has been dubbed 'Cash 22'. This arises where an investor has made a combination of unfortunate decisions. One of the first requirements when setting investment strategy is to model your liabilities, at least for the next three to five years, and plan to have these cash flow needs covered by assets which can easily be turned into cash. Where Cash 22 has arisen, it has tended to be as a result of investors getting both sides of this equation wrong.

In modelling their liabilities they have tended to look only at their operational liabilities (e.g. a college endowment modelling the projected costs of running the college) without also taking into account cash outflows that may occur as a result of Capital Calls within their Private Equity programme. In looking at liquid assets, they have tended to eschew government bonds in favour of corporate or emerging market bonds. This arises as a result of a misunderstanding of the function of bonds in a portfolio; they are a cash substitute, designed to ensure liquidity in any circumstances. They are not an investment, designed to generate a significant rate of return. In trying to treat them as the latter rather than the former, investors have been punished when liquidity has been required in extreme conditions (for example September 2008) and there has been effectively no market for corporate or emerging market bonds.

Perhaps predictably, investors have rushed to blame Private Equity as an asset class for this result rather than their own faulty planning and execution of asset allocation. There is actually a germ of validity in such criticism in that average Private Equity holding periods have lengthened, as we will see when we look at planning an investment programme, but no more than a germ. Whatever the case, this is another situation where an investor may feel forced into the secondary market to raise some cash in order to honour Capital Calls.

Housekeeping

There is a considerable cost to managing and monitoring Private Equity fund investments, or at least there is if one seeks to do it well. For this reason, if a fund has reached a point where it has only one or two investments left, and none of these are likely to be unexpectedly big winners (what is usually called the 'tail' of the portfolio, but within a Venture fund may be referred to unflatteringly as the 'living dead'), then it can make a lot of sense simply to sell this interest on, particularly if it can be bundled up with other similar interests to make what might be an attractive job lot. This is usually referred to as 'housekeeping', although 'spring cleaning' might be a more apt description since one is really just cleaning up the portfolio.

Dissatisfaction with the GP

Sadly, the balance of bargaining power during fund document negotiations in recent years has meant that once an LP has signed up to a fund, they have few remedies available if things start happening which they do not like. For many, particularly investors whose commitment to the fund is relatively small, selling their interest and simply drawing a line under their involvement with that particular GP may be seen as their only effective option.

It was the fear that this would be the perception of third parties that for many years made many GPs very hostile to the idea of any of their LPs selling their interests. However, as time has gone by, it has become better understood that this is actually quite a rare occurrence, and that the overwhelming majority of secondary sales are driven by totally different motives. In practice, selling one's interest is very much a measure of last resort, as most GPs are at least open to discussion should an LP have a grievance, and most LPs know only too well that they are likely to lose money should they seek to sell.

RESTRICTIONS ON TRANSFER

The way in which fund documentation has evolved with regard to secondary interests mirrors the evolution of attitudes which was just described.

Originally there was, in many cases, quite simply a ban on selling a secondary interest. The documents would stipulate that the transfer could not take place without the consent of the GP, which meant that the GP could simply forbid any such transaction. This reckoned without the ingenuity of the legal profession, however, who invented something called a synthetic secondary, whereby the LP who wanted to sell their interest but had been prevented from doing so would enter into a declaration of trust, agreeing to hold it on trust for the party to whom they had wished to sell it, thus putting both parties in pretty much the same position[6] they would have been in had the sale gone through.

The next phase of development in fund terms saw the introduction of rights of pre-emption; in other words, if you wanted to sell your interest you had first to offer it, through the GP, to the other LPs in the fund. GPs saw this as offering them protection against an interest passing outside their chosen LP base, but greatly underestimated the 'hassle factor' involved in implementing it. First, all LPs had to be circulated with details of the interest and invited to state both their appetite and their offer price. Then, any amount still remaining had to be re-offered, perhaps several times. Finally, extensive documentation might be required to record all this. Bear in mind, too, that before the age of email, this would all have to be done by letter or fax.

Gradually, GPs became more comfortable with the idea of professional secondary purchasers. This was due to two things: a growing perception that selling an interest did not automatically imply dissatisfaction with the GP (if there were problems with the GP, then why would anybody else wish to buy the interest?), and learning through experience that secondary purchasers acted properly as responsible LPs once they came on board.

This has brought us to the present stage of development which, while by no means universal, is becoming increasingly widespread. This is that the GP's consent is required to a transfer, but that the GP's consent may not be unreasonably withheld.

An example may serve to illustrate this. Suppose that you hold an interest in a Fund of Funds managed by, say, Pantheon. You decide, for whatever reason, to sell your interest to a Dutch pension fund. In this situation, Pantheon could have no possible reasonable excuse to refuse their consent to the transfer, unless perhaps the interest was in an ERISA-compliant vehicle and the presence of such an investor might put its ERISA status at risk.

Consider, however, if you wanted to sell your interest to someone like Harborvest. Now it would be relatively easy for Pantheon to justify refusing their consent on the grounds that Harborvest were a direct competitor, and that having them as an LP in one of their funds would put Pantheon in an invidious position.

Stapled Primaries

Obviously one of the main objections by a GP to the idea of one of their LPs selling their interest to a secondary purchaser would run along the lines 'this is all very well, but this is going to leave me with a hole in my LP base the next time I go fundraising.' Thus, in the negotiations for GP consent and co-operation, there was often an intricate shadow boxing routine going on whereby the GP would be saying 'I would be much happier going ahead with this if I knew that you (the secondary purchaser) were going to commit money to my next fund as an LP' while the secondary player was (effectively) trying to explain the difference between a portfolio secondary and a treasury secondary. Of course, where the purchaser was a specialist secondary player, they had a more direct response, which was simply 'we are a secondary investor; we don't do primaries.'

Since we have already looked (above) at the concept of a synthetic secondary, it might seem strange that this discussion would even take place. Surely the secondary player could simply take a synthetic secondary and short-circuit this whole debate? The answer to that lies

---

[6]Not ideal, though, since the 'vendor' would remain liable in the first instance for future Capital Calls as against the GP and the fund.

in the word 'co-operation' in the last paragraph. As we will see when we come to look at the methodology of a secondary transaction, the whole process becomes both much easier and less risky given the whole-hearted participation of a friendly GP. In extreme cases, it may be difficult, in the absence of GP consent, for the potential vendor even to show you the quarterly accounts of the fund because of confidentiality constraints. There is, accordingly, a benefit here for which secondary purchasers will be prepared to pay a price; the only question then becomes 'how much'?

So, despite the objection that this was a treasury secondary and did not imply a desire for any ongoing relationship, or that a secondary fund's investors did not expect it to make primary commitments, there did grow up, at least in some cases, a practice of committing a certain amount of money to a GP's next fund as the price for their consent and co-operation on the acquisition of a secondary interest in their current fund. These commitments became known as 'stapled primaries' in the sense that one document (the pre-commitment to the next fund) was effectively stapled to another (the GP's consent to the secondary transaction). In fact, making a marketing virtue out of what they perceived to be an operational necessity, some secondary fund managers ended up establishing a separate primary fund for their investors specifically to make such commitments.

SECONDARY METHODOLOGY

The purchase of a secondary interest in a fund is essentially a much less risky operation than making a primary commitment to it in the first place, at least if one equates risk with uncertainty. This is because before the fund begins operations, one clearly has no idea at all precisely in which companies it will invest, nor when. By the time that a secondary purchaser comes along the fund will frequently be fully, or at least substantially, invested. Thus, one will know not only in which companies the GP has invested, but where (both in terms of geography and business sector) and when. The latter point is at least equally important, since prevailing market conditions may make the purchase price paid seem either inviting or otherwise.

The job of a secondary purchaser is simple in principle but complicated (or at least complex) in practice. They must look at each portfolio company in turn and come to a view as to when it is likely to be exited, and for how much. This information is then modelled with any remaining cash flows (for example, ongoing management fees) to calculate an IRR. The price at which the secondary purchaser can afford to buy the interest will be that which delivers at least the target rate of return at their own transaction level (i.e. before their own fees and carried interest).

Simple in principle, yet not in practice. In reality this is a task which calls both for considerable skill and judgement, but also for the ability to make decisions in conditions of uncertainty. Nobody can 'know' for sure when a company will be exited, not even the GP. A GP's honest assessment of their portfolio in the autumn of 2006, for example, would have been totally different to their honest assessment of those same companies a year later, let alone two years later, not least because of the dramatically different prevailing market conditions.

These do not impact solely on price expectations. Anyone who has worked in investment banking will know that there are times, sometimes for no clear reason, when the IPO window 'opens' or 'closes', and this may have little to do with pricing, but with more insubstantial factors such as investor appetite, which is, in turn, impacted by such things as the apparent relative attractions of other asset classes.[7] With Venture portfolios, there is an additional complication, which is the possibility of a competitor having achieved rapid penetration of a particular market, or a particular technology breakthrough, despite the merits of one's own portfolio company.

All this assumes that you can actually access the information sources that you need. Suppose, on the contrary, that the GP is resolutely opposed to your deal, and refuses either to give you information, release the LP from their confidentiality obligations or ask any of their portfolio CEOs to talk to you.

This latter issue is of particular importance, since, just as when performing due diligence for a primary commitment, portfolio CEOs are perhaps the most valuable source of information. Yet they are hugely busy people, and their priority is to run and develop their business, not to talk to outsiders. Without the GP asking them to do so, they are unlikely to be prepared to co-operate with something which they will see as being nothing to do with them. They would also be naturally wary of disclosing confidential business information which could be of use to their competitors. This is yet another reason why, disregarding the strict legal landscape, there is, in practice, almost always a price which it is worth paying for GP co-operation.

Obviously even if all the required information is forthcoming there can still be no certainty, yet another blow to those who see all investment propositions as situations in which it is possible to find the one 'right' answer. Here there is no possibility of being entirely right or wrong, but only of being either cautious or bold in one's pricing, and lucky or unlucky in one's timing. In practice, secondary purchasers will model a range of alternative outcomes, and use their skill and experience to pitch an offer somewhere in a region which makes sense for both sides.

TAILS

A 'tail' is an expression which has sprung up to describe those companies which a fund has left in its portfolio as it approaches, or even enters, its extension or 'run-off' period. These can, particularly in the case of a Venture fund, be referred to less flatteringly as 'the living dead'.

An IRR is a harsh task-mistress. The time value of money is represented by some very cruel arithmetic which dramatically reduces the impact of cash receipts occurring towards the end of a fund's life. One well-known Fund of Funds had a fund which, in the fifteenth year of its existence, returned to LPs in cash the whole of its original committed capital. Yet this heroic effort succeeded only in lifting its lifetime IRR from inception from 14% to just 15%.

It is therefore becoming increasingly well recognised that once a Private Equity fund, almost regardless of type, passes its first decade of existence, then whatever happens to its remaining investments from that time onwards will make very little difference to the fund's overall performance. Indeed, given the time value of money, they will have to perform very well indeed even to maintain the fund's IRR at its present level.

---

[7]In the late 1990s, for example, the IPO window for non-technology companies remained very quiet for some time, despite steadily rising stock markets. Yet, at the same time, the IPO market for technology and 'dot com' companies was rampant, particularly on NASDAQ.

To cater for this situation, most secondary players have also started acquiring tails as a second string to their bow, and here, of course, the ability of a secondary player effectively to restart the J-curve is of particular significance. However, the difficulties involved in such purchases should not be underestimated. If a company has neither the growth rate nor the excitement factor to facilitate an IPO, then the only remaining possibilities are a trade sale, an MBO or some sort of recapitalisation. These are difficult areas and not to be embarked upon lightly. Why, for example, should someone want to buy a company that the GPs have presumably already been trying to sell with increasing desperation for some years?

A further problem arises, of course. Secondary purchasers are, by and large, set up to acquire and manage fund interests, not portfolio companies. Not only is a whole new range of administrative processes required, but a whole new range of investment skills. For this reason, most of these transactions take the form of the tail being effectively bundled up as a new fund, with a new GP being appointed to manage it. Their fees and carried interest will obviously be yet one more factor to build into the secondary player's calculations of how much it makes sense to pay for the tail in the first place. There is yet a further level of sophistication here, in that in appropriate circumstances the LPs in the existing fund might be offered the opportunity to become LPs in the new fund, essentially just swapping one LP interest for another, and usually injecting some new capital at the same time.

A further development in this area has been the establishment of specialist GPs who will take on these tails and manage them themselves.[8] They will also offer themselves as the GP of the new funds established by secondary purchasers as described above.

Transactions of this nature are likely to become increasingly prominent if, as widely predicted, a period of intensive consolidation is now beginning within the Private Equity industry worldwide. These are likely to be driven by a whole range of issues which would previously have been totally outside anyone's contemplation. Examples might include: LP default, inability to raise a new fund, change of control within the GP and even the winding up of the GP or related vehicle.

FEES ETC.

An obvious objection which is raised by potential LPs to the idea of committing money to a secondary fund is 'why should I pay additional layers of fees, not to mention costs and carried interest, since these will already be payable on the underlying fund interests which are to be acquired?'

This seems an obvious common sense objection, but in fact is much less so on closer examination. Remember that the secondary purchaser will be modelling the future cash flows of the underlying fund, at least so far as they can project them, and using these cash flows to establish the maximum price which they can afford to pay the vendor while still delivering their own minimum target IRR. Thus, the impact of the underlying fees and carry has already been taken into account. So, yes, they will still be payable, but no, they should not impact upon the secondary fund's own performance.

---

[8]The author once suggested the establishment of a 'Terminator' fund to do this, largely because I wanted to be able to call its successor 'Terminator 2'.

SECONDARY BUYOUTS – A WARNING

In examining the different types of Buyout activity, it is necessary to consider something which is called a Secondary Buyout. Confusingly, this has nothing to do with secondary activity at all, and it is unfortunate that the word 'secondary' has to be used in both cases. Because of this, many people quite understandably confuse a Secondary Buyout (which is a transaction between GPs at the company level) with a secondary transaction or secondary purchase (which is a transaction between LPs at the fund level).

Please see Chapter 5 for a fuller description of a Secondary Buyout, but let us simply note here that it has no place in any consideration of the secondary market.

SUMMARY

Secondary transactions involve the sale of an interest in a Private Equity fund by one LP to another, or by one LP to a specialist secondary purchaser.

Secondary transactions, sometimes called secondary purchases, have nothing to do with Secondary Buyouts, which are entirely different, and involve the sale of a company from one GP to another.

The secondary market provides practical liquidity for Private Equity fund investors, though it can be difficult to sell Venture fund interests, particularly if non-US and/or at an early stage of the fund's life.

The normal state of the secondary market implies the purchaser paying no more than net asset value, and typically a discount. While periods do occasionally occur where high demand pushes pricing into a premium to net asset value, these periods should be regarded as abnormal.

People buy secondary interests for a wide range of purposes, including targeting exposure to earlier vintage years and/or a particular sector or geography. This can be particularly helpful to an investor entering the market for the first time.

As a rule, when a secondary interest is sold, it is because the seller, rather than the asset, is distressed. Reasons for selling can involve an unexpected need for cash, a change of investment strategy or overexposure to a particular vintage year, sector, geography or GP.

GPs are often hostile to the idea of secondary purchases as they believe outsiders will perceive them to be a symptom of LP dissatisfaction, though in practice this is rarely the case.

The J-curve of a secondary fund or of an individual secondary investment will be shorter than that of a primary commitment, and may appear to show no initial negative period at all. In practice, though, this can only happen where the entire purchase price is recovered within the first year in which the investment is made, and this is highly unusual.

The need for GP consent gave rise to synthetic secondaries, where an interest is held in trust by the vendor for the purchaser. However, in most cases, secondary purchasers are now able to obtain GP approval.

A stapled primary is where a secondary purchaser will pre-commit to the GP's next fund as a quid pro quo for GP consent to the transfer of the LP interest in their current fund.

Professional secondary purchasers will now also consider the purchase of the remaining portfolio of a fund as it nears the end of its life, this being known as a tail.

Secondary-type transactions may also be driven in future by a whole new range of strategic and industry considerations such as LP defaults, fundraising failure and the change of control or winding up of GP vehicles.

13
Due Diligence

The making of any Private Equity investment is a twofold process. First comes the decision in principle as to whether this looks like an attractive prospect. If this ends with a 'yes' vote then you will have decided to make the investment 'subject to due diligence' and this second part of the process will now follow. In practice, the distinction between the two is becoming increasingly blurred, since you will have needed to investigate a lot of the facts very thoroughly in order to make your decision in principle in the first place, particularly if these have been identified as specific issues. However, for ease of discussion, we will assume that these two parts of the process are separate and discrete.

Due diligence is a huge subject, particularly so in this case since we need to cover all the different types of Private Equity investment. However, there is much that is common in the approach to each one, and so I will begin by describing the process in general and then focus on what you should look for in each particular case.

I would recommend that during the initial decision process you keep a list (putting it on a flipchart works very well) divided into three columns headed 'pros', 'cons' and 'issues' respectively. The objective of due diligence is to focus on each of the issues until it is possible to resolve it, hopefully transferring it to one of the other columns in the process. Of course, this is not always possible and there will be some issues that remain issues right up to the time the final decision is taken. Generally speaking with Private Equity you make any decision to invest despite the existence of various issues. This is just the way it is (chiefly because in many cases your decision is largely a decision to back certain individuals, and human beings are notoriously difficult to understand and classify) and if you seek a perfect situation where there can never be any possible doubt what the right decision may be, then you may well never make a single investment. You must do your best, exhausting every reasonable avenue of enquiry in the process, but you cannot achieve certainty. Indeed, it is in this final layer of uncertainty that the skill and judgement which distinguish a truly good Private Equity investor from an also-ran reside.

The fact that due diligence carries on from the initial stages of the investment process is, in fact, a great help, since you should already have identified those issues which you need to explore. Incidentally, there is an important lesson here which is ignored by the vast majority of Private Equity investors, both at the fund and at the company level. Due diligence does not take place in a vacuum. If you have a standard due diligence checklist which you dutifully and meticulously follow in each case (or, even worse, a standard questionnaire which you expect the investee to complete), then you are completely missing the point. Yes, of course there are certain things which you will always need to check, but the main purpose of due diligence is to satisfy yourself on those specific issues which you have identified during your initial investigations and analysis. Sadly most investors seem to fail to recognise that the aim of due diligence is to help them make better decisions, and prefer to see it as a means of covering their backs in advance should anything go wrong with the investment in the future (what Americans call 'papering the file').

In many cases, particularly where the LP relies on the investee supposedly to do their work for them by filling in interminable questionnaires asking for their grandmother's date of birth, due diligence at the fund level may consist largely of re-calculating the relevant historic cash flows to check that the stated IRRs are indeed correct. In passing, we should query whether this is really necessary these days when, for example, the figures have already been specifically audited by a major accounting firm, or verified by a reputable placing agent, but let that go. Such investigation may be a very good way of papering the due diligence file, but fails to address the key questions, which are not 'what is the IRR?' but 'how does it compare to the IRRs of similar funds from the same vintage year?', 'if it is different, why is it different?', 'how have the returns been influenced by the relevant drivers?', 'what evidence do the figures show of this firm doing things differently to other firms, or differently to how the same firm used to do things in the past?', etc. In other words, even financial due diligence needs to be intelligent and geared towards answering specific questions, not just verifying the data which have been proffered.

At the company level, of course, particularly in the case of Buyouts, verification *is* vitally important and will usually be addressed by way of an investigating accountant's report. Yet even here, financial due diligence will go way beyond verification and the exploration of contingent liabilities, etc. The Buyout firm will be flexing the forecasts and management accounts to see how much extra cash flow can be squeezed out to service debt, or investigating the effects of possible asset or business unit sales. There will also be legal, environmental and regulatory audits.

However, it is on the 'soft' issues that due diligence becomes the most difficult, partly because people are always reluctant to speak frankly about their associates, and in particular reluctant to say anything negative about them. For some reason this problem is particularly acute in France, where effective 'people' due diligence is all but impossible; even if you make the effort to have the conversation in French, all anyone will usually say is that the object of your enquiries is 'well-connected'. A good way of getting around this problem, if you can, is to track down anyone who has left the firm recently; even the insights of quite junior staff on things like team dynamics can be very helpful. This raises a further important point, by the way. By all means make a few calls to the names you have been given as a reference list, but this should be largely a matter of form, since they are most unlikely to tell you anything really valuable. Most of your calls should be 'off the list'. In addition to recent leavers, try to find the CEOs of portfolio companies which may have got into difficulties, any other Private Equity firms who co-invested in such deals, and any LPs who committed to previous funds but have now stopped doing so.

Also as a matter of form you should verify the personal details you have been given by contacting previous employers and educational institutions. It is amazing how many people lie about their class of degree, for example. It is a pity that this is not done more often as a matter of routine when checking offering documents and the like. The author has so far come across someone who claimed to have a degree from a prestigious British university when in fact he had been expelled in his first year, and someone who put the letters 'LLD' after his name – something which went unnoticed for some time despite the fact that this can only be awarded as an honorary degree to a major public figure, whereas this particular gentleman turned out to be a struck-off solicitor's clerk. The cast of characters over the years has also included a phoney barrister, and someone who changed the spelling of his name in an attempt to conceal a string of bankruptcy orders (and who also turned out to have spent time at Her Majesty's pleasure, described rather inventively as 'voluntary work overseas').

Incidentally, in some countries it is no longer possible to approach academic and professional institutions on the basis of enquiring for information which is available as a matter of public record. In such cases, the subjects of your enquiries can be asked to provide transcripts of their qualifications, and in most cases these can be issued electronically.

All this should be routine, but often is not. The scope of due diligence is bounded only by your imagination and the amount of time which you have available, but you should never lose sight of the real objective, which is to resolve any outstanding issues which you have with the fund or company. In the case of a fund, all your enquiries should be leading you towards one thing: exactly how does this group do its deals, and how does this differ from other people in the same space? This will include things such as dealflow (industry veteran Ian Simpson memorably drew attention one April Fools' Day to a virus which had invaded the computers of Private Equity practitioners inserting the phrases 'proprietary dealflow' and 'upper quartile performance' at random into GPs' presentations) but also how they develop their portfolio companies during the post-investment phase.

BUYOUT FUNDS

We have seen in earlier chapters how to model and analyse Buyout returns. You need to be able to examine exactly what contribution each of the three drivers has made, since this will give you a good idea of how the firm creates value for its investors. Top of your list of preferences should be any firm that is able consistently to increase company earnings in real terms (i.e. after adjusting for inflation), since this is a group that is likely to be able to make money in any market conditions.

However, you should also use your driver analysis to compare what the firm has been doing against other Buyout firms over time; obviously this will only become possible as you add more Buyout firms to your portfolio over the years, but once comparative data *is* available, this can become a very revealing exercise. Is one firm using more or less debt than the others, for example, or paying higher multiples for its companies? There is often a surprising variation in the former measure, while the latter can be an indicator of a group that is either overcapitalised or struggling for dealflow (and, in either case, likely to be over-eager to do deals).

Incidentally, this is one reason why doing due diligence on a firm is never wasted. Even if you decide at the end of the day not to invest, then your due diligence material can be saved and used for comparative purposes when analysing other funds. However, there is a very important point to be made here. You should never embark upon due diligence routinely just to acquire data for these purposes. There are quite a few LPs who do seem to do this, and they rapidly acquire a poor reputation amongst GPs and placing agents. Due diligence should only follow a decision in principle to invest, and if you are not committing to at least two-thirds of the funds on which you perform due diligence then something is wrong; specifically, you are starting a full due diligence process when a little limited information gathering could probably have killed the project at a much earlier stage. Due diligence time is precious both to you and others, particularly if you are going to do things properly by speaking to lots of people. Use it wisely to do really meaningful work on those few funds you believe to be key prospects. If you acquire a reputation for wasting other people's time, this will definitely count against you after a while in terms of access to the best funds.

Dealflow is key for Buyout firms and one of the things you should be analysing is exactly where each deal comes from. For the larger players, just about every deal will nowadays go through some sort of auction process, so be very wary of deals which are described as 'proactive' or 'exclusive' in origin. Similarly, most will today involve a consortium of investors, possibly with equity syndication outside the consortium as well. A word of warning here: every Buyout firm involved in a consortium will claim to have led it, and that their involvement was the reason why the deal was offered to the consortium in the first place (e.g. 'we had been chasing this deal for five years', 'we knew the company very well', 'we have recognised expertise in the sector', etc.). Take such claims with a pinch of salt and see if you can find independent verification (perhaps from the investment bank which handled the deal, from a lending bank or from someone who has recently left one of the Buyout firms involved) of exactly what really happened.

Equally important is to try to find out which deals they were chasing but did not manage to close. Were they on the short list of potential purchasers? If not, which of their competitors were preferred, and why? If they were on the list but did not close the deal, why was this? Is it possible to check, for example, that the price they offered was lower than that of the winning consortium, and, if so, by how much, and why?

With smaller Buyout firms due diligence can take on a more traditional flavour since here it is perfectly possible that they may be sourcing deals on an exclusive and/or proactive basis, but again do maintain a healthy scepticism. The tentacles of the auction process now reach a very long way down the size scale. Times have changed since a management team used to hire an accountancy firm and go to see two or three Buyout firms. These days most company vendors will use some sort of intermediary who will solicit offers from a wide variety of purchasers.

Team dynamics are key and require careful teasing out. How many of the executives share in the carry and the management fee profits, and in what percentages? There can be some very large sums of money involved, particularly in the case of mega funds, and having the equity ownership contained within too tight a group of people is generally an unwelcome sign, as it can be an omen of executive departures or an unhappy ship.

Similarly, exactly who takes the investment decisions, and how are these made? Is it by majority voting? Does any one person have a veto? Does it have to be unanimous? Incidentally, do look out for situations where an outsider, i.e. someone who is not a member of the executive team, plays any part in the investment decision process. This will not normally be an issue since it will typically only occur where a group is not independent but is part of a larger organisation (usually a bank or an insurance company), and you would not normally consider a fund managed by such a team in the first place. However, it is still quite common in some quarters for one or two prominent outsiders to play a role. Another way in which the issue can occur is if an outsider has previously played a role, but the team has got the message that this is bad news for investors and has removed the person from that role. The problem here is that sometimes all that happens is that the name disappears from the Offering Memorandum but the individual carries on playing the role de facto; you need to be very careful (but discreet) in checking what is going on here. The general rule is that if you have any doubt at all that decisions are not being made exclusively by the executives themselves, then do not proceed.

VENTURE FUNDS

Many of the points which have already been made in relation to Buyout funds are relevant here too, particularly in so far as they relate to team dynamics. Indeed, within a Venture firm this is even more important, as they tend to be more of a collegiate, equal partnership type of organisation rather than the more hierarchical structure of the typical Buyout firm. Some Venture firms, for example, have an 'only partners' policy, and thus they do all the work themselves rather than delegating it to principals, associates, analysts, senior vice presidents, junior vice presidents, middling vice presidents, etc. In such a situation the relationship of each partner to the others is all-important and should form a large part of your initial discussions and due diligence work. Again, the best people to ask are almost certainly not the partners themselves but people who have dealings with the firm and who, ideally, have been involved in one or more of their transactions (including ones that have not worked out).

We have already seen that what distinguishes a good Venture firm from its competitors is home-run mentality, and all your due diligence should be focused on identifying the presence or otherwise of this. Unfortunately, just as every Buyout firm will claim to have proprietary dealflow, so every Venture firm will claim to have a home-run mentality, since this is something they have learned that LPs expect, so this is very much an area where you will have to rely on what you see and hear for yourself, rather than on what you are told.

With an established firm which has been in business for ten years or more, there is a very simple litmus test which can tell you straightaway if this is an offering on which you wish to spend any time or not. If they are now on, say, Fund IV and none of their earlier funds seem likely to return at least three times their money or to produce a home run (and to do one without the other is difficult), then you are probably entitled to assume that this is a good indicator that the firm is unlikely ever to achieve this. Remember, we are defining a home run as something which has the potential to return the whole capital of the fund at least once, so even if there has been a big winner (25× or better) it does not count as a home run if it only made up, say, 1% of the fund.

This raises an important point, and something which is not appreciated (and certainly not carried out) by most LPs who do due diligence on Venture firms. It is crucial that you analyse the money multiple made by each deal relative to what percentage of the fund it made up. Ideally, of course, what you want to see is a good correlation between big bets and big winners. This is a very good indicator of home-run mentality; a firm that is identifying and killing off its losers quickly and devoting its resources to those few companies which emerge as having home-run potential. While a perfect result (a trend line from bottom left to top right) will rarely be possible, a cluster of companies in either the top left-hand or bottom right-hand corners would almost certainly be a clear reason not to invest with that firm.

The percentage of a company's equity which is held by the fund is also often a good indicator of how they are doing business. The ideal is a fund which can get into a company early, secure a good equity percentage (anything up to about 40%) and protect that against subsequent dilution as much as possible, ending up with 15% to 20%. If a fund shows consistently low percentage holdings, then either (1) they are not doing a good job of protecting their position or (2) they are predominantly coming into other people's deals at a later stage.[1] Neither of these approaches is likely to result in the scoring of home runs. Obviously there are exceptions when a company's valuation really explodes, as happened recently with Skype, but the general principle is clear. It is much easier to score a home run if you have a large

---

[1] The author was once making a reference call to the CEO of a company in which a Venture fund had taken a very small stake late in the day, and when it was explained that the call was about XYZ Partners, the CEO asked 'who?'

percentage of a company's equity, since you will capture proportionately more of the gain, and if it represents a good percentage (at least 4%) of your fund, since it will have a much greater effect on the fund's money multiple. We want to invest with Venture firms which have the maximum chance of scoring home runs, so we will tend to avoid those which exhibit either of the above tendencies.

The other aspect of a home-run mentality which needs to be thoroughly tested is the ability to contribute value add. This is best done by speaking to other Venture Capitalists who have invested alongside them, and CEOs whose companies have been backed by the firm in the past, and quizzing them about what the individual GPs actually did for the company. Here, there may well be a dramatic difference in the responses depending on whether you are in Europe or America.

In the US you will hear about GPs helping with product development, drawing up sales presentations, making introductions to key customers, hiring executives, etc. The CEO is likely to be very clued-up about Venture best practice, particularly if they are an experienced entrepreneur, and may well be able to draw direct comparisons with other Venture firms. When conducting due diligence on a traditional European Venture firm, CEOs are likely to say 'well, they come to the board meeting once a month – after all, that's what Venture Capitalists do, you know.' Happily, things are changing in Europe, but clearly a response like this is not likely to inspire confidence in a firm's ability to score home runs.

There are lots of other things that you can do when looking at a Venture fund. You can check to see how their pre-money valuations compare to other deals, how their performance may differ by sector and whether their investment focus is moving earlier or later by stage (this may well be a function of fund size – larger Venture funds typically push a firm later in stage focus). At the end of the day, however, home runs are all that really matter in Venture Capital and all your due diligence, no matter what form it takes, should be geared to answering the fundamental question: how likely is it that this fund will end up with at least one home run in it?

With Venture becoming an increasingly global business, you also need to look very carefully at how a firm might be able to grow a company across national boundaries if they are operating in sectors where this might prove necessary. For example, if a Californian firm is doing deals in the mobile space, how is it going to access European markets? Similarly, how might a European firm relocate a software company to the US? This is usually seen as much more of an issue for European firms, who commonly complain that it is impossible for them to get the attention of the leading US Venture firms when they try to interest them in becoming a US co-investor in their deals. However, what is less well appreciated is that the failure of most of the best US Venture firms successfully to colonise Europe may well prove to be a source of major strategic weakness in the future.

Co-investors

As an essential part of the due diligence on a Venture fund you should look carefully at the Venture firms which co-invested in portfolio companies. Quality Venture firms want to invest in quality companies alongside other quality Venture firms, and the identity of co-investors is a very good indicator of levels of peer recognition and respect, both for the firm generally and for its portfolio companies. Indeed, if you want a 'quick and dirty' indicator of firm quality, you could simply look at the identity of their co-investors and the number of home runs they have scored. However, please be aware that this measure, though still valid, is less applicable in Europe, where capital is typically in short supply and Venture firms frequently have to take co-investors where they can find them.

Incidentally, this is an issue, too, in Buyout funds, but for different reasons. We have already noted the practice of Buyout funds gathering together in consortia to bid for various companies. We are now also starting to see evidence of equity being syndicated immediately after completion to other Buyout funds, who may have been members of unsuccessful consortia bidding for the same deal. This needs to be carefully monitored, as it threatens to commoditise Buyout returns. In particular, if you see evidence of two or three Buyout firms habitually acting together, then you need to think very carefully about whether you can validly invest with any more than one of them. Conversely, if you see evidence of a Buyout firm that can act alone and still win deals, or perhaps involve other firms infrequently and on a random basis, then this offers genuine potential for a unique pattern of returns.[2]

CROSS-FUND INVESTING

With both Buyout and Venture funds you need to keep a very careful eye on instances of cross-fund investing. This deserves a mention here because traditionally it has been more of an issue with Venture funds, although there have been a couple of high profile cases involving Buyout funds in recent years. The reason it is more of an issue in normal circumstances with Venture funds is that Venture companies will have serial funding rounds, whereas typically Buyout companies will have only one. Thus, in Buyout situations it normally arises either where a company is making an acquisition, or where it has got into severe difficulty and an injection of new equity is proposed, or (and this may surprise you) where it is being sold by way of a Secondary Buyout and the Buyout firm involved decides to make a new investment into the deal from its current fund alongside the purchaser.

Space forbids a detailed examination of these situations but suffice it to say that each of these Buyout situations involves at least the potential for massive conflict of interest (since the LP membership of each fund will be different) and the need for a strong and disinterested advisory board of independent views is paramount (but unfortunately rarely realised). The best advice that can be given is that if you come across such a situation that seems a particularly unfair use of current fund capital, then this is probably a firm whose offerings would best be avoided in future.

Note, however, the proviso 'in normal conditions'. We are not currently experiencing normal conditions, and many Buyouts which have been transacted in recent years require, or will shortly require, re-financing. As we noted when we looked at the way in which Buyouts work, in the past these situations were often used as an opportunity to squeeze a little more debt into the deal, thus releasing some equity for return to investors. Not so now.

Today it is much more likely that Buyout funds will be required to inject fresh capital into a deal, or face the consequences. Recent re-financings such as Incisive Media and Gala Coral, for example, have seen large slices of value effectively being relinquished in favour of the banks. While there is, as yet, no evidence that this is actually happening, there must at least exist the temptation for GPs to use the capital of their current fund (for which they presently have little or no use anyway) to rescue deals from prior funds.

---

[2] But beware – this could be uniquely bad as well as uniquely good!

Within a Venture fund, other issues arise in addition to the obvious one of valuation. Principally you will need to ask what went wrong with the reserves for future funding rounds within the firm's prior fund, and question to what extent the effect of such follow-on investing may shift the investment stage focus of the new fund away from early stage towards late stage. The general principle should be that an early-stage Venture fund should not be investing in a company for the first time at a later stage, full stop. To do so is to diminish its chances of scoring a home run, to which end every penny of fund capital should be utilised.

BUYOUT COMPANIES

Buyout firms perform due diligence on prospective portfolio companies in much the same way that any prospective corporate acquirer would in any M&A transaction and this is one reason why Buyout professionals are often drawn from the ranks of investment bankers, accountants or Chartered Financial Analysts; the disciplines of M&A and Buyout are very similar in the investment and exit modes, though a Buyout firm will be looking at a company with different objectives in mind.

So, full financial due diligence is the order of the day and, as we have already seen, this will usually include commissioning a report from an investigating accountant. This is partly in the nature of an audit process but more importantly (since the most recent audited accounts will usually form the subject of reps and warranties anyway) looks at things like the company's currency exposure, leasing and borrowing arrangements and working capital generally. The objective is to make quite sure that the cash flow assumptions which the Buyout firm is making can, in fact, be relied upon. This is hugely important since, as we saw in an earlier chapter, the ability to service and repay the acquisition debt is an essential requirement for the success of any Buyout.

The Buyout firm will also want to make sure that key personnel will stay in place during the post-deal stage. Typically, they will try to do this by persuading the individuals concerned to take some part of the sweet equity personally as well as some share options, and at the same time sign agreements which tie them to the company for a certain length of time as a condition subsequent to their equity entitlement. However, in some cases the Buyout firm is not allowed access to the management team, or only under strictly regulated conditions, so this is very much a delicate area and one where some of the black arts of the Buyout world come into play.

You will also need to examine the various supply and distribution channel agreements to which the company is party. This should be not only in the nature of a legal audit (there may, for example, be a change of control provision) but also to investigate what is likely to happen in practical terms. If, for example, the relationship with a key customer has been handled by one individual for a number of years and that individual is leaving the company, you might consider inserting some sort of earn-out provision to protect you should turnover and earnings fall sharply. If they are staying as part of the management team, then you might also be thinking about what you put in that individual's contract, as well as introducing further people into the relationship as a practical measure.

Where a very large business is concerned, which is increasingly the case given the much bigger fund sizes we are seeing, you will also need to carry out due diligence on the competitive situation for fear of falling foul of anti-trust (US) or monopolies (Europe) legislation. This can lead to a lengthy and costly investigation at the end of which the deal may be vetoed or only allowed under certain conditions (usually involving business units or rights being relinquished artificially to create greater competition).

Another area which has become of vital importance in these days of pension deficits is the question of the company's pension scheme. This can be a particular problem where the company being bought is part of a larger group and the group scheme is in deficit. Here, the acquiring entity (Buyout fund) may be required not only to make good the deficit (measured artificially for accounting and regulatory purposes) but also to bring it up to what is called 'buy-out' level. Confusingly, this has nothing to do with the Private Equity meaning of the term but refers to the cost of buying annuities for all the scheme members, which can be up to 40% higher.[3] At the time of writing this is a very topical issue. According to Mercers, even in 2006, when the problem was much less acute than it is today over 20% of Buyout firms polled said they had pulled out of a deal solely for this reason.[4] There are also now in various countries what are effectively financial penalties for closing down a business and then resuscitating it without its pension fund. Whatever the case, detailed actuarial analysis of the company's pension position will continue to be an essential part of Buyout due diligence.

VENTURE COMPANIES

The issues surrounding Venture companies will be different, and thus due diligence needs to be aimed in different directions.

The main concern which any Venture firm will have concerning a new investment will be whether the product or service will be successful commercially, and successful on a large enough scale to provide the potential for growing a very large company. This can be addressed in different ways, but much will come down to the particular sector knowledge of an individual GP, and this is why personal entrepreneurial experience is so important. A Venture Capitalist who can look at a prospect from the perspective of his own recent start-up, and who is acquainted with the company's potential key customers, clearly has a huge advantage. This is a vital part of the US Venture model which has, until very recently, been largely absent in Europe.[5]

This process will inevitably be largely subjective and collegiate – the GP will discuss the prospect on an ongoing basis with the other partners in the firm, and Venture Partners and EIRs will also often be able to add their personal perspective. The process can be more formalised, however. One leading European Venture firm, for example, will not make a new investment until after they have taken the entrepreneurial team on tour around a number of prospective customers worldwide, and have watched and discussed their reaction to the team's 'pitch'. Should the firm continue with the investment then this process, of course, serves multiple purposes since it represents not only valuable advance marketing to possible alpha and beta customers, but also provides input on product design and specification.

At a scientific level, the Venture firm will need to assure itself of the soundness of the design, i.e. that the product will actually work. Many of the best GPs have these technical skills themselves, but most Venture firms also maintain a panel of consultant technical experts, many of whom will be senior academics or research scientists.

---

[3]See an article by Phil Davis in the *Financial Times*, 11 September 2006.
[4]Pension Liabilities bad for Private Equity, www.globalpension.com, 14 September 2006.
[5]An informal survey conducted by the author a few years ago across ten leading European Venture firms suggested that only about 4% of their IT and Telecoms partners had themselves founded a start-up company.

The firm will also need to satisfy itself on ownership of the intellectual property of the technology involved. Here, again, use will be made of outside specialists, this time patent agents and lawyers. This is often referred to as 'IP due diligence' or an 'IP audit'.

Venture investing is a question of investing in people, perhaps even more so at the company level than at the fund level. After all, the typical Venture company proposition is, at least at seed and early stage, 'two guys with an idea'. Thus, much time will be spent getting to know the individuals involved on a personal basis (frequently by one or more GPs, VPs and/or EIRs from the firm going and working with the team for a period of time). Another important point will arise here. The team members need to understand that they will almost certainly not be the right people to lead the company long term, and unless the Venture firm is absolutely sure that this recognition is both clear and genuine, then it should not proceed. The prospects of many a promising Venture company have been destroyed by the refusal of an intransigent founder to stand down in favour of a professional CEO, and this has been a particular problem in Europe, where Venture firms have typically striven heroically (but misguidedly) to avoid any undue confrontation in such situations.

If all this sounds a little unstructured that is probably because if Buyout investing is a science, then Venture investing is an art, in which soft issues such as people qualities and market instinct are more important than financial engineering. However, while this is undoubtedly true, we should not overplay it. The Venture firm which neglects hardcore due diligence on things like background checks and intellectual property will soon find itself in trouble, no matter how sound its instincts.

FUNDS OF FUNDS

The issues before an investor when considering investment in a Fund of Funds will vary according to the structure, time horizon and investment focus which the investor desires. Sadly, the subtlety of realising that different Fund of Funds managers can offer different things is frequently lost on LPs, particularly those who resort to the tender process, but this is nonetheless the ideal at which one should aim. Yes, of course, there are large multinational Fund of Funds players whose funds are both generalist and global in scope,[6] but there are also niche players who might specialise, for example, in US Venture or European Buyout and a sophisticated LP, even if embarking on a Fund of Funds programme (which is not only a perfectly valid approach but probably very sensible in many cases), should be seeking to understand exactly what coverage is offered, not only so that they may fine tune this as necessary but also to know in what directions their due diligence should be aimed.

Due diligence on a Fund of Funds is almost a vicarious experience, as much of it will consist of examining how the Fund of Funds manager carries out due diligence on its own potential investee funds. Having a good idea now of the sort of things to look for when examining both Buyout and Venture funds, you will, in turn, have an idea of what they should be doing and (importantly) why.

The most important area of due diligence, though, particularly as regards any firm which promises a large coverage of US Venture, is the question of access. Test the level of exposure which they have actually achieved for their investors in golden circle US firms (beware, here,

---

[6]Officially, at least. In fact, European Venture is usually conspicuous by its absence.

that they may well try to stretch this definition very considerably). In many cases it will be 5% or less of their total fund capital (sometimes considerably less). If so, this should raise questions as to why they are raising so much money. If their target for US Venture is, say, 30% overall, then even if they wanted to match their golden circle exposure dollar for dollar with other hopefully first quartile funds, they should still only be raising about one-third as much total fund capital. It should also raise questions about their asset allocation. If they can only get 5% into the golden circle, then is it really sensible to be putting five times as much into other US Venture funds? They may have perfectly good answers to these questions, but it is here that the bulk of your due diligence should be focused, not filing away voluminous questionnaires full of largely irrelevant information.

In fact, this is so important that let us make this point just once more. The most important factor in analysing any Private Equity fund (and Funds of Funds are no exception) is the investment model. Is it valid? Can the firm keep to it? Does it make sense in the context of current and possible changing market conditions? Is it consistent with the amount of money which they are raising? As you will have seen from earlier chapters, it is this last question in particular which many firms may struggle to answer convincingly. Similarly, it bears repeating one final time that the way to do this is by full and frank face-to-face meetings, the content of which is targeted at specific issues and discussed internally afterwards, not by papering the file with questionnaires. If you want to make the transition from a simple functionary to an intelligent investor, for goodness sake tear up your questionnaire and throw it away.

The final points with a Fund of Funds are, of course, people and performance. The latter should be fully set out in whatever OM is available. If not, it is a good idea to prepare a one-page summary of fund history, showing the age, vintage year, TVPI and IRR to date of each individual fund. Indeed, a good OM should already contain this as a matter of course. So far as people are concerned, all the earlier remarks in this chapter apply.

Incidentally, while conducting due diligence, it is worth remembering the following principle, sometimes known as 'the 3 Ps':

$$People + Process = Performance$$

This has now been used by many firms in different disciplines (most recently by Hedge funds) and authorship is claimed by many people. However, for what it's worth, the author's belief is that, as with so many things in Private Equity, it probably originated many years ago with Phil Horsley.

GROWTH AND DEVELOPMENT CAPITAL

There is no need to discuss these remaining areas of Private Equity activity at any great length, since almost all of what we would have to say about them has already been considered under either Buyout or Venture due diligence above.

Remembering the specific requirements of each type of investment will, however, give you a clue as to particular things for which to look when analysing their transactions. For Development Capital GPs, it will be key to examine their holding periods and their exit practice. For Growth Capital GPs this is important too, but not quite so vital since they will hopefully have higher money multiples on which to fall back.

In both cases it will be necessary to carry out due diligence on the amount of minority protection and exit protection which is taken, and how it is enforced. This can be done partly by asking to see some transaction documentation, if necessary with some details blacked out to preserve confidentiality, and check exactly which clauses are present. So much for what it says in the documents, but what about establishing how it actually works out in practice? This is best done by quizzing the GPs on what actually happened within their portfolio when problems arose and the relationship with the entrepreneur started to erode.

Above all, do not allow yourself to be deflected by excuses such as 'we can't take that sort of protection in our market because the entrepreneurs wouldn't stand for it' or 'if we tried to do that we'd never do a single deal'. Negative control and exit protection are fundamental essentials, not optional extras, and if a GP is determined to invest without them, make sure that they do so with other people's money.

MONITORING PRIVATE EQUITY FUNDS

Many people feel that once they have done all the hard work of the investment decision process and due diligence they can relax and sit back. In fact, this is what many actually do, simply attending the fund's annual meeting and, one suspects, gathering up all the quarterly reports for their auditors once a year.

This is not, however, how a sophisticated investor will approach things. Once made, the investment must be monitored. You want to know that the firm is sticking to its agreed investment model, that it is investing efficiently and that the team dynamics are still as they were when you carried out your due diligence. In particular, you want to know at once if any key player within the team is thinking of leaving.

In short, unless the firm is actually hiding things (which would obviously carry very serious implications), you should never discover anything new at the annual meeting, and if you do then you have probably not been doing your job properly. Of course, if a firm does choose to hide things there is little you can do save determine not to invest with that firm again or, in an extreme case, seek to sell your LP interest in the secondary market so as to bring your relationship with that firm to an end.

It should be noted, however, that the vast majority of GPs are honest, professional and highly reputable, and will not only practise full disclosure but will seek to bring any particular issues to your attention specifically, and in many cases canvass your views before taking any action. The author has only personally experienced downright concealment on three occasions, in each case concerning the departure of a partner or partners, but when it does occur then loss of trust tends to be both rapid and total.

Formal monitoring will take two forms. First, you will be entering the deal data contained in the quarterly reports into your Buyout or Venture model as appropriate and analysing them on an ongoing basis. You will find that most funds do not provide the level of detail you need to be able to do this, but most are happy to provide supplemental information, particularly if you promise to show them, on a blind basis, how they rank against some of their competitors on the key drivers.

Armed with this information, the second part of your monitoring process will be regular update visits to the group, ideally at least twice a year. It may be an idea to show them your analysis material in advance and to stipulate those issues upon which you wish to focus. Otherwise, there is a real danger that the firm will simply 'run the clock' and the meeting will degenerate into a general chat about the market. By the way, an hour is rarely adequate for these meetings and you should try to insist on two hours being set aside, particularly if there is a potentially significant issue which you wish to discuss (such as why an early-stage

Venture fund is suddenly making lots of late-stage investments, or why a Buyout fund seems to be paying higher earnings multiples than its competitors).

Informal monitoring consists of keeping one's ear to the ground generally. In addition to everyday conversations with other people, there are now a number of good online news sources. It is necessary to distinguish between the useful and the dangerous, however. Into the former category would fall hearing from a banker friend that a Buyout transaction's debt is being offered at a discount in the marketplace. Into the latter would fall comments of the 'I spoke to (insert name as desired) at an annual meeting and he doesn't like them' variety.

There are other things that can give you a clue that all is not well. Chief among these is timely reporting, and it is puzzling that so many GPs should, over the years, have failed to realise this. Not only are consistently late reports and accounts indicative of sloppy processes within the firm, but they can give certain classes of investor, most notably Funds of Funds, very real problems regarding the provisions in their own legal agreements governing their reporting to their own clients. It can be easy, and even appealing, to write this off as a minor administrative irritant, but you would be well advised not to neglect this key indicator. It may be a coincidence, but of only two cases of really bad and consistent late reporting encountered by the author, one of them was also one of the three 'concealment' firms alluded to above.

Remember, too, that what you learn through your monitoring of the current fund will form part of your due diligence for the next fund, so the better your monitoring, the easier and quicker your next round of due diligence is likely to be. In particular, the report pages from your Venture or Buyout model will form the starting point for your quantitative due diligence.

Finally, do remember the passage in the Introduction about the relationship between the GP and the LP. In normal circumstances (as to which see Chapter 15) the power is all with the GP, provided you are committing to quality funds. There is accordingly no point at all in trying to throw your weight around during the monitoring process; indeed, this is likely to prove counter-productive. Ignoring, for a moment, no-fault divorce provisions (since (1) a detailed discussion of fund terms falls outside the scope of this book and (2) this is not something that you can use by yourself, but only in association with a majority of the other LPs), then your options as a disgruntled Private Equity fund investor are two, and two only. You may choose not to invest in the firm's next fund, and you may choose to sell your existing interest in the secondary market.

The monitoring process is designed to help you primarily with the first of these decisions. Your monitoring activities may have already disclosed, by the time the next fundraising cycle comes around, that this is not a firm you wish to back again. It should be stressed, though, that such situations are comparatively rare and will usually only occur where a firm has had key GP departures, failed to keep to the agreed investment model, acted in perceived conflict of interest, or whose investment metrics have deteriorated unacceptably. Fortunately, such situations are unusual, and the norm will be that when you sign up for a fund, you are, in reality, signing up for at least the next one, and possible two, as well (since the performance of the first one may not have become apparent even by the time the third one is raised).

Since you are thus committed to a long-term relationship with the firm no matter what happens, conducting your monitoring in a friendly and considerate manner is not only a matter of practical common sense, it is also your best chance of getting something you don't like changed. Incidentally, this can be a good reason for not sitting on advisory boards (though there are different schools of thought on this).[7] Advisory boards generally do not make a good job of what they are supposed to do (protect LPs against conflicts of interest), and open discussion in a formal setting is not the best way to approach sensitive issues. As an independent voice who has cultivated a good personal relationship with at least some of the GPs, you often have a far better chance of getting something done through friendly chat than by attempting to use a bargaining position that it is effectively non-existent.

THE CHANGING NATURE OF DUE DILIGENCE

Some may find it surprising that we have managed to spend a whole chapter on due diligence without once mentioning the need to investigate the possibility of any possible financial wrong-doing. This view is particularly prevalent in those who find it difficult to distinguish between Private Equity funds and Hedge funds. The simple answer is that the world of Private Equity is basically a very honest one and, in any event, the way in which the mechanics of a Private Equity fund operate makes it almost impossible to use one as a vehicle for fraud. If one were an international criminal looking to relieve institutional investors of large amounts of money, then there would be many much easier ways of going about this than setting up a Private Equity fund.

Other areas of investment are different, and here it is increasingly commonplace to find personal due diligence farmed out to professional investigators. This has not yet spread to the world of Private Equity, and hopefully never will if stories of investigators sifting through household garbage, obtaining bank account details, visiting children's schools and quizzing estranged spouses are even partly correct.

Without wishing to wander too far into the realm of philosophy, it is, in any event, questionable how far the features of one's private life are (1) fair game, given understandable privacy concerns, or (2) at all relevant to one's abilities as an investor. The fact that one may be an alcoholic, drug addict or compulsive gambler almost certainly are, but should one's sexual preferences and activities be? Or one's religious beliefs or political views? It will be clear that to encroach on this particular area, as some investors are beginning to do, is to tread on difficult moral ground. After all, even American Presidents could not agree on this subject. Jefferson thought that if you sought out the trust of others then you had no right to privacy about any aspect of your life, whereas LBJ said that everyone had the right to know that their personal life would remain private.

SUMMARY

The decision to invest in a particular fund or company is usually a twofold process, although in practice the boundaries between these two neatly defined areas tend to become somewhat blurred. In theory, an investment to invest in principle will be taken first, and this decision will be subject to satisfactory due diligence which will then follow.

It may be found helpful to maintain a running record of 'pros', 'cons' and 'issues'. Due diligence is aimed at resolving all outstanding issues, and should be specifically targeted

---

[7]This argument holds broadly true with quality US and European Venture firms, who typically do a very good job of keeping their investors informed. The situation with Buyout firms, particularly in Europe, may be different as there is a regrettable tendency to cultivate an inner circle of those few LPs who sit on the advisory board while keeping the rest in relative ignorance. However, provided that you are having update meetings on a regular basis and conducting them properly, then unless a firm is actively concealing something, not being on the advisory board should not be a problem.

in this way. It should not be regarded as an unfocused information-gathering process. Still less should it take the form of a standard questionnaire. It is a way of facilitating decision making, not a process of papering the file to protect individuals from the internal consequences of making bad decisions.

It is generally far more helpful to seek out your own 'referees' than to rely on those given to you by the fund or company. In particular, try to find individuals who have left the organisation recently, and find out why. Co-investors and portfolio company CEOs can also be sources of very useful information, particularly where the investment concerned has not performed well.

Buyout fund due diligence should be based on the Buyout transaction analysis discussed earlier, and on how well placed the firm may be in terms of dealflow channels, and how expert it is in its financial engineering.

Venture fund due diligence should be based on the Venture transaction analysis discussed earlier and should focus on the firm's ability to score home runs.

Buyout company due diligence will be very similar to the standard M&A due diligence performed by a prospective corporate acquirer. However, particular attention should be paid to key members of the executive team and their level of commitment to the proposed transaction.

Venture company due diligence will focus on the qualities of the individuals concerned, and the level of market risk which their product or service will need to overcome. Also key is the potential for the company, if successful, to be sufficiently successful to become a home run.

Fund of Funds due diligence will focus on historic performance (track record) and the firm's ability to access the very best Private Equity funds.

Due diligence on Growth and Development Capital funds will tend to focus on how successful they may have been in taking and (where necessary) enforcing negative control and exit protection.

Due diligence flows naturally into monitoring. However, here, at the fund level, your focus will be on facilitating your decision whether to invest in successor funds, while at the company level it will be on checking the financial performance of the company and, in the case of Venture companies, the healthy and timely development of the company's product or service.

There are some investors who are beginning to stray into the realm of GPs' private lives in the cause of due diligence. It is submitted that this is a very dangerous practice and should only be undertaken after the most stringent discussion and consideration of its (1) moral implications and (2) relevance.

14

Planning Your Investment Programme

Hopefully having read this far you will have a good idea of what the different types of Private Equity are, what drives their returns and what to look for when selecting funds in which to invest. You have also had a chance to consider the historic returns of each asset class, arranged by geography, to take a look at how these might be influenced by transitory outside factors such as bubbles and market conditions and also to discern the workings of more lasting trends.

We should turn now to the nuts and bolts of how actually to put money to work in the Private Equity field. It is all very well having a working understanding of Buyout and Venture, but if you are suddenly presented with an allocation of, say, $100M for Private Equity, how should you go about drawing up an action plan and implementing it?

CASH FLOW PLANNING

Let's just remind ourselves of the way in which any individual Private Equity fund works by looking again at something we saw earlier (Figure 14.1).

Remember, this is the profile of one individual fund, whereas we will be looking to commit to quite a number (ideally at least six in each vintage year). In planning our programme, therefore, we will have to overlay the profiles of a large number of funds onto an overall cash flow model. Thus, at any one time within our planned programme, we will have some funds that are in investment mode, some that may not yet have drawn down any significant amount of capital at all and some that will already be harvesting their investments and returning money to investors.

You will, of course, need to assume some money multiples, since the cash that is flowing back to the investor will always be greater than the money which is flowing out by way of drawdowns. I would suggest that you start with some quite conservative default multiples – say 1.6× for a Buyout fund and 2.0× for a Venture fund – and adjust these to match actual performance as you go along. Remember these are net of fees and carry.

Remember, too, that just as the J-curve will be the same basic shape for each fund but may be either squashed or elongated according to the fund type and market conditions (and may move within different ranges according to the amount and timing of cash flows), so too the pattern which you see set out in the above figure will occur either more quickly or over a more extended interval depending on whether the investment focus of the fund will be early-stage Venture (longest/slowest), Buyout or later stage Venture (somewhere in the middle), or secondary transactions (shortest/quickest). As we will see later, it is the positioning on the time line of the anticipated payback point which is currently a very contentious issue.

We are looking here specifically at Private Equity *funds* but it is, of course, quite possible that, in deciding your overall investment policy, you might decide also to participate directly in individual Private Equity *transactions*, particularly in the secondary market where various

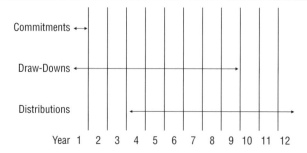

Figure 14.1   How a Private Equity fund works

LPs do commonly operate alongside specialist secondary funds. We will be looking specifically at this area later in this chapter.

The purpose of this sort of outline cash flow modelling is not to provide a forecast of income and expenditure for accounting purposes. We are dealing here with cash flows which are essentially unpredictable both as to their timing and their amount, over a period which stretches a long way out into the future. Such an exercise cannot possibly produce anything other than a guesstimate, at best. The chances of your cash flows in any one year conforming exactly to what has been predicted at the outset are virtually nil. If you are an accountant, you might find it hard to understand why, in these circumstances, we would wish to embark upon the exercise at all. Yet to criticise it in this way, or label it as pointless, is fundamentally to misunderstand the reason for embarking upon it. It is not to have something available as a yardstick against which to judge just how closely actual cash flows in future years may conform to what we predicted at the outset (indeed, the very word 'predicted' is inappropriate – it would be much more correct to say 'projected'). It is to ensure that we plan our exposure from the outset in a methodical manner; it is always open to us to fine tune this as we go along, but it is essential to have an overall plan within which to operate (and not to allow ourselves to be unduly distracted from it as we go along by short-term issues).

ALLOCATED, COMMITTED AND INVESTED CAPITAL

In Chapter 2 we looked at the difference between allocated, committed and invested capital. It might be an idea just to glance at these definitions in the glossary to remind yourself of the distinction, since an understanding of it is crucial to what we are now going to be discussing.

Almost as soon as you embark on the cash flow modelling exercise which has just been described, this distinction will be brought home to you very strongly. In the early years of a Private Equity programme you will find, for example, that, left to its own devices, invested capital may represent only a tiny fraction of allocated capital and it may seem that almost as much is getting drawn down in fees as is getting put to work in investee companies. You will notice the qualification 'left to its own devices' since there are actually some very straightforward things that can be done to alleviate this situation and which, bafflingly, many investors and their advisers simply ignore. We will look at these in detail later.

Successful management of a Private Equity programme requires these three different, but directly related, entities to be managed intelligently and proactively. This, in turn, requires active and knowledgeable monitoring of your portfolio funds. If many European Buyout funds suddenly start exiting companies at the same time, for example (which is entirely possible given that such things are usually driven by exit market conditions), their LPs will fall into two broad categories: those who saw this coming and have planned in advance as far as possible how to deploy these cash flows back into some sort of Private Equity or quasi-Private Equity bucket, and those who did not, and end up being forced to give it to their treasury department to invest on the money markets.

Similarly, if GPs invest their money either more quickly or more slowly than their usual fund cycle would suggest, then the time to do something about it, in terms of considering what this means for your future commitment programme, is straight away, not when you find yourself performing due diligence on five funds but realising that you need to commit to at least ten, or no more than one.

Please bear this distinction between allocated, invested and committed capital in mind, as it will be crucial as we now turn to look at two of the main mistakes which are made by investors when entering the Private Equity arena: failure to diversify by time, and failure to set proper commitment levels in the first place.

DIVERSIFICATION BY TIME

When studying the historic returns of both Venture and Buyout we came to the conclusion that they were subject to two broad categories of influence: those that are relatively constant and long-lasting, such as fundamental return drivers and long-term trends, and those which are transitory such as bubbles, exit windows, equity market conditions, fundraising levels, etc.

It is the job of a Private Equity investor, whether at the fund or the company level, to study and understand the former and shape investment policy accordingly. It is not part of the job to react to the latter, or, even worse, try to predict them and 'market time' one's investments. How, then, do we treat these? The answer is that we simply ignore them. Private Equity investors deal with cash flows which are unpredictable both as to their timing and as to their amount, which stretch a long way into the future, becoming even more unpredictable with every extra year added to our projections. This unpredictability is such that any attempt to 'market time' involves the prediction of market conditions and investor sentiment a long way in the future, and also involves assuming not only that this prediction will be correct, but that it will continue to be correct for a long enough period for all the planned and necessary inflows or outflows to take place. This is effectively impossible. Yet this fact goes almost entirely unrecognised: witness the number of times you will hear people say 'we don't think this is a good time to be putting money into Private Equity'.

Instead, the sophisticated investor aims to commit capital evenly every vintage year so that there will be a roughly equal exposure to every vintage year within the portfolio. Consider what would have happened, for example, if one had taken the view that 2000 was going to be a bumper year for US Venture and had decided to commit one's entire allocation to 2000 vintage year US Venture funds. Or if one had decided to stop investing in US Venture between 1994 and 1996 because the likely returns of your 1991 vintage year funds were not looking good. It is impossible to assess in advance how a particular vintage year is going to perform; one does not even usually have a final figure for total fundraising until at least three months (in the US) or about six months (in Europe) into the following calendar year.

You may think that the first example quoted in the preceding paragraph is fanciful. It is not. Not only is it drawn from life, but there were a number of new entrants to the market who did exactly that. A well-known organisation came to the author for advice in or about late 1999 on how to plan its new Private Equity programme and was given roughly the counsel which is contained in this chapter. It subsequently emerged that this advice had been totally ignored, and that not only had the Private Equity team blown its entire allocation in the space of about six months almost entirely on US Venture funds with a dot com focus, but had gone back to the board for a greatly increased allocation, much of which they proceeded to treat in similar fashion. The same company closed down its Private Equity operations a couple of years later.

This is obviously a counsel of perfection, and like all counsels of perfection there are times when it is just not possible to do exactly what you would like to. European Buyout, for example, can be a particular problem because there tends to be 'bunching', with several funds coming to market at the same time and intervening fallow periods. There is no particular reason for this; it just happens, rather in the same way that you wait for a bus for an hour and then four arrive all at once (although it was revealed recently that there *is* apparently some arcane mathematical explanation for this after all). Do you pass up the opportunity of investing with a quality fund in one year simply to keep your commitment levels in trim, or do you try to steal a bit of capital from another vintage year?

The answer is threefold. First, it is inconceivable that any LP is going to be investing solely in European Buyout, so there may be scope for undercommitting slightly that vintage year to other Private Equity classes in order to overcommit slightly to European Buyout. Second, if you want to borrow a little money from any particular year then probably little harm is done. Thirdly, many fund closings stretch in practice across year ends – this is done deliberately for precisely this reason. However the key words here are 'slightly' and 'a little'; some fine tuning is perfectly acceptable, and indeed probably even desirable, but significant tweaks are not.

Diversification by time is probably the single most important concept that should drive any Private Equity fund investor. Write it on the wall of your office. Chant it to yourself as you take your morning shower. Practising diversification by time will not, of itself, make you a successful fund investor (you still need to be able to identify and access the right funds), but it will very significantly boost your chances.

PROPER COMMITMENT LEVELS

The second common mistake made by LPs who are new to the asset class is not to set proper commitment levels. Basically, this comes down to a failure to understand the difference between allocated, invested and committed capital.

If you run the sort of broad brush cash flow exercise that we were talking about at the beginning of the chapter, you will quickly see that in normal market conditions you can expect to have money coming back from your earliest funds well before you finish paying in to those to which you commit in later years. This will, of course, be exacerbated by the fact that, in normal circumstances, the money coming back will be some multiple of the money paid in. To those who cherish the principle of the payback period, this is good news; historically, some fund programmes became self-financing after the first seven years or so. To those who understand investment returns it is a disaster, as it means that money coming back having earned a Private Equity return is going to end up invested on the money markets, and you are never going to get anywhere near your overall target allocation figure. So, how do we get around this problem?

Until very recently, the answer appeared quite simple. Many LPs overcommitted. The first edition of this book, for example, recommended using a default multiple of about 1.6× allocated capital and committing it equally over eight years. This is probably still fundamentally sound advice (though probably with a lower multiple), not least because it ensures perfect diversification by vintage year, but clearly requires some clarification and qualification in the light of recent events. In particular, and as we shall be discussing in the final chapter, holding periods within all types of Private Equity funds (but particularly Venture) have lengthened dramatically since the first edition of this book was written, thus delaying the anticipated payback point.

This, in turn, has been a contributory factor (but only one) to a phenomenon which has been given the name 'Cash 22', whereby a number of LPs have found themselves under an obligation to honour Capital Calls on their Private Equity fund portfolio, but unable to generate sufficient cash from their liquid assets in order to do so. This, in turn, has led, for the first time in the history of the industry, to both actual and threatened LP defaults, an issue we will consider more fully in the next chapter.

It is important to understand exactly how Cash 22 has come about, since, as usual, investors have found it easier to blame an asset class than their own actions. For it is not Private Equity, or even overcommitment to Private Equity funds, which have been the primary cause of this distress.

A discussion of investment strategy lies beyond the scope of this book[1] but it must be an essential part of any asset allocation exercise that one models one's likely cash outflows for the next three to five years, and holds this amount in a liquidity reserve of bonds. Unfortunately many LPs have got both sides of this process wrong, and have been found out.

When modelling their cash outflows, they properly listed all their operational cash flows (for example, the costs of running a college in the case of an endowment), but did not take account of things such as Private Equity fund Capital Calls, since they assumed there would always be sufficient distributions coming in to cover these. This has proved a most dangerous assumption.

To make matters worse, many LPs also overlooked the fact that bonds are not an investment, but a cash substitute. In their efforts to make 'a proper investment return' they moved away from boring old US government bonds to corporate, or even emerging market, bonds. As these bond markets simply collapsed in September 2008, the air was heavy with the flapping wings of chickens coming home to roost. The whole point of a liquidity reserve is that it should provide liquidity even in the case of abnormal market conditions. If you take this away, then it is like having a parachute that won't open when you need it. It is no good blaming gravity rather than the negligence of whoever packed the parachute.

Rubbing salt in the wound, many investors have reacted very inflexibly to the whole question of asset allocation. As stock markets collapsed, they insisted that their allocation levels had to stay in line with each other as a percentage of total assets, forcing LPs to stop committing to funds, and thus risking not being able to gain access to funds, as well as lack of diversification by vintage year. This can be deeply harmful to long-term returns. There is much evidence to suggest that Private Equity funds (particularly Buyout) raised at a time of recession do significantly better than others. For European Buyout, for example, 1991 was

---

[1]See *Multi Asset Class Investment Strategy*, already referenced and Swensen (2009) *Pioneering Portfolio Management*, Free Press, New York.

better than the four or five previous years (depending on which measure you adopt), while 2001 was better than the previous five or six. This is a classic example of the dangers of attempting to 'market time', and LPs who stop committing almost always do so at the worst possible time.

So, the qualifications which need to be added are flexibility and intelligence. Your asset allocation process needs to be flexible enough to allow allocation levels to different asset classes to move within ranges as valuations fluctuate, and intelligent enough to understand that you should never stop committing to Private Equity funds – almost any outcome is preferable. You should even consider selling off prior year funds in the secondary market before you stop committing in the primary market. It should also be intelligent enough to realise that you hold bonds for liquidity, not investment return.

Similarly, your Private Equity programme needs to be both flexible and intelligent. If it becomes obvious that your initial assumption as to holding periods was too short, then change it, and discuss how this might affect future commitment and allocation levels. Nobody has ever suggested that you should calculate a fixed figure and commit it each year regardless of changing circumstances. Should you be faced with the need to reduce it (and this should happen long before you get anywhere near 100% of allocated capital), then consider selling some prior year fund interests as secondaries, both to generate more capital and to even up your distribution between vintage years.

DIVERSIFICATION BY SECTOR AND GEOGRAPHY

This is a more controversial subject on which there are a number of different views. Let us consider the two arguments at different ends of the spectrum.

On the one hand there will be the traditional investment view that diversification is always attractive in its own right, and that an ideal Private Equity portfolio should therefore aim, in any one vintage year, for a roughly equal split between Venture and Buyout, and between Europe and the US, perhaps with a dash of Asia thrown into the mix for the sake of completeness.

Properly constructed, any such portfolio should tend to give a composite return that is the Private Equity equivalent of a passively managed global equities programme. It would effectively return the global Private Equity index, so the argument goes, if such a thing existed.

The reader will, by now, know more than enough about Private Equity to be able to spot various flaws in the above approach.

First, not all Private Equity classes have returned equal returns; indeed, the returns of some classes vary widely even within themselves, most notably US Venture and European Buyout. It is clear, then, that not only must manager selection play a great role in selecting a Private Equity fund portfolio, but also that the stage and sector (in Venture) or the size and geography (in Buyout) of a fund's investment focus will be legitimate considerations. The author is not aware of any portfolio anywhere in the world, for example, which currently gives anything like an equal weighting to European Venture.

Yet we have seen that the returns of any one Private Equity class fluctuate from one vintage year to another, and that it is impossible to predict such returns in advance. So are we not, an advocate of the balanced approach might argue, simply adopting a sort of market timing by stealth if we start tweaking our mix in this way? Should we not simply try to choose the best managers within each class in each vintage year and leave the relative performance of each class to fall where it may?

Second, we have seen that in each class there are a small number of managers who may consistently outperform, most notably in US Venture but also, to a less extreme extent, in other areas. Suppose that in order to make up our quota of, say, the US Buyout funds which were raising money that year we were obliged to choose a respectable but potentially unexciting candidate, when we could use that money instead to commit to a leading US Venture fund. Is it not more likely that whatever happens to the respective returns of US Buyout and Venture as a whole, the leading Venture fund is likely to give us a higher return than the unexciting Buyout manager? Ah, says the balanced investor, but suppose the vintage year in question turns out to be 2000? In that case you might end up thanking your lucky stars that you stuck to your principles and did not throw extra capital into US Venture, no matter how attractive it might have seemed at the time.

This leads us rather neatly into the opposite view, which we might term the Silicon Valley theory, for want of anything better. This runs as follows. There is one asset class within Private Equity, US Venture, that has consistently outperformed all others. Further, there is a small group of firms within it, the golden circle, that has consistently outperformed the rest of the class. So why not simply seek to identify and access these potential golden circle funds and simply ignore everything else within Private Equity? Yes, there will be the occasionally poor vintage year but you are protected against this by diversification by time and, in the case of golden circle US Venture, the dramatic returns which you make in the good years will more than compensate you for the occasional bad one.

These are interesting arguments and each has its attractions, though in fairness we should note that the Silicon Valley theory was, until recently, totally vindicated by those who chose to apply it and were able so to do. However, in the words 'and were able so to do' lies the Achilles heel of this approach, which you will probably have spotted already.

In order to be able to adopt it, you must be able both to identify *and access* potential golden circle funds. Yet access is a huge issue in US Venture Capital; even Horsley Bridge, traditionally the supreme exponent of this approach, is not able to access every single US Venture fund. To be fair, in their case this hardly matters since they have so many of the others, but just consider what your position might be if you are not fortunate enough to be Horsley Bridge, or to have invested with them over the years.

The author has, in the past, attempted to analyse how much money might be raised in any one vintage year by the US golden circle firms, but this has become a thankless task with the fundraising figures going up and down like a yo-yo and, given that they are published in arrears, efforts are often superseded almost as soon as they have been published. Suffice it to say that in any one year the amount of demand for golden circle fund capital hugely exceeds available supply.

It is not well understood, even within the Private Equity industry itself, that much of golden circle capital is committed by the GPs themselves and their strategic investors (which will include the likes of successful entrepreneurs whom they have previously backed and with whom they may wish to work again, and Technology companies who may be potential key customers and development partners for portfolio companies). Depending on the firm, this can be anywhere up to two-thirds of the fund size. Then there are the Horsley Bridge type players who have backed the firm for many years and are guaranteed a sizeable chunk of what is left. Then there are a number of Endowments and Foundations who will again typically have been long-term supporters of the firm. Finally there are a large number of institutions fighting on the fringes of the pack for whatever scraps may remain.

It is in trying to estimate the amounts involved in any one particular year that one can come to grief, but it is probably safe to assume that in any one year the amount available for fringe players (into which category would fall any new entrants to the asset class) would be certainly no more than $1B and probably a lot, lot less, perhaps as little as $100M. Given that every investor in the world would logically want as much of this as they could have, then it is probably safe to say that whatever amount it is will be at least a hundred times and maybe a thousand times oversubscribed.

In other words, access to the golden circle for the average investor is as near impossible as makes no difference. Unfortunately this is yet another very basic truth which appears to be little understood, prompted in part by the less scrupulous Fund of Funds managers who fudge the true figures (and the classification of what may or may not genuinely be a golden circle fund) and claim to be able to achieve significant coverage for their clients when, in fact, this simply is not (and indeed cannot) be the case.

It bears pointing out that the vindication of the Silicon Valley theory has been shifted into the past tense in the current edition of this book. Yes, it certainly worked, if you could apply it, in the 1990s, but it is most unclear whether it will prove as successful thereafter. To find an upper quartile TVPI multiple of even 1.7 for US Venture, one has to go back to vintage year 1998, whereas European Buyout has achieved it five times in the same period. Those who continue to hold this particular faith will require a strong nerve and a lot of patience.

For most investors, however, the issue of whether the Silicon Valley theory is still valid is irrelevant, since lack of access renders it a very dangerous approach. If you cannot gain access to the golden circle, and the same problems as to access apply with gradually diminishing severity as you descend the quality scale, then you will be struggling to achieve US Venture results which even match the upper quartile; in fact, it is quite likely that some significant number of your fund picks will end up in the second or third quartiles.

If you are struggling to achieve upper quartile US Venture returns, is it still a valid approach to say that you will target that Private Equity class, and that class only? Clearly not. Can one, then, fall back on the balanced theory in the hope that you will be able to achieve some sort of blended global return? Well, in theory yes, but the objections which we raised to such an approach merit careful consideration, and probably argue against a strict application of such a pure and uncompromising policy. In particular, we should be really troubled by the possibility of having to pass up a very high quality opportunity in one category just because one would not otherwise fulfil one's quota in a different area. In fact, practical experience suggests very strongly that any sort of rigid pre-allocation at all is the enemy of optimal returns.

We have seen several times during the book so far that Private Equity differs from other classes in various ways and this is another important one. The differential in return which can be earned through successful manager selection is almost infinite. Choosing one quoted equity manager over another might make a difference of 1–2% a year; choosing the right Private Equity manager can make a difference of 100% a year in Venture or maybe 10–15% a year in Buyout. Viewed in this light, the risk of missing out on an outstanding manager is just too great to allow pre-allocations of this sort to get in the way.

So, the answer lies somewhere between the two extremes. By all means discuss some broad outlines as to how you would like your portfolio to look in terms of Venture (sector, stage and geography) and Buyout (size and geography), but be flexible, and concentrate on selecting the best managers in any one category as you go along rather than strictly fulfilling a quota policy in any one vintage year. Finally, as we will see in the next chapter, it is increasingly difficult to ignore the emerging Private Equity markets.

TOTAL RETURN

With an understanding of the differences between allocated, committed and invested capital comes a realisation that the return which you earn across your whole Private Equity allocation will be very different from the wonderful IRRs that are peddled to you during presentations on Private Equity funds and Funds of Funds. This is, in one sense, a necessary consequence of the way in which Private Equity returns are measured, but can also betray a lack of understanding of the asset class generally.

As we saw in Chapter 2, a Private Equity fund is a sequence of cash flows, and the proper measure of its performance is an IRR. We should not seek to criticise this is any way; far from it. Save only for money multiples, an IRR is the only valid way in which Private Equity fund performance can be measured. Certainly we have hopefully well and truly dispelled any notion that annual returns can ever be appropriate. However, what an IRR or a money multiple measures when used in this way is the performance of a *fund*, whereas what you will be (or should be) concerned about is the performance of your *programme*.

Now, as we have seen, even if you do everything humanly possible to reduce its impact, you are going necessarily to suffer from underinvestment (or, perhaps more accurately, sub-optimal utilisation) of capital. You will not be committing some of your money for several years, and even when you do, it will take the GP of each individual fund a few years to draw all that money down and put it to work in investee companies. Hence, sub-optimal utilisation. The optimal use of that money is to be invested in the portfolio companies of Buyout and Venture funds. Thus, any time that any money is not so invested, it is being used in a less than optimal fashion.

Yet, if this is so obvious why is it that so few LPs take any serious steps to plan what they are going to do with their cash while it is not actually invested in underlying companies? 'I'm only 10% invested after three years' is the sort of thing which you hear on a regular basis, to which, once you have read this book, you will probably respond 'well, what did you expect?' The way in which a Private Equity fund programme operates is hardly rocket science. You can model the cash flows in outline, as we have seen above, and it will become instantly apparent that there is always going to be a very slow and protracted take-up of capital.

This, in turn, means that when many investors refer to 'our Private Equity return' what they really mean is 'our return on that small portion of our allocation which we have actually managed to invest in Private Equity assets'. Even for someone with a mature programme this is only ever likely to be some part of the whole, and in the case of a new entrant it may be practically nothing. That is why it would be helpful for people to think in terms of their total return across the whole allocation rather than just that amount which is actually sitting in underlying companies.

Which prompts the question: what should we do with our allocation in the meantime?

How to Deal with Uninvested Capital

The need to think in terms of total return means that we can re-think our philosophy of Private Equity returns. Accepted wisdom teaches that you should chase the very best possible returns and this, of course, is true when thinking about committing money to primary funds; if you have $20M to commit in any one vintage year then you want to try to ensure that you choose, from amongst those funds which you can access, those which are likely to produce the very best returns. However, where capital which is allocated but as yet uninvested is concerned, different considerations apply.

In this situation we should be content to accept slightly lower rates of return. Logically, we should accept any rate of return which is likely to be higher than that which we could earn through any alternative use of that capital. In order to assess this it would, of course, be necessary to know what that alternative use might be, and this would almost certainly vary from one investor to another. Some leave the money with their treasury department, while others might leave it within their allocation to quoted equities. Some even invest it in quoted Private Equity vehicles.

It would be cheering to report that they adopted this latter course in order to earn some sort of Private Equity proxy return, but in fact this is not the case, and many do so merely as a way of ticking the 'Private Equity' box on their checklist. In any case the overall allocation to Private Equity is frequently so small that, in truth, it is not going to make any significant difference anyway. The author's first book[2] reveals the reasons why this is not a good idea. Such vehicles are sometimes cash rich themselves and thus the problem is shifted rather than resolved. Largely because of this, it is effectively impossible to earn anything like a proper Private Equity return from them (why do you think that sophisticated investors the world over prefer to invest in institutional partnerships, even though these come at a much higher cost?). Also, since such vehicles are quoted, they are subject, in large part, to the vagaries of public equity markets and thus, rather than reducing correlation with your quoted equity holdings (a key aim of any allocation to 'alternative' assets[3]), you will actually almost certainly increase it. All this has been borne out by the events of the last few years; a good example would be 3i.

For the sake of argument, let us assume that the alternative use of funds would be quoted equities. This is probably not a bad assumption to make, since quoted equities are still generally regarded as the most 'high risk' (whatever that might mean) asset within many institutional portfolios. Thus, to use classic corporate finance theory, we should accept all projects for the use of our capital that offer a potential rate of return which exceeds the likely return on quoted equities. Given our concerns about correlation and diversification, as well as the internal requirements of staying within our investment mandate, we should however qualify 'projects' by saying something like 'projects of a Private Equity nature, or offering a Private Equity-like return which exhibits low correlation with the rest of our portfolio'.

This clearly opens up other possibilities which should be considered but, alas, rarely are by investors in this position.

Secondaries

Secondaries are an obvious candidate here. They are interests in Private Equity funds and are thus not only the closest substitute we can find, but exactly the same thing! Yet, despite their obvious attractions, many LPs ignore them. Until a few years ago LPs could, and did, play in the secondaries market themselves, but today this is really open only to the biggest and most sophisticated, since it is now a much more competitive market than it was in, say, 2000, particularly outside the US. However, secondary funds offer a valid alternative.

---

[2] *Multi-Asset Class Investment Strategy*, already referenced.
[3] The other being the ability to access high return asset classes such as Private Equity.

Mezzanine

Mezzanine, that is to say convertible debt, would also be a candidate for the use of non-invested capital. As we saw earlier when we analysed how Buyouts work, this is the financing strip that sits between the equity and the senior debt of a Buyout and thus, unsurprisingly, is designed to give less than a Buyout's equity return but more than a Buyout's debt return. Its attractions to us in our present position are twofold. First, it is part of a Private Equity trans-action and thus is undeniably Private Equity in nature (this may be important for the more officious of internal processes). Second, the debt-servicing element of its cash flows is entirely predictable both as to timing and as to amount, since this will be laid out in legally binding documentation, and this makes it possible to plan exactly where such investments might fit into our overall cash flow planning model.

For those who do not wish to venture into the convertible debt market directly, there are specialist funds, just as there are for secondaries, but these usually function on a primary basis, i.e. providing the mezzanine element of Buyouts over a period of three years or so in just the same way as a Buyout fund does with equity. This obviously makes mezzanine much less attractive for our present purposes, since we are giving up one of the key advantages (predictability).

However, it is becoming increasingly possible to invest in existing (secondary) mezzanine interests and this is another area where we may see increased sophistication in the future as total return investing becomes more widely accepted, possibly with funds offering a selection of interests with specific maturity profiles.

Co-investment

Many LPs have historically sought to co-invest in the portfolio companies of their GPs. Interestingly, the motivation for this approach has probably changed significantly over the course of the last decade. Originally its main attraction was the ability for large LPs to put extra capital to work, but dramatically increased fund sizes have made this much less of an issue, particularly for those who favour Buyout.

More recently, it has been seen as a way of reducing the overall burden of fees and carry, since these are typically not charged on co-investments, or charged at a reduced rate. In other words, the LPs are using them to narrow the gap between net and gross returns.

The argument against co-investment is that it reduces diversification within a portfolio. Indeed, it can skew it quite spectacularly. The whole idea behind a Private Equity fund pro-gramme is that no one company should be able to make a significant difference to the overall return (unless it happens to be a huge Venture home run, two examples of which have been recorded as in excess of 2000×). Does it really make sense deliberately to throw away this advantage simply to remove a small piece of the fee burden? Obviously many LPs think the answer to this is 'yes', but it is a matter of personal taste.

Private Equity proxies

Here we stray into the more controversial area of using the returns of completely different asset classes which have no direct connection with Private Equity to produce a return which might, in some way, approximate or be correlated with a Private Equity fund return. Indeed, some pension funds and other institutional investors believe that they can use such an approach as a substitute for making any Private Equity investments at all. Some, for example, use some selection of quoted equities and try introducing some leverage through debt, or some hedging through derivatives.

This approach does not work any better than the alternative policy of investing in quoted Private Equity vehicles. Advocates of this approach commonly use much too low a benchmark Private Equity return, or even assume that Private Equity returns will always be some fixed multiple of quoted equity returns, ignoring the historic data which show relatively low correlation between Private Equity and quoted markets.[4] They also look to annual, rather than compound, returns.

There are also so-called Private Equity indices available, though these are of dubious 'investability' and are also dubiously named, since they simply represent a basket of quoted Private Equity vehicles, whereas what we should be trying to approximate as far as possible are the returns of Private Equity funds. It should be noted that there is considerable heterogeneity. Some are US specific, or heavily weighted in favour of the US. Some are capital weighted and others not, and so on. Again, this does not seem an attractive approach.

TOWARDS A NEW WORLD OF PRIVATE EQUITY PROGRAMMES?

This is a new and controversial concept which was set out for the first time ever in the previous edition of this book, but which has since been widely discussed. It now seems to many observers that it is both unrealistic and unreasonable to judge a Private Equity programme on the basis only of that very small part of it which is actually invested at any one time, given that the elimination, or at least amelioration, of the results of slow capital take-up is something that can, and should, fairly easily be addressed. Once we view this as a key skill of a Private Equity LP, just as much as choosing the right funds, then surely it is appropriate to judge LP performance across the whole allocated amount? This is the argument for total return investing for institutional investors.

This clearly impacts not just upon the LP but also upon those who offer products and services to them. Why should a Fund of Funds manager, for example, be paid a fee on the whole committed capital of their fund when only a small part of it will actually be invested at any one time? To take one obvious example, if a Fund of Funds has a 1% management fee and after one year is only, say, 5% drawn down (not impossible), then the effective management fee for that year is not 1% but 20% – quite a difference!

Would it not be more logical to expect the Fund of Funds manager to draw down the money up front and be judged on a total return basis over the life of the fund? After all, the only thing that has really changed is that the money is now in the hands of the manager rather than the investor; yes, ownership of the problem has been transferred, but the manager is likely to be better placed to address it than the investor, and is being paid to do so. Granted the increased (and different types of) work would merit an increased management fee overall, but (1) when measured as a percentage of invested capital this would be a fraction of what the present fee arrangement really represents and (2) the manager will be disinclined to charge too much as his performance (upon which depends his ability to raise future funds) will still be measured on a net cash flow basis, i.e. net of fees and carried interest.

It is only fair to point out, however, that no matter how attractive such an approach might seem in theory, no moves have been made to adopt it in practice.

---

[4]Though logically this may be much higher in the case of the mega Buyout funds.

SUMMARY

When planning a Private Equity fund programme it is essential to draw up an outline cash flow model showing the various funds to which it is intended to commit, even though it must be recognised that, given the essential unpredictable nature of Private Equity fund cash flows, this will serve as only a rough guide.

When creating your model it is probably advisable to use default multiples of 1.6× for a Buyout fund and 2.0× for a Venture fund. These should be kept constantly under review in each individual case and changed if necessary as specific data on that individual fund and the market as a whole become available.

A failure to understand and remember the difference between allocated, committed and invested capital lies at the heart of many of the problems experienced by Private Equity LPs.

Historic overcommitment has resulted in significant problems for some LPs. However, it is submitted that some measure of overcommitment may still be appropriate, but given the important qualifications of the ability and readiness to adopt a flexible and intelligent approach.

To achieve acceptable levels of total return, endeavour to find alternative Private Equity uses for uninvested capital rather than allowing it to be drawn into bonds or quoted equities. Secondary and mezzanine interests and funds are the prime candidates.

Some LPs also co-invest in their GPs' portfolio companies. This will have the effect of slightly reducing the overall fee burden, but at the expense of much lower diversification.

Total return investing is a new concept but merits careful consideration.

15

Trends and Issues

It is time now to come full circle, back to some of the opening observations set out in the Introduction. The last few years have seen unprecedented amounts of capital being raised by the Private Equity industry, and unprecedented rates of change.

Let us pause for one final time and reflect that 75% of all the capital ever raised for Private Equity funds anywhere in the world has been raised from 2001 onwards, and about 50% of it from 2005 onwards.[1] It is very easy to toss these figures about glibly, but what do they actually mean for those who are investing in Private Equity funds?

First, and most importantly, they mean that if one is looking to get at long-term figures for the industry as a whole (perhaps on a pooled basis), then the returns of any year before 2000 are beginning to look increasingly irrelevant. US Venture had an upper quartile return in excess of 100% for vintage year 1996, for example, but the total capital raised for US Venture in that vintage year represents less than half of one percent of all Private Equity capital. This has particular implications for very large investors, such as some US public pension plans and sovereign wealth funds, which need to put large amounts of money to work and cannot simply try to cherry pick very good, but possibly very small, funds.

Second, it means that Private Equity has entered a distinct new phase of its existence, and of whose investment model the validity is yet to be established. This is another very important point, the significance of which does not seem to have been grasped. If the industry can no longer point to its pre-2000 record as representing a realistic pre-estimate of future returns, then this means that the industry effectively is under an imperative to justify itself to investors all over again, and there is little in the track record to date to suggest that this has been done. Whether this has been due simply to a solar storm of unexpected problems hurtling in from the wider environment outside to batter the industry, or whether to the fact that traditional investment models may no longer work in greatly changed circumstances remains to be seen.

Through all of this froth of change, however, it is possible to discern some distinct trends and issues rising up to the surface.

The most obvious of these has been the financial crisis and associated credit crunch which first started to rear its head in the summer of 2007. We need to consider not just the direct impact which this has had, most obviously on the world of mega Buyout, but also the indirect consequences which are starting to play out within the LP community, which may, in turn, have obvious ramifications for the secondaries sector.

Then there is the question of holding periods which, while primarily a problem for the Venture industry, are also washing across into all areas of Private Equity activity. This issue was already starting to cause concern at the time that the first edition of this book was published. Arguably, it should now be at the very top of any sophisticated LP's worry list, since

---

[1] Figures from Thomson Reuters.

it has implications not only for levels of Private Equity returns, but also for fundamentally important matters such as allocation and commitment levels.

Something else which was already felt to be an issue at the time the first edition was published was the size and attractiveness of the emerging Private Equity markets. Sadly, at the time there simply were insufficient data available to discuss the area sensibly. Now, while still not perfect, the available pictures paint a very clear picture, at the very least of LP appetite and GP investment levels.

FINANCIAL CRISIS

The narrative and chronology of the financial crisis which began (or, at least, started to become apparent) around the middle of 2007 are well known and this is not the place to recount them. Let us look instead at the specific implications for the Private Equity industry. These relate to credit, valuation, exits, fundraising and LP distress.

Credit

The credit market generally, and the leveraged Buyout debt market was no exception, underwent a period of irrational exuberance during the run up to the crisis. It is easy to illustrate this by the growth in multiples at which debt providers were prepared to value Buyout. Banks, like GPs, apply multiples of measures such as EBITDA to arrive at a valuation of a company, and different layers of Buyout debt will be offered at higher valuations (which means higher multiples) but correspondingly higher rates of interest (and usually higher rates of arrangement fees as well). For many years, senior debt valuations bumped along at about 4× EBITDA, with higher multiples becoming progressively more difficult (and more expensive) to obtain. Suddenly in about 2004 the banks threw caution to the winds. As late as 2003, for example, only about 5% of global Buyouts were being financed at EBITDA multiples above 6×, yet by 2006 this had risen to over 35%.[2]

Yet, illogically, the banks also chose this moment, when they were taking on significantly more risk, to take less rather than more protection, and so cov-lite lending was born. A full treatment of the terms of Buyout debt arrangements lies beyond the scope of this book, but the financing agreement will typically contain many covenants on behalf of the borrower, not just the obvious ones such as the obligation to pay interest on the due dates, but also covenants that the amount of the loan shall not exceed a certain percentage of the value of the company (loan to value) and that there shall, at any time, be sufficient cash flow available for any particular layer of debt to represent a certain multiple of the interest payable upon it (interest cover). In the feeding frenzy which now ensued, with bankers desperate for fees and GPs skilfully (and unsurprisingly) playing them off against each other, the banks were somehow persuaded to relax many of these covenants, hence the term 'cov-lite'.

Incidentally, while this fact could also have been noted above while talking about the rate of market growth, this may have been the biggest deal feast the Buyout industry will ever

---

[2]Figures from Standard & Poor's.

see, at least in Europe. It has been estimated that between the beginning of 2005 and the middle of 2007 there were over 100 Buyouts with an enterprise value in excess of €1 billion. Phrased in slightly more alarming language, this represents an awful lot of capital that was invested at historically high valuations, and almost certainly with historically high levels of gearing.

Banks are very bad drivers. They can only operate a car by either stamping on the accelerator or stamping on the brake. Just as in previous financial crises, the banks, having been hammering ahead with their foot to the floor, now took fright and tried to execute an emergency stop. The result, of course, was that senior debt dried up completely and so leveraged Buyout activity, which, after all, cannot operate without debt (the word 'leverage' being a bit of a give-away here), simply ground to a halt.

This, in turn, raised all sorts of questions, not least what Buyout GPs were going to do with the large amounts of money which they had raised as recently as 2007 (and, perhaps surprisingly, continued to be able to attract for much of 2008). Incidentally, there is an interesting parallel here with the world of US Venture firms, which found themselves, following the bursting of the bubble in 2001, with far too much capital effectively to deploy, having increased their fund sizes on the back of rising company valuations, sometimes by a factor of three and perhaps to as much as $1.5 billion.

Recognising that the world had changed, the most professional and reputable of them simply gave the excess money back to their LPs by releasing some of their commitments, and agreeing to repay the management fee which they had received on the excess amount in the interim. Some firms, in fact, ended up doing this not once but twice. Perhaps naïvely, some assumed that something similar would occur in the world of mega Buyout but in fact such honourable conduct has been notable by its absence. We know that about $670 billion of capital was committed to European and US Buyout in vintage years 2007 and 2008 combined,[3] very little of which can have been invested before the shutters came down. Even at a conservative estimate, that means there may have been at least $20 billion in management fees that has been drawn down on this money, money that the GPs acknowledged they had no chance of being able to put to work for the purposes for which they raised it; equity-only deals, mid-cap deals and PIPEs were all bruited as alternative uses for the money.

Again, there is an interesting parallel here. Those US Venture firms which did *not* reduce their fund sizes also talked about putting money to work through PIPE deals. It is, therefore, probably a valid, though cynical, conclusion to draw that when Private Equity firms start targeting PIPE deals, it probably means they have raised too much money and do not know what to do with it.

This issue is obviously of diminishing relevance the more time passes, since the LBO market is showing signs of coming back to life, albeit slowly and cautiously. However, LPs are entitled to enquire what value they have received in the meantime in return for the management fees they have been paying on 2007 and 2008 vintage year funds. To put this in context, $20 billion is more than the total amount of capital that was raised for European Buyout funds in 2002, 2003 or 2004.

---

[3] Figures from Thomson Reuters.

Valuation

We have touched on the vexed question of valuation already in Chapter 9. Readers may be interested to know that, until 2007, there was little demand for this to be included as part of training workshops on Private Equity, and that some brief references to the EVCA Guidelines were normally all that was required. Today, valuation has become a key area of concern, to the extent that a whole separate session on it is routinely requested.

There are, of course, two different aspects to this: (1) valuation in the sense of Private Equity GPs deciding how much to pay for a company and (2) valuation in the sense of an accounting exercise. As we saw earlier, the latter is chiefly an issue for auditors, both internal and external, rather than investors, but it is a hugely important one. Let us first, however, briefly consider the former aspect.

In the case of Venture, and to a lesser extent Growth, valuation is, of course, largely subjective and a matter partly of the GPs' gut feel and partly of their negotiation with entrepreneurs and other GPs. Efforts on the part of an American university to argue that they have developed a definitive Venture valuation model are nothing more than an extreme symptom of the inability of many finance theorists to accept that some aspects of investment are simply not capable of precise calculation or a universally valid solution.

In the case of Buyout, however, we find ourselves on firmer ground since valuation can be assessed, or at least expressed, in terms of multiples of earnings and cash flows. We also know that these, in turn, are heavily influenced by stock market multiples, since they are used as comparables. There can be no doubt that during the three years or so before mid-2007, many Buyouts were executed at high multiples since, just as in the run-up to all past financial crises, quoted PE ratios were at historically high levels. The S&P500, for example, was trading in the mid-20s.

Now, Buyout GPs find themselves both with companies whose earnings have declined, and with lower multiples to apply to those earnings, or at least which *would* apply to those companies if they were strictly marked to market, which leads into the second valuation issue. However, just before we leave this first discussion, let us note that all of this means that Buyout funds are currently sitting on many Buyouts (probably just about all of those 100 or so that we mentioned earlier) which effectively have zero equity value since they may now be worth less than the amount of the debt package which was entered into to finance the deal. Various recently announced refinancing packages have seen the Buyout fund concerned lose some, or even all, of its equity stake in the process. Of course this can, and almost certainly will, change in the future, but it will take time, and time is in increasingly short supply since much of the bank debt concerned is due for redemption and/or restructuring in 2011 and 2012. Unless and until this situation is resolved, there must exist at least a significant possibility that much of the equity that went into those 100 Buyouts is at serious risk.

Note that in the previous paragraph we used the word 'worth', and this where the second limb of the valuation issue comes in. Investors recognise that many Private Equity assets are difficult to value with any accuracy at any one time, particularly the farther one goes in the direction of early-stage, or even start-up, Venture. However, they also recognise that none of this is really important, as all that matters are the eventual cash flows when they occur, and both their amount and their timing are unpredictable.

This is undoubtedly a sensible frame of mind to adopt. After all, once one is committed to a Private Equity fund as an LP there is little one can do except to stay on for the ride.

However, all businesses require accounting processes and in the case of many LPs this may be further complicated by the additional demands of internal policy, oversight and even regulatory constraints and requirements.

A detailed treatment of this area belongs in a book on accountancy. It is enough for our purposes to note two particular issues which have arisen, the first of which is well recognised, but the second of which much less so.

Until the financial crisis erupted, the International Accounting Standards which underpin the accounting and audit process around the world operated largely unremarked upon in the shadows of the business world as accountants and analysts went about their daily tasks. As the full horror of the financial situation became apparent, particularly in or about September 2008, they were thrust into the full light of day, examined closely and found wanting.

To be fair, one can, of course, argue that the market conditions in which they found themselves were way outside any environment which had ever been envisaged for them, but that does not alter the fact that suddenly they seemed to be raising more questions than they answered, and questions furthermore which everyone thought had been safely taken care of.

How do American and International Standards interact when they appear to be inconsistent with each other, and how should foreign investors with US assets on their balance sheets proceed? Can a notional forced sale form the only valid basis for a valuation, and what happens when the market for a particular asset has effectively disappeared? To what extent is it even possible to calculate 'fair value' in any given situation? On what basis should assets be marked to market, and which assets, and when and how? These are just some of the debates currently raging in accounting and regulatory circles. In the meantime, many investors remain frustrated and irritated by the lack of clear guidance.

This whole area is, of course, relevant to the whole world of investment generally, not just Private Equity. Indeed, it probably affects areas such as corporate bonds and credit derivatives far more than Buyout, Growth, etc. There is, however, another question which is specific to Private Equity and to which there currently appears to be no clear answer.

As we saw, partnerships are creatures of contract, and the contract (in this case the Limited Partnership Agreement) may say that in the accounts of the partnership the portfolio companies shall be valued according to EVCA Guidelines. What happens, though, if the accounts of the LP themselves have to be audited, and the auditors come to the view that the EVCA Guidelines do not satisfy the requirements of International Accounting Standards, or perhaps of some of the American FASB requirements? Does this mean that they have to go down to the level of the underlying fund investments and revalue the portfolio companies, effectively second-guessing the GP's valuations? Pure logic might suggest 'yes', whereas commercial practicality would clearly suggest 'no'.

Holding Periods

Perhaps in no other area have investors been forced to revise their expectations more dramatically than in the case of holding periods (at the company level), and thus payback periods (at the fund level). Back in the 1990s there used to be a fairly settled expectation that Buyout firms would sell their investments after about three years on average, and Venture firms after about five. Based on these assumptions, there was a general expectation that Buyout funds would have returned at least 1× paid-in capital after about four and a half years, and Venture firms after about six.

For some years, certainly towards the end of that decade, the actual figures supported these views. During the years 1998 to 2000, for example, the average holding period of Private Equity-backed companies that went to IPO was 45 months for Venture and 40 months for Buyout, but with an upper (or should it be 'lower' in this case?) quartile of only about 30.[4]

Since then, however, things have changed dramatically. From the period from 2001 onwards the averages rise alarmingly to 79 months and 68 months respectively. Nor is it possible to argue that this is a function of poor manager selection. The average pre-IPO holding period of KKR, for example, measured over ten years and fifteen transactions, is exactly in line with the industry average.[5]

Whether the exit environment changes any time soon or not, it cannot have any appreciable effect on what has already happened, and this has two fairly obvious implications.

First, unless exit money multiples increase dramatically, then LPs are going to have to grow accustomed to much lower fund IRRs for this period. To illustrate this, to deliver a gross (not net) transaction return of 30% over three and a half years requires a money multiple (V/C multiple) of 2.5%. To deliver exactly the same gross IRR over five and a half years would require a money multiple of 5×, which would have been thought unrealistic even in the 'happy hunting time' of European Buyout back in the early 1990s.

Second, LPs who were happily assuming that their Private Equity fund programme would become more or less self-funding after about eight years (which still seemed a not unrealistic assumption at the time the first edition of this book was being written in 2006) will have been forced to modify their approach. Indeed, if they have been sensible, they will have started to do so as soon as it became apparent in the autumn of 2007 that the world had changed. As we saw in an earlier chapter, this dramatic prolongation of the payback period has been one of the major causes of the 'Cash 22' phenomenon, particularly in the United States.

Since those LPs worst affected usually have heavy allocations to US Venture, let us take a look at those particular figures in more detail. Measuring the DPI multiple for each vintage year after six years for each vintage year from 1998 to 2002 shows a very clear picture (Figure 15.1).

You will see that, whereas once it was reasonable to assume that the payback period of a US Venture fund would occur within its first six years, this is no longer the case. In fact, even measured during 2009, vintage years 2000 and 2001 have paid back only about 40% of their capital. Nor is the upper quartile much better (only about 50%), nor are subsequent years. Not since 1998 has any vintage year come anywhere near returning its capital, even using the upper quartile as a measure.

So, for US Venture, as with the whole Private Equity asset class, the jury is out, as the Americans say, on whether the sort of model which worked well during the 1990s is going to prove resilient and survive in an environment which is much more heavily funded, and an exit market which is much more challenging. Whatever the outcome, LPs will have to recast their cash flow models, as the evidence for lengthening payback periods is incontrovertible.

---

[4] Figures from Thomson Reuters throughout this analysis.
[5] These points were first made in a column in *Real Deals*.

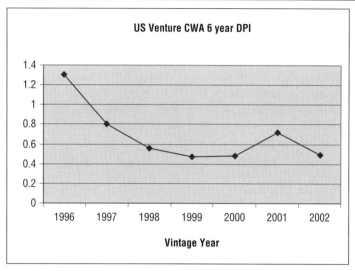

Source: Thomson Reuters

Figure 15.1   US Venture: the death of six year payback

Secondaries

With the temporary cessation of activity in the Buyout space, and a growing belief (whether justified or not) that Buyout debt may have played a significant part in the problems which began to grip financial markets from the summer of 2007 onwards, there has been a distinct change in the nature of the relationship between LPs and GPs, even those of the latter who were but recently viewed as the most glamorous and desirable of business partners.

Something similar (but on a much smaller scale) started to happen around the middle of 1989 as Buyouts began to get into trouble servicing their debt. Then, as now, the nature of the LP/GP relationship shifted dramatically. Then, as now, the banks hit the brakes on lending of any type, let alone that which involved high levels of gearing. In October 1989 a proposed Buyout of United Airlines fell apart when the banks refused to authorise the required debt package. The news was seen as sufficiently significant for the Dow to fall 7% in a single hour following the announcement. In 1990, KKR had to go back to its LPs to seek additional funding to rescue RJR Nabisco.[6]

Then, as now, this all seemed very grim news, even leading the financial writer and journalist George Anders to declare that the Age of Leverage was dead. However, in the event it turned out to be a temporary blip and Buyout fundraising and investment activity began to pick up almost immediately.

This time things may be more severe. A number of LPs, particularly those who came into the market fairly recently, and who may have allowed the lure of the mega Buyout funds to pull them into some very undiversified portfolios, have become seriously unsettled by the whole idea of Private Equity. Others may still be believers but have fallen into the trap of

---

[6]For a full (and entertaining) account of these times see Anders (1992) *Merchants of Debt*, Jonathan Cape, London.

Cash 22. At the time of writing (late 2009) we have already seen a number of situations where LPs have found reasons to refuse drawdowns or investment period extensions, and even to force fund size reductions.

For both these reasons, there are many who believe that the secondary market is likely to prove a highly attractive one for the next couple of years. This view seems logical, but should be treated with care. Yes, the market will be an attractive one for the buyers of secondary interests, in marked contrast to the period in 2005 and 2006 when some fund interests were changing hands at a premium to book value, but there appear to be huge pent-up amounts of capital still looking to be deployed in Private Equity, as witnessed by the industry's fundraising success even in 2008, perhaps the worst year that financial markets will ever know. If any significant part of this should start flowing into secondary funds, then the market will adjust very quickly. So, yes, there is a real opportunity here, but it is likely to be arbitraged away, as Hedge fund managers say, fairly quickly.

EMERGING MARKETS

Given the saturation of traditional Private Equity sectors, such as US Venture and both US and European Buyout, with capital, and uncertainty as to levels of future return in consequence, it makes increasing sense to look wider afield for one's Private Equity coverage. Most sophisticated investors will already pursue a mix of primary and secondary investing, and it is probable that this trend will grow even stronger in future. Another obvious candidate for wider coverage lies in emerging markets.

The geographic scope of emerging markets for Private Equity is not necessarily the same as for the world of investment generally. To take but two obvious examples, Japan is a major industrial economy and financial centre but still an emerging market for Private Equity purposes, and European Venture is almost certainly still an emerging market. Since we have already considered the latter, however, we will not discuss it further in this chapter.

Emerging markets have seen many false Private Equity dawns. Large amounts (or what then seemed like large amounts) of capital were thrown into China funds in the early 1990s, as well as into various South American markets (particularly Mexico) and what was then still firmly labelled Eastern Europe. In many cases such investment was clearly premature, even when viewed dispassionately at the time, and even more so when viewed with the benefit of hindsight.

China funds were, at the time, allowed only to invest in local government joint ventures. Obvious issues such as investing alongside a non-commercial partner, lack of exit route and lack of Western-style legal, fiscal and regulatory regimes were blithely ignored, with predictable results. Such was US LPs' enthusiasm for Asian markets, however, that these events were quickly forgotten and a fresh round of funds began to be raised in the latter years of the decade.

Things have, of course, moved on very considerably, and many of these markets have evolved significantly in the process. In Brazil, for example, much Private Equity fundraising is now routed through traditional Limited Partnership structures. However, significant issues remain, and while these countries now represent exciting opportunities, it is important to be aware of what these are in particular countries, and how you propose to deal with them. This can be even more difficult than it seems, since the waters are often muddied by inconsistent government statements, ambiguously drafted regulations, resistance to change and hideously complicated (and unfriendly) tax environments.

The main issues to which an investor needs to be alive are:

- taxation of gains at the local level;
- rulings as to establishing a permanent establishment;
- restricted foreign ownership, both by industry sector and percentage shareholding;
- non-recognition of Limited Partnerships;
- onerous registration requirements for foreign investors;
- repatriation of proceeds and related local currency issues;
- lack of consolidated accounting for tax purposes (without which Buyout activity is effectively made impossible);
- effectiveness of local exit routes, and bars to exits overseas;
- local fund management and regulation issues.

This may seem a daunting list, and indeed it is, but usually only some of these problems will exist in each country, and the possible attractiveness of the market will justify a great deal of time-consuming and expensive consultation with lawyers and local advisers. One wonders, however, how many LPs actually went through this process before they committed money to such funds.

The development of such markets lies firmly in the hands of their respective governments, and it is actually to be regretted that so many LPs have been happy to commit their money to be invested in sub-optimal circumstances, thus releasing any pressure which local governments might otherwise feel to make legal, fiscal and regulatory reforms. The Australian government, for example, changed its laws on the taxation of gains at local level specifically to attract foreign capital into Australian private companies.

Whatever the case, emerging markets have definitely arrived in Private Equity terms, and are here to stay. No less than $66 billion was raised for emerging market funds in 2008,[7] nearly as much also having been raised in 2007. In 2008, this was spread across 210 funds, 25% of which were first-time funds, emphasising the fact that this is still a fairly new area of investment.

To put that in context, emerging market funds raised pretty much the same amount of money in 2007 and 2008 as did US Venture funds, and they were particularly good fundraising years for US Venture. Sadly it is not possible to consider emerging markets in any detail as yet, since many GPs still do not register their data, and so available data sets are small, and analysis tentative. Surely this will change, though, and future editions of this book will hopefully be able to cover emerging markets in the depth which they deserve.

CONCLUDING THOUGHTS

The more one looks at the figures as the years go by, the more it seems that a whole new age of Private Equity began in 2001. It was from 2001 onwards that fundraising levels went into a dramatic upward curve. It was from 2001 onwards that holding periods, and thus payback periods, began to lengthen dramatically. It was from about 2001 onwards (though the full figures are not available) that much greater amounts of money also began to flow into emerging market Private Equity funds.

---

[7]Figures from *Emerging Markets PE Fundraising and Investment Review 2008*, Emerging Markets Private Equity Association.

There are some obvious forces working at a lower level as well. For US Venture, 2001 marked the first year of operating in a normal, non-bubble environment. For European Buyout, 2001 marked the beginning of a period where hugely increased fundraising created much larger fund sizes and thus much larger transaction sizes. The larger Buyout deals being done in Europe after 2000 were very different to those which had been done in the 1990s. For European Venture, 2001 marked the beginning of a period when fundraising nose-dived into serious decline, a decline which may yet prove terminal, though the true situation is masked by the official figures.

Indeed, it could be argued that Private Equity as an asset class is a completely different animal in 2010 than it was in 2000. If so, how valid is GP track record from before 2000 to possible future performance? If so, does Private Equity need to prove itself all over again as an attractive area for investors? If so, are the same fee structures which were put in place before 2000 still appropriate in a changed world?

Track Record

It would clearly be ridiculous to assert that track record achieved before 2000 is of no value. However, in some circumstances it may be evidential rather than conclusive in the future. Much will depend, for example, on the type of investment, and the purpose for which the track record is tendered. The circumstances in US Venture would have been dramatically different, whereas for US Buyout they would have been different, yes, but less so. If track record is tendered to show that the GP has demonstrated an ability to hold a team together and execute sound, well-considered investments, fine. If, however, it is tendered to convince you that because a GP earned an IRR of 120% on a 1995 vintage year US Venture fund they are likely to achieve the same thing on a 2010 US Venture fund, not fine.

Returns

Given that the circumstances of Private Equity are so very different now from what they were before 2001, it seems reasonable to argue that it will need to prove itself all over again to investors. After all, we have just seen that much pre-2001 track record will be of diminished value as a decision aid. However, there is no sign of a slowdown in Private Equity fundraising (except in the very short term). On the contrary, there has been a dramatic increase, and there seems no reason why this growth should not be continued once the present hiccup is over.

All of which seems to suggest that most LPs do not share the opinion that Private Equity has changed so radically that it is now something different to what it once was. This is not to say that Private Equity no longer offers attractive investment potential – far from it. However, there is no guarantee that it will continue to behave as it once did, and we have already seen that old track record cannot be accepted blindly as an indicator of future returns. A more intelligent approach is required, which would include both a more diversified portfolio and much more emphasis during analysis and due diligence on really picking apart a GP's investment model and trying to discern what they can do better than other people.

At the asset class level, things will change too. The Private Equity industry has grown complacent after so many years of comfortably outperforming other asset classes. Investors are growing increasingly sophisticated, and willing to consider a broad range of investment products and approaches. GPs may therefore find themselves competing within an 'alternative assets' allocation with anything from Hedge funds to commodities, and from active currency mandates to unlisted infrastructure or private real estate funds. The outcome may no longer be as clear cut as it once was, particularly since, in the short term, many LPs are likely to remain nervous of illiquid investments and those involving leverage. These are serious issues, which the industry will need to address.

At the end of the day, all that counts is performance, and there will be no substitute for GPs across all Private Equity disciplines demonstrating that they really can continue to deliver superior returns. It seems likely that this will, in fact, occur, though there are some serious structural concerns over both mega Buyout and US Venture, but it seems only reasonable to caution that the measure of that outperformance, relative to other asset classes, may well be less in the future than it was in the 1990s.

Fee Structures

Much has been said about fee structures and the way in which they seem to work unfairly in the favour of the GP and against the LP. These concerns are really just a recognition that the basic economic model of Private Equity has changed dramatically along with everything else, although here the change occurred much earlier than 2001.

In the early days of Private Equity funds, in the late 1980s, say, there was a well-recognised model which drove their economics. The management fee was designed to pay the GP's costs of operating the fund, including some modest salaries for the GP team. The GP's financial motivation was provided by the carry. If the fund made money, then the GPs made money through their participation in carried interest, and the value of that carry would be very significant indeed to the small amount they were taking out of the management fee in salary. If they made money for their LPs then they made money; if they didn't, they didn't. This is what people mean when they talk about economic interests being aligned.

Of course fund sizes were then very small compared with today. Even in 1990, for example, the average size of a US Buyout fund was only $125 million. Running a Private Equity fund is an expensive business, and so 2% of the fund's capital per year was deemed about right. It is important to understand that it was the needs of the fund's operations which set the level of the management fee, rather than the other way around. It was quite common for LPs to ask the GP to submit their operational budget for review and discussion as part of the fund-raising process. For a $125 million fund, then, 2% would provide an annual management fee of $2.5M. That is still a substantial amount of money, even today, but seen in the context of a team of professionals renting an office, employing staff and travelling to consider and execute deals, it is hardly excessive.

Today things have changed dramatically. Consider the situation if a GP raises a $15 billion fund with a 1.5% management fee. That provides the GP with $225 million a year, regardless of performance; in fact, regardless even of whether the GP actually makes any investments or not. This is clearly a very different situation from that which was originally envisaged. Economic interests are no longer aligned. In fact, they are dramatically and outrageously misaligned. GPs can now become very rich indeed on their management fee, exactly the *opposite* of what was intended.

All of this is clear and obvious. What seems less clear is why so many LPs should seem to have no real problem with it as a state of affairs. Certainly there have been few efforts in the past to form a united front to set standard industry fees at a sensible level, and wherever informal groupings have come together, the bargaining power of the GPs has always proved too great. This may seem illogical; after all, LPs have what GPs want and could simply with-hold it, couldn't they? Well, yes and no.

There are some GPs who have genuinely outperformed over substantial periods of time. They have deservedly become 'invitation only', so LPs should be, and are, prepared to pay high fees for access to their funds. However, the number of these genuine stand-out GPs is far lower than most GPs' investor relations people would have you believe. We are really talking only about the golden circle of US Venture – perhaps a dozen firms or so – plus perhaps the same sort of number in the mid-market Buyout space. In the mega Buyout sphere, returns have become increasingly commoditised and it is difficult to see it as a disaster to have to exclude any one particular GP from your starting line-up. So, logically, in respect of the overwhelming majority of GPs, LPs should be prepared not to invest unless they can do so on terms which they consider to be fair and reasonable.

This argument ignores two important factors, however. First, Private Equity fund pro-grammes acquire a momentum of their own. We have seen what a disaster it is not to have proper diversification by time. That means that an LP simply cannot afford not to invest one year, or to invest significantly less than in other years. There is, thus, an imperative to commit to funds, an imperative which GPs well understand. Second, there are a small number of very large LPs who can, and do, make commitments in bite sizes of several hundred million dollars at a time. A GP only needs to sign up a few of these and they effectively have a small mega Buyout fund straight away. Furthermore, they can point to the fact that these large LPs have already signed up to the proposed terms, and say (quite truthfully) that it would be a very difficult and complex matter to get them to go back through their various committee processes all over again to approve amended documentation.

So, in practice, though the system is obviously unfair, it seems likely to continue. The only thing that could conceivably alter this would be if the world's largest twenty or so LPs came together to agree a set of standard terms on which they were prepared to commit money to Private Equity funds. Even this would only be half the story, anyway, since having agreed the terms they would then need to stick to them, and it would inevitably only be a matter of time before a GP was able to bring influence to bear to get at least one of them to break ranks.

PRIVATE EQUITY AT A CROSSROADS?

So, it is clear, then, that Private Equity has, over the last few years, been buffeted by more change and disruption than it has ever experienced before, and that it now stands at a cross-roads, much more so even than it did in either 1989 or 2000. What does this mean for GPs and LPs?

It is a truth generally acknowledged that LPs hate change. They hate it at the micro level, with a GP's team or activities, and they hate it at the macro level, within the wider environ-ment. In consequence many, even those who were until recently active supporters of the asset class, have grown nervous of Private Equity, and especially its highly leveraged form. These nerves must be soothed, and quickly, or Private Equity may yet face the sort of investor backlash that Hedge funds have experienced over the last couple of years.

So, as the Introduction says, the industry as a whole still has a lot of work to do in educat-ing people around the world: educating those investors who are currently unable to take an informed view of the asset class; educating regulators to understand the different character-istics of different types of investment funds both within and outside the asset class; educating politicians, particularly in Asia, to see that Private Equity can safely be embraced, and can represent a powerful economic driver.

The long-term future of the industry may well depend on how well it proves able to rise to these challenges over the next few years.

SUMMARY

The financial crisis which began to unfold in 2007 has had a hugely negative effect on Private Equity generally. Buyout has been most badly affected, by lack of debt, falling valuations and companies struggling to maintain earnings levels. However, the closing of the exit window affected the whole industry, exacerbating the lengthening of holding periods (see below).

As we saw in an earlier chapter, a combination of longer Private Equity holding periods, unexpected cash flow problems and over-relaxed attitudes to liquidity have led to some investors finding themselves in Cash 22. Others, though not similarly distressed, now find themselves emotionally challenged by the asset class. For both these reasons, secondary activity is widely expected to represent an attractive opportunity over the next year or two, but it is likely this opportunity will then be arbitraged away as more and more capital seeks to enter the secondary space.

The Private Equity industry has undergone huge change since 2001. Indeed, so pronounced are these changes, particularly with regard to fundraising and holding periods, that it is possible to argue that a new age of Private Equity began at that time.

One consequence of this is that GP track record earned before 2001 may be of increasingly less value when testing a GP's investment model, particularly in the case of large Buyout funds.

Another consequence is that the industry now has to prove itself all over again as a source of long-term outperformance.

Given the likelihood of lower returns (across the whole industry – some individual firms will continue significantly to outperform), the imperative for proper diversification with a Private Equity fund programme is stronger than ever. Thus, emerging markets are likely to feature more strongly in LPs' thoughts.

The GP/LP economic model is obviously badly broken, and has been for some time. Traditional fee structures have come under renewed scrutiny. However, it is, as yet, unclear whether any significant long-term change will occur.

The long-term future of Private Equity may depend on its ability to educate and reassure investors, politicians and regulators alike of its resilience, persistence of returns and utility.

Glossary of Private Equity Terms

3G

Abbreviation or acronym for so-called 'third generation' mobile telephone technology. Strictly speaking this should only apply to UMTS, but partly due to delays in rolling this out it has come to be applied by some to GPRS, which is much less powerful but much more widely and cheaply available.

A round

Successive rounds of funding for a Venture company are given successive letters, i.e. the A round will come first, followed by the B round, etc. New Venture Capital investors can be introduced in each round.

An A round is usually defined as the first round in which a professional Venture investor participates, but this is misleading as this could equally refer to a seed round, depending on the stage in a company's development at which it takes place.

An A round may be preceded by one or more angel rounds as well as by a seed round.

A shares

Different classes of share are customarily created for different funding rounds in a Venture company. Traditionally, A shares are issued for the A round, B shares for the B round, and so on.

ADSL

Asynchronous Digital Subscriber Line. A means of using traditional copper telephone lines to carry broadband.

Advisory board

A committee of LPs within an individual fund delegated by the GP to give clearance and guidance on any situations involving a possible conflict of interest.

AFIC

The French Venture Capital association.

Allocated capital

The amount (usually calculated as a percentage) of its overall capital that an investor chooses to devote to Private Equity. Can be thought of as representing the rough amount of capital which an investor would ideally like to have invested in Private Equity at any one time.

Allocation

Another expression for allocated capital, usually when expressed as a percentage of the whole, e.g. 'a 15% allocation to Private Equity'.

Alpha and Beta (customers and product)

'Alpha' and 'beta' are used differently in different situations by different people. I would offer the following classification.

Alpha customers are those who are trialling product which is still very much at a pilot stage, i.e it is likely that, based on the customers' feedback, significant changes and development may yet be made to the product.

Beta customers are those who are trialling something that is supposed to be essentially the finished article. The intention is that only minor changes will need to be made, principally to correct technical glitches that arise during the trial.

Angel

Someone who invests in Venture companies, typically at a very early stage, but is not a professional Venture Capitalist. In the US these are quite likely themselves to have been successful entrepreneurs, and to be well adapted to dealing with the Venture industry.

In Europe, angels tend to be successful business executives, to have less money available for investment than their American counterparts, and frequently to view Venture firms with suspicion rather than seeing them as useful co-investors.

Angel round

A round of Venture funding in which only angels participate, i.e. in which no professional Venture firm is present.

Annexe fund

A separate fund formed by the LPs of a fund to provide a pool of top-up capital when the reserves of the fund have proved inadequate, with the aim of avoiding the issues raised by cross-fund investing.

Anti Dilution

Provisions commonly found in the funding agreements governing rounds of investment in Venture companies under which the shareholdings of certain shareholders (typically early-stage investors and entrepreneurs) cannot fall below a specified percentage of the whole.

Average (when applied to returns)

The arithmetic mean of any sample population of fund returns. This measure suffers from a grave drawback in that it gives equal weighting to all funds within the sample, even the very small ones which will probably not be of institutional investment grade. The capital weighted average (see below) is greatly to be preferred.

Average holding period

$$\sum HoldingPeriod \Big/ n$$

Where n is the number of companises

Average leverage (or gearing or debt)

$$\frac{\sum Debt \Big/ n}{\sum EnterpriseValue \Big/ n}$$

Where n is the number of companies
   See also Gearing ratio.

B2B
Online businesses which deal with business customers, e.g. wholesale, business services, business exchanges, etc.

B2C
Online businesses which deal with retail customers. Amazon would be one of the best-known examples.

Baggage
American expression used to describe the amount of time which GPs are going to have to spend looking after the portfolio companies of prior funds.

Basis point
One hundredth of one per cent. Thus, 50 basis points is 0.5%, and so on.

Bid premium
That part of a public company's value which may be ascribed to the possibility of it being taken over (bid for). Where there is a controlling or blocking shareholding there can, by definition, be no bid premium.

BIMBO
Acronym for Buy-In/Management Buyout. A type of Buyout transaction which combines the features of both an MBO and MBI (see below). In most cases a senior executive who has worked within the same sector (and may even have worked for the target company in the past) forms a management consortium with existing managers from within the target company.

Blind or blinded (of data)
Fund data are blinded when it is impossible to identify exactly which individual fund matches which individual data entry. Thomson Financial's VentureXpert system operates in this way.
   The disadvantage is that you cannot assess the performance of any one fund. The advantage is that GPs who may otherwise be reluctant to submit their data are reassured sufficiently to do so.

Book

'The Book' is the selling document (often called a Sale Memorandum) which is prepared by the investment bank retained on behalf of a business seller (vendor). It describes the business to be sold and will be circulated to a (usually restricted) group of potential purchasers, who will typically include at least two or three Buyout houses.

Note: this term may also be used in other ways, i.e. by brokers during share issues as meaning a list of underwriters or subscribers.

Bootstrap

To bootstrap a company means to develop it without the assistance of professional Venture Capital. Instead, the founders make do with their own assets, capital from angel investors and any cash flows which they can generate from the company's own business activities or assets.

Bottom up

The way in which analysis of Private Equity funds must be carried out, by modelling the individual transactions within a fund in order to build up a picture of the whole.

Buyout

Generic name for a group of transactions in which debt is used to assist the acquisition of a control position in a company. One of the two main categories of Private Equity, the other being Venture Capital.

Buyout drivers

There are usually said to be three main drivers of Buyout returns: earnings, (earnings) multiple and leverage. In fact there is also a fourth: time.

BVCA

British Venture Capital Association. Despite its name, it represents overwhelmingly by fund value the interests of pan-European Buyout firms based in London, not the British Venture Capital community.

EVCA (see below) is subject to similar terminological inexactitude.

Capital Call

A demand by a Private Equity fund for some part of the money which has been committed (i.e. promised) to it by investors. Each such demand, and the payment made pursuant to it, is called a drawdown.

Capital weighted average (CWA)

An average return calculated for any given sample population by reference to the capital size of each individual constituent fund. Save only for upper quartile returns, it is submitted that this is the most realistic measure of Private Equity returns.

Carried interest

That share of the profits made by a Private Equity fund which is reserved for the management team ('GPs'). This is typically 20%, but can be as high as 30% for some top US Venture funds and usually drops to 10% for a Fund of Funds.

Carry
Another term for carried interest (see above).

Cash sweep
As part of the banking arrangements for a Buyout transaction, a cash sweep refers to the process of checking all the company's bank accounts on specified dates and automatically gathering up any spare cash balances to offset some or all of the outstanding loan balances.

Catch-up
Where a hurdle rate applies, a procedure under which all of the gains of a fund can be applied to the GP once the hurdle rate is achieved until the underlying carry percentage is reached.

For example, where an 8% hurdle rate applies, the next 2% of return would be applied wholly to the GP so that the underlying agreed 80/20 split would be achieved.

Change of control provision
A clause in a business contract which stipulates that if ownership of a majority of the equity of a company changes hands, then the other party to the contract has a right to cancel, usually without liability for paying any compensation.

Class rights
Rights (such as a liquidation preference) attaching to a particular class of shares in a company which cannot be varied except with the consent of the holders of that class of share.

Clawback
An arrangement whereby at the end of a fund's life, the LPs may recover from the GP any overpayment of carry (i.e. where full account has not been taken of loss-making deals). Often coupled with some measure of security such as an escrow arrangement.

Close or Closing
The signing of an LPA (see below). Every fund will have a First Close, after which it has legal status and may begin operations, usually followed by a series of other closings. Typically the Final Close will be required to take place not later than one year after the First Close.

Closed-End or Closed-Ended
A vehicle such as a Limited Partnership, which has a stated lifetime at the end of which it will be wound up. Contrast with Open-Ended or Evergreen vehicles (see below).

Commitment
A legally binding promise by an investor to make a certain amount of money available to a Private Equity fund on demand.

Committed capital
When used by an investor, the total of all current commitments to all funds by that investor.

When used by a fund, the total amount of capital currently committed to that fund by all investors.

Condition subsequent
Used where a certain legal entitlement (for example to some share options in a Buyout company) is granted subject to a certain thing remaining true, e.g. the individual remaining employed by the company for a specified time.

Constituent fund
A fund which forms part of a specified group for return purposes. For example, a European Buyout fund formed in 1997 which turns out to have a return equal to or greater than the upper quartile will be a constituent fund of the '1997 vintage year upper quartile' group.

Controlled auction
A process whereby the potential seller of a business will appoint an intermediary (today usually an investment bank) to prepare a Sale Memorandum ('the Book') and send it to an agreed list of potential buyers, who will then enter an auction process. Practice varies, but classically there will be at least two stages, with only some of the candidates being selected to move on to the next stage. The ability to figure on this list of potential buyers represents a huge barrier to entry for first-time large Buyout funds.

Convertible
A share (usually a preference share) or loan note which carries the right, in specified circumstances (i.e. on a particular date, or on the occurrence of a specified event), to be exchanged in whole or in part for equity in the company. The conversion ratio may be fixed or on a sliding scale contingent, for example, on the performance of the company.

Cov-Lite
Short for 'Covenant Light', this refers to loan agreements that provide for less than the customary traditional range of covenants from the borrower. These were a key feature of the Buyout environment worldwide throughout 2005 and 2006.

Cross-fund investing
Where a firm invests in the same company at different times from different funds, i.e. uses its current fund towards a financing round in a company which forms part of the portfolio of one of its earlier funds.

Deal by deal (used in relation to carried interest)
An arrangement under which the GP takes their full carry entitlement on the exit of each deal, regardless of whether or not the LP has yet received full payback of capital. In its most extreme form, the GP may take their share of profitable transactions, but ignore those which incur losses.

Development Capital
A Private Equity transaction relating to a mature business, which can typically be distinguished from Buyout by the lack of (1) shareholder control and (2) any significant amount of acquisition debt. Sometimes referred to as Expansion Capital, especially in the case of a 'money in' deal (see below).

Distributed to committed capital (DCC)

The multiple (ratio) of total money distributed to date to the total committed capital of the fund. Like DPI (below) this is only really meaningful right at the end of a fund's life.

Distributed to paid in (DPI)

A multiple commonly used in analysing Private Equity funds. It represents the ratio of money distributed (i.e. paid out) by the fund to money paid in (i.e. drawn down). This ratio is referred to as the realisation ratio, but is only really meaningful in the very late stages of a fund's lifetime.

Distribution

The process of a fund paying money to an investor after exiting an investment. This can sometimes take the form of an in specie distribution of shares, particularly in the case of US Venture funds.

Diversification by time

The need to invest Private Equity money, whether at the company or fund level, steadily over several vintage years in roughly equal amounts. Lack of diversification by time is one of the most common mistakes committed by new LPs entering the asset class.

Dollar-weighted (returns)

A misleading term when compared to time-weighted returns (see below).

Simply the calculation of the IRR of a series of fund cash flows, i.e. the compound return over time. This is the classic measure of Private Equity returns, and is to be commended.

Great care should be taken not to confuse this measure with time-weighted returns which, contrary to first impressions, actually means something completely different (and should be avoided at all costs).

Dot com

There are both narrow and wide senses in which this phrase is used.

Narrowly, it refers to e-commerce businesses, ranging from the spectacularly successful such as Google.com and Amazon.com to the spectacularly unsuccessful such as Pets.com, eToys.com and Boo.com. In most people's minds it is probably most closely associated with online retailers (B2C).

Widely, it became applied to all participants in the technology and Internet bubble of the late 1990s, to the extent that this is often referred to as 'the dot com bubble'.

Downside

Negative returns within a fund or a fund programme. May be used in particular when looking at which companies within a fund lost money compared to those that made money. When used by an investor, may refer to the risk of any one fund failing to return its capital.

Drag Along

A form of exit protection whereby shareholder A can force shareholder B to sell B's shares alongside A's should A receive an offer from a third party. See also Tag Along (below).

Drawdown
See Capital Call.

Please be aware that this term is used in a completely different sense in other areas, e.g. Hedge funds, where it can mean periods of downside.

Drawdown Notice
Another term for a Capital Call.

Drawn down capital
When used by an investor, the total amount of committed capital which has actually been requested by its Private Equity funds.

When used by a fund, the total amount of committed capital which it has actually drawn down from its investors.

In either case, drawn down capital is the same thing as paid-in capital.

Dry Powder
Unused capital which is, as yet, still available for drawdown and investment. See Uninvested capital.

Due diligence
The process of performing background checks and rigorous financial analysis on a Private Equity fund (for an LP) or on a potential investee company (for a GP).

Since due diligence is a lengthy and costly exercise, it will normally only be entered into once a decision to invest in principle (i.e. 'subject to due diligence') has been taken.

Earn out
A provision which used to be commonplace but is now increasingly rare whereby the buyer of a company agrees to pay the seller a fixed multiple of the actual profits of each of the next two or three years.

The alternative is often to try to get certain minimum levels of future profits made the subject of a warranty, but this is now very difficult to achieve except in the case of a forced sale or a classic traditional-style MBO.

The one case in which an earn out is still frequently found is in Development Capital deals which are wholly or partly 'money out' in nature.

Earnings
Usually thought of as a company's earnings after deduction of all accounting items, e.g. interest and tax. Can be thought of as the earnings which would normally be available for distribution to shareholders. Forms the basis for the PE ratio (see below).

EBIT
Earnings Before (deduction of) Interest and Tax.

Probably a more appropriate Buyout measure than earnings, but still not a true cash flow proxy since it includes non cash items such as depreciation.

EBITDA
Earnings Before Interest, Taxes, Depreciation and Amortisation.

Probably the best of all Buyout earnings measures and certainly the one used by Buyout firms themselves. Of limited use for comparative purposes, however, since it is a non GAAP measure and the manner of its calculation can fluctuate from year to year.

EIR

Entrepreneur in residence. Many American Venture firms will have three or four of these at any one time, encouraging them to incubate their next business start-up idea in their offices.

End game

The management of quoted distributions. This is a much underestimated requirement of any investor in US Venture funds, calling for specialist skills and processes.

Enterprise value

The total value of a business, the price at which it may be sold. Can be thought of as earnings × PE ratio (or any of the other earnings measures × the appropriate multiple) or as Equity value + Debt.

EPS

Earnings per share.

Equity value

The value of the equity in a company. Can be thought of as Enterprise value − Debt.

ERISA

Employee Retirement Income Security Act, which governs the way in which US pension plans can invest in Private Equity. Private Equity funds must be 'ERISA compliant' in order to qualify for capital from these sources.

Escrow

A legally defined account, the contents of which may not be dealt with save with the consent of both parties, or by an escrow agent in accordance with pre-agreed conditions. In the context of Private Equity funds, often used as a mechanism to give LPs some measure of security against possible clawback (i.e. some part of the carry is paid not to the GP, but into an escrow account).

EVCA

European Venture Capital Association.

Evergreen

Refers to an investment vehicle which is open-ended, unlike an institutional Limited Partnership, which will always have a stated lifetime and will thus be closed-ended. These used to be very prevalent in continental Europe where there were both legal and cultural obstacles to investing in Limited Partnerships, but a number are quoted on the London Stock Exchange, 3i being the best-known example.

These vehicles can give rise to particular problems when it comes to analysing returns, since they typically do not return capital to investors, and thus think in terms of Net Asset Value and dividends rather than compound returns based on cash flows.

Exclusivity

An agreement that the potential seller of a company will deal only with one specific potential vendor for a specified period, on pain of financial penalties (usually refunding the buyer's costs) for any breach. See also Walkaway Fee (below).

Exit protection

Contractual provisions within a shareholders' agreement which seek to protect the right of the Private Equity investor to force an exit, usually after the expiry of a set period. See, for example, Drag Along and Tag Along.

Expansion Capital

A generic term for both Development and Growth Capital, used particularly in the USA.

Extension

The right of a GP to prolong the life of a fund beyond its originally specified length. A common provision is that the GP has the right to extend the fund twice, for one year each time, but that any further extensions require LP consent.

Extension period

Any such period of extension referred to above, but can also mean the state of existence of a fund once the first such extension has occurred.

See also Run-off.

FDA

The (American) Food and Drug Administration. Responsible for licensing all medical products for use in the USA. Chiefly relevant to drug discovery and related areas, e.g. genomics.

Firm

Yet another area of transatlantic ambiguity. I use the word in its European sense of a Private Equity management entity, whereas in North America it is frequently taken to mean a Venture company, i.e. an entity in which a fund will invest.

In North America the words 'group' or 'GP' are typically used for a European 'firm'.

Flotation

Known as an IPO in America (see below), the process by which a company's shares become quoted on a stock market and thus publicly tradeable.

French auction

Named after some infamous goings-on in France during the early and mid 1990s. An auction in which there is no guarantee that the highest bidder will win, and that may be re-opened to allow the preferred bidder to re-bid.

French solution

A euphemism employed by French politicians, investment banks and business sellers. Translated, it means 'we are going to offer this company on the open market, and anyone can buy it as long as they are French.'

Full payback
An LP-friendly alternative to a deal by deal carry, whereby full payback of either invested or (more rarely) drawn down capital has to occur before any carry becomes payable to the GP.

Fund I, etc
Private Equity funds are traditionally given roman numerals. Thus, Doughty Hanson II would be the second fund to have been raised by Doughty Hanson, Apax V would be the fifth fund to have been raised by Apax, and so on.

Fund cycle
The natural rhythm of a fund's operations. Very broadly, this will usually take the form of an investment period (typically about three years, though Venture funds will continue to invest money into companies for some years), followed by a development period and a harvesting period, when exits are effected.

Fund of Funds
A Private Equity firm which invests in funds, rather than directly into companies. Fund of Funds managers are frequently also active participants in the secondary market.

Fundraising
The process of finding investors (LPs) to commit to a new fund.

Fundraising cycle
The period between raising one fund and its successor fund. Typically about three years for primary funds and about two years for secondary funds.

GAAP
Generally Accepted Accounting Principles.

Gearing
Another word for leverage (see below), describing the effect of debt of a transaction or company.

Gearing ratio

Usually expressed as $\dfrac{TotalDebt}{EnterpriseValue}$

Go shop
A contractually agreed period during which the owner of a business can solicit offers for its sale at a price in excess of that already agreed with a vendor, in default of which the sale to the vendor will proceed. Should the owner be successful in soliciting a higher offer, then a walkaway fee will usually be payable (see below).

Golden circle
A phrase invented by the author and now in common use to refer to that very small number of US Venture firms who have managed more than one fund which has significantly

outperformed. While it defies precise definition, it is probably no more than about twenty names.

GP

In the US, and increasingly in Europe, a manager of a Private Equity fund is known as a GP (General Partner) since most Private Equity funds take the form of Limited Partnerships, and these are required by law to have a General Partner to manage their affairs.

GP can refer either to the management entity or to individual partners within such entities. (In Europe this ambiguity is avoided by using the word 'firm' for the entity but this creates fresh confusion as the word 'firm' is used in North America to denote a Venture company – oh, dear!)

GPRS

General Packet Radio Service, sometimes called 2½G, as it was meant to be a stepping stone on the way to 3G (see above). In the event, technical problems delayed the introduction of 3G and GPRS has, in many cases, come to be adopted (but wrongly described) as 3G.

Great Train Robbery

Colloquial epithet for the railway privatisation deals entered into in the UK in the mid-1990s, in conditions of considerable political risk.

Group

Frequent American usage for a 'firm' or 'GP'.

Hard circle

Reference to an investor, or group of investors, who have made a firm decision to commit money to a Private Equity, subject only to agreement on the legal terms and any outstanding due diligence.

Hockey stick

Another name used for the pattern made by the J-curve (see below). This should be avoided if possible, since it can properly be applied to all sorts of situations including where annual returns are being considered, whereas the J-curve applies specifically to returns plotted on a cumulative compound basis.

Home run

A baseball term that has been imported into Venture capital parlance. In baseball it is when the batter hits the ball out of the park into the crowd (equivalent to hitting a six in cricket, but more so in that its scoring is potentially open-ended and can have a dramatic effect on the overall team score, since all the players who are currently on base can run home).

Strictly speaking it means an investment (company) that returns the entire capital of the investing fund all by itself, but as a matter of practice, this has come to be generally accepted as being any investment which returns at least 25×.

Home-run mentality

The attitude of mind which recognises the overwhelming importance of home runs, and sets out to achieve them. Includes the need to reject an investment opportunity which does not have the potential to be a big winner, and the focus on building a business quickly into a large company.

Sometimes called 'swinging for the fence' (another baseball expression).

Housekeeping
Tidying up a portfolio of Private Equity fund interests by selling those which are both very old and very small into the secondaries market. Sometimes also called 'spring cleaning' (see below).

Hurdle or Hurdle rate
Used in its commonly accepted sense of a hurdle return, i.e. the lowest possible return which a particular investor will accept.

However, also used specifically to describe a return which a GP has to at least equal before any carry is calculated or payable. This mechanism is commonly found in Buyout and Development Capital funds, but rarely in Venture funds.

In specie
A Latin phrase meaning literally 'in its actual form'. It is used to describe a distribution of shares, rather than a distribution of the money raised from selling those shares.

See also End game and Quoted distributions.

Invested capital
The total amount of drawn down capital which has actually been invested in companies. In practice, this will be equal to the amount of drawn down capital less amounts which have been used to pay fees, or which are awaiting investment.

Investee company
A company within a Private Equity fund, i.e. an entity in which the fund buys shares, and/ or to which it provides finance in some form of convertible instrument.

IPO
Initial Public Offering. American term for a flotation (see above), which is steadily coming into common usage in Europe as well.

IRR
Internal rate of return (so called because it was originally used to calculate the return on different projects within a company). The compound return of a series of cash flows over a specified period (usually several years), used as one of the two main measures of Private Equity returns.

The strict business school definition is that compound return, found by iteration, which will reduce the NPV of any stream of cash flows to zero.

J-curve
The effect of all Private Equity funds, irrespective of final performance, exhibiting strongly negative returns in the early years as money is drawn down into the fund, reversing as distributions begin to be made. So called from the shape made by the returns when plotted on a cumulative compound basis.

Kicker

A kicker, or equity kicker, is that part of the terms of a share of loan note which confers the convertible rights (see above).

LBO

Leveraged Buyout. In one sense all Buyouts are LBOs, since they all involve the use of debt. However, this now has two main connotations: (1) a very large transaction, frequently with multiple business activities and (2) a transaction which is not initiated by a management team. It may be convenient to think of it as an industrial acquisition where the acquirer just happens to be a Buyout firm (or consortium).

Leverage

Describes the effect of debt on a company or transactions.
    See also Gearing.

Liquidation preference

Commonly found in Venture funding agreements, particularly in the US. A particular class of shareholder will reserve the right to have their investment paid back either once or some other multiple from any exit proceeds before the interests of any other investors are considered. Originally designed, as the name suggests, to provide protection in the event of a winding up, these have now come to be used almost routinely in all circumstances.

Historically less common in other parts of the world, such as Europe, where simpler capital structures and a more friendly, co-operative relationship between investors have been preferred.

Living dead

Companies which, towards the end of a fund's life, have done neither badly enough to be killed nor well enough to be sold. Usually applied only to Venture funds, though may also be appropriate in other circumstances.
    See also Tail.

LP

In the US, and increasingly in Europe, an investor in Private Equity funds is known as an LP (Limited Partner), since most Private Equity funds take the form of Limited Partnerships.

LPA

Limited Partnership Agreement, the document which constitutes a Limited Partnership. These will be the subject of discussion and negotiation prior to First Closing.

M&A

Merger and Acquisition. The process of buying and selling companies.

Manager

In Europe, a GP was traditionally referred to as a manager, and many still use this term.

Market timing

The practice of adjusting your investment approach in reaction to, or as a result of prediction of, conditions in financial markets.

In brief, because this approach requires a relatively short-term approach and, in particular, the ability to liquidate investments at short notice, it is an impossible approach to Private Equity investing, regardless of whether it may or may not work in relation to other asset classes. A failure to appreciate this is one of the most fundamental mistakes made by Private Equity investors (particularly LPs).

See also Diversification by time.

MBI

Management Buy-In. A type of Buyout transaction where a group of experienced executives buy not their own business but one which is operating in the same sector. Also includes a situation where an executive leads the Buyout of a business where he has worked previously, but this will usually be a BIMBO (see above).

MBO

Management Buyout. A type of Buyout transaction in which the team of executives managing a business buy it out from the parent company with the support of a Buyout firm.

Median

The observation within a sample population that sits exactly in the middle of the observations ranked by value. Sometimes used as a measure of Private Equity returns (especially by those outside the industry) but its value as such is questionable, particularly where there is a small sample size or a heavily skewed range of values.

Mezzanine

Convertible unsecured debt which sits between the equity and senior debt layers of a Buyout structure. In the US, the term can also be found applied to pre-IPO funding rounds for Venture companies.

MMOG

Massively Multi-player Online Game. A rapidly developing area of Venture Capital investment.

Money in

Describes a Development Capital deal where the Private Equity fund acquires new shares in the target company, thus providing it with funds for growth. Such deals are frequently referred to as Expansion Capital.

Money out

Describes a Development Capital deal where the Private Equity fund acquires existing shares from the business owner. In other words, the money goes to him rather than into the company and is thus seen as analogous to him taking money out of the company.

Negative control

Where a Buyout firm, though it may not control a majority of the target company's shares, imposes a right of veto over certain decisions, most notably executive remuneration, share dividends, capital expenditure, borrowing and changes in business activity.

Newco
A term used in structuring discussions and diagrams by lawyers, accountants, investment bankers and Private Equity professionals to describe a new company that will be formed specially to take some defined role in a corporate transaction or series of transactions, frequently as the acquisition vehicle (i.e. the new holding company) in a Buyout transaction.

NVCA
National Venture Capital Association (of America).

NVCA Guidelines
Inaccurate name for a set of guidelines actually produced by PEIGG (see below) and for which the NVCA has never done more than express broad support.

Observation
Any single value within a sample population.

Offering Memorandum
An OM is a document issued by, or on behalf of, a Private Equity firm with the object of raising money from the investment community. Sometimes referred to as a Private Placing Memorandum (see below).

Open-Ended
See Evergreen.

Operating debt
Debt which is present naturally within a company as working capital for its business activities. This can be reduced through lowering stock levels, extending the time taken to pay creditors or persuading debtors to pay their invoices more quickly.

Operating experience
Refers to what is used in contributing value add (see below). Chiefly used in a Venture context, though some Buyout firms also refer to it, and maintain a panel of key executives with different business backgrounds.

OPM (other people's money)
Any part of the consideration for a transaction other than that being provided by the Private Equity fund concerned. Most usually third party debt or mezzanine, but could also include a contribution by the vendor in the form of deferred consideration, or a vendor loan (see below).

Overhang
Capital raised by Private Equity funds but as yet uninvested. This can become acute when levels of investment fail to keep pace with levels of fundraising.

Overhang will tend to put upward pressure on valuations, raise suspicions that deal quality may be sacrificed in order to put money to work, and may also stretch out the fund cycle.

P2P
Public to Private transactions.
See also Take Private.

Paid-in capital
See Drawn down capital.

Payback period
The length of time which it takes to recover your initial capital on any investment, i.e. for the investment to return 1×.

Once widely used as a means of evaluating rival projects or investments for capital allocation purposes but now largely superseded by IRR.

Can also be applied to mean the period leading up to the payback point of a Private Equity fund.

Payback point
The moment in the life of a Private Equity fund when the amount of money returned to LPs as distributions exactly matches (or exceeds for the first time) the amount of money drawn down.

PE ratio
The Price/Earnings ratio is a way of stating the valuation of a company in a way which can be applied to and compared with those of other companies.

Either $\dfrac{Shareprice}{EPS}$ or $\dfrac{EnterpriseValue}{earnings}$

PEIGG
Private Equity Industry Guidelines Group, a body which has produced a set of advisory valuation guidelines in the US.

Pharma
A term used to refer to drug discovery activities, and also collectively for the very large multinational companies in this area.

PICC (Paid in to committed capital)
The ratio of total money drawn down by a fund to date measured against its committed capital. Can be a useful measure where there is a suspicion that a firm has raised too much money for its current fund and is struggling to put it all to work.

PIPE
Private Investment in Public Equity. Where a quoted company agrees to produce an instrument, which is typically not itself quoted, but which can potentially offer a Private Equity-type return. These transactions have, so far, largely been confined to the US.

Placing (or Placement) agent
A business which acts as adviser and a source of introductions to LPs for GPs who are looking to raise a fund.

Pooled return
A method of calculating returns whereby all the constituent funds are consolidated together and treated as if they were one large fund.

Portfolio secondary
A phrase invented by the author to mean a secondary investment which is made not for reasons of cash flow or capital management but specifically because the investor wants exposure (or additional exposure) to that particular Private Equity fund.
    See also Treasury secondary.

Post money
Refers to a valuation of a Venture company including the amount of money contributed by the Venture round in question.

Pre money
Refers to a valuation of a Venture company before taking into account the amount of money contributed by the Venture round in question.

Primary
Primary interests are commitments by investors to new funds, as distinct from secondary interests (see below). Once the fund is operating, i.e. making investments, then the interest would become a secondary interest.
    A good way of remembering the difference is to consider the parties involved. In making a commitment to a fund, the only relationship will be that between the LP and the GP. In disposing of an existing interest, the key relationship is between the LP and the other investor who is seeking to buy the interest and take the place of the LP.

Private Placing Memorandum
Or PPM. Another expression for an Offering Memorandum (see above).

Quoted distributions
Distributions in specie. That is to say, a distribution by a Private Equity fund to investors which takes the form of shares in an underlying company rather than cash produced by selling those shares. Such shares may frequently be restricted stock (see below).
    See also End game.

Realisation ratio
The ratio of money paid out by a fund compared to money paid in.
    See also DPI.

Recapitalisation or 'Recap'
A very important but little understood contributor to Buyout returns. Where a company has more earnings and/or cash flow than was originally envisaged, equity is returned to investors and replaced where necessary with new debt.

Reps and warranties
Representations and warranties by the vendor placed in the sale agreement when a company changes hands. They usually cover things such as contingent liabilities, the company's tax position and the accuracy of the most recent audited accounts.

Reserves

Fund capital which is notionally set aside to provide subsequent funding rounds for portfolio companies. The level of reserves should be kept under constant review, particularly since, when a company is written off, it will be necessary to decide how to use the reserves set aside for that company which will now no longer be needed.

Except in the case of a Roll-up, this is almost exclusively an issue for Venture funds.

Residual value to paid in (RVPI)

The ratio of the current value of all remaining investments within a fund to the total amount of capital paid in to date.

Restricted stock

Shares which form part of a flotation (IPO) but which are not freely tradeable for a specified time – usually six months. In the US this occurs automatically by operation of market regulation. In Europe it is a matter for contractual agreement, and thus can be varied if, for example, there is greater demand for stock than anticipated.

Roll-up

A Buyout transaction where a fragmented industry is targeted and a number of small businesses are bought before being consolidated together into one large entity.

Run-Off

A fund is said to be in run-off at any time after an extension event has occurred.

See also Extension and Extension period.

Secondary

A secondary interest is an ownership position in an existing fund which may or may not be fully invested, but has not been fully exited and wound up. Such interests are usually more or less freely transferable and a thriving secondary market has grown up to cater for such transactions, a number of specialist firms having been set up for the purpose.

See also Primary.

Secondary Buyout

A company within the portfolio of a Buyout fund which is then bought not by a trade purchaser, but by another Buyout fund.

Sector

Strictly speaking, both Buyout and Venture deals can be subdivided by sector, but it is of less importance in Buyout than it is in Venture, where it is one of the two main ways of classifying Venture deals (the other being by stage). Historically, Venture companies have been divided into three broad categories: Life Science, Information Technology and Telecoms. The latter two are often referred to together as 'Technology', and the distinction between them is becoming increasingly blurred.

Seed round

A round of Venture funding which takes place during the seed stage. May be preceded by an angel round, but in this case it risks being defined as an A round instead, unless it occurs fairly soon after the seed round.

Seed stage

The start-up stage of a company's existence.

Senior debt

Strictly, debt which takes priority over other layers of debt in the Buyout structure, both as to repayment and on liquidation. However, today it is used generally to refer to 'straight' debt which will not usually have a convertible element and will usually enjoy some form of security.

Sharpe ratio

A measure of the excess return of any asset or asset class relative to its own volatility.

Skin in the game

The existence of a significant financial contribution and commitment to the business by the entrepreneur(s). Can also take other forms, e.g. the willingness of the entrepreneur(s) to leave their existing job(s) to start up the company before Venture funding is in place. What is 'significant' is measured subjectively relative to the position of each individual entrepreneur.

The term can also be used in MBO transactions.

Soft circle

Reference to an investor, or group of investors, who have indicated that they are likely to make a commitment to a fund, but who have not yet taken a firm decision.

Spring cleaning

See Housekeeping.

SPV

Special Purpose Vehicle. A specially created company, often employed as a holding company in Buyout structures.

Stage

The period in a Venture company's life at which investment is made. Stage is one of the two main ways of classifying and distinguishing Venture transactions (the other being by sector) and is divided into seed, early, mid and late.

Stapled primary

An agreement by a secondary investor to commit to a GP's next fund as a primary investor (LP) in consideration of the GP granting consent for the secondary investor to acquire an LP's interest in a present or former fund of the GP.

Stepdown
A reduction in the level of management fees payable by LPs on the occurrence of a specified event (e.g. the raising of a new fund, or the extension of the fund's term by the GP) or after a specific period (e.g. the end of the investment period).

Strip
Not as exciting as it sounds. A vertical slice of the Buyout financing structure, usually taking a piece of each of the senior and mezzanine debt layers.

Survivorship bias
The artificial upward weighting of industry returns caused when underperforming managers stop submitting data, thus dropping out of the database population. Believed to be a particular issue with US Venture returns, as well as with various Hedge fund data providers.

Sweet equity
Shares issued on preferential terms (most commonly for nominal value, i.e. at a much cheaper price) which are used to give management teams a much larger equity stake in a Buyout than would be justified strictly by the amount of money which they are able to invest. Such cases are frequently structured as an option to acquire such shares based on pre-agreed performance targets and conditional upon staying with the company until an exit is achieved. More controversially, they have also been used occasionally by Buyout firms as a substitute for, or even additional form of, carry.

Synthetic secondary
A way of getting around restrictions on the transfer of a Limited Partnership interest whereby one party (the vendor) agrees to hold their interest on trust for a second party (the purchaser).

Tag Along
A form of exit protection, whereby shareholder A can force shareholder B to sell A's shares alongside B's should B receive an offer from a third party.
　　See also Drag Along.

Tail
Those few companies which still remain within a fund's portfolio as it enters, or draws close to, an extension period.
　　See Living dead.

Take Private
A Buyout transaction where a public company is acquired and then de-listed to become a private company. Sometimes referred to as P2P (Public to Private).

Telco
Literally, any provider of telecommunications services, but taken usually to mean one of the incumbent players, i.e. one of the old monopolistic utilities such as BT (in the UK), Deutsche Telekom (in Germany) and the various Bell companies in the US.

Thin equity
A capital structure in which there is a large amount of debt and very little equity. Various countries have adopted 'thin equity' rules in an attempt to limit the tax effectiveness of financial engineering by Buyout houses.

Time-weighted (returns)
A most misleading term as it actually means the exact opposite of what it suggests.
   Instead of calculating the actual IRR of a series of cash flows over a given period (i.e. the compound return over time), time-weighted returns calculate the geometric mean, i.e. the average of the annual percentage return in any one year.
   This measure of returns exists for historic reasons only. It is completely irrelevant (worse – misleading) for Private Equity purposes and should be ignored.

Total return
A phrase invented by the author which refers to the return which an LP earns on the whole Private Equity allocation, as opposed to just that part of it which is at any one time invested in underlying Buyout or Venture companies.

Total value to paid in (TVPI)
The ratio of the current value of remaining investments within a fund plus the total value of all distributions to date to the total amount of capital paid into the fund to date.
   Perhaps the best available measure of performance at the end of a fund's life.

Treasury secondary
A phrase invented by the author to mean a secondary investment which is made purely for reasons of capital and cash flow management, and the exact nature of which (save as to the likely amount and timing of the return) is thus irrelevant.
   See also Portfolio secondary.

Turn (an investment)
To turn an investment is to buy it and then sell it again quickly. In such situations, a high IRR can be generated from a low multiple.

Turnaround
A Buyout of a company which is struggling and possibly even loss-making. Such deals are relatively rare and are an exception to the principle that a Buyout target company will usually have earnings (or at least cash flow) which can be used to service debt.

UMTS
Universal Mobile Telecommunications System, popularly known as 3G. A technology that allows digital communications to be carried at broadband-type speeds to mobile telephones. A great idea, the successful introduction of which was plagued by technical problems, including the development of a sufficiently powerful battery.

Uninvested capital
Capital which is available for investment but has not yet been utilised.
See Dry powder.

Upper decile

The individual fund which sits 10% of the way down the statistical sample, or colloquially all funds which sit above this point. It is used conceptually when talking about the golden circle (see above) as in 'Venture is an upper decile game', but data including it as a statistical measure are not publicly available.

Upper quartile

Commonly used as a measure of vintage year returns. It is the return of that individual fund which sits at the bottom of the upper quartile, i.e. one quarter of the way down a ranked list of observations. It is *not* the pooled returns of all the funds which sit within the upper quartile.

However, it is used colloquially to refer to all the funds which sit within the upper quartile, hence the confusion.

While statistically useful, its limitations should be recognised. In particular, it gives no indication of the spread within the upper quartile, which can be enormous, especially where Venture funds are concerned. It can also be very misleading if the sample from which it is drawn is not properly representative (as is often the case where European Venture is concerned).

US model

This refers to the traditional approach of US Venture firms, particularly those active at early stage. Its main components are (1) a focus on the seed stage, (2) home-run mentality and (3) value add.

Interestingly and excitingly, there are a number of European firms now adopting the US model.

Value add

An American expression referring to the ability to contribute company-building skills gained at first hand to the development of a Venture company, usually on a hands-on basis.

VCOC

Venture Capital Operating Company, a term used in the ERISA regulations (see above).

Vendor loan

A loan provided by the vendor of a business to its purchaser partially to finance the acquisition. For an obvious example, see the announced (but abortive) sale of i-Shares to CVC by Barclays Bank in 2009.

Venture Capitalist

An individual professional within a Venture firm.

Venture company

An investee company within a Venture fund. Often referred to as a 'firm' in North America.

Venture Partner

Might be thought of as something between an EIR and a GP within a Venture firm. A Venture Partner will usually be someone who has been a successful entrepreneur and will be used by the firm to look at prospective investment opportunities within their own area of specialist expertise.

Venture Partner is frequently a temporary status. Typically a VP will be expected either to join the management team of an opportunity which he finds exciting, or to progress into being a GP. The status is also sometimes used for someone who has retired as a GP, but wishes to retain a part-time role within the firm.

Vintage year
The year in which a fund, or group of funds, was formed

Vintage year returns
Vintage year returns show (in respect of any one vintage year) the compound return of all constituent funds formed during the vintage year, from the vintage year to the date specified.

Walkaway fee
A contractually agreed fee payable by the owner of a business to a potential vendor should the owner decide to sell the business to a third party instead. Usually arises where there has been a breach of an exclusivity period, or under a Go shop provision (for both, see above).

Write down
To reduce the stated valuation of a portfolio company. Under both the EVCA and BVCA guidelines, there are some situations where a 25% write down is mandatory.

Write off
To reduce the stated valuation of a portfolio company to zero.

Write up
To increase the stated value of a portfolio company.

Index

Page numbers in **bold** refer to terms defined in the Glossary

Index compiled by Annette Musker